Communications
in Computer and Information Science 200

Tai-hoon Kim   Hojjat Adeli
Rosslin John Robles   Maricel Balitanas (Eds.)

Information Security and Assurance

International Conference, ISA 2011
Brno, Czech Republic, August 15-17, 2011
Proceedings

 Springer

Volume Editors

Tai-hoon Kim
Hannam University, 133 Ojeong-dong, Daeduk-gu, Daejeon 306-791, Korea
E-mail: taihoonn@hannam.ac.kr

Hojjat Adeli
The Ohio State University
470 Hitchcock Hall, 2070 Neil Avenue, Columbus, OH 43210-1275, USA
E-mail: adeli.1@osu.edu

Rosslin John Robles
Hannam University, 133 Ojeong-dong, Daeduk-gu, Daejeon 306-791, Korea
E-mail: rosslin1@sersc.org

Maricel Balitanas
Hannam University, 133 Ojeong-dong, Daeduk-gu, Daejeon, Korea
E-mail: maricel@sersc.org

ISSN 1865-0929   e-ISSN 1865-0937
ISBN 978-3-642-23140-7   e-ISBN 978-3-642-23141-4
DOI 10.1007/978-3-642-23141-4
Springer Heidelberg Dordrecht London New York

Library of Congress Control Number: 2011933824

CR Subject Classification (1998): C.2, D.4.6, K.6.5

Typesetting: Camera-ready by author, data conversion by Scientific Publishing Services, Chennai, India

Printed on acid-free paper

Springer is part of Springer Science+Business Media (www.springer.com)

Foreword

Information security and assurance is an area that has attracted many academic and industry professionals in research and development. The goal of the ISA conference is to bring together researchers from academia and industry as well as practitioners to share ideas, problems and solutions relating to the multifaceted aspects of information security and assurance.

We would like to express our gratitude to all of the authors of submitted papers and to all attendees for their contributions and participation. We believe in the need to continue this undertaking in the future.

We acknowledge the great effort of all the Chairs and the members of the Advisory Boards and Program Committees of the above-listed event. Special thanks go to SERSC (Science & Engineering Research Support soCiety) for supporting this conference.

We are grateful in particular to the speakers who kindly accepted our invitation and, in this way, helped to meet the objectives of the conference.

July 2011   Chairs of ISA 2011

Preface

We would like to welcome you to the proceedings of the 2011 International Conference on Information Security and Assurance (ISA 2011), which was held during August 15–17, 2011, at Brno University, Czech Republic.

ISA 2011 focused on various aspects of advances in information security and assurance with computational sciences, mathematics and information technology. It provided a chance for academic and industry professionals to discuss recent progress in the related areas. We expect that the conference and its publications will be a trigger for further related research and technology improvements in this important subject. We would like to acknowledge the great effort of all the Chairs and members of the Program Committee.

We would like to thank all of the authors of submitted papers and all the attendees for their contributions and participation.

Once more, we would like to thank all the organizations and individuals who supported this event as a whole and, in particular, helped in the success of ISA 2011.

June 2011

Tai-hoon Kim
Hojjat Adeli
Rosslin John Robles
Maricel Balitanas

Organization

Honorary Chair

Hojjat Adeli   The Ohio State University, USA

General Co-chairs

Martin Drahanský   Brno University, Czech Republic
Wael Adi   Technische Universität Braunschweig, Germany

Program Co-chairs

Tai-hoon Kim   Hannam University, Korea
Yang Xiao   The University of Alabama, USA
Filip Orság   Brno University, Czech Republic

Workshop Co-chairs

Muhammad Khurram Khan   King Saud University, Saudi Arabia
Byeong-joo Park   Hannam University, Korea

International Advisory Board

Haeng-kon Kim   Catholic University of Daegu, Korea
Kouich Sakurai   Kyushu University, Japan
Justin Zhan   CMU, USA
Hai Jin   Huazhong University of Science and
                              Technology, China
Edwin Sha   University of Texas at Dallas, USA
Dominik Slezak   Infobright, Poland and Canada

Publicity Co-chairs

Debnath Bhattacharyya   SERSC, India
Ching-Hsien Hsu   Chung Hua University, Taiwan
Duncan S. Wong   City University of Hong Kong, Hong Kong
Deepak Laxmi Narasimha   University of Malaya, Malaysia
Prabhat K. Mahanti   University of New Brunswick, Canada

Publication Chair

Maricel O. Balitanas   Hannam University, Korea

Program Committee

Abdelwahab Hamou-Lhadj
Ahmet Koltuksuz
Albert Levi
Andreas Jacobsson
Bonnefoi Pierre-Francois
Chantana Chantrapornchai
Chun-Ying Huang
Daniel Port
Debasis Giri
Dharma P. Agrawal
Dvorák Radim
Eduardo Fernandez
Fangguo Zhang
Filip Orsag
Hájek Josef
Han-Chieh Chao
Hejtmánková (Lodrová) Dana
Hiroaki Kikuchi
Hironori Washizaki
Hongji Yang
Hyun Sung Kim
J.H. Abawajy
Jan deMeer
Jari Veijalainen
Javier Garcia-Villalba
Jeng-Shyang Pan
Jonathan Lee
Josef Bigun
Kenichi Takahashi
Mario Freire

Martin Drahansky
Marvan Aleš
Mrácek Štepán
N. Jaisankar
Novotný Tomáš
Paolo D'Arco
Paolo Falcarin
Petr Hanacek
Pierre-François Bonnefoi
Qi Shi
Reinhard Schwarz
Rodrigo Mello
Rolf Oppliger
Rui Zhang
S.K. Barai
Serge Chaumette
Slobodan Petrovic
Stan Kurkovsky
Stefanos Gritzalis
Swee-Huay Heng
Tony Shan
Vána Jan
Victor Winter
Wei Yan
Yannis Stamatiou
YeongDeok Kim
Yi Mu
Yong Man Ro
Yoshiaki Hori

Table of Contents

Information Security Awareness Campaign:
An Alternate Approach

Bilal Khan[1], Khaled S. Alghathbar[1,2], and Muhammad Khurram Khan[1]

[1] Center of Excellence in Information Assurance,
King Saud University, Kingdom of Saudi Arabia
[2] Department of Information System, CCIS,
King Saud University, Kingdom of Saudi Arabia
{Bilalkhan,Kalghathbar,mkhurram}@ksu.edu.sa

Abstract. The destruction due to computer security incidents warns organizations to adopt security measures. In addition to technological measures, individual's information security awareness is also necessary. Different psychological theories have been proposed to make an effective information security awareness campaign. These information security awareness campaigns are limited in their ability in raising awareness of the participants of the campaign. Although much research has been done in the area of information security awareness, however, this paper considers the applications of healthcare awareness and environmental awareness strategies to make an effective information security awareness campaign. In this paper, we study some of the useful research work conducted in the healthcare and environmental safety awareness domains. These researches have been carried out by well-known researchers in the field of psychology. Finally, we apply these healthcare and environmental awareness best practices to propose an effective information security awareness campaign.

Keywords: information security awareness, healthcare, environmental, effective.

1 Introduction

Everyday new incidents such as data breaches, threats, risk etc are reported and almost every time these incidents are due to human errors and lack of information security awareness. Many analysts claim that human component of any information security framework is the weakest link. Information is one of the resources that an organization is heavily dependent on. If the critical information of an organization is leaked, the organization can suffer serious consequences, e.g., in the form of loss of income, loss of customers' trust and maybe legal action etc. therefore, information should be protected and secured.

According to information security forum [9], information security awareness can be defined as the extent to which every member of staff understands the importance of information security, the levels of information security appropriate to the organization, their individual security responsibilities, and acts accordingly. Information security awareness has been defined in different ways, however; this definition establishes

T.-h. Kim et al. (Eds.): ISA 2011, CCIS 200, pp. 1–10, 2011.

relation between behavior and awareness. Therefore a user is considered aware of information security if he/she behaves accordingly. The research work in this paper is based on the definition of information security awareness according to ISF [9].

Incidents of information loss can occur due to less conscious information security behavior of the end-users. Information security behavior of the end-users or employees is changed by raising the level of information security awareness by educating all employees in the basics of information security. To achieve this, information security awareness campaigns are initiated such as information security awareness presentations, computer based training, information security awareness posters, email messaging etc. However, not all campaigns are good enough to raise the awareness level of employees due to the less effectiveness of these campaigns in changing the information security behaviors of the targeted audience.

Researchers working in the healthcare and environmental safety domains have proposed some theories and models for the improvement of the human behavior to safeguard the human health and natural environment respectively. In this paper we study some of the best practices of healthcare awareness and environment awareness and explain that the use of such practices in information security awareness campaigns is beneficial. Table 1 lists some measures where human awareness is needed to maintain human safe natural environment. In addition, table 2 shows the list of different diseases where human behavior change is needed to prevent from such diseases.

Table 1. Natural environmental campaigns for public awarness

Serial No.	Natural environment
1	Energy conservation
2	Curbside recycling
3	Road safety
4	Oil spill

Table 2. Healthcare campaigns for public awareness

Serial No.	Healthcare
1	Alcohol use
2	HIV
3	Skin cancer
4	Flossing teeth for dental hygiene
5	Cancer screening and prevention
6	Diabetes
7	Eating disorder

It is worth to mention that when a health related awareness campaign is ignored, it usually affects one person consequently whereas in the case of information security awareness it affects the whole network of computers and therefore the whole organization.

In contrast to the health and environmental awareness exercises the participants are usually a population of general public whereas in information security awareness programs they are the employees of an organization.

This paper is organized as follows: section 2 is related work; section 3 is research design and methodology where we explain some of the best practices of human awareness in healthcare and environmental safety and explain their use in information security awareness campaigns. Section 4 proposes a comprehensive information security awareness model and section 5 finally concludes the paper.

2 Related Work

To measure the effectiveness of an information security awareness program Kruger and Kearney developed a prototype [1]. The prototype is based on the knowledge, attitude and behavior of individual about information security.

Tay R. evaluated the effectiveness of mass media and found out that mass media campaigns on drunk driving reduce the incidence of alcohol related crashes [3]. He also found that mass media is effective in large savings in medical costs, property damage etc.

Ng et al. uses the health belief model to study user's computer security behavior [4]. They proposed a model which was validated from 134 employees.

Yeo et al. proposed a web-based program based on the principles of pervasive technology [5]. The aim of using such approach is to improve information security behavior of end-users. They claim that pervasive technology is effective in raising information security aware behavior. In addition, a web-based portal was proposed by Niekerk et al. for information security education [6]. They claim that web-based portal acts as a knowledge repository and is an efficient and cost effective method of raising information security awareness.

According to Schultz nothing in security measures yield as much return on investment (RoI) as information security education [2]. Although much work has been done in the area of information security awareness, however a thorough review of literature lacks the study of using health and environmental awareness best practices for making an effective information security awareness campaign. Therefore, this study proposes the use of best healthcare and environmental awareness approaches for information security awareness.

3 Research Design and Methodology

Research design is based on the description of best practices of health awareness and environmental awareness and their use in the information security awareness campaigns to make them more effective in changing user's information security behavior.

3.1 Best Practices in a Health Awareness Campaign

Many theories and models have been proposed by researchers to change the health behavior of patients and general public [10][11] [16][17] . For example, HIV prevention, diabetes self-care, breast cancer, etc. shown in table 2.

IMB (Information-motivation-behavior skills) model for healthcare
Fisher et al. proposed IMB (information-motivation-behavioral skills) model to change the patient behavior regarding HIV prevention [11]. According to IMB model, HIV prevention information, motivation and behavioral skills are the fundamental determinants of HIV preventive behavior. Basically there are three prerequisites of this model. They are information, motivation, i.e., personal and social motivation and behavioral skills [11].

Interventions based on such model are likely to be more effective at producing the desired behavior change than purely knowledge-based campaigns alone such as educational presentation etc.

A basic tenet of the IMB model is that behavioral performance is a function of the extent to which someone is well informed and motivated to perform a behavior.

IMB model was also proposed by Osborne and Egede for the diabetes self-care behavior [17]. According to this research, IMB model is a comprehensive health behavior change framework for diabetes self care.

The above two research in HIV prevention and diabetes self-care behavior show that IMB is an effective model to change human behavior. Here we use the IMB model as shown in fig. 1that will change the user information security behavior.

Using IMB model for information security awareness campaign
In the Information-Motivation-Behavioral skills model for information security awareness or behavior change, the Information is the knowledge about information security, Motivation is personal motivation, i.e., positive attitude towards performing an action and social motivation (support from colleagues in the organization to individual's information security performance/behavior) and behavior skills is whether the individual is skilled to perform a specific action. Information security awareness campaigns are delivered using information security presentation, newsletters; magazines etc. These campaigns fulfill one of the prerequisites of the IMB model, i.e., Information. These methods of campaigns are good in disseminating the required information security education or information to the audience. However these campaigns lack the remaining two components of the IMB model, i.e., motivation and behavioral skills. One of the effective components of the IMB model is motivation, which is usually ignored while delivering an information security campaign. Figure 1 shows the IMB model for the information security behavior change. The motivation component of the IMB model motivates the user to act according to the information gained through the campaign. According to the IMB model, motivation has two subcomponents, i.e., personal motivation and social motivation. Information security awareness campaigns should be designed in such a way that motivates the user to act according to the security policy of the organization.

Most of the information security awareness programs apply to an employee's personal life. For example, employees use email, laptop, computers, PDAs for their personal use at home; therefore, an information security campaign should talk about the benefits of employee for practicing information security behavior. It is very boring for

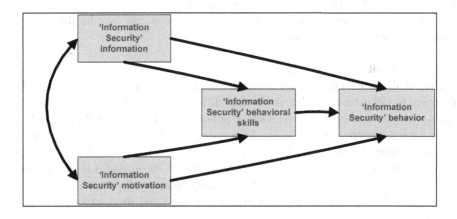

Fig. 1. Information Security Awareness campaign based on IMB model

employees to tell them what they can do and cannot do for the benefits of the company. The focus of the program should not be to focus on organization but to focus on employee benefits. Once the employee start behaving in secure manner in their personal life, his/her behavior will be automatically changed in the organizational environment. This way of motivating employees can effectively change their behaviors. In addition to personal motivation, social motivation can also be developed by making the campaign environment more social. For example, information security group discussion is an informal meeting in which there is no one way communication [18]. This type of intervention meets all prerequisites of the IMB model. In this meeting participants take full advantage of sharing information security knowledge and experience. Different information security key issues are picked one by one and openly discussed. Such strategy of discussion is good in increasing information security related information which is the first prerequisite of the IMB model. The second prerequisite of the IMB model i.e. motivation, is also present in this type of intervention. Group discussions are interactive and engage all the participants. Due to the ideal environment participants come to know about information security attitudes and behaviors of each other. In this way participants get personal as well as social motivation to act according to the gained information. Such interventions are informal and good in teaching the required skills for behaving information security. In contrast, the traditional information security awareness campaigns do not use the remaining two components of the IMB model i.e., motivation and behavioral skills. The traditional campaigns provide knowledge however; they are unsuccessful in motivating the audience to behave accordingly. Therefore the lack of motivation to learn behavioral skills make the traditional information security campaigns ineffective.

3.2 Best Practices in an Environmental Awareness Campaign

Like healthcare awareness, many theories and models have been proposed by researchers to increase public awareness regarding natural environment safety [7]

[8][12][13][14] [15]. For example waste recycling, road safety, energy conservation and oil spill etc. shown in table 1. Below is one of the concepts used for the improvement of the public's curbside recycling behavior.

Normative feedback interventions

Schultz et al. studied the behavior of people for curbside recycling [12] [13] [14]. His proposed model is based on the provision of different types of knowledge in the campaign to improve recycling behavior of the public. They divided knowledge into three types for interventions (1) procedural knowledge that gives information about when, how and where to recycle? (2) Impact knowledge that refers to an individual's belief about the consequences of recycling and (3) normative knowledge is the belief about behaviors of others. According to Schultz, many educational campaigns are based on procedural and impact knowledge which has small and short term influence on behavior.

Normative beliefs are descriptive social norms and injunctive social norms. Descriptive social norms refers to the belief about what other people are doing whereas injunctive social norms refer to the belief about what other people think should be done. Social norms are formed through social interaction. It has a powerful influence on human behavior and can be provided using presentations, magazines, newsletters and posters etc.

Use of Normative Social Norms for information Security awareness Campaigns

Using the techniques outlined by Schultz et al. [14] to improve the curbside recycling behavior of people, it is possible to make an effective information security awareness campaign. Some of the popular information security campaigns are information security presentations, posters, newsletters and magazines. All of these campaigns are information based campaigns. They are less effective in increasing information security awareness of the audience or changing information security behavior of the audience. These campaigns increase the procedural information security knowledge and impact information security knowledge of the audience. These types of campaigns teach what to secure? How to secure? When to secure? And what will be the consequences if an acceptable behavior is not adopted. Such types of campaigns are limited in their ability to produce changes in behavior. These information security educational campaigns are not sufficient to change user's behavior since they lack the normative information security knowledge. Fig. 2 shows a campaign based on the three types of knowledge that integrates the necessary components of normative knowledge to change the information security behavior of the users.

In case of information security campaigns, descriptive and injunctive social norms (normative knowledge) can be induced in the campaigns by describing the acceptable information security behavior and by giving examples of the colleagues in the organization who perform information security conscious behavior so that the audience are motivated in adopting information security behavior.

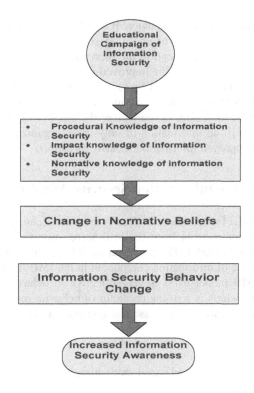

Fig. 2. Information Security Awareness campaign based on Normative Knowledge

Many information security awareness campaigns do not provide social interaction among the audience which is an ideal environment for the transfer of normative knowledge among the audience as shown in fig. 3.

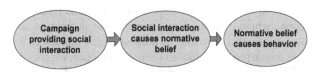

Fig. 3. Behavior Change due to Social Interaction

Social norms result from social interaction; therefore it is necessary for the information security awareness campaign to provide social interaction among the audience or employees of the organization. Social norms approach seems to be an effective method in increasing effectiveness of information security campaign. The best way to give normative knowledge to the participants of the campaign is to distribute the printed leaflets among them. As shown in fig. 3, the campaign should provide social interaction by disseminating normative knowledge that creates a social environment. These leaflets should give figures of the improved information security environment of the competing organizations as well as the good performance of the colleagues regarding the information security behavior. It should systematically mention the decreasing number of incidents due to choosing strong password and other security measures. In addition, it should mention the increased number of customers joining the competing organizations due to the improved information security measures. This strategy of creating social environment by knowing the other's behavior causes normative belief which in turn changes behavior of the employees of an organization (fig. 3). The strategy is successful in motivating the employees in adopting information security behavior if the information of only those organizations and employees are given which has improved information security measures.

4   A Comprehensive Information Security Awareness Model

A comprehensive model for information security awareness campaign can be made by combining effective components from the healthcare awareness model and natural environmental awareness model. The proposed model uses the component of normative knowledge in place of information component in the IMB model to make it more effective (fig. 4). IMB model itself is very effective in behavior change; however normative knowledge which is a strong predictor of behavior makes it more effective in raising information security awareness. The comprehensive model has the following components:

(1) Normative Knowledge.
(2) Motivation, i.e., personal and social motivation.
(3) Behavioral change.

Normative knowledge plays an important role in this model as it is not only providing the information about information security but also knowledge. As shown in fig. 4, normative knowledge motivates audience to act according to the gained knowledge about information security.

Normative knowledge is the beliefs about the information security behaviors of others. Normative social norms are developed through social interaction. It has a powerful influence on behavior. Campaigns considering normative social norms are effective in raising information security awareness of the audience. It has a good influence to motivate employees towards adopting information security behavior.

The model in fig. 4 shows that the campaign starts from disseminating knowledge in general and normative knowledge in particular. The normative knowledge causes personal as well as social motivation by giving the improved information security statistics of the fellow colleagues and the competing organizations. Once the employees or audience understand the information security behavior of the fellow colleagues, they are inclined towards adopting the relevant behavior. All positive changes in information security atmosphere of other organizations should be brought in the mind of the audience. The phenomena behind the model in fig. 4 is that normative knowledge causes motivation whereas motivation further results in changing behavior of the audience. The change in behavior results in the increased information security awareness.

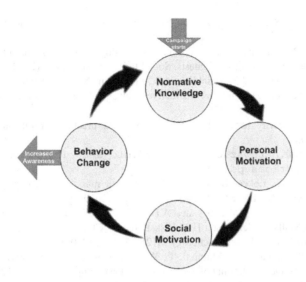

Fig. 4. A comprehensive model for Information Security Awareness campaign

5 Conclusion

This paper highlights the importance of some of the effective theories and models used for awareness campaigns in the healthcare and natural environmental domains. It takes the motivation component in general and social motivation in particular from the IMB model to be used in the information security awareness campaigns to make them more effective. In addition this study shows that for an effective knowledge based information security campaign, normative knowledge should be considered. Social norms can play an important role in changing information security behavior. Finally it proposes a comprehensive model for information security awareness campaigns. The proposed model replaces the normative knowledge component with the information component in the IMB model, which is a well-known model for the healthcare awareness campaigns.

References

[1] Kruger, H.A., Kearney, W.D.: A prototype for assessing information security awareness. Journal of Computer and Security 25(4), 289–296 (2006)
[2] Schultz, E.: Security training and awareness-fitting a square peg in a round hole. Computers & Security 23, 1–2 (2004)
[3] Tay, R.: Mass media campaigns reduce the incidence of drinking and driving. Evidence-Based Healthcare and Public Health 9(1), 26–29 (2005)
[4] Ng, B.Y., Kankanhallia, A., Xu, Y.: Studying Users' Computer Security Behavior: A Health Belief Perspective. Decision Support Systems 46(4), 815–825 (2009)
[5] Yeo, A.C., Rahim, M.M., Ren, Y.Y.: Use of Persuasive technology to change end user's IT security aware behavior: a pilot study. International Journal of Psychological and Behavioral Sciences 1(1), 48–54 (2009)

[6] Niekerk, J.V., Solms, R.V.: A web-based portal for information security education (2007)

[7] Schultz, W.P., Khaziana, A.M., Zaleskia, A.C.: Using normative social influence to promote conservation among hotel guests. Social Influence 3(1), 4–23 (2008)

[8] Schultz, P.W., Nolan, J.M., Cialdini, R.B., Goldstein, N.J., Griskevicius, V.: The constructive, destructive, and reconstructive power of social norms. Psychological Science 18(5), 429–434 (2007)

[9] Information security forum. The standard of good practice for information security (March 2003),
http://www.netbotz.com/library/Info_Security_Forum_Standard_Good_Practices.pdf

[10] Wakefield, M.A., Loken, B., Hornik, R.C.: Use of mass media campaigns to change health behavior. The Lancet 376(9748), 1261–1271 (2010)

[11] Fisher, J.D., Fisher, W.A., Bryanc, A.D., Misovichd, S.J.: Information-Motivation-Behavioral Skills Model–Based HIV Risk Behavior Change Intervention for Inner-City High School Youth. Health Psychology 21(2), 177–186 (2002)

[12] Schultz, P.W., Oskamp, S., Mainieri, T.: Who recycles and when: A review of personal and situational factors. Journal of Environmental Psychology 15(2), 105–121 (1995)

[13] Schultz, P.W.: Knowledge, education, and household recycling: Examining the knowledge-deficit model of behavior change. In: Dietz, T., Stern, P. (eds.) New Tools for Environmental Protection, pp. 67–82. National Academy of Sciences, Washington DC (2002)

[14] Schultz, P.W.: Changing behavior with normative feedback interventions: A field experiment of curbside recycling. Basic and Applied Social Psychology 21, 25–36 (1999)

[15] Nolan, J., Schultz, P.W., Knowles, E.: Using public service announcements to change behavior: No more money and oil down the drain. Journal of Applied Social Psychology 39, 1035–1056 (2009)

[16] Baranowski, T., Cullen, K.W., Nicklas, T., Thompson, D., Baranowski, J.: Are current health behavioral change models helpful in guiding prevention of weight gain efforts? Obesity Research 11(10), 23–43 (2003)

[17] Osborne, Edgede: Validation of an Information–Motivation–Behavioral Skills model of diabetes self-care (IMB-DSC). Patient Education & Counseling 79(1), 49–54 (2010)

[18] Albrechsten, E., Hovden, J.: Improving information security awareness and behavior through dialogue, participation, and collective reflection. An intervention study. Journal of Computer & Security 29(4), 432–445 (2010)

Equivalent Key Recovery Attack on H^2-MAC Instantiated with MD5[*]

Wei Wang[1,2]

[1] School of Computer Science and Technology, Shandong University,
Jinan 250101, China
[2] Key Laboratory of Cryptologic Technology and Information Security,
Ministry of Education, Shandong University, Jinan 250100, China
weiwangsdu@sdu.edu.cn

Abstract. This paper presents the first equivalent key recovery attack on H^2-MAC-MD5, which conduces to a selective forgery attack directly. H^2-MAC is similar with HMAC except that the outer key is omitted. For HMAC-MD5, since the available differential paths are pseudo-collisions, all the key recovery attacks are in the related-key setting, while our attack on H^2-MAC-MD5 gets rid of this restriction. Based on the distinguisher of HMAC-MD5 proposed by Wang et al., a pair of intermediate chaining variables, i.e., the equivalent keys $(\tilde{K}, \tilde{K}')$, is detected which fulfils the specific conditions on (IV, IV') of the pseudo-collision. Then the inner key recovery attack on HMAC-MD5 explored by Contini and Yin is adopted to recover $(\tilde{K}, \tilde{K}')$. Consequently, the adversary can compute the valid MAC value of $M_0 \| M^*$ effortlessly, where M_0 is a fixed one-block message, and M^* can be any bit string.

Keywords: Cryptanalysis, H^2-MAC-MD5, Distinguishing attack, Equivalent key recovery attack.

1 Introduction

A Message Authentication Code (MAC) algorithm is a keyed hash function, which takes a secret key K and a message M of arbitrary length as input, and produces a short tag as output. MAC is used to ensure the integrity and authenticity of messages, and has been widely used in internet security protocols (e.g., SSL/TLS, SSH, IPsec, etc.) and the financial sector for debit and credit transaction.

There are mainly three earlier methods to construct MAC algorithms, which are secret prefix, secret suffix and secret envelope [14] methods. The secret prefix method prepends a secret K to the message M before the hashing operation, and is the basic design unit for HMAC, which is a commonly-used, widely standardized MAC construction nowadays [1]. HMAC can take advantage of the

---

[*] Supported by Research Fund for the Doctoral Program of Higher Education of China (Grant No. 20100131120015) and Independent Innovation Foundation of Shandong University (Grant No. 2010TS069).

T.-h. Kim et al. (Eds.): ISA 2011, CCIS 200, pp. 11–20, 2011.

modern cryptographic hash functions directly, and is provable secure under the two assumptions that the keyed compression function of the hash function and the key derivation function in HMAC are PRFs (Pseudo Random Functions) [2]. For an iterated Merkle-Damgård hash function H, HMAC is defined by

$$HMAC(K, M) = H(IV, (K_0 \oplus opad)\|H(IV, (K_0 \oplus ipad)\|M)),$$

where M is the message, K is the secret key shared between the originator and the intended receiver, IV is the initial value of H, K_0 is K's completion to a single block of H, $opad$ and $ipad$ are two fixed one-block constants. It is noted that, HMAC has to make an access to the secret key twice in the process, which causes some inconvenience.

H^2-MAC, which was proposed by Kan Yasuda in Information Security Conference (ISC) 2009 [22], is a new secret-prefix MAC, which is almost the same as HMAC except the second call to the secret key is omitted, i. e., the outer key is replaced by the fixed IV of the hash function. In this way, the secret key is only accessed once in the computation of H^2-MAC, and H^2-MAC gets rid of the disadvantage of the secret key management without losing the original advantage of HMAC. However, the absence of the outer key also causes negative sides, which do not exist in HMAC. As pointed out by the designer, the security of H^2-MAC requires its compression function be a secure PRF, and the adversary can easily compute any extension of that message locally once one of the intermediate chaining variables (ICVs) is leaked, i. e., the ICVs are equivalent to the secret key, and the security of H^2-MAC heavily depends on the secure computation of them. Thus, it is worth investigating into the impact of the outer key on security.

This paper studies the above question by cryptanalysis of H^2-MAC instantiated with a concrete hash function of MDx family, especially MD5 [13]. It is obvious that the secret key of H^2-MAC preforms in a similar way as the inner key of HMAC. Thus the inner key recovery attack on HMAC instantiated with specific hash functions can be applied to H^2-MAC directly, and the equivalent key of H^2-MAC is recovered.

In 2005, Wang informally discussed the impact of high probability collision path on early hash based MAC constructions like the secret prefix, secret suffix, and secret envelope methods [16]. Then a series of work had been proposed [6,7,8,9,12,15,17,23]. When it comes to corresponding H^2-MAC, all the inner key recovery attacks can work with the same complexity.

While for HMAC-MD5, the situation becomes interesting. As the available differential paths are pseudo-collisions [5], which consist of two different IVs, (IV, IV'), all the key recovery attacks are in the related-key setting [7,8,12,15]. One recent work presented a distinguishing attack on HMAC-MD5 without related keys, which is extended to a partial key recovery attack on MD5-MAC [19]. This motivates us to explore the first equivalent key recovery attack on H^2-MAC-MD5. To discard the related-key setting, we construct the distinguisher similar with [19], except that the length of the chosen messages has to be 3 blocks after padding in order to recover the equivalent key. The first blocks guarantee the existence of a one-block pair (M_0, M'_0) which produces the related IV pair (IV, IV') of the pseudo-collision, the second blocks help to detect the specific (M_0, M'_0), and the third make sure that the padding information is not contained in the second block so that we can change any bits of the second block in the key recovery phase. Once the related (IV, IV') of the pseudo-collision is achieved by (M_0, M'_0), they become the intermediate variables of H^2-MAC-MD5 actually, and can be recovered by the bit flipping algorithm introduced in [7]. The complexity of our equivalent key recovery attack is 2^{97} queries. Consequently, we can compute the valid MACs for any extension of M_0 or M'_0.

This paper is organized as follows. Section 2 recalls the related backgrounds and definitions. Section 3 constructs a concrete distinguisher of H^2-MAC-MD5 first, and then extends it to an equivalent key recovery attack, which leads to a selective forgery directly. Finally, Section 4 concludes this paper.

2 Preliminaries

We first explain the notations related to this paper, then present brief descriptions of MD5, the pseudo-collision of MD5 and H^2-MAC in this section.

2.1 Notations

H : a concrete hash function, such as MD5
$\tilde{H}$: a hash function without message padding
h : a compression function
IV : the initial value for H
ICV_k : the intermediate chaining variables for the k-th iteration of H
K : a secret key
$\tilde{K}$: an equivalent secret key
$x\|y$: the concatenation of two bit strings x and y
$\oplus$: the bitwise exclusive OR
$\lll s$: the left-rotation by s-bit

2.2 Brief Description of MD5

MD5 takes a message of arbitrary length as input and produces a 128-bit hash value by iterating a compression function h [13]. First, the input message M with length l is padded to a multiple of 512 bits. Then the padded message is divided into 512-bit blocks $(M_0, M_1, \cdots, M_{b-1})$, and processed by Merkle-Damgård iterative structure. For the k-th ($1 \le k \le b$) iteration, the compression function $h(ICV_{k-1}, M_{k-1})$ performs in the following manner:

1. The 512-bit message block M_{k-1} is split into 16 message words $(m_0, m_1, \cdots, m_{15})$, and the 128-bit output of the $(k-1)$-th iteration, ICV_{k-1}, is split into four registers (A_0, B_0, C_0, D_0), where ICV_0 is the fixed initial value IV.

2. For $0 \leq i \leq 63$, compute

$$A_{i+1} = D_i, B_{i+1} = B_i + (A_i + f(B_i, C_i, D_i) + w_i + c_i) \lll s_i,$$
$$C_{i+1} = B_i, D_{i+1} = C_i,$$

where w_i is one of the 16 message words, c_i and s_i are step-dependent constants, f is a round-dependent Boolean function.

3. Output: $ICV_k = (A_0 + A_{64}, B_0 + B_{64}, C_0 + C_{64}, D_0 + D_{64})$, where $+$ means the addition modular 2^{32}.

After all the b blocks are processed, ICV_b is the hash value of the message M, i. e., $H(IV, M) = ICV_b$.

2.3   Pseudo-collisions of MD5

All the previous attacks on HMAC-MD5 are based on the dBB pseudo-collisions found by den Boer and Bosselaers [5], so does this paper. The dBB pseudo-collisions satisfy the following relations:

$$h(IV, M) = h(IV', M), \tag{1}$$
$$IV \oplus IV' = (2^{31}, 2^{31}, 2^{31}, 2^{31}) = \Delta^{\mathrm{MSB}}, \tag{2}$$
$$\mathrm{MSB}(B_0) = \mathrm{MSB}(C_0) = \mathrm{MSB}(D_0), \tag{3}$$

where $IV = (A_0, B_0, C_0, D_0)$, M is a one-block message, and MSB means the most significant bit. The probability of the dBB pseudo-collision is 2^{-46}.

We adopt the definitions presented in [19]. The dBB conditions means relations (2) and (3) on the intermediate variables, and a collision of two-block messages $(x\|y, x'\|y)$ is called a dBB-collision if

1. (ICV_1, ICV_1') satisfies the dBB conditions, where $ICV_1 = h(IV, x)$, and $ICV_1' = h(IV, x')$.
2. $(x\|y, x'\|y)$ is a colliding pair, i. e., $H(IV, x\|y) = H(IV, x'\|y)$.

2.4   Brief Description of H^2-MAC

In ISC 2009, a new MAC construction, H^2-MAC [22], was presented, which is similar to the widely used HMAC algorithm [1]. For a message M of arbitrary length, and an n-bit secret key K, where n equals to the length of the MAC value, H^2-MAC is computed as follows (See Fig. 1):

$$H^2\text{-MAC}(K, M) = H(IV, H(IV, K\|pad\|M)),$$

where H is a concrete hash function, and pad is a fixed constant chosen according to H, in order to make sure that the length of $K\|pad$ is one block.

Compared with HMAC, H^2-MAC can also utilize current hash functions directly, moreover, it achieves higher performance and reduces the cost of managing the secret key since K is accessed only once. However, the absence of the outer

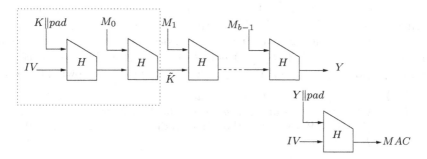

Fig. 1. H^2-MAC Algorithm

key also leads to negative sides, such as the adversary can perform a selective forgery attack as soon as one of the intermediate chaining variables is leaked, and the security is based on a stronger assumption that the compression function must be a secure PRF.

Define an equivalent key $\tilde{K}$ as the intermediate chaining variable after $K\|pad\|M_0$ is processed, i. e., $\tilde{K} = \tilde{H}(IV, K\|pad\|M_0)$, where $\tilde{H}$ is a hash function without message padding. Once $\tilde{K}$ is recovered, the adversary can compute the valid MAC value of message $M_0\|M^*$ without knowing the secret key K, where M^* is an arbitrary message.

We denote H^2-MAC initiated with MD5 as H^2-MAC-MD5, and this paper presents an attack to recover the equivalent key $\tilde{K}$ of H^2-MAC-MD5 without related-key setting.

3   Equivalent Key Recovery Attack on H^2-MAC-MD5

We first present a distinguishing attack, which distinguishes H^2-MAC-MD5 from H^2-MAC instantiated with a random function. Then an equivalent key recovery attack is proposed based on the distinguisher. Finally, a selectively forgery attack can be performed. The complexity of the equivalent key recovery attack is 2^{97} MAC queries, which is dominated by the distinguisher.

3.1   Distinguishing Attack on H^2-MAC-MD5

The distinguishing attack on H^2-MAC-MD5 is inspired by Wang et al.'s attack on HMAC-MD5 which introduced new ideas to detect the inner near-collisions [19]. However, our distinguisher makes use of messages of three blocks instead of two, in order to proceed the key recovery attack.

To take advantage of the dBB pseudo-collision and get rid of the related-key setting, the key point is to replace the specific (IV, IV') of the pseudo-collision with the intermediate chaining variables (ICV, ICV') satisfying the dBB conditions, and find a method to identify such a pair. We adopt the definitions described in [19]. Suppose that we get a collision of H^2-MAC with the form

$(M_0\|M_1\|M_2, M_0'\|M_1'\|M_2')$, where $M_1 = M_1'$, $M_2 = M_2'$, and all the padding information appears in M_2. According to the definition of ICV_k in Section 2.1, the intermediate chaining variable after $M[i]$ is processed is ICV_{i+2}, and the corresponding on for $M'[i]$ is ICV_{i+2}'. Denote $ICV_i \oplus ICV_i'$ as ΔICV_i. The collisions caused by $(M_0\|M_1\|M_2, M_0'\|M_1'\|M_2)$ are divided into the following types:

- If $\Delta ICV_2 = 0$, it is an *Internal collision*.
- Else, $\Delta ICV_2 \neq 0$, it is an *External collision*. Moreover,
  - If (ICV_2, ICV_2') satisfies the dBB conditions, and $\Delta ICV_3 = 0$, it is a *dBB-collision*.

The core of the attack is to guarantee the existence of (ICV_2, ICV_2') satisfying the dBB conditions by a one-block message pair (M_0, M_0'), and identify it by appending different M_1 (See Fig. 2). If such a (ICV_2, ICV_2') exists, another collision can be obtained with less complexity than the birthday attack [24]. In this way, the adversary can identify the specific (ICV_2, ICV_2'), and conclude that the H^2-MAC is instantiated with MD5 rather than a random function. In a word, the adversary needs to distinguish the dBB-collision from others. The details are as follows:

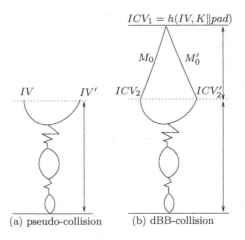

$ICV_1 = h(IV, K\|pad)$

(a) pseudo-collision   (b) dBB-collision

Fig. 2. Distinguishing Attack Based on a Pseudo-Collision Path

1. Generate a structure S that composes of 2^{89} three-block messages, where

   $$S = \{M_0\|M_1\|M_2|\ M_0 \text{ is chosen randomly, } M_1 \text{ and } M_2 \text{ are constants,}$$
   $$\text{and } M_2 \text{ contains all the padding information}\}.$$

   Query the MAC with each message in S, and collect all colliding pairs $(M_0\|M_1\|M_2, M_0'\|M_1\|M_2)$ by the birthday attack.
2. For all colliding pairs collected in step 1, append another $\tilde{M}_1\|\tilde{M}_2$ to (M_0, M_0'), and query the two MACs for the new pair $(M_0\|\tilde{M}_1\|\tilde{M}_2, M_0'\|\tilde{M}_1\|\tilde{M}_2)$. If their MACs still collide, it is an internal collision. And the others are external collisions.

3. For each external collisions, detect the dBB-collisions. Append 2^{47} different $\tilde{M}_1 \| \tilde{M}_2$ to (M_0, M_0'), respectively, and obtain their MACs. Among the 2^{47} new message pairs, if one collision is found, the corresponding (ICV_2, ICV_2') satisfies the dBB conditions. Then, append a randomly chosen $\tilde{M}_2$ to $M_0 \| M_1$, and query their MACs. If they still collide, there must be $\Delta ICV_3 = 0$, and a dBB collision is identified. The adversary concludes that the H^2-MAC is instantiated with MD5.

4. If there is no dBB-collision found after all external collisions are sieved, the H^2-MAC is based on a random function.

Complexity evaluation:

For 2^{89} randomly chosen messages, there is expected to produce $2^{89} * 2^{89} / 2 = 2^{177}$ pairs, so that step 2 collects $2^{177} / 2^{128} = 2^{49}$ internal collisions, 2 dBB-collisions and $2^{49} * 3 \approx 2^{50.6}$ non-dBB external collisions. Thus, the complexity of step 3 is $2^{50.6} * 2^{47} = 2^{97.6}$ queries, which dominates the complexity of the whole distinguishing attack. To sum up, the complexity of our attack is about $2^{97.6}$ MAC computations, and the data complexity is about $2^{97.6}$ chosen messages.

3.2 Recovering the Equivalent Key $\tilde{K}$

As defined in Section 2.4, the equivalent key $\tilde{K}$ is the same as ICV_2 appeared in the distinguisher, and can be taken as the inner key of HMAC for fixed M_0. Thus, we can combine the above distinguisher with the bit flipping algorithm proposed by Contini and Yin [7] to construct an equivalent key recovery attack on H^2-MAC-MD5 without the related-key setting.

Suppose $(M_0 \| M_1 \| M_2, M_0' \| M_1 \| M_2)$ is a dBB-collision detected by the distinguisher, the corresponding (ICV_2, ICV_2') satisfies the dBB conditions, i. e., $(\tilde{K}, \tilde{K}')$ fulfills the dBB conditions, which performs as the two related inner keys in the different attack of [7], so that it can be recovered in the same way. We just recall their main idea as follows:

1. Obtain a message $M_1 \| M_2$ which causes a dBB-collision under the fixed $(\tilde{K}, \tilde{K}')$. We can utilize the one obtained in the distinguishing attack.

2. Determine 80 bits of the intermediate registers $R_{14} = (A_{14}, B_{14}, C_{14}, D_{14})$ involved in the computation of $h(\tilde{K}, M_1)$. To do this, the adversary modifies certain bits of M_1 to create many new message pairs $(M_0 \| M_1^* \| M_2, M_0' \| M_1^* \| M_2)$ smartly, and deduces the corresponding bits of R_{14} according to whether any new pairs collides or not. Since M_2 contains all the padding information, we can change M_1 randomly without affecting M_2. For more details, please refer to [7].

3. Compute candidates of $(\tilde{K}, \tilde{K}')$. Guess the other 48 bits of R_{14} and compute backwards. For $i = 13, 12, \cdots, 0$, compute

$$B_i = C_{i+1}, C_i = D_{i+1}, D_i = A_{i+1},$$
$$A_i = (B_{i+1} - B_i) \ggg s_i - f(B_i, C_i, D_i) - w_i - c_i.$$

In this way, $R_0 = (A_0, B_0, C_0, D_0)$ is derived, which is a candidate of $\tilde{K}$. And the corresponding candidate of $\tilde{K}'$ can be obtained by the dBB conditions.

4. Finally, there will be 2^{48} candidates for $(\tilde{K}, \tilde{K}')$, and the the correct one can be identified according to the equitation $\tilde{H}(\tilde{K}, M_1 \| M_2) = \tilde{H}(\tilde{K}', M_1 \| M_2)$.

Complexity evaluation:

The complexity of step 1 depends on the distinguishing attack, which is about $2^{97.6}$ queries and 2^{89} table lookups, and step 2 and step 3 takes the same as the inner-key recovery attack of Contini and Yin, which is 2^{45} MD5 operations. Therefore, the complexity of the equivalent key recovery attack is $2^{97.6}$ queries.

Remark. From the above analysis, it is noted that to proceed the key recovery attack, the first thing is to construct a pair $(\tilde{K}, \tilde{K}')$ meeting the dBB conditions, and identify it. As soon as we detect such a pair caused by (M_0, M_0'), we can construct a dBB-collision in the following way:

1. Randomly choose 2^{47} two-block messages $M_1 \| M_2$, where the padding information only appears in M_2.
2. Obtain the MAC value of 2^{47} pairs $(M_0 \| M_1 \| M_2, M_0' \| M_1 \| M_2)$. Among them, two collisions are expected to exist because the probability of a dBB-collision is 2^{-46}.

The complexity of the above steps is 2^{47} queries.

Therefore, in the distinguishing attack, the adversary can adopt the distinguisher proposed by [19] to find a pair $(\tilde{K}, \tilde{K}')$ satisfying dBB conditions, and utilize the above technique to obtain a dBB collision, which is required in step 1 of the equivalent key recovery attack. In this way, the complexity of the whole attack is dominated by the distinguishing attack, which is reduced to 2^{97} queries.

3.3   Selective Forgery Attack

Selective forgery attack means that an adversary is able to create a valid MAC σ for a message M of his choice, where M has not been signed or MACed in the past by the legitimate signer/MAC generator, and must be fixed before the start of the attack.

Once the adversary recovered the equivalent key $\tilde{K}$, he can perform the selective forgery immediately, and only takes 1 MAC computation. From

$$H^2\text{-MAC}(K, M_0 \| M^*) = H(IV, H(IV, K \| pad \| M_0 \| M^*)) = H(IV, \tilde{K} \| M^*),$$

where M_0 is the one that leads to $\tilde{K}$ in the distinguishing attack, and M^* can be any arbitrary messages, the adversary can compute the legal MAC value of the message $M_0 \| M^*$ without knowing K. Similarly, the legal MAC value of message $M_0' \| M^*$ can be obtained because of the recovery of $\tilde{K}'$.

4   Conclusions

In this paper, we further study the impact of the outer key from the cryptanalysis side, and insight about the gap in security between H^2-MAC and HMAC when they are applied with one of the current hash functions, MD5.

Since H^2-MAC is equivalent to HMAC without the outer key, the inner key recovery attacks on HMAC instantiated with any concrete hash functions can be applied to H^2-MAC immediately. While for MD5, the situation becomes interesting. Since there only exists a distinguishing attack on HMAC-MD5 without related keys [19] in published literatures. In contrast, we present an equivalent key recovery attack on H^2-MAC-MD5 getting rid of the related-key restriction. It is noted that our results accord with the security proof associated with H^2-MAC, which is provable secure on the assumption that the underlying compression function is a secure Pseudo-Random Function (PRF) [22], while HMAC's security based on a weaker-than-PRF property of the compression function [2].

Inspired by Wang et al.'s idea of detecting the inner near-collision of HMAC-MD5 [19], the adversary can guarantee the existence of a pair of intermediate chaining variables, i. e., the equivalent keys $(\tilde{K}, \tilde{K}')$, which satisfies the specific conditions on (IV, IV') of the pseudo-collision, by one-block message M_0, and identify it by appending different one-block messages M_1. If such $(\tilde{K}, \tilde{K}')$ is identified, the equivalent key recovery attack can be processed, where the bit flipping algorithm proposed by Contini and Yin [7] is adopted. The complexity of the equivalent key recovery attack is 2^{97} queries, which is dominated by the distinguishing attack. Moreover, the equivalent key recovery attack leads to a selective forgery attack, since the adversary can compute the valid MAC value of any extension of M_0 effortlessly , where M_0 is the one-block message corresponding to $\tilde{K}$.

References

1. Bellare, M., Canetti, R., Krawczyk, H.: Keying Hash Functions for Message Authentication. In: Koblitz, N. (ed.) CRYPTO 1996. LNCS, vol. 1109, pp. 1–15. Springer, Heidelberg (1996)
2. Bellare, M.: New Proofs for NMAC and HMAC: Security without Collision-Resistance. In: Dwork, C. (ed.) CRYPTO 2006. LNCS, vol. 4117, pp. 602–619. Springer, Heidelberg (2006)
3. Biham, E., Chen, R.: Near-Collisions of SHA-0. In: Franklin, M.K. (ed.) CRYPTO 2004. LNCS, vol. 3152, pp. 290–305. Springer, Heidelberg (2004)
4. Biham, E., Chen, R., Joux, A., Carribault, P., Lemuet, C., Jalby, W.: Collisions of SHA-0 and Reduced SHA-1. In: Cramer, R. (ed.) EUROCRYPT 2005. LNCS, vol. 3494, pp. 36–57. Springer, Heidelberg (2005)
5. den Boer, B., Bosselaers, A.: Collisions for the Compression Function of MD5. In: Helleseth, T. (ed.) EUROCRYPT 1993. LNCS, vol. 765, pp. 293–304. Springer, Heidelberg (1994)
6. Chabaud, F., Joux, A.: Differential Collisions in SHA-0. In: Krawczyk, H. (ed.) CRYPTO 1998. LNCS, vol. 1462, pp. 56–71. Springer, Heidelberg (1998)

7. Contini, S., Yin, Y.L.: Forgery and Partial Key-Recovery Attacks on HMAC and NMAC Using Hash Collisions. In: Lai, X., Chen, K. (eds.) ASIACRYPT 2006. LNCS, vol. 4284, pp. 37–53. Springer, Heidelberg (2006)
8. Fouque, P.-A., Leurent, G., Nguyen, P.Q.: Full Key-Recovery Attacks on HMAC/NMAC-MD4 and NMAC-MD5. In: Menezes, A. (ed.) CRYPTO 2007. LNCS, vol. 4622, pp. 13–30. Springer, Heidelberg (2007)
9. Kim, J., Biryukov, A., Preneel, B., Hong, S.: On the Security of HMAC and NMAC Based on HAVAL, MD4, MD5, SHA-0, and SHA-1. In: De Prisco, R., Yung, M. (eds.) SCN 2006. LNCS, vol. 4116, pp. 242–256. Springer, Heidelberg (2006)
10. Preneel, B., van Oorschot, P.: MDx-MAC and Building Fast MACs from Hash Functions. In: Coppersmith, D. (ed.) CRYPTO 1995. LNCS, vol. 963, pp. 1–14. Springer, Heidelberg (1995)
11. Rechberger, C., Rijmen, V.: On Authentication with HMAC and Non-Random Properties. In: Dietrich, S., Dhamija, R. (eds.) FC 2007 and USEC 2007. LNCS, vol. 4886, pp. 39–57. Springer, Heidelberg (2007)
12. Rechberger, C., Rijmen, V.: New Results on NMAC/HMAC when Instantiated with Popular Hash Functions. Journal of Universal Computer Science 14(3), 347–376 (2008)
13. Rivest, R.L.: The MD5 Message Digest Algorithm. Request for Comments (RFC 1321), Network Working Group (1992)
14. Tsudik, G.: Message Authentication with One-Way Hash Functions. ACM Comput. Commun. Rev. 22(5), 29–38 (1992)
15. Wang, L., Ohta, K., Kunihiro, N.: New Key-Recovery Attacks on HMAC/NMAC-MD4 and NMAC-MD5. In: Smart, N. (ed.) EUROCRYPT 2008. LNCS, vol. 4965, pp. 237–253. Springer, Heidelberg (2008)
16. Wang, X.: What's the Potential Danger Behind the Collisions of Hash Functions. In: ECRYPT Conference on Hash Functions, Krakow (2005), http://www.ecrypt.eu.org/stvl/hfw/
17. Wang, X., Lai, X., Feng, D., Chen, H., Yu, X.: Cryptanalysis of the Hash Functions MD4 and RIPEMD. In: Cramer, R.J.F. (ed.) EUROCRYPT 2005. LNCS, vol. 3494, pp. 1–18. Springer, Heidelberg (2005)
18. Wang, X., Yu, H.: How to Break MD5 and Other Hash Functions. In: Cramer, R.J.F. (ed.) EUROCRYPT 2005. LNCS, vol. 3494, pp. 19–35. Springer, Heidelberg (2005)
19. Wang, X., Yu, H., Wang, W., Zhang, H., Zhan, T.: Cryptanalysis on HMAC/NMAC-MD5 and MD5-MAC. In: Joux, A. (ed.) EUROCRYPT 2009. LNCS, vol. 5479, pp. 121–133. Springer, Heidelberg (2009)
20. Wang, X., Yu, H., Yin, Y.L.: Efficient Collision Search Attacks on SHA-0. In: Shoup, V. (ed.) CRYPTO 2005. LNCS, vol. 3621, pp. 1–16. Springer, Heidelberg (2005)
21. Wang, X., Yin, Y.L., Yu, H.: Finding Collisions in the Full SHA-1. In: Shoup, V. (ed.) CRYPTO 2005. LNCS, vol. 3621, pp. 17–36. Springer, Heidelberg (2005)
22. Yasuda, K.: HMAC without the "Second" Key. In: Samarati, P., Yung, M., Martinelli, F., Ardagna, C.A. (eds.) ISC 2009. LNCS, vol. 5735, pp. 443–458. Springer, Heidelberg (2009)
23. Yu, H., Wang, G., Zhang, G., Wang, X.: The Second-Preimage Attack on MD4. In: Desmedt, Y.G., Wang, H., Mu, Y., Li, Y. (eds.) CANS 2005. LNCS, vol. 3810, pp. 1–12. Springer, Heidelberg (2005)
24. Yuval, G.: How to Swindle Rabin. Cryptologia 3, 187–190 (1979)

Recent Progress in Code-Based Cryptography

Pierre-Louis Cayrel, Sidi Mohamed El Yousfi Alaoui,
Gerhard Hoffmann, Mohammed Meziani, and Robert Niebuhr

CASED – Center for Advanced Security Research Darmstadt,
Mornewegstrasse, 32
64293 Darmstadt
Germany
pierre-louis.cayrel,elyousfi,hoffmann,meziani,niebuhr@cased.de

Abstract. The last three years have witnessed tremendous progress in
the understanding of code-based cryptography. One of its most promising applications is the design of cryptographic schemes with exceptionally
strong security guarantees and other desirable properties. In contrast to
number-theoretic problems typically used in cryptography, the underlying problems have so far resisted subexponential time attacks as well as
quantum algorithms. This paper will survey the more recent developments. *Keywords:* Post-quantum cryptography, coding-based cryptography, encryption, digital signatures, identification, secret-key.

Introduction

Code-based cryptography is one of the most promising candidates for post-
quantum cryptography, i.e. cryptosystems that resist attacks by quantum
computers. Examples are the McEliece and the Niederreiter encryption
schemes [12,14]. The underlying problem, the Syndrome Decoding problem, has
been proven NP-complete in [1]. In 2008, Overbeck and Sendrier [70] published
a comprehensive state-of-the-art of code-based cryptography. In the last three
years, there have been many new publications in various areas of cryptography.

Our Contribution

In this paper, we provide a state-of-the-art of code-based cryptography. We
present the publications since 2008 in several areas of this field, including encryption and identification schemes, digital signatures, secret-key cryptography,
and cryptanalysis.

Organization of the Paper

In Section 1, we present the recent improvements in the design of encryption
schemes attempting to reduce the public key sizes. In Section 2, we detail the
recent results in zero-knowledge identification schemes. Section 3 deals with the
new improvements of code-based signature schemes and Section 4 presents the
new results in code-based secret-key cryptography. The subsequent Section 5
details the latest results in cryptanalysis. We conclude in Section 6.

T.-h. Kim et al. (Eds.): ISA 2011, CCIS 200, pp. 21–32, 2011.
© Springer-Verlag Berlin Heidelberg 2011

1   Encryption

In code-based cryptography there are at least three encryption schemes: the McEliece [12], the Niederreiter [14] encryption schemes, and, more recently, the HyMES [9] (Hybrid McEliece encryption scheme). All those schemes have already been described in [78] pages 97–100 and 127–129.

The McEliece encryption scheme never caught the attention like e.g. RSA, mostly because of the relatively large size of the public generator matrix. Things changed when it turned out that the scheme is unscathed by quantum-computer attacks, and several contributions have been made in the last few years [5,7,48,65,11].

1.1   Reducing the Key Size of the McEliece Cryptosystem

Since [10], the idea of using compact representations of the public matrix used in the McEliece encryption scheme has been investigated. After several cryptanalyses, Berger et al. [48] and Misoczki and Barreto [65] proposed to use QC alternant codes and QD Goppa codes respectively to reduce the public key size from several hundred thousands bits (500 Kbits for the original proposal) to only 20 Kbits. The idea of those constructions is to generate the whole matrix via permutations of the first row. Furthermore, those constructions allow to encrypt the message without computing the whole matrix but by using the first row only. After several attacks (see Section 5), the binary parameters are still secure in both cases.

1.2   Implementation on Different Platforms

Due to a lack of space we will not detail the section in this version of the paper.

2   Identification

In the last few years there were many attempts to build secure identification schemes based on error-correcting codes. Such schemes allow a prover holding a secret key to prove his/her identity to a verifier holding the corresponding public key without revealing any additional information that might be used by an impersonator. At Crypto'93, Stern [20] presented the first identification scheme based on the SD problem. This scheme is a multiple-rounds zero-knowledge protocol, where each round is a three-pass interaction between the prover and the verifier, and for which the success probability for a cheater is $2/3$. The number of rounds depends on the security level needed; for 80 bits security level, one needs about 150 rounds (the norm ISO/IEC-9798-5 proposes the two cheat probabilities 2^{-16} and 2^{-32} for which one needs 28 resp. 56 rounds).

2.1   Quasi-Cyclic Stern

Due to the usual drawback of code-based cryptosystems, the large public key size, Gaborit and Girault proposed in 2007 [17] a way to reduce this disadvantage. The idea consists in using QC codes instead of random codes.

Using this class of codes, Cayrel et al. proposed in [15] an efficient implementation of Stern's protocol on a smart-card. For a security level of 80 bits, they obtained an authentication in 6 seconds and a signature in 24 seconds without cryptographic co-processor. This is a promising result when compared to an RSA implementation which would take more than 30 seconds in a similar context.

2.2 Cayrel et al.'s Identification Scheme

Recently, Cayrel et al. presented in [16] an identification scheme using q-ary codes instead of binary codes which constitutes an improvement of the Stern and Véron constructions. This scheme is a five-pass protocol for which the success probability of a cheater is bounded by $1/2$ per round. In addition to the new way to calculate the commitments, this protocol uses another improvement which is inspired by [18,19]. It consists of sending a random challenge value from $\mathbb{F}_q$ by the verifier after receiving the two commitments from the sender, who sends back the secret key scrambled by a random vector, a random permutation and the random challenge.

3 Signature

In code-based cryptography, there have been many attempts to design signature schemes using linear codes. Some proposals like [22,30,21] have been proved to be insecure; however, the two following schemes remain secure. The first one, by Kabatianskii, Krouk, and Smeets (KKS) [31] in 1997, is based on random codes and claimed to be secure. However, [26] showed that a passive attacker intercepting just a few signatures can efficiently find the private key. The second one, introduced by Courtois, Finiasz and Sendrier (CFS) in 2001, is the first code-based signature scheme with a security reduction [27] to two NP-complete problems: the SD and the GD problem. This latter has lately been shown to be solvable, but only under very specific parameter constraints (see Section 5).

3.1 Quasi-Dyadic-CFS

Motivated by the drawback of having large memory requirement, Barreto et al. [23] proposed an improved version of CFS using QD Goppa codes instead of the standard Goppa codes. This class of codes is mentioned earlier in Section 1. This modification allows to reduce the key size by a factor of 4 in practice and to speed-up the computation by using the QD structure.

3.2 Parallel-CFS

In view of Bleichenbacher's attack described in [59], the preliminary parameters of the CFS had to be increased. This leads to an increase of the public key size or of the signature cost by an exponential factor in parameters m or t, where 2^m the code length and t the degree of the Goppa polynomial, respectively.

Recently, Finiasz suggested in [28] a way to increase the security of the CFS while keeping the parameters as small as possible. The idea of his proposal consists in performing a parallel complete decoding to generate two CFS signatures using two different hash-functions for the same message. In this case, an attacker has to produce two forgeries for the same message, which makes the decoding attack much harder compared with the regular CFS.

3.3   Barreto et al's OTS

In 2010, Barreto et al. [24] developed a syndrome-based one-time signature scheme (BMS-OTS) by combining the idea of Schnorr [32] and KKS [31]. The security of their proposal is based on the hardness of decoding random binary codes, which is believed to be hard on average [25].

4   Secret Key Code-Based Cryptography

Until 2006, only two results have been proposed in code-based cryptography in the area of hash functions and stream ciphers. Regarding stream ciphers, Fischer and Stern [42] (FS) presented the first pseudo-random generator at Eurocrypt 1996, whose security stems from the intractability of the SD problem for random binary linear codes.

In context of hashing, two different versions have been proposed following the Merkle-Damgård [45,41] design principle: the first one is the Syndrome Based hash function (SB) in 2003 [34] whose compression function uses a random binary matrix and the algorithm from [44] for embedding data in a constant weight word. However, this algorithm is the most time-consuming part of the scheme. That is why a second and faster variant of SB, called Fast Syndrome Based hash function (FSB) [47], has been developed in 2005 by replacing the latter encoding function by a faster one called regular encoding. This algorithm embeds data into a regular word. This word is composed of a number of equal-sized blocks, each of which contains exactly one non-zero entry.

4.1   FSB SHA-3 Proposal

The first round SHA3-submission FSB due to Augot et al. [33] is an enhanced variant of FSB with two main features: It uses truncated QC codes to reduce the storage capacity and it provides a security reduction to the SD problem. It is designed following the well-known Merkle-Damgård transform [45,41] and parameterized by four positive integers. Each set of these parameters defines a unique compression function, which is a composition of an encoding function and a syndrome mapping. This mapping is based on a parity check matrix derived from digits of π (about 2 million bits) by circular shifting a number of vectors of the same length.

So far, the FSB SHA-3 proposal is secure. It can be proven that breaking it (finding collisions or preimages) is at least as difficult as solving certain problems introduced and proved NP-complete in [47]: the RSD and the 2-RNSD problem. The complexity of solving the latter problem is less than that of the conventional SD as demonstrated lately in [39] (see Section 5). Despite this feature, FSB suffers from the drawback of having a long initialization time and handling large states, and therefore it remains far slower than widely-used hash functions like the SHA-2 family (which is a SHA-3 candidate as well).

4.2 RFSB

Motivated by the inefficiency of FSB, Bernstein et al. [40] proposed a further improved variant of FSB in 2011, named RFSB (stands for Really Fast Syndrome-Based hashing), also following the Merkle–Damgård construction [45,41]. Its design is inspired by the Set Hash due to Zobrist [46] (and other related works [41,36,37]). In order to compute a hash value, the message is first broken into small pieces, each passed through a random function and finally combined using the bitwise XOR operator. The random function can be described by a random binary matrix. Unlike FSB, no encoding algorithm is used here and the matrix is not quasi cyclic, smaller than the FSB-matrix and defined as follows. Each entry is created by first encrypting a number of 16-bytes strings using the AES algorithm and then rotating the results certain times depending on the block position of the message.

4.3 SYND Stream Cipher

This cipher, proposed by Gaborit el al. [43] in 2007, is an improved variant of the Fisher-Stern pseudo-random generator [42] with two main improvements. Firstly, replacing a random matrix by a random QC matrix decreases the storage requirements without diminishing the hardness of the SD, as shown in [48]. Secondly, using the regular encoding technique instead of the algorithms proposed in [42] speeds up the encoding process.

5 Cryptanalysis

The two main types of attacks in code-based cryptography are structural and decoding attacks. The former exploit the structure of the underlying code, and usually they attempt to recover the secret key. The latter can be used independently of the code structure and are thus also called generic attacks.

This section details the recent cryptanalytic improvements and corresponds to Sections 3.4 and 4.3 in [78].

5.1 Structural Attacks

In the past, most structural attacks against code-based cryptosystems have targeted specific classes of codes. They exploited the code structure in order to break cryptosystems which use these codes. Examples include the Sidelnikov-Shestakov attack against the Niederreiter PKC using GRS (Generalized Reed-Solomon) codes [74], Overbeck's attack against rank-metric codes [69], and cryptanalysis of Reed-Muller codes using Stern's algorithm [75].

Since a large public key size is one of the drawbacks of code-based cryptography, there have been many proposals attempting to reduce the key size, as presented in Sections 1 and 3. Often, the authors used highly structured codes which can be stored more efficiently. Examples include QC [48] and QD [65] codes, as well as LDPC codes. In recent years, there have been several publications on structural attacks against such highly structured codes.

Otmani et al. [68] cryptanalyzed a McEliece cryptosystem based on QC LDPC codes. The attack exploits the QC structure to find a punctured version of the secret key, and then uses Stern's algorithm to reconstruct the entire secret key.

In [60], Gauthier and Leander presented an attack against QC and QD codes. The attack is based on an attack framework which exploits linear redundancies in subfield subcodes of GRS codes. While the attack breaks several codes over larger fields $\mathbb{F}_q$, binary codes remain secure against it.

Faugère et al. presented an algebraic attack against the McEliece cryptosystem using non-binary QC and QD codes at Eurocrypt 2010 [57], and an extention of this work at SCC 2010 [58]. The attacker sets up a system of algebraic equations, the solution of which will be an alternant decoder for the underlying code. While this system cannot be solved efficiently for the original McEliece cryptosystem, the additional QC or QD structure allows to significantly reduce the number of unknowns of this system. Additionally, improved Gröbner basis techniques further decrease the attack complexity. With this approach, the authors were able to break several non-binary parameters presented in [48] and [65]. Again, binary parameters remain secure. In [53], Bernstein et al. described how to improve ISD-based algorithms if the target codeword is a 2-regular word (a vector consisting of blocks, each having Hamming weight zero or two). The attack is an improvement over a previous attack against 2-regular words described in [47] and achieves an exponential speedup.

Wieschebrink presented a new attack [77] against the Berger-Loidreau public-key cryptosystem. In 2010, Faugère et al. presented a Goppa code distinguisher [56]. The algorithm allows to distinguish Goppa codes from random codes, provided that the code rate (code dimension divided by code length) is very high. While the paper does not attack a specific cryptosystem, it is an important result for past and future security proofs. Overbeck presented a security analysis of the Gabidulin version of the McEliece cryptosystem [69].

5.2 Decoding Attacks

Information-set decoding (ISD) and the generalized birthday algorithm (GBA) are the two most important types of generic attacks against code-based cryptosystems. The basic ISD algorithm is due to Prange [72], with major improvements by Leon [63], Lee-Brickell [62], Stern [75], and Canteaut-Chabaud [54].

Wagner [76] generalized the well-known birthday algorithm to more than two lists which greatly improved the algorithm efficiency.

In [51], Bernstein et al. proposed several techniques to speed up ISD-based attacks, e.g. by re-using pivot values to speed up the matrix inversion step. These improvements reduce the cost to attack the original McEliece parameters

$(1024, 524, 50)$ to $2^{60.5}$ binary operations. Together with van Tilborg, the above authors presented a comparison of different generic decoding algorithms [55]. Using upper and lower bounds for the cost of these algorithms, they also compared the asymptotic behaviour. While the analyzed decoding algorithms (asymptotically) save a non-constant factor compared with Lee-Brickell, they only save a factor of $1 + o(1)$ compared with Stern's algorithm.

In [59], Finiasz and Sendrier proposed lower bounds for the complexity of birthday, ISD and GBA attacks against code-based cryptosystems. The approach is to define a generic model for each attack, identify the essential steps, and use only the cost of these steps to compute the attack complexity.

In [71], Peters generalized Stern's and Lee-Brickell's algorithms (both are variants of ISD) to $\mathbb{F}_q$. Based on this generalization, the author provided an estimation of the cost of these algorithms.

Bernstein et al. published an improved ISD-algorithm in [52]. This algorithm manages to decrease the complexity slightly below the corresponding lower bound from [59]. Note that the improved algorithm does not fit into the generic model used in [59], so this result did not invalidate the lower bound formula. Niebuhr et al. [67] generalized these lower bounds to $\mathbb{F}_q$.

While Wagner's GBA has improved the time complexity compared with previous birthday algorithms, the lists used by the algorithm can be very large. Minder and Sinclair [64] proposed a more flexible algorithm that allows to trade off time vs. memory efficiency. The modified algorithm allows to limit the list size to arbitrary values, including the size of the input lists. The drawback is a decreased time efficiency.

In [66], Niebuhr et al. showed how to increase the efficiency of GBA when attacking structured matrices. Covered by the improvement are all matrices where each row is a permutation of the first. The improvement allows to increase the time and memory efficiency by a factor of r, the co-dimension of the code. A basic problem on which several code-based cryptosystems are based is the SD problem. It was proved to be NP-complete in 1978. In most cases, however, the cryptosystems rely on specific instances of this problem that are subject to additional constraints. While code-based cryptography is assumed to be secure against quantum computer attacks, a modification of the parameters will nonetheless be required. The conventional wisdom is that Shor's algorithm [73] requires a twofold increase in the key size of these cryptosystems. In [49], Bernstein analyzed the impact of Grover's algorithm [61]. Using this algorithm to speed up specialized attacks like ISD will require a quadrupling of the McEliece key size, for instance. While this effect is smaller than the worst-case assumption of a square-root speedup in all attacks, it is greater than some more optimistic assumptions, e.g. in [70, Section 3.5].

6   Conclusion

In this paper, we have described the recent results in code-based cryptography. These results include the new improvements in several different areas of cryptography (encryption, identification, signature, secret-key and cryptanalysis). This paper provides a comprehensive state-of-the-art and an extension of the chapter "Code-based cryptography" of the book [78]. The study of code-based cryptosystems needs still more work to obtain efficient and secure schemes, but also schemes with additional properties like identity-based encryption, batch-identification, blind signature or block cipher.

Encryption References

1. Berlekamp, E., McEliece, R., van Tilborg, H.: On the Inherent Intractability of Certain Coding Problems. IEEE Transactions on Information Theory IT-24(3) (1978)
2. McEliece, R.: A Public-Key Cryptosystem Based on Algebraic Coding Theory. The Deep Space Network Progress Report, DSN PR, 42–44 (1978), http://ipnpr.jpl.nasa.gov/progressreport2/42-44/44N.PDF
3. Niederreiter, H.: Knapsack-type Cryptosystems and Algebraic Coding Theory. Problems of Control and Information Theory 15(2), 159–166 (1986)
4. Overbeck, R., Sendrier, N.: Code-Based Cryptography, pp. 95–146. Springer, Heidelberg (2008)

Identification References

5. Barreto, P.S.L.M., Lindner, R., Misoczki, R.: Decoding Square-Free Goppa Codes over $\mathbb{F}_p$. Cryptology ePrint Archive, Report 2010/372 (2010), http://eprint.iacr.org/
6. Berger, T.P., Cayrel, P.-L., Gaborit, P., Otmani, A.: Reducing Key Length of the McEliece Cryptosystem. In: Preneel, B. (ed.) AFRICACRYPT 2009. LNCS, vol. 5580, pp. 77–97. Springer, Heidelberg (2009)
7. Bernstein, D.J.: List Decoding for Binary Goppa Codes. Preprint (2008), http://cr.yp.to/papers.html#goppalist
8. Bernstein, D.J., Buchmann, J., Dahmen, E.: Post-Quantum Cryptography. Springer, Heidelberg (2008)
9. Biswas, B., Sendrier, N.: Mceliece Cryptosystem Implementation: Theory and Practice. In: Buchmann, J., Ding, J. (eds.) PQCrypto 2008. LNCS, vol. 5299, pp. 47–62. Springer, Heidelberg (2008)
10. Gaborit, P.: Shorter Keys for Code-based Cryptography. In: International Workshop on Coding and Cryptography – WCC 2005, pp. 81–91. ACM Press, Bergen (2005)
11. Loidreau, P.: Designing a rank metric based McEliece cryptosystem. In: Sendrier, N. (ed.) PQCrypto 2010. LNCS, vol. 6061, pp. 142–152. Springer, Heidelberg (2010)
12. McEliece, R.: A Public-Key Cryptosystem Based on Algebraic Coding Theory. The Deep Space Network Progress Report, DSN PR, 42–44 (1978), http://ipnpr.jpl.nasa.gov/progressreport2/42-44/44N.PDF
13. Misoczki, R., Barreto, P.S.L.M.: Compact McEliece Keys from Goppa Codes (2009) (preprint), http://eprint.iacr.org/2009/187.pdf
14. Niederreiter, H.: Knapsack-type Cryptosystems and Algebraic Coding Theory. Problems of Control and Information Theory 15(2), 159–166 (1986)

Signature References

15. Cayrel, P.-L., Gaborit, P., Prouff, E.: Secure Implementation of the Stern Authentication and Signature Schemes for Low-Resource Devices. In: Grimaud, G., Standaert, F.-X. (eds.) CARDIS 2008. LNCS, vol. 5189, pp. 191–205. Springer, Heidelberg (2008)
16. Cayrel, P.-L., Véron, P., Alaoui, S.M.Y.: A Zero-Knowledge Identification Scheme Based on the q-ary Syndrome Decoding Problem. In: Biryukov, A., Gong, G., Stinson, D.R. (eds.) SAC 2010. LNCS, vol. 6544, pp. 171–186. Springer, Heidelberg (2011)
17. Gaborit, P., Girault, M.: Lightweight Code-based Authentication and Signature. In: IEEE International Symposium on Information Theory – ISIT 2007, pp. 191–195. IEEE, Nice (2007)
18. Shamir, A.: An Efficient Identification Scheme Based on Permuted Kernels. In: Brassard, G. (ed.) CRYPTO 1989. LNCS, vol. 435, pp. 606–609. Springer, Heidelberg (1990)
19. Stern, J.: Designing Identification Schemes with Keys of Short Size. In: Desmedt, Y.G. (ed.) CRYPTO 1994. LNCS, vol. 839, pp. 164–173. Springer, Heidelberg (1994)
20. Stern, J.: A New Identification Scheme Based on Syndrome Decoding. In: Proceedings of the 13th Annual International Cryptology Conference on Advances in Cryptology, pp. 13–21. Springer-Verlag New York, Inc., New York (1994)

Secret Key References

21. Alabbadi, M., Wicker, S.B.: Security of Xinmei Digital Signature Scheme (1992)
22. Alabbadi, M., Wicker, S.B.: Digital Signature Scheme Based on Error-Correcting Codes. In: IEEE International Symposium on Information Theory, pp. 9–19. IEEE, Los Alamitos (1993)
23. Barreto, P.S.L.M., Cayrel, P.-L., Misoczki, R., Niebuhr, R.: Quasi-dyadic CFS signatures. In: Lin, D. (ed.) Inscrypt 2010. LNCS, vol. 6584, pp. 336–349. Springer, Heidelberg (2011)
24. Barreto, P.S.L.M., Misoczki, R., Simplício Jr., M.A.: One-Time Signature Scheme from Syndrome Decoding over Generic Error-Correcting Codes. Journal of Systems and Software 84(2), 198–204 (2011)
25. Berlekamp, E., McEliece, R., van Tilborg, H.: On the Inherent Intractability of Certain Coding Problems. IEEE Transactions on Information Theory 24(3), 384–386 (1978)
26. Cayrel, P.-L., Otmani, A., Vergnaud, D.: On Kabatianskii-Krouk-Smeets Signatures. In: Carlet, C., Sunar, B. (eds.) WAIFI 2007. LNCS, vol. 4547, pp. 237–251. Springer, Heidelberg (2007)
27. Dallot, L.: Towards a Concrete Security Proof of Courtois, Finiasz and Sendrier Signature Scheme. In: Proceedings of WEWoRC 2007, Bochum, Germany (2007), http://users.info.unicaen.fr/~ldallot/download/articles/CFSProof-dallot.pdf
28. Finiasz, M.: Parallel-CFS: Strengthening the CFS Mc-Eliece-Based Signature Scheme. In: Biryukov, A., Gong, G., Stinson, D. (eds.) SAC 2010. LNCS, vol. 6544, pp. 159–170. Springer, Heidelberg (2011)

29. Finiasz, M., Sendrier, N.: Security bounds for the design of code-based cryptosystems. In: Matsui, M. (ed.) ASIACRYPT 2009. LNCS, vol. 5912, pp. 88–105. Springer, Heidelberg (2009), http://eprint.iacr.org/2009/414.pdf

30. Harn, L., Wang, D.C.: Cryptoanalysis and Modification of Digital Signature Scheme Based on Error-Correcting Codes (1992)

31. Kabatianskii, G., Krouk, E., Smeets, B.J.M.: A Digital Signature Scheme Based on Random Error-Correcting Codes. In: Darnell, M.J. (ed.) Cryptography and Coding 1997. LNCS, vol. 1355, pp. 161–167. Springer, Heidelberg (1997)

32. Schnorr, C.P.: Efficient Identification and Signatures for Smart Cards. In: Brassard, G. (ed.) CRYPTO 1989. LNCS, vol. 435, pp. 239–252. Springer, Heidelberg (1990)

Cryptanalysis References

33. Augot, D., Finiasz, M., Gaborit, P., Manuel, S., Sendrier, N.: SHA-3 Proposal: FSB. Submission to the SHA-3 NIST Competition (2008)

34. Augot, D., Finiasz, M., Sendrier, N.: A Fast Provably Secure Cryptographic Hash Function. Cryptology ePrint Archive, Report 2003/230 (2003), http://eprint.iacr.org/

35. Augot, D., Finiasz, M., Sendrier, N.: A Family of Fast Syndrome Based Cryptographic Hash Functions. In: Dawson, E., Vaudenay, S. (eds.) Mycrypt 2005. LNCS, vol. 3715, pp. 64–83. Springer, Heidelberg (2005)

36. Bellare, M., Goldreich, O., Goldwasser, S.: Incremental Cryptography: The Case of Hashing and Signing. In: Desmedt, Y.G. (ed.) CRYPTO 1994. LNCS, vol. 839, pp. 216–233. Springer, Heidelberg (1994)

37. Bellare, M., Micciancio, D.: A New Paradigm for Collision-Free Hashing: Incrementality at Reduced Cost. In: Fumy, W. (ed.) EUROCRYPT 1997. LNCS, vol. 1233, pp. 163–192. Springer, Heidelberg (1997)

38. Berger, T.P., Cayrel, P.-L., Gaborit, P., Otmani, A.: Reducing Key Length of the McEliece Cryptosystem. In: Preneel, B. (ed.) AFRICACRYPT 2009. LNCS, vol. 5580, pp. 77–97. Springer, Heidelberg (2009)

39. Bernstein, D.J., Lange, T., Peters, C., Schwabe, P.: Faster 2-regular Information-Set Decoding (2011)

40. Bernstein, D.J., Lange, T., Peters, C., Schwabe, P.: Really Fast Syndrome-Based Hashing. Cryptology ePrint Archive, Report 2011/074 (2011), http://eprint.iacr.org/

41. Damgård, I.: A Design Principle for Hash Functions. In: Brassard, G. (ed.) CRYPTO 1989. LNCS, vol. 435, pp. 416–427. Springer, Heidelberg (1990)

42. Fischer, J.-B., Stern, J.: An Efficient Pseudo-Random Generator Provably as Secure as Syndrome Decoding. In: Maurer, U.M. (ed.) EUROCRYPT 1996. LNCS, vol. 1070, pp. 245–255. Springer, Heidelberg (1996)

43. Gaborit, P., Laudauroux, C., Sendrier, N.: SYND: A Fast Code-Based Stream Cipher with a Security Reduction. In: Proceeedings of ISIT 2007 (2007)

44. Guillot, P.: Algorithmes pour le codage á poids constant (unpublished)

45. Merkle, R.C.: One Way Hash Functions and DES. In: Brassard, G. (ed.) CRYPTO 1989. LNCS, vol. 435, pp. 428–446. Springer, Heidelberg (1990)

46. Zobrist, A.L.: A New Hashing Method with Application for Game Playing. Technical Report 88, U. Wisconsin CS Department (April 1970), https://www.cs.wisc.edu/techreports/1970/TR88.pdf

Others References

47. Augot, D., Finiasz, M., Sendrier, N.: A Family of Fast Syndrome Based Cryptographic Hash Functions. In: Dawson, E., Vaudenay, S. (eds.) Mycrypt 2005. LNCS, vol. 3715, pp. 64–83. Springer, Heidelberg (2005)

48. Berger, T.P., Cayrel, P.-L., Gaborit, P., Otmani, A.: Reducing Key Length of the McEliece Cryptosystem. In: Preneel, B. (ed.) AFRICACRYPT 2009. LNCS, vol. 5580, pp. 77–97. Springer, Heidelberg (2009)

49. Bernstein, D.J.: Grover vs. McEliece. In: Sendrier, N. (ed.) PQCrypto 2010. LNCS, vol. 6061, pp. 73–80. Springer, Heidelberg (2010)

50. Bernstein, D.J., Buchmann, J., Dahmen, E.: Post-Quantum Cryptography. Springer, Heidelberg (2008)

51. Bernstein, D.J., Lange, T., Peters, C.: Attacking and Defending the McEliece Cryptosystem. In: Buchmann, J., Ding, J. (eds.) PQCrypto 2008. LNCS, vol. 5299, pp. 31–46. Springer, Heidelberg (2008)

52. Bernstein, D.J., Lange, T., Peters, C.: Ball-Collision Decoding. Cryptology ePrint Archive, Report 2010/585 (2010), http://eprint.iacr.org/

53. Bernstein, D.J., Lange, T., Peters, C., Schwabe, P.: Faster 2-regular Information-Set Decoding. Cryptology ePrint Archive, Report 2011/120 (2011), http://eprint.iacr.org/

54. Canteaut, A., Chabaud, F.: A New Algorithm for Finding Minimum-Weight Words in a Linear Code: Application to Primitive Narrow-Sense BCH-Codes of Length 511. IEEE Transactions on Information Theory 44(1), 367–378 (1998)

55. Peters, C., Bernstein, D.J., Lange, T., van Tilborg, H.C.A.: Explicit Bounds for Generic Decoding Algorithms for Code-Based Cryptography. In: Pre-proceedings of WCC 2009, pp. 168–180 (2009)

56. Faugère, J.-C., Gauthier, V., Otmani, A., Perret, L., Tillich, J.-P.: A distinguisher for high rate mceliece cryptosystems. Cryptology ePrint Archive, Report 2010/331 (2010), http://eprint.iacr.org/

57. Faugère, J.-C., Otmani, A., Perret, L., Tillich, J.-P.: Algebraic Cryptanalysis of McEliece Variants with Compact Keys. In: Gilbert, H. (ed.) EUROCRYPT 2010. LNCS, vol. 6110, pp. 279–298. Springer, Heidelberg (2010)

58. Faugère, J.-C., Otmani, A., Perret, L., Tillich, J.-P.: Algebraic Cryptanalysis of McEliece Variants with Compact Keys – Towards a Complexity Analysis. In: SCC 2010: Proceedings of the 2nd International Conference on Symbolic Computation and Cryptography, RHUL, pp. 45–55 (June 2010)

59. Finiasz, M., Sendrier, N.: Security Bounds for the Design of Code-based Cryptosystems. In: Matsui, M. (ed.) ASIACRYPT 2009. LNCS, vol. 5912, pp. 88–105. Springer, Heidelberg (2009), http://eprint.iacr.org/2009/414.pdf

60. Gauthier, V., Leander, G.: Practical Key Recovery Attacks on Two McEliece Variants. Cryptology ePrint Archive, Report 2009/509 (2009), http://eprint.iacr.org/

61. Grover, L.K.: A Fast Quantum Mechanical Algorithm for Database Search. In: STOC, pp. 212–219 (1996)

62. Lee, P.J., Brickell, E.F.: An Observation on the Security of McEliece's Public-Key Cryptosystem. In: Günther, C.G. (ed.) EUROCRYPT 1988. LNCS, vol. 330, pp. 275–280. Springer, Heidelberg (1988)

63. Leon, J.S.: A Probabilistic Algorithm for Computing Minimum Weights of Large Error-Correcting Codes. IEEE Transactions on Information Theory 34(5), 1354–1359 (1988)

64. Minder, L., Sinclair, A.: The Extended k-tree Algorithm. In: SODA, pp. 586–595 (2009)
65. Misoczki, R., Barreto, P.S.L.M.: Compact McEliece Keys from Goppa Codes (2009) (preprint), http://eprint.iacr.org/2009/187.pdf
66. Niebuhr, R., Cayrel, P.-L., Buchmann, J.: Improving the Efficiency of Generalized Birthday Attacks Against Certain Structured Cryptosystems. In: WCC 2011 (April 2011)
67. Niebuhr, R., Cayrel, P.-L., Bulygin, S., Buchmann, J.: On Lower Bounds for Information Set Decoding over $\mathbb{F}_q$. In: SCC 2010, RHUL, London, UK (2010)
68. Otmani, A., Tillich, J.-P., Dallot, L.: Cryptanalysis of Two McEliece Cryptosystems Based on Quasi-Cyclic Codes (2008) (preprint), http://arxiv.org/abs/0804.0409v2
69. Overbeck, R.: Structural Attacks for Public Key Cryptosystems Based on Gabidulin Codes. J. Cryptology 21(2), 280–301 (2008)
70. Overbeck, R., Sendrier, N.: Code-Based Cryptography, pp. 95–146. Springer, Heidelberg (2008)
71. Peters, C.: Information-Set Decoding for Linear Codes over $\mathbb{F}_q$. In: Sendrier, N. (ed.) PQCrypto 2010. LNCS, vol. 6061, pp. 81–94. Springer, Heidelberg (2010)
72. Prange, E.: The Use of Information Sets in Decoding Cyclic Codes. IRE Transactions on Information Theory, 5–9 (1962)
73. Shor, P.W.: Polynomial-Time Algorithms for Prime Factorization and Discrete Logarithms on a Quantum Computer. SIAM Journal on Computing 26, 1484–1509 (1995)
74. Sidelnikov, V., Shestakov, S.: On Cryptosystems based on Generalized Reed-Solomon Codes. Discrete Mathematics 4(3), 57–63 (1992)
75. Stern, J.: A Method for Finding Codewords of Small Weight. In: Wolfmann, J., Cohen, G. (eds.) Coding Theory 1988. LNCS, vol. 388, pp. 106–113. Springer, Heidelberg (1989)
76. Wagner, D.: A Generalized Birthday Problem. In: Yung, M. (ed.) CRYPTO 2002. LNCS, vol. 2442, pp. 288–304. Springer, Heidelberg (2002)
77. Wieschebrink, C.: Two NP-complete Problems in Coding Theory with an Application in Code Based Cryptography. In: IEEE International Symposium on Information Theory – ISIT 2006, pp. 1733–1737. IEEE, Seattle (2006)

Conclusion References

78. Bernstein, D.J., Buchmann, J., Dahmen, E.: Post-Quantum Cryptography. Springer, Heidelberg (2008)

GPU Implementation of the Keccak Hash Function Family

Pierre-Louis Cayrel[1,2], Gerhard Hoffmann[2], and Michael Schneider[2]

[1] CASED – Center for Advanced Security Research Darmstadt, Germany
pierre-louis.cayrel@cased.de
[2] Technische Universität Darmstadt, Germany
hoffmann@mathematik.tu-darmstadt.de,
mischnei@cdc.informatik.tu-darmstadt.de

Abstract. Hash functions are one of the most important cryptographic primitives. Some of the currently employed hash functions like SHA-1 or MD5 are considered broken today. Therefore, in 2007 the US National Institute of Standards and Technology announced a competition for a new family of hash functions. Keccak is one of the five final candidates to be chosen as SHA-3 hash function standard. In this paper, we present an implementation of the Keccak hash function family on graphics cards, using NVIDIA's CUDA framework. Our implementation allows to choose one function out of the hash function family and hash arbitrary documents. In addition we present the first ready-to-use implementation of the *tree mode* of Keccak which is even more suitable for parallelization.

Keywords: Cryptography, Hash Functions, Keccak, GPU Computation.

1 Introduction

Before the modern era, cryptography was concerned solely with message confidentiality, conversion of messages from a comprehensible form into an incomprehensible one and back again at the other end, rendering it unreadable by interceptors or eavesdroppers without secret knowledge (namely the key needed for decryption of that message). Encryption was used to (attempt to) ensure secrecy in communications, such as those of spies, military leaders, and diplomats. In recent decades, the field has expanded beyond confidentiality concerns to include techniques for message integrity checking, sender/receiver identity authentication, digital signatures, interactive proofs, and others.

Cryptographic hash functions are a specific type of cryptographic algorithm. Without the existence of hash functions, modern cryptography is not imaginary. Among many others, hash functions are required for digital signatures, message authentication codes, or password authentication. A hash function takes as input a bit string of arbitrary length, and outputs a short, fixed length hash value. Since existing hash functions like MD4, MD5, and SHA-1 are considered broken today, the NIST (US National Institute of Standards and Technology) announced in 2007 an open hash function competition. A new SHA-3 is supposed to replace

T.-h. Kim et al. (Eds.): ISA 2011, CCIS 200, pp. 33–42, 2011.

the older SHA-1 and SHA-2 hash functions. The competition started with 64 hash function candidates. 14 candidates were chosen for the second round. Now there have been five SHA-3 candidates selected by NIST for the third final round: BLAKE, Grøstl, Skein, JH, Keccak [7]. For a detailed classification of the SHA-3 candidates, see [11]. The main concern for selection into the final, third round was security. Nonetheless, performance has been a relevant factor as well. We chose Keccak for a GPU implementation, because it has been the fastest one out of the five remaining NIST SHA-3 candidates [10].

Brief Description of Keccak. This paper is about the Keccak family of hash functions, which is based on the sponge construction [6]. The construction consists of two phases: an *absorbing phase* and a *squeezing phase*. In the absorbing phase the variable-length input is padded and decomposed into blocks of equal length. Each block is then handled successively: first, it is XORed onto some fixed memory area (called the *state*), then an internal permutation is applied on the state. As long as there are input blocks left, this step is repeated. After that the construction switches into the squeezing phase, providing arbitrary-length output. To this end the permutation is repeatedly applied to the state. After each step, some bits of the state are read as additional output. The nominal version of Keccak operates on a 1600-bit state. There are 6 other state widths, though, ranging from 25 to 800.

Why a GPU Implementation. Since 2005 a transition to multiple-core CPU took place, it is no longer possible just to wait for a new CPU model to speed up a sequential application. Programs have to be designed with parallelism in mind to use the computational power of modern CPUs and modern graphic processing units (GPUs). Even more than the CPUs, modern graphic processing units have evolved into massively parallel processors. Their performance doubles every 12 to 18 months, exceeding even the rate of Moore's law [9,15]. They are increasingly used for non-graphical calculations, an approach which is known as general-purpose GPU computing (GPGPU), or just GPU computing. As outlined in [9], in little more than five years a GPU will be equipped with more than 2.400 cores. Hardware companies are about to combine the computational power of the GPUs and the flexibility of multi-core CPUs into new architectures [12,1]. Highly parallel machines will be quite common in the future.

Related Work. There are two other GPU implementations of Keccak available [17,8]. Both only implement the tree-based mode proposed in [5], which will also be explained to some extent later in this document. The work of [17] is publicly available and implements Keccak-f[800]. Its implementation does not allow to hash arbitrary documents. The source code of [8] is closed at the moment, so we cannot compare to it. The Keccak version submitted to NIST is Keccak-f[1600]. Keccak-f[800] needs less memory and fits more naturally into the 32-bit GPU architecture. The prize to pay is that there is no publicly available reference implementation and that Keccak-f[800] possesses smaller values for the bit rate r and the capacity c. The bit rate r gives an estimation for the performance, whereas the capacity c determines the security of Keccak. Details on these parameters will be given in Section 2.1. Another difference to our implementation is that there are as many copies of Keccak-f[800] running as there are threads. In our implementation 25 threads cooperate to execute only one copy of Keccak.

Our Contribution. As Keccak is the fastest of the five remaining SHA-3 candidates, it is natural to ask how well Keccak can be implemented on todays parallel machines. Specifically, we will show in a first step how the internal sponge permutation of Keccak can be parallelized on modern GPU models. Even a parallel version of Keccak's permutation can not overcome the fact that the sponge construction is an inherently sequential process, resulting in a very low occupancy of the GPU. We will address this restriction in a second step and show two approaches of how the GPU can be used more efficiently to implement Keccak, namely batch and tree modes. Furthermore, we provide a public implementation of the Keccak hash function family.

Organization of the Paper. The remainder of this paper is organized as follows. First, we will give a general overview of Keccak in Section 2. After introducing a pseudo-code version of Keccak's internal permutation, we will first give some details of the GPU in Section 3. Then we describe a GPU implementation of Keccak's internal permutation in Section 3. We discuss the batch-mode and the tree-mode, which allow a much higher usage of the GPU in Section 4. Finally, we present some experimental results in Section 5.

2   The Keccak Hash Function Family

Before introducing the Keccak hash function family, we give a short explanation of the security properties of hash functions.

2.1   Structure of Keccak

Keccak is a family of hash functions based on the sponge construction (cf. Figure 1), which is an iterated algorithm [6,4]. The algorithm takes a variable-length

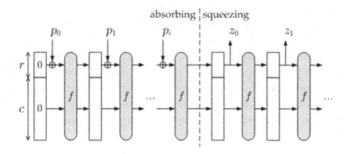

Fig. 1. The sponge construction [6]. p_i are the message blocks, f denotes the compression function, and z_i are the output blocks of the hash function.

bit string as input and produces an arbitrary-length output. The core of the algorithm is a permutation f repeatedly applied to a fixed-length *state* of $b = r + c$ bits. The value r is referred to as the *bit rate* and the value c as the *capacity*. Higher values of r improve the speed, higher values of c its security level. As described in [6], the sponge construction proceeds in the following steps:

(i) Reset the state to zero.
(ii) Pad the input message, such that its length is a multiple of r bits.
(iii) Absorbing phase: all input blocks of r bits are successively sent to the sponge construction in two steps: the r bits of each block (p_i) are XORed onto the first r bits of the state, which is then followed by an application of the permutation f.
(iv) Squeezing phase: After all blocks have been processed in the absorbing phase, the first r bits of the state are returned as output block (z_i). Should the user have requested more output blocks of r bits, then each repeated application of f will provide the next r-bit output block.

Note that the last c bits of the state are only changed by f itself, not by the XOR-operation in the absorbing phase. They are also never output in the squeezing phase.

2.2 Detailed View of Keccak

Seven possible Keccak hash functions form the Keccak family. They are denoted by Keccak-f[b], where $b \in \{25, 50, 100, 200, 400, 800, 1600\}$ is the width of the underlying permutation (in bits), which is also the width of the state A in the sponge construction. As noted above, $b = r + c$. The state consists of an array of 5×5 so-called *lanes*, each of length $w \in \{1, 2, 4, 8, 16, 32, 64\}$ bits, i.e. $b = 25w$. On a 64-bit processor, a lane of Keccak-f[1600] fits exactly in a 64-bit CPU word, which is why Keccak-f[1600] is the default version in the Keccak family. A more detailed pseudo-code of Keccak is shown in the full version.

2.3 Proposed Parameters

The recommended number of rounds for Keccak-f[1600] is 24. For SHA-3 the following parameter values have been proposed [2]: Keccak-f[$r = 1156, c = 448$], Keccak-f[$r = 1088, c = 512$], Keccak-f[$r = 832, c = 768$], Keccak-f[$r = 576, c = 1024$]. The default parameters are $r = 1024$ and $c = 576$, which are also the values we used in our implementation. The cost of finding a collision is 2^{288} binary operations. If an attacker has access to one billion computers, each performing one billion evaluations of Keccak-f per second, it would take about 1.6^{1061} years (1.1^{1051} times the estimated age of the universe) to evaluate the permutation 2^{288} times [3].

3   GPU Implementation

3.1   CUDA Programming Model

CUDA (*Compute Unified Device Architecture*) [14] is a GPGPU technology (*General-Purpose Computing on Graphics Processing Units*). Instead of executing an application exclusively on the central processor (CPU), some computational intensive parts of the application can be transferred to the graphic processor (GPU). Using the GPU for high-performance computing has been in practice for years already, but the lack of a suitable API made it a painstaking experience for the programmer, formulating his ideas in an API designed for pure graphics programming. In contrast, CUDA uses as API an extension of C or Fortran, which makes general-purpose programming on the GPU a lot easier. However, to program the GPU efficiently, a good knowledge of the internal workings of the GPU is still necessary.

Some NVIDIA GPU Internals. An extensive description of hardware details of NVIDIA GPUs can be found at [14,15], and we will restate some of the main points here in the context of the GPU model used for this paper, the GTX 295. But even for the new GPU architecture, called Fermi, the description will be adequate. At the highest level, the GPU consists of a number of so-called streaming multiprocessors (SM). Each SM contains a fixed number of so-called streaming processors (SP), typically 8. The GPU supports hardware-multithreading: a stalled thread waiting for data can be quickly replaced by another thread in exactly one processor (SP) cycle. The threads are organized in bigger units, so-called *warps*, which typically consist of 32 threads. Warps are the units which are actually scheduled on an SM. They are in turn organized in blocks (*cooperative thread arrays (CTAs)*) of typical sizes of 128 up to 256 threads or 4 to 8 warps. Threads belonging to the same CTA can communicate via a special and very fast memory area called *shared memory*. There is no way for the CTAs themselves to communicate: CUDA requires the thread blocks to be independent to allow them to be executed in any order, which leads to portability and scalability of CUDA programs. Using shared memory is in theory as fast as using registers. In practice, some care is advisable, though. Shared memory is composed of DRAM: each read or write operation has to be followed by a refresh cycle. To allow for maximal parallelism, shared memory is therefore built up of so-called *memory banks*. As long as different threads of a warp (more exactly, of a half-warp) access different memory banks, there is no problem. Otherwise so-called *bank conflicts* occur, leading to a contention situation, which reduces performance. Another important fact for the GPU implementation is that threads in the same warp are always synchronized. That means that data written to shared memory by the threads of a warp are visible to all threads in the warp in the next computational step. Finally, the code to be executed on the GPU is called a *kernel*. It is a C (or Fortran) function which has to be called on the CPU. With older GPU models only one kernel can be active on the GPU at the same moment.

3.2   Basic GPU Implementation of Keccak on the GPU

It is inherently difficult to parallelize Keccak on the GPU. The main reason is the very nature of the sponge construction. For instance, if using Keccak-f[1600] with bit rate $r = 1024$ and capacity $c = 576$, then each new 1024-bit part of the data to be hashed is XORed onto the first 1024 bits of the current state A, leading to a very sequential process. Before addressing this limitation, we will show how to parallelize the main functionality of Keccak, namely the rounds of the hash permutation. We give here C-code for a CUDA kernel, which executes a 64-bit version of Keccak-f[1600] with only one warp consisting of 25 threads.[1]. Although the GTX 295 is a 32-bit machine, the 64-bit version performed better. The 32-bit version uses some extra tables and operations to reduce the number of bank conflicts, but also extends its source code.

Source Listing (Algorithm 1). GPU code is typically very susceptible against conditionals for this often results in divergence of threads. Also, all the calculations in Keccak are done modulo 5, which is an expensive operation on the GPU. Therefore we designed some tables to get a compact code with implicit modulo settings, which will then be executed by 25 threads in parallel. The tables are given in the full version of this paper and have to be copied from the host to the GPU at runtime. Once the tables are in place, the actual code for Keccak-f[1600] consists of only 5 lines of code. As usual, A denotes the state of the permutation, consisting of $1600/8 = 200$ bytes. C and D are temporary variables. Only the innermost permutation step of Keccak-f[1600] consisting of 24 rounds is shown. Each round itself consists of five steps named θ, ρ, π, χ, and ι, respectively. When loading more than $1600/8 = 200$ byte, or when switching to the squeezing phase of Keccak, it has to be called repeatedly.

Lines 9 and 10 of Algorithm 1 represent the first part of the θ step. Using the index s into A results in the same access pattern as using $A[index(x, y)]$, where x and y run from 0 to 4 and $index(x, y)$ as given in Line 3. As the line is executed by 25 threads accessing only 5 different memory locations, bank conflicts occur. They could be resolved by the use of another table, but runtime measurements have shown that performance does not improve substantially. Bank conflicts in Lines $10 - 11$ are more serious, but also more difficult to avoid due to the general access pattern of Keccak. For instance, the tables are kept in constant device memory. While this type of memory is cached, it is also afflicted with bank conflicts. Line 11 is made up of the last part of the θ operation. Using to the encoding tables, it also contains ρ and π. Finally, Line 12 represents χ, whereas Line 13 is the ι operation.

4   Additional Keccak Modes on the GPU

Hashing a single document with Keccak is an inherently sequential process. The GPU supports thousands of threads in hardware, so the question arises how to

---

[1] Even when started with 25 threads, the runtime system of CUDA will always make sure that a warp has 32 threads.

Algorithm 1. Keccak-f[1600], 64-bit, r=1024, c=576

INPUT: *data*, A
OUTPUT: The scrambled state A.
1: #define ROUNDS (24)
2: #define R64(a,b,c) (((a) $\ll$ b) ^ ((a) $\gg$ c))
3: #define index(x,y) (((x)%5)+5*((y)%5))
4: int const t = threadIdx.x;   int const s = threadIdx.x%5;
5: __shared__ uint64_t A[25], C[25], D[25];
6: **if** t < 25 **then**
7:     $A[t] \leftarrow data[t]$;

8:     **for** $i \leftarrow 0$ **to** ROUNDS **do**
9:         $C[t] \leftarrow A[s] \ ^\wedge\ A[s+5] \ ^\wedge\ A[s+10] \ ^\wedge\ A[s+15] \ ^\wedge\ A[s+20]$;   ▷ First part of θ.
10:        $D[t] \leftarrow C[b[20+s]] \ ^\wedge\ R64(C[b[5+s]], 1, 63)$;   ▷ End of the θ operation.
11:        $C[t] \leftarrow R64(A[a[t]] \ ^\wedge\ D[b[t]], ro[t][0], ro[t][1])$;
12:        $A[d[t]] \leftarrow C[c[t][0]] \ ^\wedge\ ((\sim C[c[t][1]]) \ \& \ C[c[t][2]])$;   ▷ χ operation.
13:        $A[t] \leftarrow A[t] \ ^\wedge\ rc[(t == 0)\,?\,0\,:\,1][i]$;   ▷ ι operation.
14:    **end for**
15: **end if**

---

use more than just the 25 threads as shown above. One possibility is to hash more than one document at once in a *batch mode*. This way, the above kernel is applied on many data streams on the GPU, thereby greatly enhancing the achieved parallelism. Another approach is hashing a single document in *tree mode*. In this case, parts of the document are first loaded into the leaves of a tree. These leaves are then hashed using the basic kernel above. The result values are pushed onto the next level in the tree, iterating the process.

Batch Mode. For the batch mode, create a CUDA kernel consisting of 128 threads, say. Each of the 8 warps executes the basic Keccak kernel above on a different document. Thus a high occupancy of the GPU is possible. Some care is necessary, though. One point to keep in mind is that the GPU has considerable less memory than the CPU. As thousands of documents might not fit in GPU memory, some kind of ordering is necessary on the GPU side. Such an ordering can be achieved using CUDA streams. Together with the ability of the new Fermi GPUs to start kernels concurrently, such a batch mode seems to be a viable option. Due to time reasons we did not include the batch mode to our implementation.

Tree Mode. The task of parallelizing cryptographic hash functions by using trees has been studied by several authors [16,13]. The idea is to distribute the input data into the leaves of a tree and to hash those leaves independently and in parallel. Their hash values are combined and sent to corresponding parent nodes. The process is then applied recursively, until the root node provides the final digest. The Keccak main document [5] describes two possible approaches for such a tree-based mode: LI (*leaf interleaving*) and FNG (*final node growing*). We implemented only LI, for more information on FNG see the main document [5]. With LI, the tree size and the number of its leaves is a fixed number. The tree itself is a balanced tree of height H. All internal nodes have the same degree D. The number of the leaves is then $L = D^H$. As the tree is fixed, its parameters can be provided as input parameters. For possible parameter ranges we refer to [5]. The data input are two binary strings: a prefix P, which can be used as a key or a salt, and the document to be hashed [5, Page 30]. In a first step, the prefix and the document are concatenated and padded to form the input message M, whose blocks are then interleaved onto the leaves, c.f. Algorithm 2.

Algorithm 2. Leaf-Interleaving

INPUT: Bit string M, the input message. A tree with $L = D^H$ leaves. B denotes the leaf block size (in bits).
OUTPUT: A tree with M interleaved into its leaves.
　　　For each leaf L_j, $0 \leq j \leq L - 1$, set L_j to the empty string.
　for $i \leftarrow 0$ **to** $|M| - 1$ **do**
　　$j \leftarrow floor(i/B) \mod L$
　　Append bit i of M to L_j
　end for

Note that it does not say that a leaf can only load B bits of data. Instead, the number B is used merely as a parameter for the interleave technique. Once the leaves are initialized, each one is hashed independently in parallel. As in our setting $D = 4$, the hash values of 4 leaves are concatenated to form the input for the associated parent node. The process is then continued recursively up to the root node, which provides the final hash value. By applying Keccak on the root node repeatedly, arbitrary-length output is possible.

5   Experimental Results

We made some tests on an NVIDIA GTX 295 GPU. The source code of our implementation is publicly available[2]. Timings for different tree parameters and document file sizes are given in Table 1 as reported by the CUDA profiler. The numbers are given in seconds. For comparison, we ran the standard hash function MD5 on the same files on an Intel(R) Core(TM)2 Duo CPU E8400 (3.00GHz) running Linux 2.6.32. We cannot compare to other GPU versions of Keccak, since they are either not public or do not allow to hash arbitrary documents. Table 1 shows the strength of the tree mode. For height H=0 (the original serial mode) the timings cannot compete with MD5, whereas Keccak-f[1600] with height H=4 is nearly as fast as MD5. Recall that MD5 is considered outdated and insecure, whereas Keccak is supposed to guarantee strong security.

Together with the SHA-3 submission, a reference implementation of Keccak was published. Table 2 presents timings we gained using the Keccak reference implementation in version 2.3. The experiments were performed on an Intel(R) Core2 Duo CPU E8400 running at 3.00GHz. Hashing 128 MB costs approximately half a second, for example. Tests on a Tesla C2050 GPU showed comparable results between MD5 and the GPU implementation of Keccak.

---

[2] http://www.cayrel.net/spip.php?article189

Table 1. Timings in seconds for Keccak-f[1600] in tree mode on a GTX 295, for different tree heights H

File size [bytes]	H = 0	H = 1	H = 2	H = 3	H = 4	MD5
1.050.112	0.415	0.104	0.020	0.014	0.019	0.003
10.500.096	4.110	0.994	0.144	0.069	0.063	0.025
25.200.000	9.854	2.375	0.332	0.151	0.129	0.057
50.400.000	19.702	4.742	0.655	0.291	0.199	0.112

Table 2. Timings for the Keccak reference implementation on CPU, using a bit rate of r = 1024. We hashed blocks of size 128 byte each

File size [bytes]	Cycles	Time [ms]
128.000	1.664.892	0.555
1.280.000	16.616.619	5.539
12.800.000	166.548.357	55.516
128.000.000	1.668.329.037	556.110

6   Conclusion and Further Work

The crucial function of Keccak is its internal permutation f, therefore an efficient implementation is very important. Its implementation (Algorithm 1) has two weaknesses: it only uses 25 threads of the 32 available ones for a warp, and it produces a relatively high number of bank conflicts. The basic scheduling unit of CUDA is the warp. Therefore, using the other seven threads in the execution of another permutation instance raises synchronization problems. As threads in the same warp are always synchronized, Algorithm 1 does not suffer from this issue. The bank conflicts themselves can be reduced using a 32-bit version of Algorithm 1, but is still not at all conflict-free. A deeper analysis of Keccak could reveal the path to a conflict-free permutation kernel. According to the CUDA profiler, Algorithm 1 executes in about $58\,\mu s$ (24 rounds, bit rate $r = 1024$), producing more than 9.000 bank conflicts. A corresponding 32-bit version of Algorithm 1 executes in about $50\mu s$ with a number of bank conflicts of ~ 1250. Another issue is that at the moment we have not used so-called *streams* and *Zero Copy*. With streams it is possible to copy data to the device or to the host asynchronously to kernel execution, whereas with Zero Copy the GPU can directly access host memory, thereby copying data to the device on demand. Zero Copy is especially interesting for integrated devices, e.g. in laptops. NVIDIA's new Fermi architecture could also be helpful here, for those new cards have more shared memory and a dedicated L1 cache, which might not suffer from bank conflicts. Fermi cards have 48 KB shared memory and 16 KB of dedicated

L1 cache per SM, whereas the GTX 295 only has 16 KB of shared memory. Fermi cards also allow for more threads per SM. As the GPU scales nearly optimal, we expect to observe corresponding speedups in Keccak's runtime on the GPU.

References

1. AMD: AMD fusion family of APUs (2010), `http://sites.amd.com/us/Documents/48423B_fusion_whitepaper_WEB.pdf`
2. Bertoni, G., Daemen, J., Peeters, M., Van Assche, G.: Note on keccak parameters and usage, `http://keccak.noekeon.org/NoteOnKeccakParametersAndUsage.pdf`
3. Bertoni, G., Daemen, J., Peeters, M., Van Assche, G.: Tune keccak to your requirements, `http://keccak.noekeon.org/tune.html`
4. Bertoni, G., Daemen, J., Peeters, M., Van Assche, G.: ECRYPT hash workshop (2007)
5. Bertoni, G., Daemen, J., Peeters, M., Van Assche, G.: The keccak sponge function family - main document. In submission to NIST, Round 2 (2009), `http://keccak.noekeon.org/Keccak-main-2.1.pdf`
6. Bertoni, G., Daemen, J., Peeters, M., Van Assche, G.: Cryptographic sponges (2011), `http://sponge.noekeon.org/`
7. Bertoni, G., Daemen, J., Peeters, M., Van Assche, G.: The keccak sponge function family (2011), `http://keccak.noekeon.org/`
8. Bos, J.W., Stefan, D.: Performance analysis of the SHA-3 candidates on exotic multi-core architectures. In: Mangard, S., Standaert, F.-X. (eds.) CHES 2010. LNCS, vol. 6225, pp. 279–293. Springer, Heidelberg (2010)
9. Dally, B.: The future of GPU computing (2009), `http://www.nvidia.com/content/GTC/documents/SC09_Dally.pdf`
10. ECRYPT. SHA-3 hardware implementations (2011), `http://ehash.iaik.tugraz.at/wiki/SHA-3_Hardware_Implementations`
11. Fleischmann, E., Forler, C., Gorski, M.: Classification of the SHA-3 candidates (2008), `http://eprint.iacr.org/2008/511`
12. Intel. Sandy bridge (2011), `http://software.intel.com/en-us/articles/sandy-bridge/`
13. Merkle, R.C.: Secrecy, authentication, and public key systems. PhD thesis, Stanford University (1979)
14. NVIDIA. NVIDIA CUDA programming guide 3.2 (2010), `http://developer.download.nvidia.com/compute/cuda/3_2/toolkit/docs/CUDA_C_Programming_Guide.pdf`
15. Patterson, D.A., Hennessey, J.L.: Computer Organization And Design. Morgan Kaufmann, Burlington (2009)
16. Sarkar, P., Schellenberg, P.J.: A parallelizable design principle for cryptographic hash functions. Cryptology ePrint Archive, Report 2002/031 (2002), `http://eprint.iacr.org/`
17. Sevestre, G.: Keccak tree hashing on GPU, using NVIDIA CUDA API (2010), `http://sites.google.com/site/keccaktreegpu/`

A Comparative Study of a New Associative Classification Approach for Mining Rare and Frequent Classification Rules

Ines Bouzouita[1,2], Michel Liquiere[2], Samir Elloumi[1], and Ali Jaoua[1,3]

[1] Computer Science Department,
Faculty of Sciences of Tunis, 1060 Tunis, Tunisia
[2] LIRMM,
161, rue ADA
34392, Montpellier, Cedex 5
[3] Qatar University
{ines.bouzouita,samir.elloumi}@fst.rnu.tn

Abstract. In this paper, we tackled the problem of generation of rare classification rules. Our work is motivated by the search of an effective algorithm allowing the extraction of rare classification rules by avoiding the generation of a large number of patterns at reduced time. Within this framework we are interested in rules of the form $a_1 \wedge a_2 \ldots \wedge a_n \Rightarrow b$ which allow us to propose a new approach based on genetic algorithms principle. This approach allows obtaining frequent and rare rules while avoiding making a breadth search. We describe our method and provide a comparative study of three versions of our method on standard benchmark data sets.

Keywords: Cover Set, Associative Classification, Rare Classification Rules.

1 Introduction

Most of the studies of classification were interested in the extraction of the frequent rules and they achieve good accuracy performance [1,2]. However, the rare rules present a real interest for a multitude of applications in the domains of the biology, the medicine, the IT security and the behavioral study. In fact, such rules are obtained when minimum support is set very low and consequently a huge number of patterns is produced. Thus, classical AC algorithms would break down while generating rare classification rules. In the literature, extracting rare associative classification rules has not yet been studied in detail, although rare classification rules can contain important information to classify new examples or objects in many applications such as intrusion detection and unsolicited commercial e-mail and email viruses.

In this paper, we address the problem of generating relevant frequent and rare classification rules. Our work is motivated by the long-standing open question of devising an efficient algorithm for finding rules with low support at reduced time.

T.-h. Kim et al. (Eds.): ISA 2011, CCIS 200, pp. 43–52, 2011.

A particularly relevant field for rare item sets and rare associative classification rules is intrusion detection. For example it may be important to identify patterns of traffic or application data presumed to be malicious and that are not frequent in database.

The remainder of the paper is organized as follows. Section 2 briefly reports basic concepts of associative classification. Related pioneering works are scrutinized in section 3 by splitting them into two pools. Section 4 introduces our proposed approach, where details about classification rules discovery and experimental results and comparisons of the three proposed versions are given. Finally, section 5 concludes this paper.

2 Basic Concepts of Associative Classification

In this section, we will recall some basic concepts of associative classification. Let us define the classification problem in an association rule task. Let D be the training set with n attributes (columns) $A_1, .., A_n$ and $|D|$ rows. Let C be the list of class attributes.

An *object* or *instance* in D can be described as a combination of attribute names and values and an attribute class denoted by $b \in C$ [3].

An *item* is described as an attribute name and a value a_i [3].

An *itemset* can be described as a set of items contained in an object.

An *associative classification rule* is of the form: $a_1 \wedge a_2 \ldots \wedge a_n \Rightarrow b$ where the premise of the rule is an itemset and the conclusion is a class attribute.

A classifier is a set of rules of the form $a_1 \wedge a_2 \ldots \wedge a_n \Rightarrow b$ where a_i is an attribute value and b is a class attribute. The classifier should be able to predict, as accurately as possible, the class of an unseen object belonging to the test data set. In fact, it should maximize the equality between the predicted class and the hidden actual class.

3 Related Work

Associative classification approaches can be categorized considering different criteria:

- Search method: classification rules extraction way (Breadth−First search or depth −First search).
- Classifier building phases: integrated approaches or two phases approaches.
- Application field: mono-class or multi-class problem.

In the following, we will consider the first criterium and split the approaches into two pools according to the way of the classification rules extraction:

3.1 Breadth−First Search

Examples of this approach include CBA [3], ARC-AC and ARC-BC [4,5], GARC [6] and IGARC[7].

CBA [3] was one of the first algorithms to use association rule approach for classification. This approach, firstly, generates all the association rules with certain support and confidence thresholds as candidate rules by implementing the Apriori algorithm [8]. Then, it selects a subset by evaluating all the generated rules against the training data set. When predicting the class attribute for an example, the highest confidence rule, whose body is satisfied by the example, is chosen for prediction.

ARC-AC and ARC-BC have been introduced in [4,5] in the aim of text categorization. They generate rules similar to the Apriori algorithm and rank them in the same way as does CBA rules ranking method. ARC-AC and ARC-BC calculate the average confidence of each set of rules grouped by class attribute in the conclusion part and select the class attribute of the group with the highest confidence average.

GARC [6] extracts the generic basis of association rules. Once obtained, generic rules are filtered out to retain only rules whose conclusions include a class attribute. Then, by applying the decomposition axiom, we obtain generic classification rules. After that, a total order is set on them. The data set coverage is similar to that in CBA. In fact, a data object of the training set is removed after it is covered by a selected generic rule.

IGARC[7] extracts generic classification rules in order to retain a small set of rules with higher quality and lower redundancy in comparison with current AC approaches. Unlike GARC, IGARC extracts generic classification rules directly from a training set without using generic basis of association rules.

3.2   Depth−First Search

Examples of this approach include CMAR [9], CPAR [2] and Harmony [10].

CMAR [9] mines the training data set to find the complete set of rules passing certain support and confidence thresholds for this it adopts a variant of FP−Growth method. CMAR introduces a CR-tree structure to handle the set of generated rules and uses a set of them to make a prediction using a weighted $\chi 2$ metric [9]. The latter metric evaluates the correlation between the rules.

The CPAR [2] algorithm adopts FOIL [11] strategy in generating rules from data sets. It seeks for the best rule itemset that brings the highest gain value among the available ones in data set. Once the itemset is identified, the examples satisfying it will be deleted until all the examples of the data set are covered. The searching process for the best rule itemset is a time consuming process, since the gain for every possible item needs to be calculated in order to determine the best item gain. During rule generation step, CPAR derives not only the best itemset but all close similar ones. It has been claimed that CPAR improves the classification accuracy whenever compared to popular associative methods like CBA and CMAR [2].

A new AC approach called Harmony was proposed in [10]. Harmony uses an instance-centric rule generation to discover the highest confidence discovering rules. Then, Harmony groups the set of rules into k groups according to their rule conclusions, where k is the total number of distinct class attributes in the training set. Within the same group of rules, Harmony sorts the rules in the same order as CBA. To classify a new test instance, Harmony computes a score for each group of rules and assign the class attribute with the highest score or a set of class attributes if the underlying classification is a multi-class problem. It has been claimed that Harmony improves the efficiency of the rule generation process and the classification accuracy if compared to CPAR [2].

It is noteworthy that all the approaches, except CPAR, sort the classification rules using support and confidence measures in order to build the classifier.

However, the support confidence measures could be misleading while classifying new objects since it would be interesting to have rare classification rules to classify them. Moreover, all the approaches, except CPAR, CMAR and HAR-MONY, make a breadth–first search to extract an overwhelming number of patterns in order to get classification rules during the learning stage. However setting the minimum support threshold too low would make processing infeasible. Consequently, interesting rare rules would be overlooked. Furthermore, none of the approaches is focusing on rare associative classification rules. In order to overcome this drawback, our proposed approach tries to gouge this fact by making a depth–first search and applying genetic algorithms principle to extract both frequent and rare rules.

4   Our Proposed Approach

As already mentioned, the extraction of rare classification rules may be particularly useful in information system security to detect, for instance, attack attempts at the source system. In this way, a frequent classification rule such $A \rightarrow Cl1$, where $Cl1$ is a label describing a kind of attack, means that this classification rule describes an expected and right way of acting. By contrast, a rare classification rule such as $A \rightarrow Cl2$ may be interpreted as the fact that $Cl2$ describes an abnormal way of acting, possibly leading to an attack attempt.

In this section, we propose an AC method that extracts rare classification rules from a learning data set. In the following, we will present and explain in detail the proposed approach. The intuition behind this method is that AC algorithms [3,4,5] utilize the frequent itemset strategy as exemplified by the Apriori algorithm. The frequent itemset strategy first discovers all frequent itemsets, *i.e.*, whose support exceeds a user defined threshold minimum support. Associative classification rules are then generated from these frequent itemsets. These approaches are efficient if there are relatively few frequent itemsets. It is, however, subject to a number of limitations:

1. Associations with support lower than the nominated minimum support will not be discovered. Infrequent itemsets may actually be especially interesting for some applications. In many applications high value transactions are likely to be both relatively infrequent and of great interest.

2. Even if there is a natural lower bound on support the analyst may not be able to identify it. If minimum support is set too high then important associations will be overlooked. If it is set too low then processing may become infeasible.

There is no means of determining, even after an analysis has been completed, whether it may have overlooked important associations due to the lower bound on support being set too high.

In this following, we will recall genetic algorithm principle and some logic basic notions necessary for covering set algorithm comprehension.

Our proposed approach is based on genetic algorithms principle to present a classifier formed by rare and frequent rules at reduced time.

In fact, some problems can be very complicated. Genetic algorithms try to find some suitable solution (ie. not necessarily the best solution). The solution found by this methods is often considered as a good solution, because it is not often possible to prove what is the real optimum.

Genetic algorithms are inspired by Darwin's theory about evolution. Solution to a problem solved by genetic algorithms is evolved. Algorithm is started with a set of solutions (represented by chromosomes) called population. Solutions from one population are taken and used to form a new population. This is motivated by a hope, that the new population will be better than the old one. Solutions which are selected to form new solutions (offspring) are selected according to their fitness - the more suitable they are the more chances they have to reproduce.

1. Generate random population of n chromosomes (suitable solutions for the problem)

2. Evaluate the validity of each chromosome x in the population

3. Create a new population by repeating following steps until the new population is complete

4. Select two parent chromosomes from a population according to their validity

5. With a crossover probability, cross over the parents to form a new offspring (children). If no crossover was performed, offspring is an exact copy of parents. his is repeated until some condition (for example number of populations or improvement of the best solution) is satisfied.

6. With a mutation probability, mutate new offspring.

7. Place new offspring in a new population.

8. Use new generated population for a further run of algorithm

9. If the end condition is satisfied, stop, and return the best solution in current population

10. Go to step 2

The chromosome should in some way contain information about solution which it represents. The most used way of encoding is a binary string. The performance is influenced mainly by crossover and mutation operators.

We can make a step to crossover. Crossover selects genes from parent chromosomes and creates a new offspring. The simplest way how to do this is to choose randomly some crossover point and everything before this point point copy from a first parent and then everything after a crossover point copy from the second parent.

After a crossover is performed, mutation can take place. This is to prevent falling all solutions in population into a local optimum of solved problem. Mutation changes randomly the new offspring. For binary encoding we can switch a few randomly chosen bits from 1 to 0 or from 0 to 1. In the case of our approach, we did not need to apply this operator because we need to extract valid knowledge.

Indeed, in the approach that we propose, rules extraction is equivalent to the problem of cover set. The algorithm 1 crosses in depth-first manner the search space, for this, it uses a function of evaluation to choose the next attribute to be tried. A classic function is based on the number of elements that this attribute covers, that we shall exploit to search rare rules.

Algorithm 1. BACKTRACK SEARCH (VERSION I)

Search
Data: Context: (E,A,R); Sub complementary context: (E',A',R'); List of
      attributes: LC, Res; Attribute b
Results: List of rules:Res
 Begin
   If *E' is empty* **then**
     If *support $\overline{LC}$ >0* **then**
        add rule $\overline{LC} \rightarrow$ b to Res
     If *A is empty* **then**
        return Res (Backtrack)
   Evaluate each attribute in A' using the evaluation function
   Order the attributes in a list LA
   While *LA is not empty* **do**
     Take the first element x of LA
     Create the new context (E",A",R") from (E',A',R') where A"←A'-
     x, and E"←E'-{e ∈ e(x)}
     Res ← Res ∪ Search((E,A,R),(E",A",R"), LC ∪x,Res,b)
     remove attribute x from LA
   return Res
 End

Algorithm 1 will supply the list of all possible covers for a given context [12]. However, to apply this principle we have to cross the search space in an exhaustive way (version I), which is very expensive. That is why, we have adopted genetic algorithms principle to minimize the search space exploration and thus reduce building classifier runtime while proposing a second version of the algorithm. Indeed, for version II, the algorithm 4 appeals a procedure given by a greedy algorithm 3 based on the following principle. An expert of the domain of the application set a number of attributes k which are randomly chosen among the list of the candidates. This set of attributes corresponds to a part of the premise of a rule, called granulate, which will be completed to cover the examples of the context in question. Then, the granulate is built by crossing premises of two existing rules. We repeat the process until reach the number of rules set from the beginning by an expert of the field of research of the application.

Algorithm 2. Main I

Data: Context: (E,A,R), Attribute b
Results: List of rules
Begin
  E'←E-e(b) Build (E',A',R')which is the complementary context of
  (E-e(b),A,R)
  return Search ((E,A,R), (E',A',R'), ∅, ∅, b)
End

Thus, the method that we propose allows from a binary database consisted of a small number of negative examples and a large number of positive examples to study the negative examples and to extract from it the information concerning the positive examples what allows to work on a small context instead of working on the totality of the examples to extract rules and to extract frequent and even rare knowledge;

The intuition behind our proposed approach is that both frequent and rare associative classification rules could be of important interest for many real applications area. Unlike previous AC approaches, our new approach permits:

- to explore the search space in a depth−first manner.
- to extract both frequent and rare classification rules by using an evaluation function.

In fact, the algorithm traverses the space search in a depth-first manner to generate rules with small premises which is an advantage for the classification framework when the rules imply the same class. For example, let us consider two rules R_1: $a \wedge b \wedge c \wedge d \Rightarrow$class and R_2: $b \wedge c \Rightarrow$class. R_1 and R_2 have the same attribute conclusion. R_2 is considered to be more interesting than R_1, since it is needless to satisfy the properties $a \wedge d$ to choose the class class. Hence, R_2 implies less constraints and can match more objects of a given population than R_1. In fact, such set of rules is smaller than the number of all the classification rules since we eliminate redundant ones. Moreover their use is beneficial for classifying new objects.

We have conducted experiments to evaluate our proposed approach under the three different versions, developed in Java langage. Experiments were conducted to compare accuracy and runtime using data sets taken from UCI Machine Learning Repository[1].

Classification accuracy can be used to evaluate the performance of classification methods. In fact, it is the percentage of correctly classified examples in the test set and can be measured by splitting the data sets into a training set and a test set.

Version 1: This version given by Algorithm 1 is based on cover set principle.

Version 2: This version given by Algorithm 3 is based on cover set principle and genetic algorithms. Table 1 shows that the best accuracy is reached with

---

[1] *Available at* http://www.ics.uci.edu/~mlearn/MLRepository.html

Algorithm 3. BACKTRACK SEARCH (VERSION II)

Search
Data: Pathinit: random attributes list; Context: (E,A,R); Sub
      complementary context: (E',A',R'); List of attributes: LC,
      Res; Attribute b
Results: List of rules:Res
Begin

> If *E' is empty* then
>> If *support* $\overline{LC}$ *>0* then
>>> └ add rule $\overline{LC}\rightarrow$ b to Res
>>
>> If *A is empty* then
>>> └ return Res (Backtrack)
>
> Evaluate each attribute in A' using the evaluation function
> Order the attributes in a list LA
> pathinit= choixalea(la,k)
> If *Pathinit is not empty* then
> Take the first element x of Pathinit
> Create the new context (E",A",R") from (E',A',R') where
> A"←A'- x, and E"←E'-{e ∈ e(x)}
> Res ← Res ∪ Search(pathinit,(E,A,R),(E",A",R"),
> $a_1 \wedge a_2 \ldots \wedge a_n \ldots \wedge x$, Res, b)
> remove attribute x from LA
> **While** *LA is not empty* **do**
>> Take the first element x of LA
>> Create the new context (E",A",R") from (E',A',R') where
>> A"←A'- x, and E"←E'-{e ∈ e(x)}
>> Res ← Res ∪ Search(pathinit,(E,A,R),(E",A",R"), LC
>> ∪x,Res,b)
>> └ remove attribute x from LA
>
> return Res

End

Algorithm 4. MAIN II

Data: Context: (E,A,R), Attribute b
Results: List of rules
Begin

> E'←E-e(b) Build (E',A',R')which is the complementary
> context of (E-e(b),A,R)
> **for** *(i<=rules number)* **do**
>> └ return Search (Pathinit,(E,A,R), (E',A',R'), ∅, ∅, b)

End

Table 1. Accuracy and runtime variation versus rules number

Data set	Spect-Heart		Tic-Tac-Toe	
# rules	Runtime	Accuracy	Runtime	Accuracy
100	14(s)	76	7(s)	42.2
500	14(s)	79	8(s)	86.59
1000	14(s)	78	8(s)	89.69
3000	17(s)	79	11(s)	89.9

Table 2. Runtime comparison

	Version I	Version II	Version III
Spect-Heart	12 (s)	8(s)	1500 (s)
Tic-Tac-Toe	16(s)	14(s)	29(s)

version II. Moreover, the latter gives a better runtime than the other two versions as shown by Table 2 thanks to the use of the principle of the genetic algorithms which allows to avoid the exploration of the research in an exhaustive way.

Version 3: introduces a random algorithm. The bad result is due to the fact that for the extraction of classification rules and more particularly the premises this algorithm is not guided it is purely a blind exploration what slows down the outcome in the result.

5 Conclusion

In this paper, we introduced and compared different versions of classification approach that extract rare classification rules while exploring the search space in a depth−first manner. To this end, the three versions adopt the covering set algorithm and uses the lift measure in order to guide the traversal of the search space and to generate the most interesting rules for the classification framework even rare ones. The best version which gives better execution time is the second one which is based on genetic algorithms principle. The main contributions of this work are:

- A depth first search algorithm for the search of rules with form $a_1 \wedge ...$ $\wedge a_n \Rightarrow b$. This is an greedy algorithm using an evaluation function avoiding the generation of an enormous number of patterns in order to get rare and frequent classification rules. We demonstrated the interest of use of the principle of the genetic algorithms in our work.
- We experiment this new algorithm on datasets by using measures of evaluation. The obtained results show that the lift parameter gives good classification results by guiding the choice of extraction of rules and facilitating those who are rare and positively correlated.

Acknowledgements. We thank Qatar National Research Fund (QNRF) for having granted the present research work.

References

1. Zaiane, O., Antonie, M.: On pruning and tuning rules for associative classifiers. In: Khosla, R., Howlett, R.J., Jain, L.C. (eds.) KES 2005. LNCS (LNAI), vol. 3683, pp. 966–973. Springer, Heidelberg (2005)
2. Xiaoxin Yin, J.H.: CPAR: Classification based on Predictive Association Rules. In: Proceedings of the SDM, San Francisco, CA, pp. 369–376 (2003)
3. Liu, B., Hsu, W., Ma, Y.: Integrating classification and association rule mining. Knowledge Discovery and Data Mining, 80–86 (1998)
4. Antonie, M., Zaiane, O.: Text Document Categorization by Term Association. In: Proceedings of the IEEE International Conference on Data Mining (ICDM 2002), Maebashi City, Japan, pp. 19–26 (2002)
5. Antonie, M., Zaiane, O.: Classifying Text Documents by Associating Terms with Text Categories. In: Proceedings of the Thirteenth Austral-Asian Database Conference (ADC 2002), Melbourne, Australia (2002)
6. Bouzouita, I., Elloumi, S., Yahia, S.B.: GARC: A new associative classification approach. In: Tjoa, A.M., Trujillo, J. (eds.) DaWaK 2006. LNCS, vol. 4081, pp. 554–565. Springer, Heidelberg (2006)
7. Bouzouita, I., Elloumi, S.: Integrated generic association rules based classifier. In: Wagner, R., Revell, N., Pernul, G. (eds.) DEXA 2007. LNCS, vol. 4653, pp. 514–518. Springer, Heidelberg (2007)
8. Agrawal, R., Srikant, R.: Fast algorithms for mining association rules. In: Bocca, J.B., Jarke, M., Zaniolo, C. (eds.) Proceedings of the 20th Intl. Conference on Very Large Databases, Santiago, Chile, pp. 478–499 (1994)
9. Li, W., Han, J., Pei, J.: CMAR: Accurate and efficient classification based on multiple class-association rules. In: Proceedings of IEEE International Conference on Data Mining (ICDM 2001), pp. 369–376. IEEE Computer Society, San Jose (2001)
10. Wang, J., Karypis, G.: HARMONY: Efficiently mining the best rules for classification. In: Proceedings of the International Conference of Data Mining, pp. 205–216 (2005)
11. Quinlan, J., Cameron-Jones, R.: FOIL: A midterm report. In: Proceedings of European Conference on Machine Learning, Vienna, Austria, pp. 3–20 (1993)
12. Bouzouita, I., Michel Liquire, S.E.: Afortiori: an associative classification approach based on covering set method. In: International Conference Of Formal Concept Analysis ICFCA 2009. Darmstadt University of Applied Sciences, Germany (2009)

Secret Key Awareness Security Public Key Encryption Scheme

Guoyan Zhang* and Qiuliang Xu

School of Computer Science and Technology,
Shandong University,
Jinan 250100, China
{guoyanzhang,xql}@sdu.edu.cn

Abstract. In this paper, firstly, we introduce a new security definition called secret key awareness security which is to guarantee anyone generating the public key to know the corresponding secret key. Following, we give a concrete implementing for secret key awareness security. Secondly, we present two applications: one is in plaintext awareness security cryptosystem, and another is in certificatless public key encryption scheme.

Keywords: Secret Key Awareness Security, DHK1 Assumption, Non-Interactive Zero-Knowledge, Non-Black-Box.

1 Introduction

For encryption scheme, a variety of goals including indistinguishability (IND), non-malleability (NM) and plaintext awareness (PA) have been introduced which are actually stronger than the notion of [1]. Indistinguishability (IND), due to Goldwasser and Micali [2], formalizes an adversary's inability to learn any information about the plaintext x underlying a challenge ciphertext y, capturing a strong notion of privacy. Non-malleability (NM)presented by Dolev, Dwork and Naor [3] formalizes an adversary's inability, given a challenge ciphertext y, to output a different ciphertext $y^{'}$ such that the corresponding plaintexts $x, x^{'}$ are meaningfully related. Plaintext awareness defined by M. Bellare, A. Desai, D. Pointcheval and P. Rogaway in [4] formalizes an adversary's inability to create a ciphertext y without knowing its underlying plaintext x. In this paper, we give the forth goal called secret key awareness security which formalizes an adversary's inability to create a valid public key pk without knowing its underlying secret key sk.

---

* This work is Supported by the National Natural Science Foundation of China(No.60873232), Open Research Fund from Key Laboratory of Computer Network and Information Integration In Southeast University, Ministry of Education, China, Shandong Natural Science Foundation(No.Y2008A22) and Shandong Postdoctoral Special Fund for Innovative Research(No.200902022).

T.-h. Kim et al. (Eds.): ISA 2011, CCIS 200, pp. 53–61, 2011.

1.1   Related Work

In fact, before we formally give the security notion of secret key awareness, it has found its application. In order to get a non-interactive $\sum$-protocol, Ivan Damgard, Nelly Fazio and Antonio Nicolosi [5] have forced the verifier to generate its public key and to register it with the random number chosen by the verifier to generate its public key. This required simultaneously that the verifier knew the secret key underlying its public key. Also in [6], Jonathan Herzog, Moses Likov and Silvio Micali got a generic construction for public key encryption scheme with plaintext awareness security via key registration, in which the sender generating public key should be engaged in a zero-knowledge proof of knowledge that he knew the corresponding secret key with registration authority.

1.2   Our Contributions

We formally introduce a new security notion called secret key awareness (SKA) security in public key cryptography, and this security notion requires any adversary generating its public key must know the corresponding secret key. It is to say, there is a secret key extractor which can extract the secret key through revising the adversary or getting the adversary's transcripts as input.

Following, we give a concrete implementing for cryptosystem with secret key awareness security by modifying ELGamal encryption protocol.

Lastly, two applications are presented. One is a construction for plaintext awareness security encryption scheme. Plaintext awareness defined by Bellare, Desai, Pointcheval and Rogaway in [4] and they showed that PA+IND-CPA should imply IND-CCA2. But most of the practical encryption protocols with plaintext awareness security need random oracle. Mihir Bellare and Adriana Palacio [7] gave a new notion of plaintext awareness in standard model, in which they presented a concrete protocol with non-black-box technology. Jonathan Herzog, Moses Likov and Silvio Micali [6] got a generic public key encryption scheme with plaintext awareness security via key registration. Compared with their construction, our construction omits the registration authority and zero-knowledge proof by the use of non-black-box technology in reduction. Another is a construction for certificateless public key encryption by modifying the construction [8] which could be proved secure against the strong Type I adversary. But in the construction [8], the Type I adversary could generate the valid ciphertext different with the challenge ciphertext for the same message by replacing the users's public key without knowing the message. Our construction makes use of a CPA secure id-based public key encryption scheme, a CPA secure public key encryption scheme with secret key awareness secure, and a non-malleable $NIZK$ proof system for any NP as components, and the construction is secure against the strong Type I adversary.

2 Preliminaries

2.1 Computational Complexity

Assumption [$DHK1$] Let G be a prime-order-group generator. Let H be an algorithm that has access to an oracle, takes two primes and two group elements, and returns nothing. Let H^* be an algorithm that takes a pair of group elements and some state information, and returns an exponent and a new state. We call H a $DHK1$-adversary and H^* a $DHK1$-extractor. For $k \in \mathbb{N}$, we say that G satisfies the $DHK1$ assumption in the following experiment, if for every polynomial-time $DHK1$-adversary H, there exists a polynomial-time $DHK1$-extractor H^* such that

$$Adv_{G,H,H^*}^{DHK1}(k) = Pr[Exp_{G,H,H^*}^{DHK1}(k) = 1]$$

is negligible.

Experiment $Exp_{G,H,H^*}^{DHK1}(k)$

$(p, q, g) \leftarrow G(1^k); a \leftarrow \mathbb{Z}_q; A \leftarrow g^a mod p$

Choose coins $R[H], R[H^*]$ for H, H^*, respectively; $St[H^*] \leftarrow ((p, q, g, A), R[H])$

Run H on input (p, q, g, A) and coins $R[H]$ until it halts, replying to its oracle queries as follows:

-If H makes query (B, W) then

$(b, St[H^*]) \leftarrow H^*((B, W), St[H^*]; R[H^*]])$

If $W \equiv B^a (mod p)$ and $B \neq g^b (mod p)$ then return 1.

Else return b to H as the reply End If

Return 0

2.2 Certificateless Public Key Encryption

Definition 1. (Certificateless Public Key Encryption). A generic certificateless public key encryption scheme consists of the following seven algorithms:

-**SetUp(SU):** a probabilistic polynomial time (PPT) algorithm run by a key generation center (KGC) given a security parameter k as input, which outputs a randomly chosen master secret key msk and master public key mpk. The master public key mpk includes a description of the message space $\mathcal{M}$ and ciphertext space $\mathcal{C}$.

-**PartialPrivateKeyExtract(PPKE):** given the master public key mpk, master secret key msk and an identifier for entity A, ID_A, the KGC runs this PPT algorithm to generate the partial private key d_A. Then the partial private key d_A is transported to entity A over a confidential and authentic channel.

-**SetSecretValue(SSV):** a PPT algorithm run by the entity A given master public key mpk and ID_A as input, which outputs a secret value x_A.

-**SetPrivateKey(SPVK):** given master public key mpk, the entity A's secret value x_A, and the entity A's partial private key d_A as input, the entity runs this PPT algorithm to generate a private key SK_A.

-SetPublicKey(SPK): given master public key mpk and the entity A's secret value x_A, and output a public key PK_A for the entity A.

-Encrypt($\mathcal{E}$): given a plaintext $M \in \mathcal{M}$, master public key mpk, an identifier ID_A and public key PK_A for an entity A as input, a sender runs this PPT algorithm to create a ciphertext $C \in \mathcal{C}$ or the null symbol $\perp$ indicating an encryption failure. This will always occur in the event that PK_A does not have the correct form.

-Decrypt($\mathcal{D}$): given master public key mpk, the entity's private key SK_A, and the ciphertext $C \in \mathcal{C}$ as inputs, the entity as a recipient runs this deterministic algorithm to get a decryption σ, which is either a plaintext message or a "reject" message.

3   Secret Key Awareness Security

3.1   Definition

Definition 2 (Secret Key Awareness Security-SKA). Let $\Pi = (\mathcal{G}, \mathcal{E}, \mathcal{D})$ be a public key encryption scheme, let $\mathcal{B}$ be a polynomial-time adversary called public key creator who can generate a valid public key. Let $\mathcal{K}$ be an algorithm that takes the user's public key and some state information, returns the corresponding secret key and a new state. We call $\mathcal{K}$ a secret key extractor. For $k \in \mathbb{N}$, we say that a public key encryption scheme Π satisfies the secret key awareness security in the following experiment, if for every polynomial time adversary $\mathcal{B}$ generating valid public key, there is a polynomial time secret key extractor $\mathcal{K}$ such that

$$Adv^{SKA}_{\Pi,\mathcal{B},\mathcal{K}}(k) = Pr[Exp^{SKA}_{\Pi,\mathcal{B},\mathcal{K}}(k) = 1]$$

is negligible.

Experiment $Exp^{SKA}_{\Pi,\mathcal{B},\mathcal{K}}(k)$

$(PK = (pk, parameters), SK) \leftarrow \mathcal{G}(1^k)$

Choose coins $R[\mathcal{B}], R[\mathcal{K}]$ for $\mathcal{B}, \mathcal{K}$, respectively; $St[\mathcal{K}] \leftarrow (parameters, R[\mathcal{B}])$

Run $\mathcal{B}$ on input $parameters$ and coins $R[\mathcal{B}]$ until it halts, replying to its oracle queries as follows:

-If $\mathcal{B}$ makes query pk' then

$(x, St[\mathcal{K}]) \leftarrow \mathcal{K}[pk', St[\mathcal{K}]; R[\mathcal{K}]]$

If x isn't the secret key corresponding with pk' then return 1.

Else return x to $\mathcal{B}$ as the reply End If

Return 0

From the above definition, the secret key extractor is non-black-box, and allows the extractor code to depend non-uniformly on the code of the public key creator. Again, this is done in order to increase the possibility of finding constructions. Evidence of the power of non-black-box formulations is provided in another context by [9].

In order to obtain this kind of security, there are two usual technology considered, one is the non-interactive zero knowledge proof system to prove the possession of the secret key, and the knowledge extractor can extract corresponding knowledge by revising the adversaries creating the valid public key, but the existence of the non-interactive zero-knowledge greatly reduces the efficiency of schemes. Another makes use of a non-black-box reduction model, in which the knowledge extractor can get the code of the adversary, and the $R[\mathcal{B}]$ including the random choice of the adversaries, and certainly can extract the corresponding secret key.

3.2 Implementing Secret Key Awareness with Non-Black-Box Technology

Intuitively, the secret key awareness security is to guarantee the public key has the correct format so that anyone generating the public key to know the corresponding secret key. In order to obtain this kind of security, a traditional public key cryptographic scheme needn't be changed a lot, it is to say, the security requirement can't make the scheme more realizable and more secure, but it is easy to make a scheme to satisfy secret key awareness security without effecting the scheme's security and efficiency, For example, we can easily modify the key generation algorithm of *ELGamal* encryption scheme to make it be secret key awareness security as follows:

- **SetUp:** Let p be a prime, and g_1, g_2 be generators of $\mathcal{Z}_p$. The private key x is an integer between 1 and $p - 2$. Let $y_1 = g_1^x mod p, y_2 = g_2^x mod p$. The public key is the tuple (p, g_1, g_2, y_1, y_2).
- $\mathcal{E}^{ELG}$ **and** $\mathcal{D}^{ELG}$**:** The encryption algorithm $\mathcal{E}^{ELG}$ and the decryption algorithm $\mathcal{D}^{ELG}$ are the same to the original *ElGamal* encryption scheme.

Theorem 1. *The above encryption scheme modified from ElGamal encryption scheme is secret key awareness secure under the DHK1 assumption and the other security properties are same with ElGamal encryption scheme.*

Proof: According to $DHK1$ assumption, obviously, the above scheme is secret key awareness secure. Furthermore, the extra public key information g_2, y_2 have not leaked any information about the secret key, and the encryption algorithm and decryption scheme are same to the original scheme, so the other security properties are remained.

4   Two Applications

4.1   A Construction for Encryption Scheme with Plaintext Awareness Security

Let $\pi_1 = (G, E, D)$ is an indistinguishable secure cryptosystem against chosen plaintext attack with secret key awareness security, and $\pi_2 = (G^{'}, E^{'}, D^{'})$ is a semantically secure cryptosystem against chosen plaintext attack. π is a non-interactive zero knowledge protocol with non-malleable for NP.

A construction for $CCA2$ secure encryption scheme with plaintext awareness security $\Pi = (\mathcal{G}, \mathcal{E}, \mathcal{D})$ is the following:

-$\mathcal{G}$: (Key Generation)

(Receiver Key Generation): Run G' to generate two public-secret key pairs (e_1, d_1) and (e_2, d_2). Choose a random δ. The receiver's public key is $pk_r = (e_1, e_2, \delta)$, and the secret key is $sk_r = (d_1, d_2)$.

(Sender Key Generation): Run G to generate the sender's public-secret key pair (e_s, d_s).

-$\mathcal{E}$: On input $(m, (e_1, e_2, \delta), (e_s))$, compute $c_1 = E'(e_1, m), c_2 = E'(e_2, m)$ and $c_3 = E(e_s, m)$. With public reference string δ, compute a non-malleable non-interactive zero knowledge protocol π to prove that c_1, c_2 and c_3 are all the ciphertexts of the same message under the public key of e_1, e_2 and e_s respectively. Output c_1, c_2, c_3 and π as the ciphertext.

-$\mathcal{D}$: Receive ciphertext (c_1, c_2, c_3, π). Verify the validity of π. If so, output $D'(c_1, d_1)$. Otherwise, output $\perp$.

Theorem 2. *Π is indistinguishable secure against the chosen ciphertext attack assuming public key encryption schemes π_1 and π_2 are indistinguishable secure against chosen plaintext attack.*

Proof: The security proof is similar to the proof of chosen ciphertext security in [4], and we simply describe it here.

Suppose there is an adversary A that succeeds in an adaptive chosen ciphertext attack against scheme Π with non-negligible advantage ε, we can construct two adversaries B_1 against scheme π_1 and B_2 against scheme π_2 in chosen plaintext attack.

Given $(e, 1^k)$, B_2 sets $e_2 = e$ and $(e_1, d_1) = G'(1^k)$. He generates a public reference string δ for non-interactive zero knowledge proof protocol π. Set $(e_s, d_s) = G(1^k)$. B_2 can finish the chosen plaintext attack using A as following:

- When A asks the decryption oracle (c_1, c_2, c_3, π), B_2 checks the validity of π. If invalid, he outputs $\perp$. Else, he returns $D'(d_1, c_1)$. According to the soundness of the non-interactive zero-knowledge protocol, B_2 always correctly answers the decryption oracle.
- When gives two equal length messages (m_0, m_1), B_2 sends out and receives the challenge c. Supposing $c = E'(e, m_a)$, he sets $c_2 = c$ and respectively chooses $b \in \{0, 1\}$ and $\beta \in \{0, 1\}$ with probability $1/2$. B_2 computes $c_1 = E'(e_1, m_b)$ and $c_3 = E(e_s, m_\beta)$. Then there are mainly three cases:
  - $b = a = \beta$: in this case, B_2 can output correctly a with probability $3/4 + \varepsilon/2$.
  - $b = a \neq \beta$: in this case, we assume that A can guess a with probability x. Then B_2 can output a with probability $1/2 + x/2$.
  - $b \neq a$: in this case, B_2 can output a with probability $1/4$.

Taking into account all cases, the probability that B_2 is correct is

$$7/16 + (\varepsilon + x)/8.$$

We can see that B_2 will succeed with non-negligible advantage if $\varepsilon + x$ is non-negligibly different from $1/2$. This conflicts with the security of scheme π_2. If $\varepsilon + x$ is negligibly different from $1/2$, we can construct B_1 to break the chosen plaintext security of π_1: Given $(e, 1^k)$, B_1 sets $(e_1, d_1) = G'(1^k)$, $(e_2, d_2) = G'(1^k)$ and $e_s = e$, B_1 can finish the chosen ciphertext attack using A as following:

- When A asks the decryption oracle (c_1, c_2, c_3, π), B_1 checks the validity of π. If invalid, he outputs $\perp$. Else, he returns $D'(d_1, c_1)$. According to the soundness of the non-interactive zero-knowledge protocol, B_1 always correctly answers the decryption oracle.
- When A gives two equal length messages (m_0, m_1), B_1 outputs the message pair and receives the challenge c. Supposing $c = E(e, m_a)$, he sets $c_3 = c$ and chooses $b \in \{0, 1\}$ with probability $1/2$. B_1 computes $c_1 = E'(e_1, m_b)$ and $c_2 = E'(e_2, m_b)$. Then there are mainly two cases:
  - $b = a$: in this case, B_1 can correctly output a with probability $1/2 + \varepsilon$.
  - $b \neq a$: in this case, Then B_1 can output a with probability $1 - x$.

  Taking into account all cases, the probability that B_1 is correct is $1/2 + \varepsilon/2$, which conflicts with the security of scheme π_1.

Theorem 3. Π *is plaintext awareness security assuming public key encryption scheme π_1 is secret key awareness secure.*

Proof: The proof is simple. Assuming that A is an attacker who generates its public key pk with random coin $R[A]$ and ciphertext (c_1, c_2, c_3, π). Because of the secret key awareness security of scheme π_1, there is a secret key extractor $\mathcal{K}$ which can extract secret key d_s, given A's random coin $R[A]$. Then if π is invalid, output $\perp$. Else, output the message $m = D(d_s, c_3)$. According to the soundness of the non-malleable $NIZK$ protocol, the output is always correct.

4.2 A Construction for Certificatless Encryption Scheme Secure in the Strong Model

Let $\Pi^{IBE} = (Setup^{IBE}, Extract^{IBE}, \mathcal{E}^{IBE}, \mathcal{D}^{IBE})$ be an IBE scheme secure against chosen plaintext attack and $\Pi^{PKE} = (\mathcal{K}^{PKE}, \mathcal{E}_{pk}^{PKE}, \mathcal{D}_{sk}^{PKE})$ denotes a traditional public key encryption scheme that is CPA-secure with secret key awareness security. Let (f, P, V, S_1, S_2) be a statistically sound and computationally simulation-sound $NIZK$ proof system for the language

$$L = \{(C_1, pk_A, ID_A, C_2, pk_B) | \exists (m, r_1, r_2),$$
$$C_1 = \mathcal{E}_{pk_A}^{PKE}(\mathcal{E}_{ID_A}^{IBE}(m, r_1)) \wedge C_2 = \mathcal{E}_{pk_B}^{PKE}(m, r_2)\}.$$

A generic construction for certificateless public key encryption scheme $\Pi^{CLE} = (SU, PPKE, SSV, SPVK, SPK, \mathcal{E}, \mathcal{D})$ can be obtained in the following:

Setup (SU): is an algorithm running the setup algorithm of Π^{IBE}. The message space of Π^{CLE} is the common part of the message space of Π^{PKE} and the message space of Π^{IBE}, while its ciphertext space is the one of Π^{PKE}.

Both schemes have to be compatible in that the plaintext space of Π^{PKE} must contain the ciphertext space of Π^{IBE}. Choose a random sring σ

Partial-Private-Key-Extract (PPKE): is the private key generation algorithm of Π^{IBE}, and runs the algorithm for the identity ID_A to get the partial private key d_A.

Set-Secret-Value (SSV): run the key generation procedure of Π^{PKE} to obtain a private key sk_A and a public key pk_A. sk_A is the secret value.

Set-Private-Key (SPVK): return $SA = (d_A, sk_A)$, where d_A is obtained by running the key generation algorithm of Π^{IBE} for the identity ID_A and sk_A is entity A's secret value obtained from Π^{PKE}'s key generation algorithm.

Set-Public-Key (SPK): output (ID_A, pk_A, σ) as the public key.

Encrypt ($\mathcal{E}$): to encrypt m using the identifier ID_A and the public key pk_A,

- check that pk_A has the right format for Π^{PKE}.
- run the key generation procedure of Π^{PKE} to obtain a private key sk_B and a public key pk_B.
- compute and output the ciphertext

$$C_1 = \mathcal{E}_{pk_A}^{PKE}(\mathcal{E}_{ID_A}^{IBE}(m, r_1)),$$

$$C_2 = \mathcal{E}_{pk_B}^{PKE}(m, r_2),$$

$x \leftarrow (c_1, pk_A, ID_A, c_2, pk_B), \pi \leftarrow P(x, m, r_1, r_2, \sigma), C = (C_1, C_2, \pi, pk_B),$

where $\mathcal{E}_{pk_A}^{PKE}, \mathcal{E}_{pk_B}^{PKE}$ and $\mathcal{E}_{ID_A}^{IBE}$ respectively denote the encryption algorithms of Π^{PKE} and Π^{IBE} for the public key pk_A, pk_B and the identity ID_A.

Decrypt ($\mathcal{D}$): to decrypt C using $SA = (d_A, sk_A)$,

- $x \leftarrow (c_1, pk_A, ID_A, c_2, pk_B)$, and verify $NIZK$, if $V(x, \pi, \sigma) \neq 1$, output $\bot$.
- else, compute $\mathcal{D}_{sk_A}^{PKE}(C_1)$ using the decryption algorithm of Π^{PKE}. If the result is $\bot$, return $\bot$ and reject the ciphertext. Otherwise, compute $\mathcal{D}_{d_A}^{IBE}$ $(\mathcal{D}_{sk_A}^{PKE}(C_1))$ using the decryption algorithm of Π^{IBE} and return the result.

The security of Π^{CLE} can be proved by the security of Π^{PKE} and Π^{IBE}.

Theorem 4. *The above certificateless encryption scheme is Strong Type I and Strong Type II secure if Π^{IBE} and Π^{PKE} are secure against chosen plaintext attack and Π^{PKE} is also secret key awareness secure.*

5   Conclusion

This paper firstly introduces a new secure notion called secret key awareness security in public key cryptography, this secure notion requires any adversary creating users' public keys must know the corresponding secret keys. Then we give a concrete implementing for it. Following, we present two applications, one is a construction for a plaintext awareness secure encryption scheme, and another is concrete construction for certificateless cryptosystem secure in strong attack model. Although there isn't great improvement in the two aspects by the use of the new security notion, we believe that secret key awareness security is of more independent interesting.

References

1. Al-Riyami, S.S., Paterson, K.G.: Certificateless public key cryptography. In: Laih, C.-S. (ed.) ASIACRYPT 2003. LNCS, vol. 2894, pp. 452–473. Springer, Heidelberg (2003)
2. Baek, J., Safavi-Naini, R., Susilo, W.: Certificateless public key encryption without pairing. In: Zhou, J., López, J., Deng, R.H., Bao, F. (eds.) ISC 2005. LNCS, vol. 3650, pp. 134–148. Springer, Heidelberg (2005)
3. Bentahar, K., Farshim, P., Malone-Lee, J., Smart, N.P.: Generic constructions of identity-based and certificateless KEMs (2005), http://eprint.iacr.org/2005/058
4. Cheng, Z., Comley, R.: Efficient certificateless public key encryption (2005), http://eprint.iacr.org/2005/012/
5. Libert, B., Quisquater, J.-J.: On constructing certificateless cryptosystems from identity based encryption. In: Yung, M., Dodis, Y., Kiayias, A., Malkin, T. (eds.) PKC 2006. LNCS, vol. 3958, pp. 474–490. Springer, Heidelberg (2006)
6. Hu, B.C., Wong, D.S., Zhang, Z., Deng, X.: Key replacement attack against a generic construction of certificateless signature. In: Batten, L.M., Safavi-Naini, R. (eds.) ACISP 2006. LNCS, vol. 4058, pp. 235–246. Springer, Heidelberg (2006)
7. Huang, X., Susilo, W., Mu, Y., Zhang, F.: On the security of certificateless signature schemes from Asiacrypt 2003. In: Desmedt, Y.G., Wang, H., Mu, Y., Li, Y. (eds.) CANS 2005. LNCS, vol. 3810, pp. 13–25. Springer, Heidelberg (2005)
8. Yum, D.H., Lee, P.J.: Generic construction of certificateless signature. In: Wang, H., Pieprzyk, J., Varadharajan, V. (eds.) ACISP 2004. LNCS, vol. 3108, pp. 200–211. Springer, Heidelberg (2004)
9. Zhang, Z., Wong, D.S., Xu, J., Feng, D.: Certificateless public-key signature: Security model and efficient construction. In: Zhou, J., Yung, M., Bao, F. (eds.) ACNS 2006. LNCS, vol. 3989, pp. 293–308. Springer, Heidelberg (2006)
10. Dent, A.W.: A survey of certificateless encryption scheme and security models (2006), http://eprint.iacr.org/2006/211
11. Dent, A.W., Libert, B., Paterson, K.G.: Certificateless encryption schemes strongly secure in the standard model. In: Cramer, R. (ed.) PKC 2008. LNCS, vol. 4939, pp. 344–359. Springer, Heidelberg (2008)
12. Barak, B.: How to go beyond the black-box simulation barrier. In: Proceedings of the 42nd Symposium on Foundations of Computer Science, pp. 106–115. IEEE Press, Los Alamitos (2001)
13. Zhang, G., Wang, X.: Certificateless Encryption Scheme Secure in the Standard Model. Tsinghua Science and Technology 14(4), 122–127 (2009)

Using SAT Solving to Improve Differential Fault Analysis of Trivium

Mohamed Saied Emam Mohamed[1], Stanislav Bulygin[2],
and Johannes Buchmann[1]

[1] TU Darmstadt, FB Informatik
Hochschulstrasse 10, 64289 Darmstadt, Germany
{mohamed,buchmann}@cdc.informatik.tu-darmstadt.de
[2] Center for Advanced Security Research Darmstadt (CASED)
Stanislav.Bulygin@cased.de

Abstract. Combining different cryptanalytic methods to attack a cryptosystem became one of the hot topics in cryptanalysis. In particular, algebraic methods in side channel and differential fault analysis (DFA) attracted a lot of attention recently. In [9], Hojsík and Rudolf used DFA to recover the inner state of the stream cipher Trivium which leads to recovering the secret key. For this attack, they required 3.2 one-bit fault injections on average and 800 keystream bits. In this paper, we give an example of combining DFA attacks and algebraic attacks. We use algebraic methods to improve the DFA of Trivium [9]. Our improved DFA attack recovers the inner state of Trivium by using only 2 fault injections and only 420 keystream bits.

Keywords: Differential Fault Analysis, algebraic attack, SAT-Solvers, Trivium.

1 Introduction

Stream ciphers are encryption algorithms that encrypt plaintext digits one at a time. Trivium is a hardware-oriented synchronous stream cipher [4]. It was selected in phase three of profile two of the eSTREAM project [12]. Due to its simplicity and speed, it can provide reliable security service for many hardware applications, such as wireless connections and mobile telecommunication. In order to assess the security of these applications, one can use cryptanalytic methods.

A differential fault analysis (DFA) is a method to analyse a cipher by examining and affecting its implementation. The idea is to induce a physical corruption to the internal state of the cipher. This leads to producing some information about the internal data that helps to recover the secret of the cipher. At INDOCRYPT 2008, M. Hojsík and B. Rudolf introduced a differential fault analysis of the stream cipher Trivium [9] by using the floating representation of Trivium instead of the classical representation of the cipher. The basic idea of this attack is to inject a one-bit fault into the inner state of Trivium. In this case

T.-h. Kim et al. (Eds.): ISA 2011, CCIS 200, pp. 62–71, 2011.

an attacker can generate, in addition to the equations system that represents a set of keystream bits, some lower degree polynomial equations that relate a set of keystream bits generated after the injection performed. Using this method one needs 3.2 fault injections on average and 800 keystream bits to recover the inner state of Trivium at certain time $t = t_0$, which leads to recovering the secret key of the cipher.

Instead of attacking Trivium with only one method, an attacker can gain more power by combining differential fault analysis with algebraic techniques. In this paper, we improve the above attack by using a SAT solver to speed up the solving part of the attack, as well as we improve the equation preprocessing phase. In this case, attacker needs exactly 2 one-bit fault injections and 420 keystream bits to recover the inner state of Trivium.

This paper is organized as follows. In Section 2 we describe the floating representation of Trivium. In Section 3 we briefly explain the differential fault analysis of Trivium and in Section 4 we explain the generation of the polynomial equation system that represents the inner state of Trivium and the DFA of it. Our attack description and the results are presented in Section 5 and Section 6 respectively. Finally, we conclude the paper in Section 7.

2 Algebraic Description of Trivium

In this section, we describe the algebraic representation of Trivium. Trivium generates a sequence of keystream bits from an 80-bit secret key and an 80-bit initial vector (IV). The inner state of Trivium consists of 288 bits which are stored in three shift registers respectively as explained in Figure 1. The so called floating representation [9] of Trivium is as follows. The inner state at time t is

$$(a_{t+1}, \ldots, a_{t+93}, b_{t+1}, \ldots, b_{t+84}, c_{t+1}, \ldots, c_{t+111}).$$

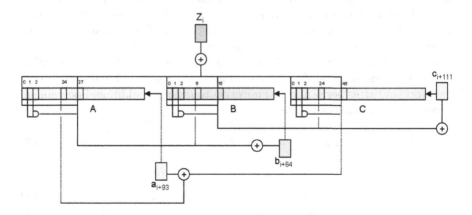

Fig. 1. Trivium construction, $i \geq 0$.

We use the secret key $K = (k_1, \ldots, k_{80})$ and IV$=(v_1, \ldots, v_{80})$ to initialize the inner state as follows

$$(\underbrace{0, \ldots, 0, k_{80}, \ldots, k_1}_{A}, \underbrace{0, 0, 0, 0, v_{80}, \ldots, v_1}_{B}, \underbrace{1, 1, 1, 0, \ldots, 0}_{C}).$$

In the initialization phase, Trivium loops 1152 times without producing any keystream. Let at time $t = 0$ (directly after the initialization phase), the inner state of Trivium be

$$(a_1, \ldots, a_{93}, b_1, \ldots, b_{84}, c_1, \ldots, c_{111}).$$

The keystream bits z_i and the new inner state bits $a_{i+93}, b_{i+84}, c_{i+111}$ of Trivium registers A,B,C are generated as follows.

$$z_i = a_i + a_{i+27} + b_i + b_{i+15} + c_i + c_{i+45}, \quad i \geq 1 \tag{1}$$

$$a_{i+93} = a_{i+24} + c_{i+45} + c_i + c_{i+1} \cdot c_{i+2} \tag{2.1}$$
$$b_{i+84} = b_{i+6} + a_{i+27} + a_i + a_{i+1} \cdot a_{i+2} \tag{2.2}$$
$$c_{i+111} = c_{i+24} + b_{i+15} + b_i + b_{i+1} \cdot b_{i+2} \tag{2.3}$$

By using equations (2.1)-(2.3), we can clock Trivium forward to generate new inner states and backward to recover previous inner states.

3   Preliminaries on the DFA of Trivium

We use the same assumptions as in [9]. Namely, the attacker is able to inject a one-bit fault at a random position within the inner state at $t = 0$. Also, he can obtain the first n keystream bits z_i, $1 \leq i \leq n$, before any fault injections and after a fault injection which we call z_i', $1 \leq i \leq n$. The attacker can do the previous step several times with the same secret key and IV.

Each one-bit fault injection leads to additional equations. We use the difference of keystream outputs ($\triangle z_i = z_i + z_i'$) and shift registers inputs ($\triangle a_i$, $\triangle b_i$, $\triangle c_i$) before and after performing an injection to generate additional polynomial equations as in (3) and (4.1)-(4.3).

$$\triangle z_i = \triangle a_i + \triangle a_{i+27} + \triangle b_i + \triangle b_{i+15} + \triangle c_i + \triangle c_{i+45}, \quad i \geq 0 \tag{3}$$

$$\triangle a_{i+93} = \triangle a_{i+24} + \triangle c_{i+45} + \triangle c_i + \triangle(c_{i+1} \cdot c_{i+2}) \tag{4.1}$$
$$\triangle b_{i+84} = \triangle b_{i+6} + \triangle a_{i+27} + \triangle a_i + \triangle(a_{i+1} \cdot a_{i+2}) \tag{4.2}$$
$$\triangle c_{i+111} = \triangle c_{i+24} + \triangle b_{i+15} + \triangle b_i + \triangle(b_{i+1} \cdot b_{i+2}) \tag{4.3}$$

In this case the difference values of the inner state at $t = 0$,

$$(\triangle a_1, \cdots, \triangle a_{93}, \triangle b_1, \cdots, \triangle b_{84}, \triangle c_1, \cdots, \triangle c_{111}),$$

are zeros everywhere except at the fault injection position. For example, suppose that the injected bit is a_{35} then the difference vector will be

$$(0, \cdots, 0, \triangle a_{35} = 1, 0, \cdots, 0)$$

The fault position is not known *a priori*, but it can be determined by observing the faulty keystream as in [9]. So we assume that we know it. In the next section, we explain how we use this differential model to generate the additional polynomial equations produced after inserting several one-bit fault injections.

4   Generating Low Degree Polynomial Equations

We explain the generation of the polynomial equation system that we use in our attack. As defined in Section 2, we let the inner state at time $t = 0$ of Trivium be

$$(a_1, \ldots, a_{93}, b_1, \ldots, b_{84}, c_1, \ldots, c_{111}).$$

Also, we suppose that we have an $n-$bit keystream output vector $Z = (z_1, \ldots, z_n)$.

The TRIV procedure constructs the polynomial equation system that describes the generation of n keystream bits using the 288 inner state bits at $t = 0$ as in Algorithm 1. It uses the strategy of generating low degree polynomials. In this case, we represent each new inner state bit generated by one of the shift-registers A, B, C ($a_{i+93}, b_{i+84}, c_{i+111}$, $1 \le i \le n$, respectively) as a new internal variable. By adding them to the 288 initial inner state bit variables, we have totally $3n + 288$ variables $(a_1, \ldots, a_{n+93}, b_1, \ldots, b_{n+84}, c_1, \ldots, c_{n+111})$. We call them the *inner state variables*.

Algorithm 1. TRIV$(Z = (z_1, \ldots, z_n))$

1: $P \leftarrow \emptyset$
2: **for** $i = 1$ to n **do**
3:      $P \leftarrow P \cup \{a_i + a_{i+27} + b_i + b_{i+15} + c_i + c_{i+45} + z_i\}$ // Eq. (1)
4:      $P \leftarrow P \cup \{a_{i+93} + a_{i+24} + c_{i+45} + c_i + c_{i+1} \cdot c_{i+2}\}$ // Eq. (2.1)
5:      $P \leftarrow P \cup \{b_{i+84} + b_{i+6} + a_{i+27} + a_i + a_{i+1} \cdot a_{i+2}\}$ // Eq. (2.2)
6:      $P \leftarrow P \cup \{c_{i+111} + c_{i+24} + b_{i+15} + b_i + b_{i+1} \cdot b_{i+2}\}$ // Eq. (2.3)
7: **end for**
8: **return** P

TRIV takes the keystream bit vector Z as an input and uses equations (1) and (2.1)-(2.3) to generate the polynomial equations. It returns the set of polynomials P that describes Z using the inner state variables. The system of equations $\{p = 0, p \in P\}$ contains $4n$ polynomial equations (n linear and $3n$ quadratic produced by (1) and (2.1)-(2.3) respectively) in the $3n + 288$ inner state variables. We call it the pure system of Trivium without using DFA.

Now we are going to explain how we generate the additional low degree polynomial equations that are obtained from the faulty key stream. For this we use the differential model that was explained in the previous section. The EQgenerator procedure constructs such equations as described in Algorithm 2. It takes as inputs m fault injection positions $(l_1, \ldots, l_m)$, the keystream vector Z before any fault injections and m keystream vectors $Z^{(1)}, \ldots, Z^{(m)}$ obtained after each one of the m fault injections, where each keystream vector $Z^{(j)} = (z_1^{(j)}, \cdots, z_n^{(j)}), 1 \leq j \leq m$.

EQgenerator initializes the set of polynomial equations (P) with the set of the pure polynomials returned by the TRIV procedure (line 1). It initializes the arrays a, b, c with the inner state variables (lines 2...4).

For each fault injection j, $1 \leq j \leq m$, EQgenerator sets the arrays da, db, dc that store the polynomials representing the *inner state difference variables*

$$(\triangle a_i)_{i=1}^{n+93}, (\triangle b_i)_{i=1}^{n+84}, (\triangle c_i)_{i=1}^{n+111}$$

to zeros (lines 7...9). In line 10 (Inject(da, db, dc, l_j)), EQgenerator inserts a fault to the inner state $(a_1, \ldots, a_{93}, b_1, \ldots, b_{84}, c_1, \ldots, c_{111})$ as follows. Let the fault injection position be $l_j \leq n$. EQgenerator sets $da[l_j]$ to 1 when $l_j \leq 93$. In case of $93 < l_j \leq 177$, it sets $db[l_j - 93]$ to 1. Otherwise, it sets $dc[l_j - 177]$ to 1.

For each keystream bit z_i and the corresponding faulty keystream bit $z_i^{(j)}$, $1 \leq i \leq n$, EQgenerator evaluates the key stream output difference dz. Then, it uses (3) to generate an additional polynomial and includes this polynomial to P (lines 13,14). Also, by using the fact that

$$\triangle(x \cdot y) = \triangle x \cdot y + x \cdot \triangle y + \triangle x \cdot \triangle y,$$

we can reconstruct equations (4.1), (4.2), and (4.3) as follows.

$$\triangle a_{i+93} = \triangle a_{i+24} + \triangle c_{i+45} + \triangle c_i + \triangle c_{i+1} \cdot c_{i+2} + c_{i+1} \cdot \triangle c_{i+2} + \triangle c_{i+1} \cdot \triangle c_{i+2}$$
$$(5.1)$$

$$\triangle b_{i+84} = \triangle b_{i+6} + \triangle a_{i+27} + \triangle a_i + \triangle a_{i+1} \cdot a_{i+2} + a_{i+1} \cdot \triangle a_{i+2} + \triangle a_{i+1} \cdot \triangle a_{i+2}$$
$$(5.2)$$

$$\triangle c_{i+111} = \triangle c_{i+24} + \triangle b_{i+15} + \triangle b_i + \triangle b_{i+1} \cdot b_{i+2} + b_{i+1} \cdot \triangle b_{i+2} + \triangle b_{i+1} \cdot \triangle b_{i+2}$$
$$(5.3)$$

The EQgenerator procedure uses these equations to construct the polynomial entries of the difference polynomial arrays (da, db, dc).

EQgenerator extracts from P all possible univariate polynomials of the form $x + v$, where x is an inner state variable and v is 0 or 1 (line 20). If there are such univariates, it simplifies P by substituting the solved variables in each polynomial $p \in P$ (line 21). It repeats these two steps as long as it generates more univariates (lines 18...23). After that, EQgenerator uses all univariates produced from the previous loop to simplify the elements of the arrays da, db, dc, a, b, c (line 24).

Finally, the EQgenerator procedure returns the set of generated polynomials P together with the set of generated univariates S.

Algorithm 2. EQgenerator($l_1, \ldots, l_m, Z, Z^{(1)}, \ldots, Z^{(m)}$)

1:   $P \leftarrow \text{TRIV}(Z)$
2:   $a \leftarrow [a_1, \ldots, a_{n+93}]$
3:   $b \leftarrow [b_1, \ldots, b_{n+84}]$
4:   $c \leftarrow [c_1, \ldots, c_{n+111}]$
5:   $S \leftarrow \emptyset$
6:   **for** $j = 1$ to m **do**
7:     $da \leftarrow [0, \ldots, 0]$ // length(da) $= n + 93$
8:     $db \leftarrow [0, \ldots, 0]$ // length(db) $= n + 84$
9:     $dc \leftarrow [0, \ldots, 0]$ // length(dc) $= n + 111$
10:    InjectFault(da, db, dc, l_j)
     // Insert a one-bit fault to one of da, db, dc based on the value of l_j
11:    **for** $i = 1$ to n **do**
12:      $S_1 \leftarrow \emptyset$
13:      $dz \leftarrow z_i + z_i^{(j)}$
14:      $P \leftarrow da[i] + da[i + 27] + db[i] + db[i + 15] + dc[i] + dc[i + 45] + dz$ // (3)
15:      $da[i + 93] \leftarrow$ right hand side of (5.1)   // replace $\triangle a_{i+24}$ by $da[i + 24]$, ..
16:      $db[i + 84] \leftarrow$ right hand side of (5.2)   // replace $\triangle b_{i+6}$ by $db[i + 6]$, ..
17:      $dc[i + 111] \leftarrow$ right hand side of (5.3)   // replace $\triangle c_{i+24}$ by $dc[i + 24]$, ..
18:      **repeat**
19:        $S_2 \leftarrow \emptyset$
20:        $S_2 \leftarrow \text{ExtractUnivariate}(P)$
21:        $P \leftarrow \text{Substitute}(P, S_2)$
22:        $S_1 \leftarrow S_1 \cup S_2$
23:      **until** $S_2 = \emptyset$
24:      $da, db, dc, a, b, c \leftarrow \text{Substitute}(da, db, dc, a, b, c, S_1)$
25:      $S \leftarrow S \cup S_1$
26:    **end for**
27: **end for**
28: **return** $P \cup S$

In the EQgenerator procedure, we use the same way of generating polynomial equations as in [9]. However, the authors of [9] substituted by the solved variables only in the higher degree generated polynomials (P), whereas we substitute solved variables in all the generated polynomials (linear and non-linear) and all constructed $\triangle a_i, \triangle b_i, \triangle c_i$ polynomials. Moreover, we replace the solved variables by their values in the set of variables to prevent their occurrence in the remaining computation. In Table 1 we compare the Hojsík-Rudolf (H-R) polynomial system generator [9] with our generator. For this comparison, we have $n = 800$ and denote the number of fault injections by m. We report the number of the produced polynomial equations of degree ≤ 4. Clearly, our generator creates systems that contain more linear equations than those created by H-R. This leads to an easier system to solve. We evaluate the average over 1000 experiments.

Table 1. Comparison between our generator and Hojsík-Rudolf generator for $n = 800$ and m fault injections

Generator	m	degree 1	degree 2	degree 3	degree 4
H-R	0	800	2400	0	0
H-R	1	825	2466	35	57
H-R	2	1017	2419	36	57
H-R	3	1258	2298	37	56
H-R	4	2402	498	8	12
our	0	800	2400	0	0
our	1	994	2394	28	27
our	2	1212	2362	64	76
our	3	1619	1990	82	66
our	4	2688	0	0	0

5   Attack Description

Algebraic cryptanalysis is based on solving a multivariate polynomial system that describes a cryptosystem. There are several methods for solving such systems. Computing Gröbner basis is one of the standard techniques for solving multivariate polynomial systems including F_4 [7], F_5 [8], and MXL_3 [10] algorithms. One of the main problems of all of these techniques is the memory usage when we try to solve large systems even if the systems are sparse. Recently SAT solvers have made a great progress in algebraic cryptanalysis. In [5], Bard et al used a SAT solver combined with the slide attack to break Keeloq block cipher. Using SAT solvers, Eibach et al. [6] attacked Bivium, a scaled version of Trivium. According to our experiments, SAT solvers yielded superior results to Gröbner basis techniques provided by Magma and PolyBoRi [3]. For our implementation of the MXL_3 algorithm, the best variant of the XL algorithm we have, solving such systems is not feasible since our implementation is based on the dense matrix representation, whereas systems considered in this paper are sparse.

The aim of our attack is to recover the inner state of the stream cipher Trivium at $t = 0$ that leads to recovering the secret key. We assume that the attacker has the following information:

1.) m fault injection positions $(l_1, \ldots, l_m)$, $l_i \leq 288, i \in \{1, \cdots, m\}$.
2.) The vector of the output keystream bits before the fault injection, $Z = (z_1, \ldots, z_n)$.
3.) The vectors of the output keystream bits that are obtained after each fault injection, $(Z^{(1)}, \ldots, Z^{(m)})$.

Algorithm 3 explains the main part of this paper. It describes the steps of our attack. The first step has been explained in the previous section. It is important to note that we used only equations of degree ≤ 2 in the attack. In this case, the maximal degree of P is 2.

Algorithm 3.

Require: m fault injection positions $(l_1, \ldots, l_m)$ and the vectors Z, $Z^{(i)}, 1 \leq i \leq m$
1: $P \leftarrow$ EQgenerator$(l_1, \ldots, l_m, Z, Z^{(1)}, \ldots, Z^{(m)})$
2: CNF$(P) \leftarrow$ Converting P to a satisfiability problem in the CNF form
3: Solution $\leftarrow$ Solve the satisfiability problem CNF(P) by using a SAT solver
4: IS $\leftarrow$ extract the inner state values $(a_1, \ldots, a_{n+93}, b_1, \ldots, b_{n+84}, c_1, \ldots, c_{n+111})$
5: Recover the secret key K from IS
6: **return** IS

SAT solvers can deal with a formula in the conjunctive normal form (CNF), a set of clauses, which is a conjunction ($\wedge$) of disjunctions ($\vee$) of some variables or negation of variables. Since we used SAT solving in our attack and the equations from P are represented using the algebraic normal form (ANF), we need to construct the CNF representation of P. We used the ANF-to-CNF converter by Martin Albrecht and Mate Soos [1] to convert our generated system to CNF. This converter uses the method of Bard-Courtois-Jefferson [2] for converting the ANF of polynomial equations to the SAT problem in CNF.

We briefly explain the ANF-to-CNF converter of [2]. In the ANF representation, a Boolean polynomial p is a sum of terms $(t_1 + t_2 + \ldots + t_m)$, where each term t_i is a product of variables. For each term t_i of degree ≥ 1, we define a new variable b such that $b_i = t_i$. In terms of corresponding the values of variables from CNF to ANF, we identify each 1 with "True" and 0 with "False". Then we generate CNF clauses that equivalent to $b_i = t_i$. For example, let $p = (x \cdot y + x \cdot z + y \cdot w + x + z + 1)$. We define three new variables b_1, b_2, b_3, where $b_1 = (x \cdot y), b_2 = (x \cdot z), b_3 = (y \cdot w)$. Since the multiplication ($\cdot$) of two variables is simply the conjunction ($\wedge$), then $(b_1 = x \cdot y) \equiv (b_1 \Leftrightarrow x \wedge y)$ which is equivalent to the following clauses

$$(\overline{b}_1 \vee x) \wedge (\overline{b}_1 \vee y) \wedge (b_1 \vee \overline{x} \vee \overline{y}) \tag{6}$$

In the same way, we construct the equivalent clauses of b_2 and b_3. The constant term 1 can be easily represented by the clause $(b \vee \overline{b})$ which is true in all cases. The addition ($+$) is equivalent to the logic operation (XOR). We can generate the set of clauses of $(b_1 + b_2)$ as

$$(b_1 \vee \overline{b}_2) \wedge (\overline{b}_1 \vee b_2) \wedge (\overline{b}_1 \vee \overline{b}_2) \tag{7}$$

Using (6) and (7) we can convert a polynomial p from ANF to CNF. The method that we used is based on splitting the equations that contain more than a certain number (called the cutting number) of terms into shorter equations by adding new variables. This is motivated by the fact with this conversion method the number of variables grows exponentially when representing XOR chains. Then we write each equation in the CNF form as explained above. We found that 4 is the best cutting number for our attack.

In steps 3 and 4, we may pass the generated CNF file to any SAT solver and extract the values of the inner state $(a_1, \ldots, a_{93}, b_1, \ldots, b_{84}, c_1, \ldots, c_{111})$. Then we clock Trivium backwards to recover the secret key K.

6   Experimental Results

We present our results to show how advanced solving techniques can improve the differential fault analysis of the stream cipher Trivium. We used our C++ implementation to generate the Trivium equations and the additional equations that are produced from DFA as in Section 4 and Albrecht's converter [1] as explained in the previous section.

We used the SAT solver Minisat2 [11] to recover the inner state of Trivium at $t = 0$. We run all the experiments on an Intel(R) Core(TM)2 Duo CPU, each CPU is running at 2.8 GHz, and we used only one out of the two cores.

Table 2. Results of using Minisat2

n	m	degree 1	degree 2	time (sec.)
800	2	1216	2365	0.261
700	2	1088	2080	0.356
600	2	1005	1771	0.414
500	2	890	1437	0.127
450	2	831	1230	1.573
430	2	799	1138	1.936
420	2	769	1117	138.653

Table 2 shows the results of solving DFA Trivium equations when we insert several one-bit faults to random positions in any of the three registers (as explained in Algorithm 2). For each case ($n = 800, \ldots, 430$) in Table 2, we have generated 100 systems and used only the equations of degree ≤ 2. Each system has been solved 100 times by Minisat2. In case of $n = 420$, we have generated 10 systems and each system solved 10 times by Minisat2. Starting from $n \leq 420$, Minisat2 has taken significantly more time to solve the generated systems. This is due to the fact that the number of low degree equations in the generated system becomes lower. We report the average of these experiments. We have observed that the complexity of solving these systems is based on the number of linear equations generated by the EQgenerator procedure and the heuristic of the SAT solver.

7   Conclusion

We introduced an improvement to the differential fault analysis of Trivium from [9]. By using the SAT solver Minisat2 we could reduce the number of fault injections needed to recover the inner state of the cipher which leads to recovering the secret key. We show that our attack can recover the secret key of Trivium by using only two fault injections and 420 keystream output bits. As a future work, we plan to improve our attack to recover the secret key of Trivium using only one fault injection by applying more advanced conversion techniques and tuning SAT solver parameters.

Acknowledgments. The first author is supported by the BMBF project RE-SIST. The second author is partially supported by the German Science Foundation (DFG) grant BU 630/22-1. We want to thank the useful comments from Marcel Medwed and anonymous referees of the COSADE workshop on this paper and their valuable suggestions which helped to improve the paper.

References

1. Albrecht, M., Soos, M.: ANF2CNF – Converting ANF to CNF for algebraic attack using SAT solver (2008), http://bitbucket.org/malb/algebraicattacks/src
2. Bard, G.V.: Algebraic Cryptanalysis. Springer, London (2009)
3. Brickenstein, M., Dreyer, A.: PolyBoRi: A framework for Gröbner-basis computations with Boolean polynomials. Journal of Symbolic Computation 44(9), 1326–1345 (2009); Effective Methods in Algebraic Geometry
4. Canniere, C.D., Preneel, B.: Trivium specifications. eSTREAM, ECRYPT Stream Cipher Project (2006)
5. Courtois, N.T., Bard, G.V., Wagner, D.: Algebraic and slide attacks on keeLoq. In: Nyberg, K. (ed.) FSE 2008. LNCS, vol. 5086, pp. 97–115. Springer, Heidelberg (2008)
6. Eibach, T., Pilz, E., Völkel, G.: Attacking bivium using SAT solvers. In: Kleine Büning, H., Zhao, X. (eds.) SAT 2008. LNCS, vol. 4996, pp. 63–76. Springer, Heidelberg (2008)
7. Faugère, J.-C.: A new efficient algorithm for computing Gröbner bases (F4). Pure and Applied Algebra 139(1-3), 61–88 (1999)
8. Faugère, J.-C.: A new efficient algorithm for computing Gröbner bases without reduction to zero (F5). In: Proceedings of the 2002 International Symposium on Symbolic and Algebraic Computation (ISSAC), pp. 75–83. ACM Press, Lille (2002)
9. Hojsík, M., Rudolf, B.: Floating fault analysis of trivium. In: Chowdhury, D.R., Rijmen, V., Das, A. (eds.) INDOCRYPT 2008. LNCS, vol. 5365, pp. 239–250. Springer, Heidelberg (2008)
10. Mohamed, M.S.E., Cabarcas, D., Ding, J., Buchmann, J., Bulygin, S.: MXL3: An efficient algorithm for computing gröbner bases of zero-dimensional ideals. In: Lee, D., Hong, S. (eds.) ICISC 2009. LNCS, vol. 5984, pp. 87–100. Springer, Heidelberg (2010) (accepted for publication)
11. Niklas Een, N.S.: MinSat 2.0 – one of the best known SAT solvers (2008), http://minisat.se/MiniSat.html
12. Robshaw, M.: The estream project. In: Robshaw, M., Billet, O. (eds.) New Stream Cipher Designs, pp. 1–6. Springer, Heidelberg (2008)

Design of a Retargetable Decompiler for a Static Platform-Independent Malware Analysis

Lukáš Ďurfina, Jakub Křoustek, Petr Zemek, Dušan Kolář, Tomáš Hruška, Karel Masařík, and Alexander Meduna

Brno University of Technology, Faculty of Information Technology
Božetěchova 2, 612 66 Brno, Czech Republic
{idurfina,ikroustek,izemek,kolar,hruska,masarik,meduna}@fit.vutbr.cz

Abstract. Together with the massive expansion of smartphones, tablets, and other smart devices, we can notice a growing number of malware threats targeting these platforms. Software security companies are not prepared for such diversity of target platforms and there are only few techniques for platform-independent malware analysis. This is a major security issue these days. In this paper, we propose a concept of a retargetable reverse compiler (i.e. a decompiler), which is in an early stage of development. The retargetable decompiler transforms platform-specific binary applications into a high-level language (HLL) representation, which can be further analyzed in a uniform way. This tool will help with a static platform-independent malware analysis. Our unique solution is based on an exploitation of two systems that were originally not intended for such an application—the architecture description language (ADL) ISAC for a platform description and the LLVM Compiler System as the core of the decompiler. In this study, we show that our tool can produce highly readable HLL code.

Keywords: decompilation, reverse engineering, malware, LLVM, Lissom, ISAC.

1   Introduction

There are two basic types of malicious software (a.k.a. *malware*) analysis— *dynamic analysis* and *static analysis*. Even though both types have the same objective—investigation of malware behavior—they differ in its accomplishment. Both methods are usually performed together to gain a better understanding of malware samples. In dynamic analysis, we inspect a run-time malware behavior by its monitoring (e.g. monitoring of WinAPI calls [1]) and we track changes of the system and network (e.g. registry modification, installation of new services, network communication, etc. [2,3]).

To gain further insight of malware (e.g. inspection of malware functions, shellcode detection, etc.), static analysis is used. In this case, the code viewing and walking is done by several reverse-engineering tools like disassemblers or decompilers [4,5]. The reverse translation of malware gives the analyst an opportunity to see its source code, either on the assembly language level (disassembly), or on

T.-h. Kim et al. (Eds.): ISA 2011, CCIS 200, pp. 72–86, 2011.
© Springer-Verlag Berlin Heidelberg 2011

a higher level, such as the C language (decompilation). With such knowledge, it is possible to create an appropriate protection (e.g. signature of a malware sample for an anti-virus or a new heuristic method).

Static malware analysis is crucial because some kinds of malware cannot be properly analysed using only dynamic analysis (e.g. polymorphic and metamorphic code [6,7]), and we will focus on it in the further text.

Malware was primarily targeted at personal computers (i.e. architectures x86 and x86-64 [8]) for the past 20 years. The techniques for malware analysis were well optimized for this platform during this time and security companies were able to keep pace with malware authors [9,6].

The expansion of smart devices (e.g. smartphones, tablets, etc.) is very rapid last years [10]. Such devices are powered by various processors and running several types of operation systems. Users often use these new platforms for manipulating sensitive user data (e.g. passwords, credit card information, etc.), which comes to the attention of malware authors. Furthermore, the variety of these platforms is problematic for security companies because their solutions are mostly oriented on the classical ones, and they are not capable to protect new platforms at the moment. Those are the main reasons why the amount of malware for these platforms increases steadily for the last years.

In this paper, we present an overview of a retargetable decompiler, which is currently in an early stage of development. Our approach is not tied to any particular target platform. The primarily utilization of this tool is a static platform-independent malware analysis. With its help, it will be possible to inspect malware code on a much more abstract and unified form of representation, while preserving the functional equivalence of the code. Therefore, malware analysts do not need to have a deep knowledge of the target platform (i.e. instruction set and processor architecture) and they can fully focus on malware analysis.

The retargetable decompiler is based on exploitation of the ADL ISAC [11], which is intended to be used for designing new application-specific instruction set processors (ASIPs). However, we use this formalism for the description of existing platforms. The front-end of the decompiler is generated from this description. The decompiler core is based on the LLVM Compiler System [12], which we use for a reverse translation from a binary form into a Python-like language.

The paper is organized as follows. Section 2 discusses the state of the art of machine code decompilers. Then, Sections 3 and 4 describe the two key concepts our decompiler is based on—the ISAC language and the LLVM Compiler System. The design of our decompiler is then presented in Section 5. Experimental results are given in Section 6. Section 7 closes the paper by discussing future research.

2   State of the Art

The era of machine code decompilers was established before more than 50 years. The D-Neliac decompiler [13], built in 1960, was the first decompiler which showed that it is feasible to develop programs working in a reverse way to compilers.

From this period, there have been a lot of attempts to create various kinds of decompilers. A project with the closest idea to our project is the PILER System [14]. This system, consisting of three parts, uses two intermediate representations. The first part is an interpreter, which has to be run on the source machine. Its output is *Micro Form*. Micro Form is a three-address low-level intermediate representation. This representation is processed by the second part— an analyzer. The analyzer exploits more analyses, such as data flow or timing analyses, to produce *Intermediate Form*. This form is a high-level intermediate representation designed to be suitable for FORTRAN, COBOL, and other languages of that time. The last part is a converter. It emits the source of code of the HLL. In its time, the PILER System was designed to be flexible and general. However, according to the available information, it was never completed.

Currently, there exist several decompilers which deserve to be mentioned. There are the dcc decompiler [15] from C. Cifuentes, the open source Boomerang decompiler [16], the REC Decompiler [17], and the Hex-Rays Decompiler [5]. The first two decompilers are not developed any more, but the second two are constantly improving. They are shortly described in the following paragraphs. The summary is shown in Table 1.

The dcc decompiler aims only to a single architecture and to a single operating system (i80286 MS-DOS executables), but it is well structured and it complexly shows and implements the most important algorithms for the reverse engineering process. It has the same structure as a compiler: there are a front-end, a middle-end, and a back-end. Every part has its own separate tasks. This decompiler uses also two types of an intermediate representation. The low one is for the communication between the front-end and the middle-end, and the high one is sent from the middle-end to the back-end, which finally transforms this representation into a C source code. Except these intermediate representations, the decompiler creates a control flow graph in the front-end, and this graph is used in the both other parts. The dcc decompiler also contains other tools which help to create a more readable result in the target HLL. The most important features of these tools are recognitions of compilers and library routines. According to the recognized compiler, the start-up code does not need to be decompiled. The same effect applies for library routines.

After the dcc decompiler was published, there was an idea to create a retargetable decompiler. This idea resulted in an open source project called Boomerang. Its main developer was M. van Emmerik. Boomerang is a retargetable decompiler with a modular architecture. This architecture is a base for its retargetability. The design is similar to dcc, but there is an emphasis on the modular principle for an easy substitution of every part. Boomerang currently supports input executables for x86 (except SIMD instructions), Sparc, and PowerPC processors, where binary file format can be either ELF or PE. The target language is C.

The REC decompiler is not open source, but it is available for free, and also the authors published the description of its design. From nowadays decompilers, it supports the most number of architectures and binary file formats. The supported processors are x86, x86-64, MIPS, m68k, Sparc, and PowerPC. The file format of an input executable can be PE, ELF, or MachO. The REC decompiler implements complex algorithms for control flow graphs. Therefore, it is able to reconstruct some advanced constructs, such as `switch` statements.

The Hex-Rays Decompiler represents a proprietary solution which can be bought as an add-on to the IDA Pro Disassembler [4]. Therefore, we lack detailed information about this solution. This decompiler has a well-developed recognition of compilers, start-up and statically-linked code. This scope is covered by Fast Library Identification and Recognition Technology (FLIRT) [18]. It provides tools for an easy addition of new library and compiler signatures, which can be subsequently used by the decompiler.

Table 1. A comparison of the described decompilers

	dcc	Boomerang	REC decompiler	Hex-Rays Decompiler
Supported architectures	i80286	x86, Sparc, PowerPC	x86, x86-64, MIPS, m68k, Sparc, PowerPC	x86, ARM
Supported file formats	MS-DOS format	PE, ELF	PE, ELF, MachO	ELF, PE
Target language	C	C	C-like	C
Intermediate representation	two types (high and low)	a single type	?	?
Detects statically-linked code	Yes	No	Yes	Yes

On the other hand, there are projects which are not complete decompilers, but they are specialized only for generating a source code from some intermediate representation. As a nice example, we can mention emscripten [19]. It is a compiler able to transform LLVM bitcode to Javascript. It is used for transforming C/C++ code for running on the web. A similar project is llvm-js-back-end [20], which is a general LLVM back-end for producing Javascript code.

3 ISAC Language

The ISAC language [11] was developed within the Lissom project at Brno University of Technology [21]. The project has two basic scopes. The first scope is a development of an ADL for the description of Multiprocessor Systems-on-Chip (MPSoC). The second scope is a transformation of MPSoC description into advanced software tools (e.g. a C compiler, a simulator, etc.) or into a hardware realization of each processor. The ISAC language belongs into a so-called mixed ADL. It means that a processor model consists of several parts. In the resource part, processor resources, such as registers or memory hierarchy, are declared. In the operation part, processor instruction set with behavior of instructions and processor micro-architecture is described. Processor model can be written in two levels of accuracy—instruction-accurate or cycle-accurate. The retargetable decompiler currently uses the first one.

The *assembler* and *coding* sections capture the format of instructions in the assembly and machine language, so they define instructions in textual and binary forms. For the behavioral model, the *behavior* section is used. In this section, a subset of the ANSI C language can be used. The behavior section defines the semantics of each operation. For example, a simple instruction with its behavior is described using the assembler, coding, and behavior sections, see Figure 1.

```
RESOURCES {                    // HW resources
  PC REGISTER bit[32] pc;      // program counter
  REGISTER bit[32] regs[16];   // register file
  RAM bit[32] memory {SIZE(0x10000); FLAGS(R, W, X); };
}
OPERATION reg REPRESENTS regs
  { /* textual and binary description of registers */ }
OPERATION op_add {             // instruction description
  INSTANCE reg ALIAS {rd, rs, rt};
  ASSEMBLER { "ADD" rd "=" rs "," rt };
  CODING { 0b0001 rd rs rt };
                               // instruction behavior
  BEHAVIOR { regs[rd] = regs[rs] + regs[rt]; };
}
```

Fig. 1. Example of a ISAC language source code

4 LLVM Compiler System

The LLVM Compiler System [12] was originally designed as a compiler framework to support transparent, lifelong program analysis and transformation for arbitrary programs, by providing high-level information to compiler transformations at compile-time, link-time, run-time and in idle-time between runs [22]. Nowadays, the use of LLVM spans over many different areas, including compilation [23,24,25,26], video decoding [27], signal processing [28], static checking [29,30,31,32], and implementation of various programming languages

[33,34,35]. The key features of LLVM include a universal, language-independent instruction set, type system, intermediate representation (LLVM IR [36]), many built-in sophisticated optimization algorithms and passes, link-time optimizations, just-in-time (JIT) code generation, and application programming interface for several programming languages.

Consider the C source code in Figure 2. This straightforward implementation of the factorial function can be directly compiled into the LLVM IR. The output of this conversion is shown in Figure 3. This example shows us some of the properties of the LLVM IR:

- The used RISC-like instruction set captures the key operations of ordinary processors, but avoids most of machine-specific constraints. Most instructions are in the three-address form—they take either one or two operands and produce a single result. The instruction set includes arithmetic instructions (e.g. add, mul), bitwise instructions (e.g. shl, and), memory access instructions (e.g. load, store, alloca), conversion instructions (e.g. trunc, zext), and other instructions (e.g. icmp, call). Furthermore, every basic block ends with a terminator instruction (e.g. br, ret) which explicitly specifies its successor basic blocks.
- As can be seen from the presence of the phi instruction in Figure 3, the virtual registers are in the Static Single Assignment (SSA) form (see [37]), where each variable is assigned exactly once. The use of this form results in a simplification of many compiler optimizations.
- A language-independent type system is used. Every instruction and SSA register has an associated type and all operations obey strict type rules. This enables several optimizations which otherwise would not be possible (at least not in such a straightforward way). Primitive types include void, boolean, variable-sized integers, and floating-point types. Derived types include pointers, arrays, structures, and functions. The cast instruction can be used for type conversions (other ways of type conversions are not possible). Address computation and address arithmetic is done by the getelementptr instruction.
- The LLVM IR can exist in the following three forms: textual (as in Figure 3), binary (compiled textual representation), and in-memory (compiler internal representation). All of these representations are equivalent—that is, one can be transformed to the others without any loss of information.

```
int factorial(int n) {
    if (n == 0)
        return 1;
    return n*factorial(n-1);
}
```

Fig. 2. A simple implementation of the factorial function in C

```
define i32 @factorial(i32 %n) {
entry:
    %0 = icmp eq i32 %n, 0
    br i1 %0, label %bb2, label %bb1

bb1:
    %1 = add i32 %n, -1
    %2 = icmp eq i32 %1, 0
    br i1 %2, label %factorial.exit, label %bb1.i

bb1.i:
    %3 = add i32 %n, -2
    %4 = call i32 @factorial(i32 %3)
    %5 = mul i32 %4, %1
    br label %factorial.exit

factorial.exit:
    %6 = phi i32 [ %5, %bb1.i ], [ 1, %bb1 ]
    %7 = mul i32 %6, %n
    ret i32 %7

bb2:
    ret i32 1
}
```

Fig. 3. The generated LLVM IR code from the code in Figure 2

5 Design of a Retargetable Decompiler

The objective of the decompiler is an analysis of a binary code and its transformation into a HLL. It is important to preserve the functional equivalence of the transformed program; otherwise, further code analyses will be inaccurate. This is a very difficult task because we have to deal with missing information in the input code (e.g. because of compiler optimizations, malware obfuscation, etc.). The usage of the retargetable decompiler is straightforward—its user describes the target architecture in the ISAC ADL and the decompiler is automatically generated by a tool-chain generator based on this description. After that, it is possible to reversely translate binary executables for this architecture. The idea of this process is discussed in the following text.

The structure of the retargetable decompiler is similar to a classical compiler. It consists of a front-end, a middle-end, and a back-end, see Figure 4. The only platform-specific part is the front-end. For this purpose, the binary coding and semantics of each processor instruction is extracted from the architecture model in ISAC. This is a major difference against other retargetable decompilers, because it is not necessary to manually reconfigure the decompiler for a new

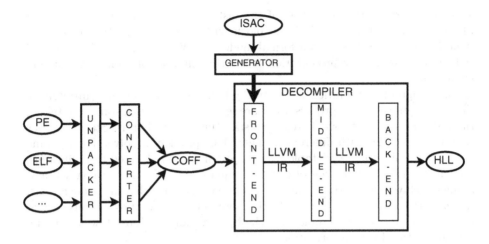

Fig. 4. The concept of the retargetable decompiler

architecture. It should be noted that in present, there is no other competitive method of automatically-generated retargetable decompilation.

5.1   Front-End

The objective of the front-end is a translation from an architecture-specific machine code into a sequence of low-level LLVM IR instructions. The input binary file is stored in a platform-specific file format (e.g. Windows PE, Unix ELF, etc.). Furthermore, in the case of malware, the input file is usually packed and protected against reverse-engineering. Therefore, the first step of the reverse translation is a code unpacking phase. As this topic is well documented in the literature (see [38,39]), we will not deal with it in our paper.

After that, it is necessary to convert the platform-specific file format into a unified form of representation. The internal COFF-based file format has been designed for this purpose, together with several conversion algorithms. At the moment, we support conversions from Windows PE, Unix ELF, Symbian E32, and Android DEX file formats.

To generate the instruction decoder (i.e. a part of the front-end responsible for the conversion from a machine code into LLVM IR), it is necessary to extract the binary coding and semantics of instructions from the ISAC model. This task is done via a tool called *semantics extractor* [40]. The semantics extractor transforms ANSI C code from the behavior section of the instruction into a sequence of LLVM IR instructions, which properly describes its behavior. Therefore, we are able to map instruction semantic in LLVM IR to its machine code.

After that, it is possible to automatically generate an instruction decoder. Its functionality is similar to a disassembler, except its output is not an assembly language representation of the instruction, but rather a sequence of LLVM IR instructions (i.e. a basic block with several instructions). The instruction decoder is based on a formal model [41]. Whenever a statically-linked code is detected, its representation is emitted instead of simple instruction semantics.

The design of our solution for statically-linked code detection is inspired by FLIRT [18]. In the whole process, there are separate steps which start from taking the static library and finish at creating a signature for this library. Static libraries contain object files with different formats. This problem is solved by the same way as it is solved for executable files. Object files are extracted from libraries, they are transformed into our object file format and finally, they are packed into a single archive. Due to this action, we can then proceed with a single file format. In comparison with FLIRT, this clearly represents an advantage because we do not have to build separate tools for each object file format. Indeed, we can easily extend the tool for transformation.

The creation of signatures consists of two parts:

– extracting the pattern for each object file from a library,
– building the signature from a group of patterns.

The process is visualized in Figure 5.

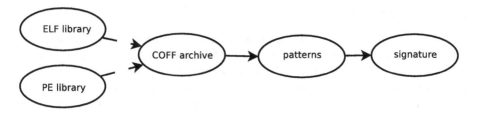

Fig. 5. The process of creating the signature for static library

The final part of the front-end is a static analysis of the emitted LLVM IR code. It is focused on control flow analyses and transformation of the LLVM IR code to produce more suitable code for the following parts of the decompiler. For example, this phase is responsible for the detection of functions, elimination of "jump register" instructions, and annotation of the resulting LLVM IR code. However, this part is not implemented yet, and more intensive research in this field is necessary.

5.2   Middle-End

In this stage, we have a very low-level LLVM IR of the input binary. Each basic block represents a single assembly instruction, there may be many redundant instructions (recall that each assembly instruction is decompiled in isolation), and there is no evidence of high-level constructs, such as loops. The key role of the middle-end part of our decompiler is to improve the properties of the generated LLVM IR code and prepare it for the final emission of the output HLL.

The following passes are performed over the LLVM IR code:

- Search for idioms. These are sequences of code whose combined semantics is not immediately apparent from the instructions' individual semantics. For example, xor'ing a single register with itself can be replaced by assigning a zero into it. This form is clearly more readable than the original form. Idioms may, however, span over several instructions. In such cases, they may be replaced with a few equivalent instructions. This pass also includes several other types of program analysis, such as constant or expression propagation.
- Retrieval of high-level constructs, such as if/else statements, switches, and loops. As we want to use unstructured goto's as little as possible, it is necessary to identify proper structured equivalents. We identify headers and bodies of loops, common destination basic blocks after a branch instruction, and other information needed to generate natural and readable output code.
- Optimization of the code. Here, we connect successive basic blocks and perform optimizations which eliminate redundant instructions.

As LLVM already includes many worked-out and sophisticated optimization and analysis passes, we naturally prefer using them over our own passes whenever possible.

To improve this middle phase in terms of effectiveness, the LLVM IR code generated by our front-end is annotated. We utilize the fact that LLVM IR allows metadata to be attached to instructions in the program that can convey extra information about the code. The used annotations include markings of the entry point of function bodies and information about application binary interface (calling conventions, system calls, etc.).

5.3   Back-End

In this final decompilation stage, we transform the optimized LLVM IR into a HLL. We currently use a Python-like (see [42]) language as the target language, briefly described next. However, a support for different back-ends is planned.

Our HLL is non-typed, block structured, and uses whitespace indentation, rather than curly braces or keywords, to delimit blocks. Since we focus on code analysis by humans, the used language emphasises code readability. Whenever there is no support in Python for a specific construction, we use C-like constructs. For example, we use C-like switch statements to implement the fall-through feature of C. Instead of arrays, we use lists, and instead of structures, we utilize dictionaries. We also use the address and dereference operators from C. As there are cases when the code cannot be structured by high-level constructs only (for example, an irreducible subgraph of the control-flow graph is detected [15]), an explicit goto represents a necessary addition to our language.

The implemented back-end takes the optimized LLVM IR and converts it into our HLL by walking over its control-flow graph. Analysis information from the middle-end is used throughout the generation to emit proper high-level constructs.

After the generation is completed, an additional post-processing phase is done to further improve the readability of the code. These modifications are done on a textual level, and include the elimination of redundant brackets and expressions introduced by the back-end.

In the next section, we present an example of a generated output code.

6   Experimental Results

In this section, we present some experimental results. Since our decompiler is in an early stage of development, we just compare our back-end with the C back-end, currently included in LLVM. Even though we have several examples of a preliminary decompilation of a real-world code, the obtained results are not in a publishable form yet.

First, we compile the source code given in Figure 6 directly into LLVM IR using llvm-gcc[1]. Due to space requirements, we omit the listing of the obtained LLVM IR code. Then, we emit a high-level representation of it by the C back-end and by our back-end (see Figures 7 and 8, respectively).

Observe the following key differences between the two back-ends:

– We do not introduce any useless variables (see llvm_cbe_tmp__1 in the output from the C back-end).
– Instead of using goto's, we inline the bodies of the corresponding basic blocks wherever possible. This also holds for other high-level constructs, such as loops and switch statements.
– Instead of accessing string literals through a structure, we inline them wherever possible.
– We eliminate as much redundant code as possible, hence increasing the readability of the resulting code. For example, consider the redundant pairs of brackets in the output from the C back-end. As they are not needed and they also do not contribute to the understandability of the code (like when brackets are used in complex expressions with many different operators), we remove them.
– As our HLL is non-typed, there is no need for any sequences of castings which make the generated code—albeit type correct—less readable.
– Finally, we generate as little boilerplate code as possible (however, this cannot be seen from the figures).

---

[1] We used llvm-gcc version 4.2.1. The source code from Figure 6 was compiled with enabled optimizations (-O3) directly into LLVM IR (-emit-llvm). The used version of LLVM is 2.8.

```
int func(int a, int b) {
    if (a != b) {
        printf("%d != %d", a, b);
    }
    return a * (b + 10);
}
```

Fig. 6. An input source code for our comparison of back-ends

```
// Removed boilerplate code
struct l_unnamed0 { unsigned char array[9]; };
static struct l_unnamed0 _OC_str = { "%d != %d" };

unsigned int func(unsigned int llvm_cbe_a,
                  unsigned int llvm_cbe_b) {
    unsigned int llvm_cbe_tmp__1;

    if ((llvm_cbe_a == llvm_cbe_b)) {
        goto llvm_cbe_bb1;
    } else {
        goto llvm_cbe_bb;
    }

llvm_cbe_bb:
    llvm_cbe_tmp__1 = printf((((&_OC_str.array[((signed
        long long)0ull)]))), llvm_cbe_a, llvm_cbe_b);
    goto llvm_cbe_bb1;

llvm_cbe_bb1:
    return (((unsigned int)(((unsigned int)(((unsigned
        int)(((unsigned int)llvm_cbe_b) + ((unsigned
        int)10u))))) * ((unsigned int)llvm_cbe_a))));
}
```

Fig. 7. Truncated output from the C back-end

```
def func(a, b):
    if not (a == b):
        printf("%d != %d", a, b)
    return (b + 10) * a
```

Fig. 8. Output from our back-end

7   Conclusion

This paper proposed the concept of a retargetable decompiler for a static platform-independent malware analysis. The front-end of this tool is generated based on a processor description in the ISAC ADL. Its middle-end and back-end are build on top of the LLVM Compiler System. The idea of exploitation of these systems is innovative and it allows an automatic retargetability of our solution. This is a major advantage of our solution over other similar projects.

The functionality of each part of the decompiler was discussed and we presented results of the current state of the implementation. As can be seen, we are already able to convert a platform-specific machine code into its semantic representation as a platform independent LLVM IR code. Such code can be translated into a human-readable HLL code by our back-end after that. This back-end can achieve better results in a reverse translation than other existing solutions.

However, there is still a lot of space for improvements. In the first place, it is necessary to finish the implementation of the static analyser in the front-end. After that, we will be able to produce a more accurate LLVM IR code, which will improve the resulting HLL code.

The middle-end of our decompiler can be enhanced by several new analyses and transformations. For example, consider the `if` condition in Figure 8. A more natural way of representing the condition would be to transfer the negation into the expression, resulting into `if a != b`. Another transformation to be considered is a replacement of a chain of `if/else if` statements by a single `switch` statement. Furthermore, current analyses and transformations have to be improved to generate better HLL.

As for the back-end of our decompiler, emission of some HLL constructs can be improved. For example, loops are currently always generated as `while True` loops. A proper detection of induction variables in the middle-end is necessary to emit more natural constructions. Furthermore, other HLLs can be considered, possibly including type information and conversions between types.

Acknowledgments. This work was supported by the research fundings MPO ČR, No. FR-TI1/038, TAČR, No. TA01010667, BUT FIT grant FIT-S-11-2, by the Research Plan No. MSM0021630528, and by the SMECY European project.

References

1. Xu, J., Sung, A.H., Chavez, P., Mukkamala, S.: Polymorphic malicious executable scanner by API sequence analysis. In: Fourth International Conference on Hybrid Intelligent Systems, pp. 378–383 (2004)
2. Wagener, G., State, R., Dulaunoy, A.: Malware behaviour analysis. Journal in Computer Virology 4, 279–287 (2008)
3. Willems, C., Holz, T., Freiling, F.: Toward automated dynamic malware analysis using CWSandbox. IEEE Security and Privacy 5(2), 32–39 (2007)
4. IDA Pro Disassembler, http://www.hex-rays.com/idapro/

5. Hex-Rays Decompiler, http://www.hex-rays.com/decompiler.shtml
6. Szor, P.: The Art of Computer Virus Research and Defense. Addison-Wesley, Upper Saddle River (2005)
7. Szor, P., Ferrie, P.: Hunting for metamorphic. In: Virus Bulletin Conference, pp. 123–144 (2001)
8. Intel Corporation: Intel 64 and ia-32 architectures software developer's manual. Basic architecture, vol. 1 (2011)
9. Aquilina, J.: Malware Forensics Investigating and Analyzing Malicious Code. Syngress Publishing, Burlington (2008)
10. International Data Corporation (IDC): Worldwide quarterly mobile phone tracker (2011)
11. Masařík, K.: System for Hardware-Software Co-Design, 1st edn., p. 156. Faculty of Information Technology BUT, Brno (2008)
12. The LLVM Compiler System, http://llvm.org/
13. Halstead, M.H.: Machine-Independent Computer Programming, pp. 143–150. Spartan Books, Washington (1962)
14. Barbe, P.: The PILER system of computer program translation. Technical report, Probe Consultants Inc. (1974)
15. Cifuentes, C.: Reverse Compilation Techniques. PhD thesis, School of Computing Science, Queensland University of Technology, Brisbane, AU-QLD (1994)
16. Boomerang, http://boomerang.sourceforge.net/
17. Reverse Engineering Compiler, http://www.backerstreet.com/rec/rec.htm
18. Fast Library Identification and Recognition Technology, http://www.hex-rays.com/idapro/flirt.htm
19. emscripten, http://code.google.com/p/emscripten/
20. llvm-js-backend, http://github.com/dmlap/llvm-js-backend
21. Lissom Project, http://www.fit.vutbr.cz/research/groups/lissom/
22. Adve, V., Lattner, C., Brukman, M., Shukla, A., Gaeke, B.: LLVA: A low-level virtual instruction set architecture. In: Proceedings of the 36th Annual ACM/IEEE International Symposium on Microarchitecture, San Diego, US-CA (2003)
23. Clang, http://clang.llvm.org/
24. LDC: LLVM D Compiler, http://www.dsource.org/projects/ldc
25. Trident Compiler, http://trident.sourceforge.net/
26. Tripp, J.L., Gokhale, M.B., Peterson, K.D.: Trident: From high-level language to hardware circuitry. Computer 40(3), 28–37 (2007)
27. Just-In-Time Adaptive Decoder Engine (Jade), http://sourceforge.net/apps/trac/orcc/
28. Faust: Signal Processing Language, http://sourceforge.net/projects/faudiostream/
29. Babić, D., Hu, A.J.: Structural abstraction of software verification conditions. In: Damm, W., Hermanns, H. (eds.) CAV 2007. LNCS, vol. 4590, pp. 366–378. Springer, Heidelberg (2007)
30. Babić, D., Hu, A.J.: Calysto: Scalable and precise extended static checking. In: ICSE 2008: Proceedings of the 30th International Conference on Software Engineering, Leipzig, DE, pp. 211–220 (2008)
31. Calysto Extended Static Checker, http://www.domagoj-babic.com/index.php/ResearchProjects/Calysto
32. Lewycky, N.: Checker: A static program checker. Master's thesis, Computer Science Department, Ryerson University, Toronto, CA-ON (2006)
33. unladen-swallow: A Faster Implementation of Python, http://code.google.com/p/unladen-swallow/

34. Rubinius, http://rubini.us/
35. The Pure Programming Language, http://code.google.com/p/pure-lang/
36. Adve, V., Lattner, C.: LLVM: A compilation framework for lifelong program analysis & transformation. In: Proceedings of the International Symposium on Code Generation and Optimization, Palo Alto, US-CA, pp. 75–86 (2004)
37. Cytron, R., Ferrante, J., Rosen, B.K., Wegman, M.N., Zadeck, F.K.: Efficiently computing static single assignment form and the control dependence graph. ACM Transactions on Programming Languages and Systems 13(4), 451–490 (1991)
38. Coogan, K., Debray, S.K., Kaochar, T., Townsend, G.M.: Automatic static unpacking of malware binaries. In: Working Conference on Reverse Engineering, Lille, FR, pp. 167–176 (2009)
39. Yan, W., Zhang, Z., Ansari, N.: Revealing packed malware. IEEE Security and Privacy 6(5), 65–69 (2008)
40. Husár, A., Trmač, M., Hranáč, J., Hruška, T., Masařík, K., Kolář, D., Přikryl, Z.: Automatic C compiler generation from architecture description language ISAC. In: 6th Doctoral Workshop on Mathematical and Engineering Methods in Computer Science, pp. 84–91. Masaryk University, Brno (2010)
41. Hruška, T., Kolář, D., Lukáš, R., Zámečníková, E.: Two-way coupled finite automaton and its usage in translators. In: New Aspects of Circuits, Heraklion, GR, vol. 2008, pp. 445–449 (2008)
42. Python Programming Language, http://www.python.org/

The Proactive and Reactive Digital Forensics Investigation Process: A Systematic Literature Review

Soltan Alharbi[1], Jens Weber-Jahnke[2], and Issa Traore[1]

[1] Electrical and Computer Engineering,
University of Victoria
{salharbi,itraore}@ece.uvic.ca
[2] Computer Science Department,
University of Victoria
jens@cs.uvic.ca

Abstract. Recent papers have urged the need for new forensic techniques and tools able to investigate anti-forensics methods, and have promoted automation of live investigation. Such techniques and tools are called proactive forensic approaches, i.e., approaches that can deal with digitally investigating an incident while it occurs. To come up with such an approach, a Systematic Literature Review (SLR) was undertaken to identify and map the processes in digital forensics investigation that exist in literature. According to the review, there is only one process that explicitly supports proactive forensics, the multi-component process [1]. However, this is a very high-level process and cannot be used to introduce automation and to build a proactive forensics system. As a result of our SLR, a derived functional process that can support the implementation of a proactive forensics system is proposed.

Keywords: Proactive Forensics Investigation, Reactive Forensics Investigation, Anti-forensics, Systematic Literature Review and Automation.

1 Introduction

Computer crimes have increased in frequency, and their degree of sophistication has also advanced. An example of such sophistication is the use of anti-forensics methods as in Zeus Botnet Crimeware toolkit that can sometimes counter-act digital forensic investigations through its obfuscation levels. Moreover, volatility and dynamicity of the information flow in such a toolkit require some type of a proactive investigation method or system. The term *anti-forensics* refers to methods that prevent forensic tools, investigations, and investigators from achieving their goals [2]. Two examples of anti-forensics methods are *data overwriting* and *data hiding*. From a digital investigation perspective, anti-forensics can do the following [2]:

- Prevent evidence collection.
- Increase the investigation time.
- Provide misleading evidence that can jeopardize the whole investigation.
- Prevent detection of digital crime.

T.-h. Kim et al. (Eds.): ISA 2011, CCIS 200, pp. 87–100, 2011.

To investigate crimes that rely on anti-forensics methods, more digital forensics investigation techniques and tools need to be developed, tested, and automated. Such techniques and tools are called proactive forensics processes. Proactive forensics has been suggested in [1-4]. To date, however, the definition and the process of proactive forensics have not been explicated [1].

In order to develop an operational definition for proactive forensics process and related phases, we have conducted a systematic literature review (SLR) to analyze and synthesize results published in literature concerning digital forensics investigation processes. This SLR has ten steps, described in sections 3.1 to 5.2, grouped under three main phases: planning, conducting, and documenting the SLR [5]. As result of this SLR, a proactive forensics process has been derived.

The SLR approach was selected for a couple of reasons. Firstly, SLR results are reproducible. Secondly, since all resources (databases) will be queried systematically there is less chance of missing an important reference.

The rest of the paper is organized as follows. Section 2 outlines the related work and the motivation behind the proactive investigation process. Section 3 lays out the plan of the systematic literature review prior to implementation. Section 4 describes the implementation of the review and the extraction of the primary studies from the selected resources. Section 5 generates the report of the review after synthesizing the data collected in the previous section. Section 6 presents the review findings, results, and the proposed process. Section 7 contains the conclusion and suggestions for future work.

2   Related Work and Motivation for the Proactive Investigation Process

According to the literature, only a few papers have proposed a proactive digital forensics investigation process. Some of these papers have mentioned the proactive process explicitly, while in others the process is implicit, but all have indicated the need for such a process.

In [6], Rowlingson stated that in many organizations , incident response team already performs some activities of evidence collection. But he added, that the need for collecting those evidence and preserving it in a systematic proactive approach still an open issue.

In [2], Garfinkel implicitly suggested that in order to investigate anti-forensics, organizations need to decide early what information to collect and preserve in a forensically sound manner.

In [1], Grobler et al. noted that live (proactive) forensic investigations are hindered by lack of definitions of live forensics and standard procedures in live investigations. In addition, the authors suggested the automation and activation of evidence-collection tools in live investigations. This automation should involve minimal user intervention to improve the integrity of the evidence. Thus, a multi-component view of the digital forensics investigation process has been proposed. However, it is a high-level view of the investigation and, as such, cannot directly be operationalized to create automated tools. Additionally, the process described in [2] contains phases, such as service restoration, that lie outside the scope of the investigation.

In [3], Garfinkel summarized digital forensics investigation processes that have been published in literature. In his summary, he stated that it would be unwise to depend upon "audit trails and internal logs" in digital forensics investigation. In addition, he noted that a future digital forensics investigation process will only be possible if future tools and techniques make a proactive effort at evidence collection and preservation.

In [4], Orebaugh emphasized that the quality and availability of the evidence collected in the reactive stage of the investigation is more time consuming to investigate. Conversely, the proactive stage collects only potential evidence, which is less time consuming to investigate. In addition, a high-level proactive forensics system is proposed as ideal. As future work, the author suggested that in order to address anti-forensics crimes, methods should be identified to handle evidence collection and proactive forensics investigation.

In summary, previous papers have shown the importance of a proactive digital forensics investigation process. The proposed notion of proactiveness is, however, still insufficient and imprecise, and more work needs to be done. To this end, we will follow a systematic literature review and derive the missing components.

3   Planning the Systematic Literature Review (SLR)

The planning stage of the systematic literature review consists of the following steps:

3.1   Specify Research Questions

This step defines the goal of the SLR by selecting the research question that has to be answered by the review. The research question is: "What are all the processes in digital forensics investigation?"

Processes include the phases of any digital forensics investigation. According to [7], the six phases of digital forensics investigation are: identification, preservation, collection, examination, analysis, and presentation. The reader can refer to [7] for elaboration of these phases.

3.2   Develop Review Protocol

The review protocol is outlined in steps 4.1 through 5.2 below. These steps show how data for the review is selected and summarized.

3.3   Validate Review Protocol

The review protocol was validated by querying the selected databases and looking at the search results. Those results were meaningful and showed the feasibility of the developed protocol.

4 Conducting the Systematic Literature Review

The review was conducted by extracting data from the selected sources using the following steps:

4.1 Identify Relevant Research Sources

Six database sources were selected as being most relevant to the fields of computer science, software engineering, and computer engineering. The expert engineering librarian at the University of Victoria corroborated the relevance of those databases, and also recommended another indexed database that is considered to contain reliable sources: *Inspec*. Two extra public indexed databases were used for sanity check: *CiteSeer* and *Google Scholar*. The *International Journal of Computer Science and Network Security* (IJCSNS) was located while conducting a sanity check in Google Scholar using "digital forensic investigation process" as keywords.

All of the searches were limited in date from 2001 to 2010.

4.1.1   IEEE Xplore: http://ieeexplore.ieee.org/Xplore/dynhome.jsp

4.1.2   ACM Digital Library: http://portal.acm.org/dl.cfm

4.1.3   Inspec: http://www.engineeringvillage2.org/

4.1.4   SpringerLink: http://www.springerlink.com

4.1.5   ELSEVIER: http://www.sciencedirect.com

4.1.6   IJCSNS: http://ijcsns.org/index.htm

4.1.7   CiteSeer: http://citeseerx.ist.psu.edu *(indexed database)*

4.1.8   Google Scholar: http://scholar.google.ca *(indexed database)*

The queries used to search the databases above, except for IJCSNS, were as follows:

(Computer OR Digital) AND (Forensic OR Crime) AND (Investigation OR Process OR Framework OR Model OR Analysis OR Examination)

For IEEE Xplore, the basic search screen window was used to search only within title and abstract (metadata, not a full text).

In ACM Digital Library, the basic search screen window was used to search for the queries within the database.

In the case of SpringerLink, the advanced search screen window was used to search within title and abstract. Furthermore, in SpringerLink the search field for queries could not take all of the queries so last two keywords, "Analysis" and "Examination," had to be excluded.

In the case of ELSEVIER, the advanced search screen window was used to search within abstract, title, and keywords.

Running the above queries against the databases gave the following numbers of papers:

- IEEE Xplore: 42 (on Nov 1, 2010)
- ACM Digital Library: 27 (on Nov 3, 2010)
- SpringerLink: 158 (on Nov 3, 2010)
- ELSEVIER: 346 (on Nov 4, 2010)

For IJCSNS, as an exception, the keywords **"Digital Forensic Investigation"** were used in the search screen window. The search returned this number of papers:

- IJCSNS: 86 (on Nov 24, 2010)

Since using the above queries for Inspec and CiteSeer would result in a considerable number of irrelevant Primary Studies (PS), Control Terms (CT) were used instead. In addition, CT were run against previous databases as well, to be able to capture more relevant PS. The CT recommended by the Inspec database as well as the subject librarian are:

(Computer Crime) OR (Computer Forensics) OR (Forensic Science)

The first two CT (computer crime OR computer forensics) were used to search IEEE Xplore, ACM, SpringerLink, and ELSEVIER. "Forensic Science" was excluded since it returns PS out of the scope of this study. For IEEE Xplore, the advanced search screen window was used in searching the metadata only. In the ACM digital library, the advanced search screen window was used to fetch the database within the keywords field. In SpringerLink, the advanced search screen window was used to search within title and abstract. For ELSEVIER, the advanced search screen window was used to search within the keywords.

In the case of Inspec, using the CT above, the database was searched in three categories. In the first category, all of the CT (including "forensic science") were used with an AND Boolean operator between them in the quick search screen window for searching within CT fields in the database. In the second category, only "computer forensics" was used in the quick search screen window to search within the CT field. In the third category, "forensic science" was used in the quick search screen window to search within CT.

For CiteSeer, the advanced search screen window was used. In addition, since CiteSeer does not have the option to search within CT, it was necessary to search its database using keywords. These keywords were **"Computer Crime" OR "Computer Forensics" OR "Digital Forensic."** The search was conducted in two categories. First, an OR operator was used between all the keywords in the abstract field. Second, only the first two keywords were used, with an OR operator between them, in the keywords field.

When the above CT and keywords were run on different dates, the following numbers of papers were returned from the databases listed above:

- IEEE Xplore: 1,053 (on Nov 6, 2010)
- ACM Digital Library: 134 (on Nov 8, 2010)
- SpringerLink: 128 (On Nov 10, 2010)
- ELSEVIER: 69 (on Nov 14, 2010)
- Inspec: 459 (on Nov 5, 2010). The PS were distributed as follows:
    - Category 1: 13
    - Category 2: 290
    - Category 3: 156

- CiteSeer: 162 (on Nov 15, 2010)
    - Category 1: 143
    - Category 2: 19

Finally, the primary studies that were collected from running all the above queries are [1], [8-26]. Additional primary studies were collected by examining the previous primary studies [7, 27-31].

4.2 Select Primary Studies

4.2.1 Selection Language
Publications in the English language only were selected from the above database resources.

4.2.2 Selection Criteria
Primary studies were selected and irrelevant ones were excluded using three filters. The criteria for those filters are as follows:

- The first filter excludes any papers whose titles bear no relation to the question in section 3.1. According to this filter, the total number of papers is 32.

- The second filter excludes any papers that do not target processes of the digital forensics investigation in their abstract or title. After this filter, the total number of papers is 26.

- The third filter excludes any papers that do not discuss processes of the digital forensics investigation in more detail in their full text. This leaves only the primary studies that need to be included in the systematic review. With this filter, the total number of PS remaining is 20 [1], [8-26] . Six additional primary studies were found by investigating the 20 PS. Out of these 26 primary studies only 18 papers dealt with the processes of digital forensics investigation.

4.3 Assess Study Quality

The quality of the primary studies was assessed according to the following categorizations, starting from the highest level to the lowest:

1. Peer-reviewed journals: Level 5 (Highest).
2. Peer-refereed book chapters: Level 4.
3. Peer-reviewed conference papers: Level 3.
4. Peer-reviewed workshop papers: Level 2.
5. Non-peer refereed papers: Level 1 (Lowest).

Table 1 shows the summary of the primary studies genre. Nine of the 18 primary studies were journals; these reveal the maturity of the processes listed in this paper and its patterns.

4.4 Extract Required Data

The processes of digital forensics investigation that were extracted from the total 26 primary studies are grouped in Table 2.

4.5 Synthesize Data

The processes of digital forensics investigation were mapped to the proposed investigation process (see Table 3).

Table 1. Paper genre and the number of primary studies

Genre	Number of Primary Studies
Peer-reviewed journals	9
Peer-refereed book chapters	1
Peer-reviewed conference papers	7
Peer-reviewed workshop papers	1
Non-peer-refereed papers	0

5 Documenting the Systematic Literature Review

This stage is about generating the systematic literature review report.

5.1 Write Review Report

The review report is contained in the current paper.

5.2 Validate Report

The same review protocol was used to validate the systematic literature review twice during execution of the review.

6 Research Findings

All the processes of digital forensics investigation in Table 3 shows that they all share the reactive component, but only one [1] includes the proactive component. (In [1], this proactive component has been named the active component.) The reactive component of all processes was inspired by [7]. Recent papers such as [2], [1], [3], and [4] have suggested that there is a need for advancement in the area of proactive forensic systems.

In [1], a multi-component view of digital forensics process is proposed. This process is at a high level and consists of three components: proactive, active, and reactive. The term "proactive" as it is used in [1] deals with the digital forensics readiness of the organization as well as the responsible use of digital forensics tools. The active component, termed the proactive component in the current study, deals with the collection of live evidence in real time while an event or incident is happening. The active component of the investigation is not considered to be a full investigation since it lacks case-specific investigation tools and techniques. The reactive component is the traditional approach to digital forensics investigation.

The process proposed in this study is derived from [1], but has only two components, proactive and reactive (see Figure 1). Even though Figure 1 shows that the investigation process is a waterfall process, in real-life it has some iteration. The proposed proactive component is similar to the active component in [1].

Table 2. Processes of digital forensics investigation

Process No.	Authors, Reference # & Genre	Digital Forensic Investigation Process Name	Number of Phases
1	Palmer [7]& Conference	Investigative Process for Digital Forensic Science	6 Phases
2	Reith, Carr, and Gunsch [8]& Journal	An Abstract Digital Forensics Model	9 Phases
3	Carrier and Spafford [27]& Journal	An Integrated Digital Investigation Process	17 phases organized into 5 major phases
4	Stephenson [12]& Journal	End-to-End Digital Investigation Process	9 phases
5	Baryamureeba and Tushabe [10]& Journal	The Enhanced Digital Investigation Process	5 major phases including sub-phases
6	Ciardhuain [28]& Journal	The Extended Model of Cybercrime Investigations	13 phases
7	Carrier and Spafford [9]& Conference	An Event-Based Digital Forensic Investigation Framework	5 major phases including sub-phases
8	Harrison [14]& Journal	The Lifecycle Model	7 phases
9	Beebe and Clark [15]& Journal	The Hierarchical, Objective-Based Framework	6 phases
10	Kohn, Eloff, and Olivier [11]& Conference	The Investigation Framework	3 phases
11	Kent, Chevalier, Grance, and Dang [31]& Journal	The Forensic Process	4 phases
12	Rogers, Goldman, Mislan, Wedge, and Debrota [29]& Conference	The Computer Forensics Field Triage Process Model	6 major phases including sub-phases
13	Ieong [16]& Journal	FORZA – Digital Forensics Investigation Framework Incorporating Legal Issues	8 phases
14	Freiling and Schwittay [30]& Conference	The Common Process Model for Incident Response and Computer Forensics	3 major phases including sub-phases
15	Khatir, Hejazi, and Sneiders [17]& Workshop	Two-Dimensional Evidence Reliability Amplification Process Model	5 major phases including sub-phases
16	Shin [19]& Conference	Digital Forensics Investigation Procedure Model	10 phases including sub-phases
17	Billard [20]& Book Chapter	An Extended Model for E-Discovery Operations	10 phases
18	Grobler, Louwrens, and Solms [1]& Conference	A Multi-component View of Digital Forensics	3 major phases including sub-phases

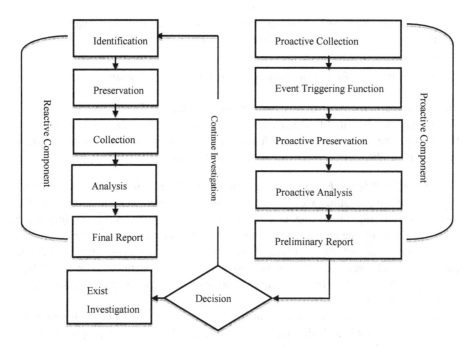

Fig. 1. Functional process for proactive and reactive digital forensics investigation system

Both the proposed process and the multi-component process share the reactive component. Table 3 maps phases of the proposed proactive and reactive digital forensics investigation process to phases of the existing processes.

Description of the two components in the proposed process is as follows:

1) Proactive Digital Forensics Component: is the ability to proactively collect, trigger an event, and preserve and analyze evidence to identify an incident as it occurs. In addition, an automated preliminary report is generated for a later investigation by the reactive component. The evidence that will be gathered in this component is the proactive evidence that relates to a specific event or incident as it occurs [4]. As opposed to the reactive component, the collection phase in this component comes before preservation since no incident has been identified yet.

Phases under the proactive component are defined as follows:

- *Proactive Collection:* automated live collection of a pre-defined data in the order of volatility and priority, and related to a specific requirement of an organization.

- *Event Triggering Function:* suspicious event that can be triggered from the collected data.

- *Proactive Preservation:* automated preservation of the evidence related to the suspicious event, via hashing.

- *Proactive Analysis:* automated live analysis of the evidence, which might use forensics techniques such as data mining to support and construct the initial hypothesis of the incident.

- *Preliminary Report:* automated report for the proactive component.

This proactive component differs from common Intrusion Detection Systems (IDS) by ensuring the integrity of evidence and preserving it in a forensically sound manner. In addition, the analysis of the evidence will be done in such a way as to enable prosecution of the suspect and admission to court of law.

2)   Reactive Digital Forensics Component: is the traditional (or post-mortem) approach of investigating a digital crime after an incident has occurred [7]. This involves identifying, preserving, collecting, analyzing, and generating the final report. Two types of evidence are gathered under this component: active and reactive. Active evidence refers to collecting all live (dynamic) evidence that exists after an incident. An example of such evidence is processes running in memory. The other type, reactive evidence, refers to collecting all the static evidence remaining, such as an image of a hard drive.

Phases under the reactive component are defined by [7]. It is worth mentioning that the examination and analysis phases in [7] are combined in the proposed process under a single phase called analysis.

In order to see how the two components work together, let us take the scenario that electronic health records with an elevated risk will be proactively collected all the time for any read access of such records. This live collection is automated and is conducted without the involvement of the investigator. When a suspicious event is triggered during collection, consequently all evidence related to that event will be preserved by calculating MD5 hashing algorithm. Thereafter, a forensic image will be made from the preserved evidence, and this image must produce the same MD5 number. Next, a preliminary analysis will be conducted on the forensic image and maybe some data mining techniques will be applied to reconstruct the event. Such analysis will help in identifying if the event has occurred or not. Finally, an automated report will be generated and given to the person in charge to decide if the reactive component needs to take over or not.

Next, if needed, the reactive component will conduct a more comprehensive approach investigation. This initial event will be used as identification for the occurrence of the incident, and additional clues can be gathered from the scene. Since this is a post-mortem of an incident or an event, the evidence will be preserved first by calculating the MD5 hashing algorithm. Then a forensic image will be made from the original source of evidence. This forensic image must produce the same MD5 number to preserve the integrity of the original evidence. Thereafter, a deeper analysis will be conducted using forensic tools and techniques to enable the investigator to reach a conclusion. Finally, a report will be generated.

Table 3. Mapping phases of the proposed proactive and reactive digital forensics investigation process to phases of the existing processes

Digital Forensic Investigation Process Name& Reference	Proactive Investigation					Reactive Investigation				
	Proactive Collection	Event Trigging Function	Proactive Preservation	Proactive Analysis	Preliminary Report	Identification	Preservation	Collection	Analysis	Report
Investigative Process for Digital Forensic Science (2001)[7]						✓	✓	✓	✓	✓
An Abstract Digital Forensics Model (2002)[8]						✓	✓	✓	✓	✓
An Integrated Digital Investigation Process (2003)[27]						✓	✓	✓	✓	✓
End-to-End Digital Investigation Process (2003)[12]								✓	✓	
The Enhanced Digital Investigation Process (2004)[10]						✓	✓	✓	✓	✓
The Extended Model of Cybercrime Investigations (2004)[28]						✓	✓	✓	✓	✓
An Event-Based Digital Forensic Investigation Framework (2004)[9]						✓	✓	✓	✓	✓
The Lifecycle Model (2004)[14]						✓	✓	✓	✓	✓
The Hierarchical, Objective-Based Framework (2005)[15]						✓	✓	✓	✓	✓
The Investigation Framework (2006)[11]						✓	✓	✓	✓	✓
The Forensic Process (2006)[31]							✓	✓	✓	✓
The Computer Forensics Field Triage Process Model (2006)[29]						✓	✓	✓	✓	
FORZA – Digital Forensics Investigation Framework Incorporating Legal Issues (2006)[16]						✓	✓	✓	✓	✓
The Common Process Model for Incident Response and Computer Forensics (2007)[30]						✓	✓	✓	✓	✓
Two-Dimensional Evidence Reliability Amplification Process Model (2008)[17]						✓	✓	✓	✓	✓
Digital Forensics Investigation Procedure Model (2008)[19]						✓	✓	✓	✓	✓
An Extended Model for E-Discovery Operations (2009)[20]						✓	✓	✓	✓	✓
A Multi-component View of Digital Forensics (2010)[1]	✓	✓	✓	✓	✓	✓	✓	✓	✓	✓

Goals to be achieved by the addition of the proactive component are as follows:

- Develop new proactive tools and techniques to investigate anti-forensics methods.

- Capture more accurate and reliable evidence in real time while an incident is happening live [1], [3], [4].

- Promote automation without user intervention in the following phases in the proactive component of the digital forensics investigation: proactive collection, event triggering function, proactive preservation, proactive analysis, and preliminary report.

- Provide reliable leads for the reactive component to take place.

- Save time and money by reducing the resources needed for an investigation.

The advantages of the proposed process over the multi-component process are as follows:

- It is a functional process compared to the high-level multi-component process.
- It will be used to develop techniques and automated tools to investigate anti-forensics methods.
- It will automate all phases of the proactive component.
- It combines both digital forensics readiness, as in proactive collection phase, and live investigation, in the other phases, under the same component.

The disadvantages of the proposed process are as follows:

- Not yet fully implemented and may be adapted to implementation requirements.
- The investigator will have to decide whether to move from the proactive to the reactive component or to exit the whole investigation. This decision is not automated yet.
- It will not be able yet to address all techniques used by anti-forensics methods.

7   Conclusion

In order to investigate anti-forensics methods and to promote automation of the live investigation, a proactive and reactive functional process has been proposed. The proposed process came as result of SLR of all the processes that exist in literature. The phases of the proposed proactive and reactive digital forensics investigation process have been mapped to existing investigation processes. The proactive component in the proposed process has been compared to the active component in the multi-component process. All phases in the proactive component of the new process are meant to be automated.

For future work, the proposed process will be used to develop and implement the proactive and reactive systems using domain-specific modeling language and automated code generation. This new method will help in creating the skeleton of the new digital investigation tools and techniques. Two major issues will be addressed in the implementation of the new process: 1) the ability to predict an event (an attack) proactively, and 2) optimizing the proactive component by providing a feedback loop whenever the proactive or the reactive component is concluded.

References

[1]   Grobler, C.P., Louwrens, C.P., von Solms, S.H.: A Multi-component View of Digital Forensics. In: ARES 2010 International Conference on Availability, Reliability, and Security, pp. 647–652 (2010)

[2]   Garfinkel, S.: Anti-forensics: Techniques, detection and countermeasures. In: 2nd International Conference on i-Warfare and Security, p. 77 (2007)

[3]   Garfinkel, S.L.: Digital forensics research: The next 10 years. Digital Investigation 7, S64–S73 (2010)

[4]   Orebaugh, A.: Proactive forensics. Journal of Digital Forensic Practice 1, 37 (2006)

[5]   Brereton, P., Kitchenham, B.A., Budgen, D., Turner, M., Khalil, M.: Lessons from applying the systematic literature review process within the software engineering domain. Journal of Systems and Software 80, 571–583 (2007)

[6]   Rowlingson, R.: A ten step process for forensic readiness. International Journal of Digital Evidence 2, 1–28 (2004)

[7]   Palmer, G.: A road map for digital forensics research-report from the first Digital Forensics Research Workshop (DFRWS), Utica, New York (2001)

[8]   Mark, R., Clint, C., Gregg, G.: An Examination of Digital Forensic Models. International Journal of Digital Evidence 1, 1–12 (2002)

[9]   Carrier, B., Spafford, E.: An event-based digital forensic investigation framework. In: Proceeding of the 4th Digital Forensic Research Workshop, pp. 11–13 (2004)

[10]   Baryamureeba, V., Tushabe, F.: The Enhanced Digital Investigation Process Model. Asian Journal of Information Technology 5, 790–794 (2006)

[11]   Kohn, M., Eloff, J., Olivier, M.: Framework for a digital forensic investigation. In: Proceedings of Information Security South Africa (ISSA) 2006 from Insight to Foresight Conference (2006)

[12]   Stephenson, P.: A comprehensive approach to digital incident investigation. Information Security Technical Report 8, 42–54 (2003)

[13]   Stephenson, P.: Completing the Post Mortem Investigation. Computer Fraud & Security, 17–20 (2003)

[14]   Harrison, W.: The digital detective: An introduction to digital forensics. Advances in Computers 60, 75–119 (2004)

[15]   Beebe, N.L., Clark, J.G.: A hierarchical, objectives-based framework for the digital investigations process. Digital Investigation 2, 147–167 (2005)

[16]   Ieong, R.S.C.: FORZA - Digital forensics investigation framework that incorporate legal issues. Digital Investigation 3, 29–36 (2006)

[17] Khatir, M., Hejazi, S.M., Sneiders, E.: Two-Dimensional Evidence Reliability Amplification Process Model for Digital Forensics. In: Third International Annual Workshop on Digital Forensics and Incident Analysis, WDFIA 2008, pp. 21–29 (2008)

[18] Pollitt, M.M.: An Ad Hoc Review of Digital Forensic Models. In: Second International Workshop on Systematic Approaches to Digital Forensic Engineering, SADFE 2007, pp. 43–54 (2007)

[19] Yong-Dal, S.: New Digital Forensics Investigation Procedure Model. In: Fourth International Conference on Networked Computing and Advanced Information Management, NCM 2008, pp. 528–531 (2008)

[20] Billard, D.: An Extended Model for E-Discovery Operations. In: Peterson, G., Shenoi, S. (eds.) Advances in Digital Forensics V, vol. 306, pp. 277–287. Springer, Boston (2009)

[21] Tanner, A., Dampier, D.: Concept Mapping for Digital Forensic Investigations. In: Peterson, G., Shenoi, S. (eds.) Advances in Digital Forensics V, vol. 306, pp. 291–300. Springer, Boston (2009)

[22] Ruan, C., Huebner, E.: Formalizing Computer Forensics Process with UML. In: Yang, J., Ginige, A., Mayr, H.C., Kutsche, R.-D. (eds.) Information Systems: Modeling, Development, and Integration, vol. 20, pp. 184–189. Springer, Heidelberg (2009)

[23] Slay, J., Lin, Y.-C., Turnbull, B., Beckett, J., Lin, P.: Towards a Formalization of Digital Forensics. In: Peterson, G., Shenoi, S. (eds.) Advances in Digital Forensics V, pp. 37–47. Springer, Boston (2009)

[24] Kizza, J.: Computer Crime Investigations-Computer Forensics. In: Ethical and Social Issues in the Information Age, pp. 343–358. Springer, London (2007)

[25] Selamat, S., Yusof, R., Sahib, S.: Mapping process of digital forensic investigation framework. IJCSNS 8, 163 (2008)

[26] Perumal, S.: Digital forensic model based on Malaysian investigation process. IJCSNS 9, 38 (2009)

[27] Carrier, B., Spafford, E.: Getting physical with the digital investigation process. International Journal of Digital Evidence 2, 1–20 (2003)

[28] Ciardhu·in, S.: An extended model of cybercrime investigations. International Journal of Digital Evidence 3, 1–22 (2004)

[29] Rogers, M., Goldman, J., Mislan, R., Wedge, T., Debrota, S.: Computer forensics field triage process model. Journal of Digital Forensics, Security and Law 1, 27–40 (2006)

[30] Freiling, F., Schwittay, B.: A common process model for incident response and computer forensics. In: 3rd International Conference on IT-Incident Management and IT- Forensic (2007)

[31] Kent, K., Chevalier, S., Grance, T., Dang, H.: Guide to Integrating Forensic Techniques into Incident Response. NIST Special Publication 800-86 (2006)

Multistep Attack Detection and Alert Correlation in Intrusion Detection Systems

Fabio Manganiello, Mirco Marchetti, and Michele Colajanni

Università degli Studi di Modena e Reggio Emilia,
Department of Information Engineering
Via Vignolese 905, Modena, Italy
{fabio.manganiello,mirco.marchetti,michele.colajanni}@unimore.it

Abstract. A growing trend in the cybersecurity landscape is represented by *multistep* attacks that involve multiple correlated intrusion activities to reach the intended target. The duty of reconstructing complete attack scenarios is left to system administrators because current Network Intrusion Detection Systems (NIDS) are still oriented to generate alerts related to single attacks, with no or minimal correlation.
We propose a novel approach for the automatic analysis of multiple security alerts generated by state-of-the-art signature-based NIDS. Our proposal is able to group security alerts that are likely to belong to the same attack scenario, and to identify correlations and causal relationships among them. This goal is achieved by combining alert classification through Self Organizing Maps and unsupervised clustering algorithms. The efficacy of the proposal is demonstrated through a prototype tested against network traffic traces containing multistep attacks.

Keywords: Network security, neural networks, alert correlation.

1   Introduction

The presence of a Network Intrusion Detection System (*NIDS*) is a cornerstone in any modern security architecture. A typical NIDS analyzes network traffic and generates security alerts as soon as a malicious network packet is detected. Alert analysis is then performed manually by security experts that parse the NIDS logs to identify relevant alerts and possible causal relationships among them. While log analysis can be aided by NIDS management interfaces, it is still a manual, time consuming and error prone process, especially because we are experiencing a growing number of *multistep* attacks that involve multiple intrusion activities.

This paper proposes a novel alert correlation and clustering approach that helps security analysts in identifying multistep attacks by clustering similar alerts produced by a signature-based NIDS (such as Snort [10]), and by highlighting strong correlations and causal relationships among different clusters. This goal is achieved through multiple steps: alerts are preprocessed by a hierarchical clustering scheme; then, they are processed using a Self-Organizing Map [5];

T.-h. Kim et al. (Eds.): ISA 2011, CCIS 200, pp. 101–110, 2011.

the alerts that likely belong to the same attack scenarios are clustered by using the k-means algorithm over the SOM output layer; finally, a correlation index is computed among the alert clusters to identify causal relationships that are typical of multistep attacks. The final output of our framework for multistep attack detection is a set of oriented graphs. Each graph describes an attack scenario in which the vertices represent alert clusters belonging to the same attack scenario, and the directed links denote alert clusters that are tied by causal relationships. In such a way, a security administrator can immediately identify correlated alerts by looking at the graphs, avoiding to waste time on checking false positives and irrelevant alerts.

This paper presents several contributions with respect to the state of the art. The application of the k-means clustering algorithm to the output layer of a SOM allows us to perform robust and unsupervised clustering of correlated NIDS alerts. To the best of our knowledge, this solution has never been proposed in network security. Moreover, several original (for the security literature) heuristics for the initialization of the SOM and for the definition of the number of clusters produced by the k-means algorithm reduce the number of configuration parameters and allow our solution to autonomously adapt to different workloads. This is an important result, because security alerts are heterogeneous and present high variability. We demonstrate the feasibility and efficacy of the proposed solution through a prototype that was extensively tested using the most recent datasets released after the 2010 Capture the Flag competition [3].

2   Related Work

The application of machine learning techniques, such as neural networks and clustering algorithms, for intrusion detection has been widely explored in the security literature. Several papers propose clustering algorithms, support vector machines [6] and neural networks as the main detection engine for the implementation of anomaly-based network intrusion detection systems. In particular, the use of *Self-Organizing Maps* (SOM) for the implementation of an anomaly-based IDS was proposed in [13], [8] and [1]. Unlike previous literature mainly oriented to anomaly detection, in this paper we propose SOM and clustering algorithms for the postprocessing of security alerts generated by a signature-based NIDS. Hence, our proposal relates to other papers focusing on techniques for NIDS alert correlation [2]. According to the comprehensive framework for NIDS alert correlation proposed in [12], the solution proposed in this paper can be classified as a *multistep correlation* component. In this context, two related papers are [7] and [4].

Our work differentiates from [7] because our evaluation is not limited to the computation of alert similarity. Indeed, mapping security alerts on the output layer of the SOM is only one intermediate steps of our framework, that uses the SOM output as the input of the alert clustering algorithms. Moreover, with respect to [7] we propose an innovative initialization algorithm for the SOM and an adaptive training strategy that makes the SOM more robust with respect to perturbations in the training data (see Section 4 for details on the design and implementation of the SOM). Finally, instead of relying just on a commutative correlation index based on the distance between two alerts, our correlation index depends also on the type of alerts and on their detection time (see Section 6). The resulting correlation index expresses the causality relationships among alerts much better than the previous one.

In [4] security alerts generated by a NIDS are grouped through a hierarchical clustering algorithm. The classification hierarchy, that is defined by the user, aggregates alerts of the same type targeting one host or a set of hosts connected to the same subnet. We use a similar hierarchical clustering scheme as a pre-processing step. We then use the alert clusters generated by this hierarchical clustering algorithm as an input for the SOM. Hence, we take advantage of the ability of the algorithm presented in [4] to reduce the number of alerts to process, and to group a high number of false positives. All the subsequent processing steps are novel.

3 Software Architecture

The architecture of the framework proposed in this paper consists of a prepro-cessing phase and of three main processing steps.

The preprocessing phase, called *hierarchical clustering* in Figure 1, takes as its input the intrusion alerts generated by a signature-based NIDS. In our reference implementation, we refer to the well known Snort. Alerts are grouped according to a clustering hierarchy in a way similar to [4]. This preprocessing phase has two positive effects. It reduces the number of elements that have to be processed by the subsequent steps, with an important reduction of the computational cost of the three processing phases. Moreover, it groups many false positives in the same cluster, thus simplifying human inspection of the security alerts. Clustered alerts are then processed by the SOM, that is able to reduce the dimensionality of the input dataset by mapping each multidimensional tuple to one output neuron. Each output neuron is identified by its coordinates on the output layer of the SOM, hence clustered alerts are mapped to two-dimensional coordinate sets on the output layer. Moreover, a SOM has the ability to map similar tuples to neurons that are close in the output layer. In particular, the distance between two output neurons on the output layer of the SOM is inversely proportional to the similarity of the related inputs.

The output of the SOM is then analyzed by the second processing step, that is a k-means clustering algorithm. The basic idea is that similar alert clusters are mapped on close neurons of the SOM, hence it is possible to group simi-lar alert clusters by executing a k-means clustering on the output layer of the SOM. The choice of the parameter k is critical. Our proposal includes a heuristic that computes the best k on the basis of the data analyzed so far, as illustrated in Section 5. This approach allows our clustering algorithm to automatically adapt its parameters without setting a static value for k that risks to be unsuitable in most instances. The output of the proposed k-means clustering algorithm, de-scribed in Section 5, is a set of clusters each representing a likely attack scenario.

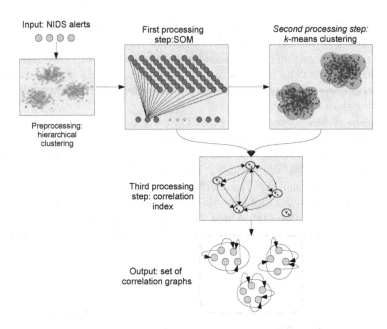

Fig. 1. Main functional steps of the software architecture

The third (and last) processing step takes as its input the output layer of the SOM and the results of the k-means, and then computes a correlation index between alert clusters that have been grouped within the same cluster by the k-means. The correlation index is based on the distance between the neurons on the output layer of the SOM, on the timing relationships between alerts and on their type. This algorithm can identify causal relationships between alerts by determining which of the two alerts occurred first, and whether historical data show that alerts of the same type usually occur one after another.

The final output of the proposed algorithm for multistep alert correlation is represented by a set of directed graphs. Each graph represents a different attack scenario, whose vertices are clusters of similar alerts. The directed edges represent relationships between different alert clusters that belong to the same scenario.

4   Self-Organizing Map

A Self-Organizing Map is an auto-associative neural network [5], that is commonly used to produce a low-dimensional (typically two-dimensional) representation of input vectors that belong to a high-dimensional input space, since input vectors are mapped to coordinates in the output layer by a neighborhood function that preserves the topological properties of the input space. Hence, input vectors that are close in the input space are mapped to near positions in the output layer of the SOM. Given a SOM having K neurons in the input layer, and $M \times N$ on the output layer, the SOM is a completely connected network having $K \cdot M \cdot N$ links, so that each input neuron is connected to each neuron of the output layer. Each link from the input to the output layer has a weight that expresses the strength of that link. In the described implementation, each alert is modelled as a numerical normalized tuple provided to the input layer. As an example, the $i - th$ alert x_i is modelled as

$\mathbf{x}_i = (alertType_i, srcIP_i, dstIP_i, srcPort_i, dstPort_i, timestamp_i)$

where $alertType_i$ is the alert type as identified by Snort, $srcIP_i$ and $dstIP_i$ are its source and destination IP addresses, $srcPort_i$ and $dstPort_i$ are the source and destination port numbers, and $timestamp_i$ is the time at which the alert has been issued.

The first step initializes the weights of the links between the input and the output layer. Since the training algorithm is unsupervised, it is important to have an optimal weight initialization instead of a random initialization. The weight initialization algorithm used in this model is similar to that proposed in [11]. It involves a heuristics that aims to map on near points the items which are dimensionally or logically close, and on distant points the items which are dimensionally or logically distant. Let us consider the training space $\mathbf{X} = \{\mathbf{x}_1, ..., \mathbf{x}_h\}$ for our network. We pick up the two vectors $\mathbf{x}_a, \mathbf{x}_b \in \mathbf{X}$, with $\mathbf{x}_a = \{x_{a1}, ..., x_{aK}\}$ and $\mathbf{x}_b = \{x_{b1}, ..., x_{bK}\}$ having the maximum K-dimensional Euclidean distance. The values of $\mathbf{x}_a$ and $\mathbf{x}_b$ are used for initializing the vectors of weights on the lower left, $\mathbf{w}_{M1} = \mathbf{x}_a$, and the upper right corner, $\mathbf{w}_{1N} = \mathbf{x}_b$. The idea is to map the most distant items on the opposite corners of the output layer. The values of the upper left corner weights vector $\mathbf{w}_{11}$ are then initialized by picking up the vector $\mathbf{x}_c \in \mathbf{X} - \{\mathbf{x}_a, \mathbf{x}_b\}$ having the maximum distance from $\mathbf{x}_a$ and $\mathbf{x}_b$. Finally, the vector $\mathbf{x}_d \in \mathbf{X} - \{\mathbf{x}_a, \mathbf{x}_b, \mathbf{x}_c\}$ having the maximum distance from $\mathbf{x}_a, \mathbf{x}_b, \mathbf{x}_c$ initializes the values of the bottom right corner $\mathbf{w}_{MN}$. The weights of the remaining neurons on the four edges are initialized through linear interpolations. This heuristic-based initialization strategy for the SOM reduces the number of steps to reach a good precision, and improves the accuracy of the network with respect to a random initialization scheme [11].

After the initialization of the weights, the network undergoes unsupervised and competitive training by using the same training set $\mathbf{X} = \{\mathbf{x}_1, ..., \mathbf{x}_h\}$ used for the initialization. For each training vector $\mathbf{x}_i \in \mathbf{X}$, $\forall i = 1, ..., h$, the algorithm finds the neuron that most likely "represents" it, that is, the neuron having the weights vector $\bar{\mathbf{w}}$ with the minimum distance from $\mathbf{x}_i$. At the t-th learning step, the map weights are updated according to the following relation:

$$\mathbf{w}_{jk}(t) = \mathbf{w}_{jk}(t-1) + \delta(\bar{\mathbf{w}}, \mathbf{w}_{jk})\alpha(t) (\mathbf{x}_i - \mathbf{w}_{jk}(t-1)) \qquad (1)$$

for $j = 1, ..., M$, $k = 1, ..., N$. The value of the function δ is inversely proportional to the distance between the two neuron weights taken as their arguments. Considering two neurons with coordinates (x, y) and (i, j), for the purposes of this paper we use the following δ function:

$$\delta(\mathbf{w}_{xy}, \mathbf{w}_{jk}) = \frac{1}{(|x - j| + |y - k|)^4 + 1} \qquad (2)$$

The following step consists in the definition of a *learning rate* for the network expressed in function of the learning step t. In many SOM applications, this value is high at the beginning of the learning phase, when the network is still more prone to errors, and it decreases monotonically as the learning phase continues. However, as discussed in [14], this approach makes the learning process too much dependent on the first learning vectors, and not suited to the high variable context of NIDS alert analysis.

To mitigate this issue, in this paper we use a learning rate function $\alpha(t)$ close to that proposed in [14]:

$$\alpha(t) = \frac{t}{T} \exp\left(1 - \frac{t}{T}\right) \tag{3}$$

T is a parameter that expresses *how fast* the learning rate should tend to 0. A low value of T implies a faster learning process on a smaller training set, while a high value implies a slower process on a larger training set. The parameter T is computed as a function of two user-defined parameters: C and t_c. C represents the value under which the learning phase feedback becomes negligible (cutoff threshold). t_c is computed by solving the equation $\alpha(t_c) = C$. It represents the number of learning steps before the cutoff threshold is reached, i.e. the number of steps after which the SOM network becomes nearly insensitive to further learning feedbacks. The parameter T in $\alpha(t)$ representation given t_c, is computed by solving $\alpha(t_c) = C$. The SOM is re-trained at regular intervals. The training phase, that is computationally expensive, is executed in a separate thread, as discussed in Section 7.

5   Clustering Algorithm

The next step is to apply a k-means clustering algorithm on the SOM output layer to extract possible information over distinct *attack scenarios*. Hence, we need to initialize k centers, for a fixed value of k. As the first two centers we choose the two points in the data set having the maximum euclidean distance. The third center is chosen as the point having the maximum distance from these two centers, the fourth center as the point having the maximum distance from the three centers chosen so far, and so on. After the initialization step, each element in the data set D chooses the centers closest to it as the identifier of its cluster. A well known drawback of the k-means algorithm consists in the necessity to fix the value of k before clustering. To limit this risk, we use the *Schwarz criterion* [9] as our heuristics for computing the best k. In particular, for $1 \leq k \leq |D|$, we compute several heuristic indexes that express, for that value of k, how large is the distortion value for that k, computed as the average distance between each point and its associated center. The best value of k, k^*, is the one having the minimum distortion. This approach is able to autonomously adapt to the heterogeneity of the data set at the price of a higher computational cost.

6   Correlation Index

In the last processing step we compute correlations among alert clusters belonging to the same scenario. The correlation index between two alert clusters A_i and A_j, whose output neurons have coordinates $(x[A_i], y[A_i])$ and $(x[A_j], y[A_j])$ is computed as a function of the Euclidean distance between these two neurons. The correlation value between two alerts is always normalized in $[0, 1]$.

This definition of correlation is commutative, and it does not express any causality correlation. As we want to express the *direction* of the causality between two alerts, a of type A and b of type B with a relatively high correlation coefficient, we pursue the following approach. If $t[b] > t[a]$, i.e. the alert b was raised *after* the alert a, and we have no historical information over time relations between alerts of type A and alerts of type B, then $a \longrightarrow b$, that is the alert a was likely to generate the alert b in a specific attack scenario. If we have logged information over alerts of both types A and B, and the number of times that an alert of type B occurred *after* an alert of type A (in a specified time window) is greater than the number of times when the opposite event occurred, then $a \longrightarrow b$.

The weight of this correlation value (denoting its accuracy), is computed as a function of the number of alerts in the alert log $\mathcal{L}$ used to train the SOM. In particular, we want to keep a relatively low weight (close to 0) when the size of the alert log used for training the network is small, and to increase it when the system acquires new alerts. Given an alert log of size $x = |\mathcal{L}|$, we compute the weight $w(x)$ of the SOM-based index through a monotonically increasing function in $[0, 1]$. In particular, we will use the *hyperbolic tangent* tanh as the weight function:

$$w(x) = \tanh\left(\frac{x}{K}\right) = \frac{e^{\frac{x}{K}} - e^{-\frac{x}{K}}}{e^{\frac{x}{K}} + e^{-\frac{x}{K}}} \tag{4}$$

The parameter K determines how fast we want the algorithm to tend to 1. It is set as a function of the parameter x_M denoting the size of the alert log $\mathcal{L}$ in order to have $w(x_M) = M$. In this paper we use $M = 0.95$.

After having computed the correlation coefficients for each pair of alerts, we consider two alerts A_i, A_j actually correlated only if $Corr(A_i, A_j) \geq \mu_{corr} + \lambda \sigma_{corr}$ where μ_{corr} is the average correlation value and σ_{corr} is its standard deviation. $\lambda \in \mathbb{R}$ denotes how far from the average we want to shift in order to consider two alerts as correlated. Feasible values of λ for our purposes are in the interval $\lambda \in [0, 2]$. For $\lambda \simeq 0$ we consider as correlated all the pairs of alerts having a correlation value higher than the average one. This usually implies a relatively large correlation graph. A value of $\lambda \simeq 2$ brings to a smaller correlation graph, that only contains the most strongly correlated pairs of alerts. Higher values for λ could result in empty or poorly populated correlation graphs, since the correlation constraint could be too strict.

7   Experimental Results

We carried out several experiments using a prototype implementation of the proposed multistep alert correlation architecture. The software has been mainly developed in C, as a module for Intrusion Detection System software *Snort*. A preliminary set of experiments, aiming to verify all the funcionalities of our software, were conducted using small-scale traffic traces, including attack scenarios performed within controlled network environment. Extensive experimental evaluations have then been carried out against the *Capture the Flag* 2010 dataset, that includes 40 GB of network traffic in PCAP format and is publicly available [3]. Our goals are to demonstrate that the computational cost of the proposed solution is compatible with live traffic analysis and to verify the capability of the system to recongize and correlate alerts belonging to the same attack scenario.

To achieve high performance, several different processing steps have been implemented as concurrent threads, that run in parallel with traffic analysis. In particular, alert clustering, training of the SOM and the periodic evaluation of the best value of k of the k-means algorithm, are performed in the background. As soon as the new weight of the SOM or the new best value of k are computed, they are substituted to the previous values. This design choice allows us to leverage multi-core CPUs to perform these expensive operations with no impacts on the performance of Snort. The two lines in Figure 2 show the memory usage of Snort while analyzing a 200MB traffic trace with and without or multistep alert correlation module. When our module is active, the memory usage of Snort is slightly higher. However, in both the cases the analysis of the traffic dump requires about 42 seconds, hence or module has no noticeable impact on the time required to analyze the traffic trace. Thanks to the self-adaptive choices of the parameters, our framework can easily adapt to heterogeneous traffic traces without the need for user-defined static configurations. The first alert clustering

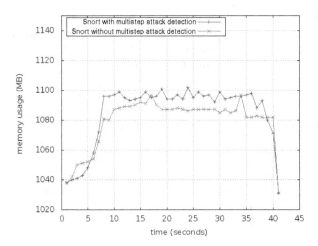

Fig. 2. Memory usage of Snort with and without multistep attack detection

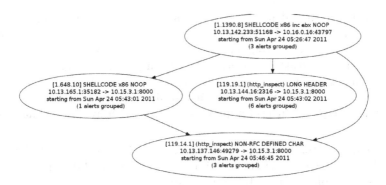

Fig. 3. Example of a correlation sub-graph

phase [4] is performed using the average heterogeneity of the alerts as grouping measure. The SOM distances depend on the size of the SOM network itself, but a greater size means a higher average distance, that anyway does not impact on the relative normalized distance values. The k-means clustering uses Schwarz criterion as heuristic for computing the best number of data clusters.

The correlation index among clustered alerts, is sensitive to the choice of the parameter λ. Feasible values are in the interval $\lambda \in [0, 2]$. A value of λ close to zero produces a graph that contains many alert correlations (all the ones having a correlation value greater than the average one). This is useful when the user wants to know all the likely correlations. A value closer to 2 highlights the few "strongest" correlations, having high correlation values. For example, by setting $\lambda = 1.7$, we obtain 4 different scenarios. Due to space limitation, only one of them is shown in Figure 3. It contains a likely shellcode execution (the grouping of several similar alerts inside of the same graph node is performed through Julisch method described in [4]) linked to an HTTP LONG HEADER alert and to a NON-RFC DEFINED CHAR alert raised by the `http_inspect` module towards the same host and port in the same time window.

On the other hand, by setting $\lambda = 1.2$ we obtain a larger number of likely scenarios, that can also be connected among them. The XML file[1] containing the 37 alert clusters that represent different attack scenarios and the corresponding correlation graphs [2] cannot be included in this paper for space limitations and are available online.

8   Conclusion

This paper presents a novel multistep alert correlation algorithm that is able to group security alerts belonging to the same attack scenario and to identify correlations and casual relationships among intrusion activities. The input of the proposed algorithm is represented by security alerts generated by a signature-based NIDS, such as Snort. Viability and efficacy of the proposed multistep alert

---

[1] Available online at `http://cris.unimore.it/files/attack_scenarios.xml`

[2] Available online at `http://cris.unimore.it/files/correlation_graph.png`

correlation algorithm is demonstrated through a prototype, tested against recent and publicly available traffic traces. Experimental results show that the proposed multistep correlation algorithm is able to isolate and correlate intrusion activities belonging to the same attack scenario, thus helping security administrator in the analysis of alerts produced by a NIDS. Moreover, by leveraging modern multi-core architectures to perform training in parallel and non-blocking threads, the computational cost of our prototype is compatible with live traffic analysis.

Acknowledgments. The authors acknowledge the support of MIUR-PRIN project DOTS-LCCI "Dependable Off-The-Shelf based middleware systems for Large-scale Complex Critical Infrastructure".

References

1. Chen, Z.G., Zhang, G.H., Tian, L.Q., Geng, Z.L.: Intrusion detection based on self-organizing map and artificial immunisation algorithm. Engineering Materials 439(1), 29–34 (2010)
2. Colajanni, M., Marchetti, M., Messori, M.: Selective and early threat detection in large networked systems. In: Proc. of the 10th IEEE International Conference on Computer and Information Technology, CIT 2010 (2010)
3. Capture the flag traffic dump, http://www.defcon.org/html/links/dc-ctf.html
4. Julisch, K.: Clustering intrusion detection alarms to support root cause analysis. ACM Transactions on Information and System Security 6, 443–471 (2003)
5. Kohonen, T.: The self-organizing map, vol. 78(9) (1990)
6. Mukkamala, S., Janoski, G., Sung, A.: Intrusion detection using neural networks and support vector machines. In: Proceedings of the 2002 International Joint Conference on Neural Networks (2002)
7. Munesh, K., Shoaib, S., Humera, N.: Feature-based alert correlation in security systems using self organizing maps. In: Proceedings of SPIE, the International Society for Optical Engineering (2009)
8. Patole, V.A., Pachghare, V.K., Kulkarni, P.: Article: Self organizing maps to build intrusion detection system. International Journal of Computer Applications 1(7), 1–4 (2010)
9. Pelleg, D., Moore, A.: X-means: Extending k-means with efficient estimation of the number of clusters. In: Proc. of the 17th International Conference on Machine Learning, pp. 727–734. Morgan Kaufmann, San Francisco (2000)
10. Snort home page, http://www.snort.org
11. Su, M.C., Liu, T.K., Chang, H.T.: Improving the self-organizing feature map algorithm using an efficient initialization scheme. Tamkang Journal of Science and Engineering 5(1), 35–48 (2002)
12. Valeur, F., Vigna, G., Kruegel, C., Kemmerer, R.A.: A comprehensive approach to intrusion detection alert correlation. IEEE Transactions on Dependable and Secure Computing 1, 146–169 (2004)
13. Vokorokos, L., Baláz, A., Chovanec, M.: Intrusion detection system using self organizing map, vol. 6(1) (2006)
14. Yoo, J.H., Kang, B.H., Kim, J.W.: A clustering analysis and learning rate for self-organizing feature map. In: Proc. of the 3rd International Conference on Fuzzy Logic, Neural Networks and Soft Computing (1994)

2SC: An Efficient Code-Based Stream Cipher

Mohammed Meziani, Pierre-Louis Cayrel, and Sidi Mohamed El Yousfi Alaoui

CASED – Center for Advanced Security Research Darmstadt,
Mornewegstr. 32, 64289 Darmstadt, Germany
{mohammed.meziani,pierre-louis.cayrel,elyousfi}@cased.de

Abstract. In this article, we present a new code-based stream cipher called 2SC, based on the sponge construction. The security of the keystream generation of 2SC is reducible to the conjectured intractability of the Syndrome Decoding (SD) problem, which is believed to be hard in the average case. Our stream cipher compares favorably with other provably secure stream ciphers such as QUAD and SYND in terms of efficiency and storage. In particular, 2SC is much faster than both these stream ciphers, requiring shorter keys and initial vectors (IVs) in order to attain comparable security levels (the runtime in terms of clock cycles is actually halved compared to SYND for around 170 bits of security, whereas the key size is about 50 bits smaller).

Keywords: Stream ciphers, Provable security, Syndrome decoding.

1 Introduction

Stream ciphers and block ciphers are two very important families of symmetric encryption schemes. The former typically operates on smaller units of plaintext one at a time, usually bits, while the latter operates on large blocks of the plaintext message at the same time. Stream ciphers have to be exceptionally fast, much faster than any block cipher, and require lower computing resources. For this reason, they are used in many applications such as secure wireless communication. A stream cipher produces what is called a *keystream*, which is a sequence of bits used as a key for encryption. The ciphertext is obtained by combining the keystream with the clear text (plaintext) on a 'bit by bit' basis, usually by mean of the bitwise XOR operation.

Over the last decades, the design of stream ciphers, and more generally, pseudo-random number generators (PRNGs), has been a subject of intensive study. There exist several constructions, most of them based on linear feedback shift registers (LFSR). However, state of the art of cryptanalysis of such ciphers showed that they suffer from many security weaknesses. Another method to construct a PRNG is to use keyed pseudo-random permutation. The first provably secure construction following this approach is due to Blum and Micali [6] whose security is based on the hardness of factoring an RSA modulus. Another PRNG was proposed by Blum, Blum, and Shub [5] is secure under the assumption that factoring large Blum integers is hard. For the modified of the

T.-h. Kim et al. (Eds.): ISA 2011, CCIS 200, pp. 111–122, 2011.

Blum-Micali construction developed by Kaliski [18], the corresponding hardness is the intractability of the discrete logarithm problem in the group of points on an elliptic curve defined over a finite field. Assuming the assumption of the RSA problem , Alexi, Chor, Goldreich and Schnorr [1] proposed a PRNG. The one-way function hard-core bit construction by Goldreich and Levin [13] has also led to the construction of the efficient pseudo-random number generator, called BMGL [22], which was developed by Håstad and Näslund using Rijndael.

Unfortunately, the theoretically secure constructions of PRNG have up to now mostly focused on methods based on number theoretic assumptions. The existing schemes are vulnerable to "quantum" attacks as shown by Shor [21]. Furthermore, despite their simplicity, most of these systems are inefficient thus impractical for many applications. It is therefore desirable to have efficient stream ciphers whose security relies on other assumptions, and which are more promising even for a future featuring quantum computers. The first construction addressing this challenge is due to Impagliazzo and Naor [17] is based on the subset sum problem. Later, Fisher and Stern [9] proposed a PRNG system whose security relies on the syndrome decoding problem for error-correcting codes. Recently, two provably secure PRNG constructions have proposed. The first one, called QUAD, due to Berbain, Gilbert and Patarin [3] under assumption that solving a multivariate quadratic system is difficult (MQ-problem). The second one, named SYND and proposed by Gaborit, Lauradoux and Sendrier [12], is an improved variant of Fisher-Stern's system [9]. The security of SYND is reducible to the SD problem, which has been proved to be NP-complete in [4].

Our Contribution

In this paper we describe a new code-based stream cipher whose security can be reduced to the SD problem. This cipher is faster than the last one proposed in [12]. We also propose parameters for fast keystream generation for different security levels.

Organization of the Paper

Section 2 provides a short introduction to error-correcting codes. Section 3 gives a brief review of related work. A detailed description of the of 2SC stream cipher is presented in Section 4, its security is discussed in Section 5. In Section 6 secure parameters and experimental results for 2SC are presented. Section 7 concludes the paper and gives some suggestions for future research.

2   Preliminaries

In this section we provide a short introduction to error-correcting codes and recall some hard problems in this area. A more detailed description can be found in [20].

In general, a linear code C is a k-dimensional subspace of an n-dimensional vector space over a finite field $\mathbb{F}_q$, where k and n are positive integers with $k < n$ and q a prime power. Elements of $\mathbb{F}_q^n$ are called words and elements of C are called codewords. The integer $r = n - k$ is called the co-dimension of C. The weight of a word x, denoted by $w = wt(x)$, is the number of non-zero entries in x, and the Hamming distance between two words x and y is $wt(x - y)$. The minimum distance d of a code is the smallest distance between any two distinct codewords. If the ratio n/w is a power of 2, we say words are regular if they consist of w blocks of n/w bits, each with a single non-zero entry. A generator matrix G of C is a matrix whose rows form a basis of C. i.e., $C = \{xG : x \in \mathbb{F}_q^k\}$. A parity check matrix H of C is defined by $C = \{x \in \mathbb{F}_q^n : Hx^T = 0\}$ and generates the code's dual space.

Throughout this paper we set $q = 2$.

The security of code-based cryptosystems is based on the hardness of several classical coding theory problems. The most relevant in our context are the following:

Definition 1 (Binary Syndrome Decoding (SD) problem). *Let n, s, and w be positive integers with $n > s > w$. Given a binary $s \times n$ matrix H, a binary vector $y \in \mathbb{F}_2^s$,and an integer $w > 0$, find a word $x \in \mathbb{F}_2^n$ of weight w, such that $H \cdot x^T = y$.*

This problem was proved NP-complete in [4]. A particular case of SD is the Regular Syndrome Decoding problem (RSD), which was defined and proved NP-complete in [2]. This problem is stated as follows.

Definition 2 (Regular Syndrome Decoding problem (RSD)). *Let n, s, and w be positive integers with $n > s > w$. Given a binary $s \times n$ matrix H, a binary vector $y \in \mathbb{F}_2^s$, and an integer $w > 0$, find a regular word $x \in \mathbb{F}_2^n$ of weight w, such that $H \cdot x^T = y$.*

Through this paper, we will denote $SD(n, s, w)$ and $RSD(n, s, w)$ to indicate instances of the above problems with parameters (n, s, w).

3   Related Works

In this section, we briefly review related work for our construction: The SYND stream cipher [12] and the sponge construction [10].

SYND stream cipher. SYND is a improved variant of Fisher-Stern's PRNG [9] with two improvements: the use of quasi-cyclic codes, which reduces the storage capacity and the introduction of the regular words technique used in [2], which speeds up the keystream generation of the system. SYND is a synchronous stream cipher, which uses a secret key and an initial value, both of length r (in bits). THe SYND cipher has three phases: initialization, update, and output.

During each step, an r-to-r bit function is applied. The update and output function, denoted respectively by g_1 and g_2, are defined as follows:

$$g_i : \mathbb{F}_2^r \to \mathbb{F}_2^r \quad (i = 1, 2)$$
$$x \mapsto g_i(x) = H_i \cdot \phi(x)^T,$$

where the mapping $x \mapsto \phi(x)$ is an encoder which transforms a bitstring of length r into a regular word of length n and weight w, and each H_i is an $r \times n$ random matrix. The three round Feistel transformation using g_1 and g_2 is the initialization function, taking as input an initial value IV and a secret K, both of them $r/2$ bits long, and returning as output an initial state of size r. The security of SYND is reduced to a special case of the syndrome decoding problem, having solutions from the space of regular words (See [12] for more details).

Sponge functions. Sponge functions were introduced in [10]. They provide a new method for iterative hash function design, called the sponge construction. A sponge function takes as input a variable-length bit string and outputs a bit string of unspecified length. It is determined by a fixed-length transformation (or permutation), operating on states of fixed size b (in bits). The value b is called width. Each state is composed of two parts: the first r bits are its outer part and the last c bits are its inner part with $b = r + c$. r is called the bitrate and c is the capacity of the construction. Furthermore, all bits of the state are initialized to 0. Denote by $e = (e_r, e_c)$ a state of the sponge construction, where e_r is the outer part and e_r the inner part of e. The function $\mathcal{F}$ is evaluated in two steps, called the absorbing, and resp. the squeezing phase.

During the former phase, for an r-bits input x, the state is updated as $e \leftarrow \mathcal{F}(e_r \oplus x, e_c)$. In the squeezing phase, only the first parts of states are returned as blocks z_i of the infinite output bit string, i.e. $z_i \leftarrow e_r$; this operation is followed by the state update as $e \leftarrow \mathcal{F}(e)$. The number of output blocks is chosen by user.

Note that the inner parts e_c of each state e are never directly modified by inputs and never returned during the squeezing phase. The desired security level of the construction is determined by the capacity c.

For the security analysis of the sponge construction, there are two cases to consider, keyed and resp. unkeyed sponge constructions. The first setting corresponds to scenarios where a sponge function is used in conjunction with a key, for example in the case of stream ciphers and message authentication codes (MACs). It was proved in [11] that the advantage in distinguishing a keyed sponge from a random oracle is upper bounded by $\max\{\left((M^2/2 + 2MN)\, 2^{-c}, N2^{-|K|}\right)\}$, where M is the data complexity, i.e. the amount of access to the keyed instance, N the number of queries to the underlying transformation (or permutation), where only "fresh" queries are considered. "Denote by $|K|$ the length of the key, and let c be the capacity. In the unkeyed setting, for example the case of hash functions, this bound is larger, and equaling to $N(N + 1)/2^{c+1}$ when $2^c >> N$ (See [11] for more details).

4   Our Proposal: 2SC

This section describes in detail a novel construction, called $\mathcal{S}$ponge $\mathcal{C}$ode-based $\mathcal{S}$tream $\mathcal{C}$ipher (2SC). We outline the construction starting from the illustration in Figure 1. Let K and IV denote the key and the initial vector respectively, with $|\text{K}| = |\text{IV}| = s/2$, where $s = w\log_2(n/w)$. Here, $n > w$ and the ratio n/w is power of 2. Furthermore, we consider two additional parameters r and c (as in the sponge construction) such that $s = r+c$.

Initialization. The initialization function f takes a key K and an initial vector IV and returns an initial state as follows:

$$f : \mathbb{F}_2^{|\text{K}|} \times \mathbb{F}_2^{|\text{IV}|} \to \mathbb{F}_2^s$$
$$(x_1, x_2) \mapsto f(x_1, x_2) = f_1\left((f_1^{[r]}(x_1|0^c) \oplus x_2, f_1^{[c]}(x_1|0^c)) \right),$$

where "|" denotes the concatenation and "0^l" is the all-zero vector of size l. We write $f_1^{[r]}(\cdot)$ and resp. $f_1^{[c]}(\cdot)$ for the outer, resp. inner part of $f_1(\cdot)$. The syndrome mapping f_1 is defined by:

$$f_1 : \mathbb{F}_2^s \to \mathbb{F}_2^s$$
$$x \mapsto f_1(x) = H_1 \cdot \phi(x)^T.$$

Here, the function $x \mapsto \phi(x)$ is a regular encoder, transforming a an s-bit string into a regular word of length n and weight w. The matrix H_1 is a random binary matrix of size $s \times n$. This initialization step requires two function evaluations and two bitwise XOR operations. Thus, if optimal parameters (n, s, w) are chosen for each security level, our proposal is more efficient than SYND (see also Section 6).

Update. During this step, an additional random function g is used to update the internal state several times (say N times). The number of times that g is run is chosen by the user, affecting both the security and the efficiency of the construction. The function g is defined by:

$$g : \mathbb{F}_2^s \to \mathbb{F}_2^s \tag{1}$$
$$x \mapsto g(x) = H_2 \cdot \phi(x)^T, \tag{2}$$

where H_2 is a binary random matrix of size $s \times n$ and the function $x \mapsto \phi(x)$ is the regular encoder used in the initialization step above.

Squeezing. Let e_N be the internal state output by the update phase. The cipher 2SC generates a keystream consisting of r bit blocks $(z_i)_{i \geq 1}$ as follows:

- z_1 consists of the first r bits of the internal state $x_1 = g(e_N)$, where e_N is the output of the N iterations of g in the update state.
- For $i \geq 2$, z_i consists of the first r bits of the recursively computed state $x_i = g(x_{i-1})$.

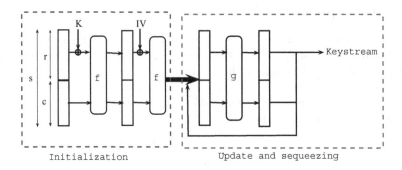

Fig. 1. A Diagram of 2SC Key Stream Generator

Encryption. Let L be the maximal keystream that may produced using a single $(\mathtt{K}, \mathtt{IV})$ pair. In our construction, we have $L = rN_g$, where N_g indicates the maximal number of calls of the function g. In order to encrypt a clear text of length $l \leq L$, each of the first l bits of the keystream sequence is XOR-ed with the corresponding clear text value as in the one-time pad encryption.

In practice the parameters n, s, and w are chosen such that $\frac{n}{w} = 2^m$ and $s = w \times m$ for some integers $m > 0$. As stated in [2], this choice is due to the following consideration: the number of regular words is exactly equal to $\left(\frac{n}{w}\right)^w$, thus our choice of n, s, and w implies the existence a simple regular encoder between $\mathbb{F}_2^{wm}$ and the set of regular words. In 2SC, we use the regular encoding algorithm introduced in [7] to speed-up the computation. The main idea of this algorithm is to compute the w indexes where the non-zero entries of a regular word are located. These indexes exactly correspond to the w columns used in the XOR operations.

5   Security Analysis of 2SC

This section assesses the security of 2SC. We first show that, in practice, it is hard to recover states or reconstruct the secret data (Key and IV) from the key stream. We then show that the output of 2SC is pseudo-random, i.e., the probability to distinguish the key stream output by 2SC from a random sequence is negligible.

5.1   Best Known Attacks

In practice, an adversary against the security of 2SC is faced with two problems. On the one hand, knowing the blocks z_i of r bits does not allow an adversary to get the remaining $c = b - r$ bits; the larger the capacity, the more secure the system is. On the other hand, even having successfully guessed those bits, the adversary must solve an instance of the RSD problem. However, solving the RSD problem efficiently is as difficult as SD in average case, for an appropriately chosen parameter set. Indeed, all known attacks for SD are fully exponential; in fact, only two kinds of algorithms can attack the SD-based systems: Information Set Decoding (ISD) and the Generalized Birthday Algorithm (GBA). Which of the two approaches is more efficient depends on the parameters and the cryptosystem. In our setting, each instance of RSD has on average one solution due to the form of the regular words; here the best known attack is the GBA, as shown in [8]. The most recent GBA against code-based crytosystems is proposed in [8] and will be used to select secure parameters for 2SC.

Remark 1. One could also use Time Memory trade-off attacks against stream ciphers. This attack was first introduced in [15] as a generic method of attacking block ciphers. To avoid it, one must adjust the cipher parameters as shown in [16,14], i.e., the IV should be at least as large as the key, and the state should be at least twice the key.

5.2 Pseudorandomess

In this section, we analyze the security of the key stream generation as well as the security of the initialization process. We first show that the key stream produced by our scheme is indistinguishable from a random sequence. Towards achieving this goal, we first define several useful concepts.

Definition 3 (Universal Hashing). *A family $\mathcal{U}$ of hash functions $u \in \mathcal{U}$ with $u : X \to Y$ is called universal if for all $x \neq x'$ we have*

$$Prob[u(x) = u(x') \mid u \text{ sampled randomly from } \mathcal{U}] \leq \frac{1}{b},$$

where $x, x' \in X$ and $b = |Y|$.

Next, we introduce the Subset Sum Problem (SSP), which is closely related to syndrome decoding problem. The SSP has been proved NP-complete by Karp in [19] and can be stated as follows.

Definition 4 (Subset Sum Problem (SSP)). *Given n integers $(h_1, \cdots, h_n)$, each of s bits, and and an integer y called the target, find a subset $S \subset \{1, \cdots, n\}$ such that $\sum_{j \in S} h_j = y \mod 2^s$.*

As stated in [17], this problem is equivalent to inverting the function

$$g_h(S) = \sum_{j \in S} h_j = y \mod 2^s. \tag{3}$$

This function maps an n-bit string to s-bit string. When the cardinality $|S|$ of S is upper bounded by a fixed integer w (i.e. $|S| \leq w$), we get an instance of the (regular) syndrome decoding stated earlier. More precisely, take $|S| = w$; then the elements in S can be interpreted as the positions of the non-zero coordinates of an incidence vector x. Thus x has weight $|S| = w$. The elements $(h_1, \cdots, h_n)$ are the rows of a matrix H of size $s \times n$. The target y is the syndrome such that $H \cdot x^T = y$.

Without loss of generality, the transformation f in the initialization step (see section 4) and the equivalent transformation g can be regarded as a mapping $x \mapsto u(x) = H \cdot x^T$, x is a regular word, because the encoding function ϕ (as defined in the initialization and update steps outlined in section 4) is bijective.

Let $\mathcal{R}$ denote the set of regular words of length n and weight w and $\mathcal{H}$ the set of binary random matrices of size $s \times n$. In order to prove that the family $\mathcal{U} = \{u : u(x) = H \cdot x^T, x \in \mathcal{R}, H \in \mathcal{H}\}$ is universal, we state the following lemma.

Lemma 1. *There exists, on average, only one solution of each instance RSD* (n, s, w), *where* $s = w \log 2(n/w)$.

Proof. Let $N_{rsd}(n, s, w)$ denotes the expected number of solutions of an instance RSD(n, s, w). This number is defined as the number of regular words divided by the number of the syndromes, i.e. $N_{rsd}(n, s, w) = \frac{\left(\frac{n}{w}\right)^w}{2^s}$.
By replacing s by $w \log 2(n/w)$, we obtain $N_{rsd}(n, s, w) = 1$.

Proposition 1. *The family* $\mathcal{U} = \{u : u(x) = H \cdot x^T, x \in \mathcal{R}, H \in \mathcal{H}\}$ *is universal.*

Proof. From Lemma 1, we know that there exists on average only one regular word that solves the syndrome decoding problem. Thus, it follows that for all for all $x \neq x'$

$$\text{Prob}[H \cdot x^T = H \cdot x'^T \mid H \text{ sampled randomly from } \mathcal{H}] = 0 \leq \frac{1}{2^s}$$

Proposition 2. *The probability of distinguishing the output of each* $u \in \mathcal{U}$ *from a random sequence of length s is negligible.*

Proof. (Sketch). The proof is inspired from [17] and works as follows. As explained above, the family $\mathcal{U}$ can be seen as a collection g_h defined as in equation (3). Due to Proposition 1 this collection of transformations is universal and therefore, as proved in [17], we can apply the Leftover hash lemma to show that if $s < \gamma n$ for some real number $\gamma < 1$, then the expected distinguishibility of $g_h(S) = H \cdot x^T$ and a random $y \in \mathbb{F}_2^s$ is at most $2^{\frac{-(1-\gamma)n}{2}}$.
In our setting, γ can be obtained as follows:

$$\psi(n, w) = \frac{s}{n} = \frac{\log_2(n/w)}{(n/w)}.$$

For simplicity, we can assume that $n > 4w$. In this case, the function ψ tends to zero when n is chosen to be large enough. Consequently, there exists an n_0 such that for all $n \geq n_0$, $\psi(n, w)$ is upper bounded by a constant $\gamma < 1/2$. Thus, for values of the code length n such that $\frac{(1-\gamma)n}{2}$ is large enough, the probability of distinguishing the output of any function $u \in \mathcal{U}$ from a random sequence of length s is negligible.

Security of the key stream generation. As explained above, the keystream output by 2SC consists of a number of blocks of length $s - c$ bits (the number of blocks depends on the number of times the squeezing operation is performed). Each block is obtained from the output of the update function g, by extracting its first $s - c$ bits. Since g is similar to the output function used in SYND [12], it is straightforward to prove that the keystream generated by our scheme is indistinguishable from a random sequence under the assumption that the regular syndrome decoding problem is intractable for some sets of parameters. The proof is inspired from [12,9] based on the proofs given in [3]. The following theorem summarizes our main result.

Theorem 1. *Let $L = \alpha(s - c)$ represent the number of keystream bits produced by our scheme after iterating the update function g α times. If there exists an algorithm A, in time T and with advantage ϵ, which distinguishes the L-bit keystream sequence produced through a known random $s \times n$ matrix (or a quasi-cyclic random matrix of the same size) multiplied by an unknown, randomly chosen regular word e from a random bit sequence, then there exists an algorithm A' that can recover e in time $T' \approx \frac{2^7 n^2 \alpha^2 T}{\epsilon^2}$.*

Proof. (Sketch) As in [3], the proof sketch consists of three steps. First we prove that distinguishing the keystream from a random sequence is equivalent to distinguishing the output of a random syndrome mapping $x \mapsto H \cdot x^T$ for an unknown, regular n-bit word x, from a random vector of appropriate size. Then, we prove that a distinguisher against the syndrome map can be used to build a predictor for any linear function of its inputs. Finally, we show that such a predictor allows us to invert the syndrome mapping for regular words.

Security of the initial state. As explained in Section 4, the initialization process of the 2SC consists of two stages. During the first stage, the secret key is introduced to generate a pre-initial state. For suitably chosen parameters (n, s, w), as indicated in [12], the underlying syndrome mapping behaves like a random function, since its outputs are indistinguishable from a random sequence. Therefore, the pre-initial state is random. During the second stage, the outer r-bit part of this state is first XORed with a secret initial value. Then, the resulting s-bit vector is fed to the function f to produce the initial state. This process can be viewed as XORing w random columns of a random matrix, resulting in a random s-bit initial state.

6   Parameters and Implementation Results

Suitable parameters (n, s, w) for 2SC should provide both efficiency and high security against all known attacks. Firstly, we account for Time Memory Trade-Off attacks (see section 5.1) and choose (n, s, w) such that:

$$s = w \log_2(n/w) \geq 2|\text{IV}| \quad \text{and} \quad |\text{IV}| \geq |\text{K}|.$$

Since $|\mathtt{IV}| = |\mathtt{K}| = s - c$, we obtain $s \leq 2c$. We use the following strategy for selecting secure parameters for 2SC: according the sponge construction, we first fix c such that $c/2$ is at least the desired security level, then choose the remaining parameters (n, s, w) accordingly.

We have implemented 2SC to test a large set of potential parameters for a number of security levels. In practice, optimal parameters for this scheme should also take into account these three main implementation-specific requirements: the ratio $\frac{s}{c}$, selecting an appropriate block size for the regular encoding, and the use of int-wise (rather than byte-wise) XORing. A large value of $\frac{s}{c}$ yields a large value of r, hence allowing for better performance. We implement the regular encoding such that it uses shift operations, thus efficiently using processor architecture. The choice $\log_2(n/w) = 16$ was the most promising block size in terms of the computation time in our implementation. Finally, int-wise XORing reduces computation time by four times compared to byte-wise XORing. Our parameters should thus ensure that we can perform int-wise XORing.

Putting everything together, the choice of w, s and c is a tradeoff decision. On the one hand, a small w leads to fewer XOR operations during matrix multiplication. On the other hand, a small w implies a small s ($s = w \log_2(n/w)$). Making n large will help in increasing s. But at the same time the matrix will become very big. Last but not least, the smaller c is chosen, the more efficient the computation is, because $(r = s - c)$ becomes larger.

Table 1 presents the optimal parameter sets (n, w, s, c) resulted from running our implementation for three security levels, 100, 160, and 250 bits. All results are tested on 2,53 GHz Pentium Core2 Duo, 32 Bit Ubuntu 10.04, 6 MB Level 2 Cache, 4 GB RAM.

In order to compare the speed of 2SC with the speed of SYND [12], we have implemented SYND with the same techniques using the parameter sets proposed in [12].

Table 1. Performance of 2SC using quasi-cyclic codes

Security Level	n	s	w	c	Key/IV size	Speed (cycles/byte)
100	1572864	384	24	240	144	37
160	2228224	544	34	336	208	47
250	3801088	928	58	576	352	72

Table 2. Performance of SYND using quasi-cyclic codes

Security Level	n	s	w	Key/IV size	Speed (cycles/byte)
80	8192	256	32	128	36
170	8192	512	64	256	85
366	8192	1024	128	512	132

Note that the results given in [12] can not be checked, since no freely-available implementation of SYND exists. For this reason, we decided to implement SYND. On our own implementation of SYND, we obtained the results presented in Table 2. For comparable security levels, 2SC runs faster than SYND. At the same time, SYND needs significantly larger key sizes compared to 2SC. However, 2SC suffers from the drawback of having to store large matrices.

7 Conclusion and Future Work

This paper describes a new code-based stream cipher, called 2SC. Its design follows the sponge construction [10]. Our proposal is more efficient than the SYND and QUAD stream ciphers and its security is reducible to the syndrome decoding problem. Moreover, 2SC uses small key/IV sizes compared to SYND and QUAD. However, our construction is slower than AES in counter mode and needs a larger storage capacity. We believe that these two issues could be considerably reduced by avoiding the use of the regular encoding, which is the most time consuming part during the keystream generation. A promising alternative to the regular encoding and matrix-vector multiplication step is to introduce a one-way mapping based only on XOR operations.

References

1. Alexi, W., Chor, B., Goldreich, O., Schnorr, C.P.: Rsa and rabin functions: certain parts are as hard as the whole. SIAM J. Comput. 17(2), 194–209 (1988)
2. Augot, D., Finiasz, M., Sendrier, N.: A Family of Fast Syndrome Based Cryptographic Hash Functions. In: Dawson, E., Vaudenay, S. (eds.) Mycrypt 2005. LNCS, vol. 3715, pp. 64–83. Springer, Heidelberg (2005)
3. Berbain, C., Gilbert, H., Patarin, J.: Quad: A multivariate stream cipher with provable security. J. Symb. Comput. 44(12), 1703–1723 (2009)
4. Berlekamp, E., McEliece, R., van Tilborg, H.: On the inherent intractability of certain coding problems. IEEE Transactions on Information Theory 24(2), 384–386 (1978)
5. Blum, L., Blum, M., Shub, M.: A simple unpredictable pseudo random number generator. SIAM J. Comput. 15(2), 364–383 (1986)
6. Blum, M., Micali, S.: How to generate cryptographically strong sequences of pseudo-random bits. SIAM J. Comput. 13(4), 850–864 (1984)
7. Finiasz, M., Gaborit, P., Sendrier, N.: Improved fast syndrome based cryptographic hash functions. In: Rijmen, V. (ed.) ECRYPT Hash Workshop 2007 (2007)
8. Finiasz, M., Sendrier, N.: Security Bounds for the Design of Code-based Cryptosystems. In: Matsui, M. (ed.) ASIACRYPT 2009. LNCS, vol. 5912, pp. 88–105. Springer, Heidelberg (2009)
9. Fischer, J.-B., Stern, J.: An efficient pseudo-random generator provably as secure as syndrome decoding. In: Maurer, U.M. (ed.) EUROCRYPT 1996. LNCS, vol. 1070, pp. 245–255. Springer, Heidelberg (1996)
10. Peeters, M., Bertoni, G., Daemen, J., Van Assche, G.: Sponge Functions. In: ECRYPT Hash Workshop 2007 (2007)

11. Peeters, M., Bertoni, G., Daemen, J., Van Assche, G.: On the security of the keyed sponge construction. In: Symmetric Key Encryption Workshop, SKEW 2011 (2011)
12. Gaborit, P., Laudaroux, C., Sendrier, N.: Synd: a very fast code-based cipher stream with a security reduction. In: IEEE Conference, ISIT 2007, Nice, France, pp. 186–190 (July 2007)
13. Goldreich, O., Levin, L.A.: A hard-core predicate for all one-way functions. In: STOC 1989: Proc. of the Twenty-first Annual ACM Symposium on Theory of Computing, pp. 25–32. ACM, New York (1989)
14. Golic, J.D.: Cryptanalysis of alleged a5 stream cipher. In: Fumy, W. (ed.) EURO-CRYPT 1997. LNCS, vol. 1233, pp. 239–255. Springer, Heidelberg (1997)
15. Hellman, M.: A cryptanalytic time-memory trade-off. IEEE Transactions on Information Theory 26, 401–406 (1980)
16. Hong, J., Sarkar, P.: Rediscovery of time memory tradeoffs. Cryptology ePrint Archive, Report 2005/090 (2005), http://eprint.iacr.org/
17. Impagliazzo, R., Naor, M.: Efficient cryptographic schemes provably as secure as subset sum. J. Cryptology 9(4), 199–216 (1996)
18. Kaliski, B.S.: Elliptic Curves and Cryptography: A Pseudorandom Bit Generator and Other Tools. Phd thesis, MIT, Cambridge, MA, USA (1988)
19. Karp, R.M.: Reducibility among combinatorial problems. In: Miller, R.E., Thatcher, J.W. (eds.) Complexity of Computer Computations. Plenum Press, New York (1972)
20. MacWilliams, F.J., Sloane, N.J.A.: The Theory of Error Correcting Codes. North-Holland, Amsterdam (1977)
21. Shor, P.W.: Algorithms for Quantum Computation: Discrete Logarithms and Factoring. In: SFCS 1994: Proc. of the 35th Annual Symposium on Foundations of Computer Science, pp. 124–134. IEEE Computer Society, Los Alamitos (1994)
22. Håstad, J., Näslund, M.: Bmgl: Synchronous key-stream generator with provable security (2001)

Towards Algebraic Cryptanalysis of HFE Challenge 2

Mohamed Saied Emam Mohamed[1], Jintai Ding[2],
and Johannes Buchmann[1]

[1] TU Darmstadt, FB Informatik
Hochschulstrasse 10, 64289 Darmstadt, Germany
{mohamed,buchmann}@cdc.informatik.tu-darmstadt.de
[2] Department of Mathematical Sciences, University of Cincinnati,
South China University of Technology
jintai.ding@uc.edu

Abstract. In this paper, we present an experimental analysis of HFE Challenge 2 (144 bit) type systems. We generate scaled versions of the full challenge fixing and guessing some unknowns. We use the MXL$_3$ algorithm, an efficient algorithm for computing Gröbner basis, to solve these scaled versions. We review the MXL$_3$ strategy and introduce our experimental results.

1 Introduction

Solving systems of multivariate non-linear polynomial equations is one of the important research problems in cryptography. The problem of solving quadratic systems over finite fields is called the Multivariate Quadratic (MQ) problem. This problem is a well-known NP-hard problem and hard on average. Types of public-key encryption and signature schemes, which are based on the intractability of solving the MQ problem, constitute Multivariate Cryptography.

Hidden field equation (HFE) is a multivariate cryptosestem introduced by Patarin in [9]. In the extended version of [9], Patarin introduced two HFE challenges. The first one is an HFE system with 80 quadratic polynomial equations in 80 variables over $\mathbb{F}_2$. The second challenge consists of 144 quadratic equations, 16 of them are hidden, in 144 variables.

Algebraic cryptanalysis has been proposed in the last few years as an effective cryptanalytic method. The secret information of a cryptosystem could be recovered by solving a system of multivariate polynomial equations which describes such cryptosystem [3,10,4]. In [6], Faugère and Joux used a version of F$_5$ algorithm to break the first challenge. In this paper, we present a cryptanalysis of HFE challenge 2 cryptosystems towards an algebraic attack that breaks the full challenge. For this analysis we the MXL$_3$ algorithm to solve some scaled versions the HFE challenge 2. We present experiments that show how the MXL$_3$ strategies can solve efficiently these scaled versions.

The paper is organized as follows. In Section 2 we review the HFE cryptosystems. In Section 3, we describe the MXL$_3$ algorithm in Section 3. Section 4

T.-h. Kim et al. (Eds.): ISA 2011, CCIS 200, pp. 123–131, 2011.

describes our attack and our experimental results. Before continuing let us introduce the necessary notation.

1.1   Notation

Let $X := \{x_1, \ldots, x_n\}$ be a set of variables, upon which we impose the following order: $x_1 > x_2 > \ldots > x_n$. (Note the counterintuitive $i < j$ imply $x_i > x_j$.) Let

$$R = \mathbb{F}_2[x_1, \ldots, x_n]/\langle x_1^2 - x_1, \ldots, x_n^2 - x_n \rangle$$

be the Boolean polynomial ring in X with the terms of R ordered by the graded lexicographical order $<_{glex}$. We represent an element of R by its minimal representative polynomial over $\mathbb{F}_2$ where degree of each term w.r.t any variable is 0 or 1.

We denote by $T_d(x_{j_1}, \ldots, x_{j_s})$ the set of terms of degree d in the variables $x_{j_1}, \ldots, x_{j_s}$, and by T_d all the terms of degree d.

Let $P = \{p_1, \ldots, p_m\}$ be set of polynomials in R. A row echelon form is simply a basis for span(P) with pairwise distinct head terms, (see [7] for definition).

We will denote by $P_{(op)d}$ the subset of all the polynomials of degree $(op)d$ in P, where (op) is any of $\{=, <, >, \leq, \geq\}$. A term ordering on R is a total ordering $<$ on $T(R)$ such that: $1 < t, \forall t \in T(R)$, $t \neq 1$ and $\forall s, t_1, t_2 \in T(R)$ with $t_1 < t_2$ then $st_1 < st_2$. There are several term orderings. In this paper we use the graded lexicographical term ordering ($glex$. Let $t_1, t_2 \in T(R)$, $t_1 >_{glex} t_2$ if and only if $\deg(t_1) > \deg(t_2)$ or $\deg(t_1) = \deg(t_2)$ and $t_1 >_{lex} t_2$.

Let $p \in \mathbb{F}_q[x_1, \ldots, x_n]$ and the terms in p is ordered by $\leq$. The leading term of p is defined by $\mathrm{LT}(p) := \max_{\leq} T(p)$, $T(p)$ the set of terms of p.

2   HFE Cryptosystem

We explain the construction of HFE cryptosystem as follows. As any public key cryptosystem, HFE uses two keys, one is public and the other is private. The private key consists of the following: The map φ which transforms a vector $x = (x_1, \ldots, x_n) \in \mathbb{F}_{2^n}$ to a vector $y = (y_1, \ldots, y_m) \in \mathbb{F}_{2^n}$. The transformation φ is a univariate polynomial of degree d in a variable x over an extension field $\mathbb{F}_{2^n}$. The inverse φ^{-1} of φ is easily evaluated over $\mathbb{F}_{2^n}$ by finding a solution for the equation $\varphi(x) = y$. The map φ is chosen such that it can be expressed as a system of n multivariate quadratic polynomial equations over $\mathbb{F}_2$. In this case each coordinate of $\varphi(x)$ is expressed by a polynomial in $x_1, \ldots, x_n$. HFE hides its secret polynomial using two randomly chosen invertible affine transformations (S, T) from $\mathbb{F}_{2^n}$ to $\mathbb{F}_{2^n}$. The public key is defined by a system of quadratic equations $P = (p_1, \ldots, p_n)$ over $\mathbb{F}_2$, $P = T \circ \varphi \circ S$.

As any MPKC, the HFE security is based on solving a polynomial system $P(x) = c$, where x is an input plaintext and c is the output ciphertext. An HFE system has two parameters that affect the complexity of solving its system. The first parameter is the number of variables (n) and the other is the degree of its secret polynomial (d). The hardness of solving HFE systems is close to solving random systems when d is very big, say $d > 512$). However, the univariate degree d should be small enough to obtain an efficient HFE cryptosystem in practice. In the extended version of [9], Patarin introduced two HFE challenges with a prize US \$500 for attacking any of them. The HFE challenge 1 has parameters $n = 80, d = 96$ and HFE challenge 2 has parameters $n = 36$ and $d = 4352$ over the finite field $\mathbb{F}_{2^4}$, where 4 of the 36 equations are not given public.

The HFE challenge 2 systems can be converted to systems over $\mathbb{F}_2$. The resulting system consists of 144 equations in 144 variables, while 16 of these equations are hidden. In this case, the HFE challenge 2 systems have a special structure over $\mathbb{F}_2$. Let $P = \{p_1, \ldots, p_{36}\}$ are HFE system in $X_1, \ldots, X_{36} \in \mathbb{F}_{2^4}$ with a univariate degree $d = 4352$. We can represent each polynomial $p_i \in P$ into 4 polynomials $q_{i_1}, q_{i_2}, q_{i_3}, q_{i_4}$ in $x_1, \ldots, x_{144}$ over $\mathbb{F}_2$. Also, each X_j is represented by 4 new variables $x_{j_1}, x_{j_2}, x_{j_3}, x_{j_4}$. In this case the constructed system over $\mathbb{F}_2$ has a special structure such that no products (terms) of two variables belongs to the same group. For example, let $X_1 \in \mathbb{F}_{2^4}$ be represented by $x_1, x_2, x_3, x_4 \in \mathbb{F}_2$. Then $x_1x_2, x_1x_3, x_1, x_4, x_2x_3, x_2x_4, x_3x_4$ are not appeared in any polynomial of the constructed system over $\mathbb{F}_2$.

3   MXL₃ Algorithm

The MXL₃ algorithm is a version of the XL algorithm [2] that based on the variable-based enlargement strategy [8,7], the mutant strategy [5], and a new sufficient condition for a set of polynomials to be a Gröbner basis [7]. In this section, we briefly explain the MXL₃.

Let P be a finite set of polynomials in R. Given a degree bound D, the XL algorithm is simply based on extending the set of polynomials P by multiplying each polynomial in P by all the terms in T such that the resulting polynomials have degree less than or equal to D. Then, by using linear algebra, XL computes $\widetilde{P}$, a row echelon form of the extended set P. Afterwards, XL searches for univariate polynomials in $\widetilde{P}$.

In [5], it was pointed out that during the linear algebra step, certain polynomials of degrees lower than expected appear. These polynomials are called mutants. The mutant strategy aims at distinguishing mutants from the rest of polynomials and to give them a predominant role in the process of solving the system. The MutantXL algorithm [5] is a direct application of the mutant concepts to the XL algorithm. It uses mutants (if any) to enlarge the system at the same degree level before it is going to extend the highest degree polynomials and increment the degree level.

In order to specify the enlargement strategy used by MXL₃, we need the following additional notation.

Let $X := \{x_1, \ldots, x_n\}$ be a set of variables ordered as $x_1 > x_2 > \ldots > x_n$. Assume the terms of R have been ordered by the graded lexicographical order $<_{glex}$. By an abuse of notation, we call the elements of R polynomials. The leading variable of $p \in R$, $\mathrm{LV}(p)$, is defined according to the order defined on X as

$$\mathrm{LV}(p) := \max\{x \mid x \in \mathrm{LT}(p)\}.$$

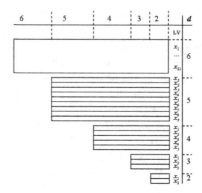

Fig. 1. variable partitions of polynomials generated by XL for a random system of size $n = 26$

Let P be a set of polynomials in R, we define the subset $L(P, x) \subset P$, the *variable partition*, as $L(P, x) = \{p \in P \mid LV(p) = x\}$.

We have studied the total system of polynomials that are generated by XL. We have observed that each degree part can be partitioned using the leading variable and construct the so called *variable partitions*. When we enlarge the system from degree d to degree $d + 1$, the set of degree d polynomials is divided into subsets based on the leading variable of its polynomials. Since the polynomials are ordered using the graded lexicographical order, then the degree d polynomials are partitioned from up to down by $x_1, x_2, \ldots, x_n$ partitions. Only some of these partitions are not empty. Figure 1 shows the structure of the total system generated by XL for a random system of size $n = 26$. Horizontal stripes represent non empty variable partitions. For example, at $d = 5$, the degree d polynomials are divided into 9 partitions (x_1-partition,...,x_9-partition). Let the set of polynomials is in the row echelon form, the variable-based enlargement strategy suggests to stepwise constructing the degree 6 polynomials by enlarging one partition per time. In this case, the partition with the smallest leading variable x_9 is enlarged first, then the next smallest x_8, and so on. MXL$_3$ proceeds in this way until it generates lower degree polynomials (mutants) that leads finally to compute a Gröbner basis of the ideal generated by the input set of polynomials. The complete description of MXL$_3$ can be found in [7].

4   Attack Description

In this section, we explain our method to cryptanalysis the second challenge. The HFE challenge 2 can be considered a multivariate digital signature scheme that signs a message of length 128 bits and generates a signature of length 144 bits. It has 36 variables and 32 equations over $\mathbb{F}_{2^4}$. When we transfer the equations over $\mathbb{F}_2$, we have 144 variables and 128 equations. Since we initially construct HFE challenge 2 systems over $\mathbb{F}_{2^4}$, so we select to scale down the parameters of HFE Challenge 2 as follows:

- $\mathbb{F}_{2^4}$: $n = 36$, $h = 4$, and $m = 32 \rightarrow \mathbb{F}_2$: $n = 144$, $h = 16$, and $m = 128$.
- $\mathbb{F}_{2^4}$: $n = 27$, $h = 3$, and $m = 24 \rightarrow \mathbb{F}_2$: $n = 108$, $h = 12$, and $m = 96$.
- $\mathbb{F}_{2^4}$: $n = 18$, $h = 2$, and $m = 16 \rightarrow \mathbb{F}_2$: $n = 72$, $h = 8$, and $m = 64$.
- $\mathbb{F}_{2^4}$: $n = 9$, $h = 1$, and $m = 8 \rightarrow \mathbb{F}_2$: $n = 36$, $h = 4$, and $m = 32$.

We can analysis these systems by applying the following steps on each one of the above systems:

1. Generate a HFE system of equations over $\mathbb{F}_{2^4}$.
2. Remove h equations from the system.
3. Convert the system of equations to be over $\mathbb{F}_2$.
4. Fix the first h variables $(x_1, \ldots, x_h)$.
5. Guess more g variables.
6. Solve the resulting system with size $(n - h - g) \times m$.
7. Repeat the previous two steps with $g = g - 4$ until we reach to g such that the system of size $(n - h - g) \times m$ could not be able to solve.

After converting the system to be over $\mathbb{F}_2$, we fix $n - m$ variables to get a determinant system. After that we guess a number of variables as many as enough for solving the resulting over determined systems easily. We decrease the number of guessing variables by 4 and repeat the previous step until we can not solve the resulting system. For the six step we use our MXL$_3$ implementation to solve the systems. By this way we can estimate the complexity of solving the HFE Challenge 2 systems. In the next section we will present our experimental results and give more analysis.

5   Experimental Results

We built our experiments to explain the performance of MXL$_3$ for solving some HFE challenge 2 systems. We run all the experiments on a Sun X4440 server, with four "Quad-Core AMD Opteron^{TM} Processor 8356" CPUs and 128 GB of main memory. Each CPU is running at 2.3 GHz. We used only one out of the 16 cores.

Table 1 shows results of the HFE challenge 2 system with $n = 144$, $m = 128$, and $h = 16$. We used the method explained in the previous section. After fixing 16 variables we have a system of $m = 128$ equations and variables. We guess more g variables. As the system is originally built over $\mathbb{F}_{2^4}$, then each sequential 4 variables $x_{4i-3}, x_{4i-2}, x_{4i-1}, x_{4i}$ ($i \in \{1, 2, \ldots, m/4\}$) are related since they represent x_i over $\mathbb{F}_{2^4}$. In this case, we choose g such that $g \mid 4$. Moreover, we select the first $g/4$ groups, for example when $g = 40$, we pass values for $x_1, \ldots, x_{40}$.

Table 2 shows the results of solving some scaled versions of a HFE challenge 2 system with $n = 144$, $m = 128$, and $h = 16$ using Magma's implementation of F$_4$. Magma can not solve any bigger system greater than 128 equations in 72 variables. This explains how our improved MXL$_3$ algorithm is efficient than Magma's F$_4$ in terms of memory. However, F$_4$ is faster than our MXL$_3$ implementation since it uses the advanced Magma's linear algebra techniques.

Table 3 shows how MXL_3 solves a scaled version of HFE2 with $n = 72$, $m = 64$, and $h = 8$. Let we fix 8 variables and guess more 8 variables, so the resulting system is 64 equations in 56 variables. As we show from the table at degree $D = 4$, we have nine rounds. Four of them come by enlarging degree 3 partitions of leading variables x_1, x_5, x_9, x_{13} that are generated from the original degree 2 partitions x_1, x_5. The other three partitions $\{x_2, x_3, x_6\}$ are generated by reduction as shown in steps 5, 8. Also, in this level we found few mutants which are not sufficient to solve the system. At $D = 5$, we found some lower degree polynomials generated by reduction in rounds 2,3,4, and 5. While, at round 6 we found a lot of mutants of degree 3 and 4 that successfully solve the system with maximum matrix size 186804×494887.

Figure 2 displays the experimental time complexity of solving scaled versions of HFE Challenge 2 system by MXL_3 as in Table 1. In this case, after fixing 16 variables (the number of removed equations) we have a HFE system with 128 equations and 128 variables. We guess more g variables and solve the resulting systems with 128 equations and $(128 - g)$ variables.

In Figure 2(a), X-axis represents the number of guessing variables g and Y-axis represents the time consuming to solve each system after guessing g variables. As we show, the time complexity increased as the number of guessing variables decreased. However, this does not give us a real feeling about the complexity of breaking the Challenge.

Figure 2(b) shows the complexity of breaking HFE Challenge 2 in the worst case after guessing different g variables. Here X-axis as in Figure 2(a) represents g, while the values of Y-axis represent the logarithm of the time consuming to solve the scaled system with 128 equations and $128-g$ variables multiplied by 2^g. For example, in the worst case we need 10^{27} seconds to break HFE Challenge 2 when $g = 88$ and around 10^{21} seconds when $g = 52$. It is clear from Figure 2(b) that the time complexity for breaking HFE Challenge 2, in the worst case, decreased as the number of guessing variables decreased.

Another study to the complexity of solving HFE Challenge 2 is showed in Figure 3. Since the most time consuming part of MXL_3 is the linear algebra step, we study the complexity of computing the row echelon form of the maximum

Table 1. results of MXL_3 for HFE Challenge 2 system ($n = 144$, $m = 128$ and $h = 16$)

g	n'	max. matrix	D	Var	Time	Memory
88	40	2600×5781	3	x_9	3	3.8
84	44	6444×10871	3	x_5	12	13.2
80	48	3668×14421	3	x_5	16	24.8
76	52	8804×23479	3	x_1	100	61.5
72	56	23452×34162	4	x_{37}	272	136
68	60	24692×127441	4	x_{21}	14031	1855
64	64	42964×238325	4	x_{17}	39547	4819
60	68	196174×419753	4	x_{13}	44037	9817
56	72	54772×549904	4	x_{13}	144173	19131
52	76	286620×887612	4	x_9	365801	47366

Table 2. results of F_4 for HFE Challenge 2 system ($n = 144$, $m = 128$ and $h = 16$)

g	n'	D	Time	Memory
76	52	3	6	203
68	60	4	983	12288
64	64	4	8117	38912
60	68	4	12482	60416
56	72	4	73515	105472
52	76	ran out of memory		

Table 3. Results for HFE2 system ($n = 72, m = 64, h = 8, g = 8$) by MXL_3

Step	D	Round	Matrix Size	Rank	Svar	M	UM	MD
1	2	1	64×1597	64	x_1	0	0	-
2	3	1	688×23697	688	x_5	0	0	-
3	3	2	3612×29317	3612	x_1	0	0	-
4	4	1	7484×165068	7484	x_{13}	0	0	-
5	4	2	18132×223897	17780	x_9	1276	232	3
6	4	3	28916×223897	28916	x_9	0	0	-
7	4	4	51182×279217	51000	x_6	0	0	-
8	4	5	105942×300042	83762	x_5	36	24	3
9	4	6	85010×300042	84542	x_5	0	0	-
10	4	7	87230×345568	86582	x_3	0	0	-
11	4	8	161564×370372	135086	x_2	0	0	-
12	4	9	221456×396607	161320	x_1	0	0	-
13	5	1	161384×400975	161368	x_{41}	0	0	-
14	5	2	162332×412111	162256	x_{37}	152	0	4
15	5	3	163228×430256	163228	x_{34}	180	0	4
16	5	4	170040×439111	169820	x_{33}	2120	0	4
17	5	5	172352×477337	172352	x_{30}	480	0	4
18	5	6	186804×494887	186304	x_{29}	4344, 376	376	4, 3

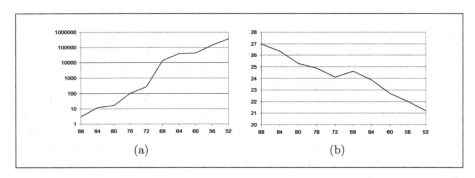

(a)   (b)

Fig. 2. Explain time complexity in seconds (y-axis) and the number of guessing variables g (x-axis)

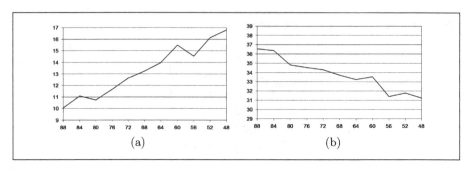

Fig. 3. Relation between the O-Notation of the maximum matrix (y-axis) and the number of guessing variables g (x-axis)

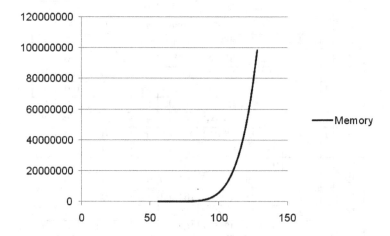

Fig. 4. Relation between the memory usage of solving HFE challenge 2 systems (y-axis) and the number of variables n' (x-axis) after guessing g variables, while the number of equation is fixed ($m = 128$)

matrix computed by MXL_3. Our implementation of MXL_3 uses the "Method of Four Russians" [1] in the linear algebra step. The complexity of this method is $O(N \cdot M \cdot R / \log N)$ [1] where N,M, and R are the number of rows, the number of columns, and the rank respectively. In Figure 3(a), we compute the O-notation for the maximum matrix computed by MXL_3 as in Table 1. In Figure 3(b), we multiply this O-notation by 2^g when we guess g variables. In both figures, Y-axis represents the logarithm of the computed O-notation. Figures 3(a), 3(b) confirm the results that we showed in Figures 2(a), 2(b) respectively. The complexity of computing the row echelon form of the maximum matrix decreased as the number of guessing variables decreased.

Finally, we interpolate the results in Table 1 to estimate the memory needed to break the full challenge using MXL$_3$ algorithm. Figure 4 shows the estimated memory consumed for solving scaled versions of HFE challenge 2 systems. We used Lagrange polynomial interpolation method in this computations. In this case, we need approximately 100000 Giga bytes to break the full version of HFE challenge 2.

Acknowledgments. We want to thank Prof. Dieter Schmidt for supporting us with his implementation of HFE systems.

References

1. Bard, G.V.: Accelerating cryptanalysis with the Method of Four Russians. Report 251, Cryptology ePrint Archive (2006)
2. Courtois, N., Klimov, A., Patarin, J., Shamir, A.: Efficient Algorithms for Solving Overdefined Systems of Multivariate Polynomial Equations. In: Preneel, B. (ed.) EUROCRYPT 2000. LNCS, vol. 1807, pp. 392–407. Springer, Heidelberg (2000)
3. Courtois, N.T., Pieprzyk, J.: Cryptanalysis of Block Ciphers with Overdefined Systems of Equations. In: Zheng, Y. (ed.) ASIACRYPT 2002. LNCS, vol. 2501, pp. 267–287. Springer, Heidelberg (2002)
4. Courtois, N.T., Pieprzyk, J.: Cryptanalysis of Block Ciphers with Overdefined Systems of Equations. Technical Report 2002/044, Cryptology ePrint Archive (2002)
5. Ding, J., Buchmann, J., Mohamed, M.S.E., Moahmed, W.S.A., Weinmann, R.-P.: MutantXL. In: Proceedings of the 1st International Conference on Symbolic Computation and Cryptography (SCC 2008), pp. 16–22. LMIB, Beijing (2008)
6. Faugère, J.-C., Joux, A.: Algebraic Cryptanalysis of Hidden Field Equation (HFE) Cryptosystems Using Gröbner Bases. In: Boneh, D. (ed.) CRYPTO 2003. LNCS, vol. 2729, pp. 44–60. Springer, Heidelberg (2003)
7. Mohamed, M.S.E., Cabarcas, D., Ding, J., Buchmann, J., Bulygin, S.: MXL3: An efficient algorithm for computing gröbner bases of zero-dimensional ideals. In: Lee, D., Hong, S. (eds.) ICISC 2009. LNCS, vol. 5984, pp. 87–100. Springer, Heidelberg (2010)
8. Mohamed, M.S.E., Mohamed, W.S.A.E., Ding, J., Buchmann, J.: *MXL2*: Solving polynomial equations over GF(2) using an improved mutant strategy. In: Buchmann, J., Ding, J. (eds.) PQCrypto 2008. LNCS, vol. 5299, pp. 203–215. Springer, Heidelberg (2008)
9. Patarin, J.: Hidden Fields Equations (HFE) and Isomorphisms of Polynomials (IP): Two New Families of Asymmetric Algorithms. In: Maurer, U.M. (ed.) EUROCRYPT 1996. LNCS, vol. 1070, pp. 33–48. Springer, Heidelberg (1996)
10. Penzhorn, W.: Algebraic attacks on cipher systems. In: Proceedings of 7th AFRICON Conference in Africa (AFRICON), vol. 2, pp. 969–974. IEEE, Los Alamitos (2004)

S-FSB: An Improved Variant of the FSB Hash Family

Mohammed Meziani, Özgür Dagdelen, Pierre-Louis Cayrel,
and Sidi Mohamed El Yousfi Alaoui

CASED – Center for Advanced Security Research Darmstadt,
Mornewegstrasse 32, 64293 Darmstadt, Germany
{mohammed.meziani,oezguer.dagdelen,pierre-louis.cayrel,elyousfi}@cased.de

Abstract. In 2003, Augot et al. introduced the Fast Syndrome-Based hash family (in short FSB), which follows the generic construction of Merkle-Damgård and is based on the syndrome decoding problem. In 2007, Finiasz et al. proposed an improved version of FSB. In this work, we propose a new efficient hash function, which incorporates the ideas of FSB and the sponge construction introduced by Bertoni et al. Our proposal is up to 30 % faster in practice than FSB. Its security is related on the Regular Syndrome (RSD) Decoding problem, which is proven NP-complete.

Keywords: cryptographic hash functions, provable security, syndrome decoding.

1 Introduction

A hash function maps strings of any length into short strings of fixed length, called *hash* or *digest*. For practical uses, hash functions should be easy to compute. That is, computing the hash value of a message m should be feasible in time polynomial in the size of m. Furthermore, if the hash function additionally satisfies certain security properties, it becomes a powerful tool for cryptographic applications such as digital signatures, conventional message authentication, password protection and pseudo-random number generation.

Over the last years, a long list of hash functions has been proposed in the literature. Following cryptanalytical advances, most of the widely used in practice (e.g. SHA-1) have been found to be insecure [12,26]. This has called into question the long-term security of later algorithms that share a similar design like SHA-2 family [23]. As a reaction, in 2007 the US National Institute of Standards and Technology (NIST) has opened a public competition, called SHA-3 (or the Advanced Hash Standard (AHS)), to develop new families of hash functions. Initially, 64 candidates have been submitted following different design principles, and only 4 of the competing designs passed to the third (and final) round of the contest. One of the first round submissions is the Fast Syndrome-Based hash Function (FSB) introduced first by Augot, Finiasz, and Sendrier [1] in 2003 and improved by Finiasz, Gaborit, and Sendrier [16] in 2007. The FSB is still

T.-h. Kim et al. (Eds.): ISA 2011, CCIS 200, pp. 132–145, 2011.

unbroken up to now. It has a security reduction to NP-complete problems from coding theory, that are believed to be difficult on average. However, the main drawback of FSB is the efficiency issue because it is slower than other competing hash functions. For that reason, FSB was removed since the second round. We compensate for this disadvantage and speed up the process of hash computing by following a different design principle.

Instead of building the hash function upon the Merkle-Damgård design principle [22,15], we improve FSB further following the sponge construction, which is used in many hash functions like the SHA-3-finalist Keccack hash function [9].

Our contribution. In this paper we describe a new code-based hash function following the sponge construction. The mapping within FSB applied in a sponge hash function scheme results in a more efficient hash family than the origin FSB. We come up with detailed security analysis, including collision resistance and (second) preimage resistance.

Even though we reuse the transformation within FSB for our hash family, we show that their security results cannot be conveyed directly. Furthermore, the security analysis for a hash function built upon a sponge construction are given only for assuming random transformation. We go into detail how the security reacts when instantiated with a transformation given in FSB. Upon this analysis and the current state of the art in cryptanalytic algorithms tackling the hard underlying problems within our scheme, we propose some parameters for fast and secure hashing.

Organization. The paper is organized as follows. Section 2 provides preliminaries. In Section 3 we briefly describe the related works that help us to construct our proposal. In Section 4 we present our construction. We analyze its security in Section 5. In Section 6 we propose some set of parameters for fast hashing. Section 7 presents the performance evaluation results of our proposal.

2   Preliminaries

Properties of Hash Functions. Hash functions are functions that map bit strings of arbitrary length into short fixed bit strings of length l. Besides the compressing property, "good" hash functions fulfill further properties like collision resistance and onewayness. Informally, collision resistance states that it is infeasible to find two distinct input values mapping to the same string when applied on the hash function. Furthermore, onewayness states that it is infeasible to return a pre-image when given an output of the hash function (hash value).

Next, we state formal definitions of collision resistance and (second) pre-image resistance.

Definition 1 (Security Properties for Hash Functions). *A family of hash functions $H_k : \{0,1\}^* \to \{0,1\}^l$ with $k \in \mathcal{K}$ for some finite set $\mathcal{K}$ is collision resistant if for any probabilistic polynomial-time (PPT) algorithm $\mathcal{A}$ the probability that the experiment $\mathsf{Col}_{\mathcal{A}}^{H}$ evaluates to 1 is negligible (as a function of λ). H_k*

is pre-image (resp. second pre-image) resistant *if for any PPT algorithm $\mathcal{A}$ the probability that the experiment* $\mathsf{PreImg}_{\mathcal{A}}^{H}$ *(resp.* $\mathsf{SecPre}_{\mathcal{A}}^{H}$*) evaluates to 1 is negligible (as a function of λ). Let* $\mathsf{Kg} : \lambda \mapsto k$ *be a generator for the keys of hash function H_k where $k \in \mathcal{K}$.*

Experiment $\mathsf{Col}_{\mathcal{A}}^{H}(\lambda)$
$\quad k \leftarrow \mathsf{Kg}(\lambda)$
$\quad (x, x') \leftarrow \mathcal{A}(k)$
$\quad$*Return* 1 *iff* $x \neq x'$
$\quad\quad$*and* $H_k(x) = H_k(x')$.

Experiment $\mathsf{PreImg}_{\mathcal{A}}^{H}(\lambda)$
$\quad k \leftarrow \mathsf{Kg}(\lambda)$
$\quad x \leftarrow \{0,1\}^*$
$\quad x' \leftarrow \mathcal{A}(k, H_k(x))$
$\quad$*Return* 1 *iff* $H_k(x) = H_k(x')$.

Experiment $\mathsf{SecPre}_{\mathcal{A}}^{H}(\lambda)$
$\quad k \leftarrow \mathsf{Kg}(\lambda)$
$\quad x \leftarrow \{0,1\}^*$
$\quad x' \leftarrow \mathcal{A}(k, x)$
$\quad$*Return* 1 *iff* $x \neq x'$
$\quad\quad$*and* $H_k(x) = H_k(x')$.

The probability is taken over all coin tosses of Kg *and* $\mathcal{A}$.

Note that the value k specifying the hash function H_k from the hash family is called key, but usually the key is not kept secret. There is an exception if we consider message authentication codes. In other words, a family of hash functions does not fulfill the security properties mentioned above only due to the secrecy of the key.

It is well known and straightforward to prove that any hash function which is collision resistant is also second pre-image resistant. That is, when designing a family of hash functions, one should aim for collision resistance and pre-image resistance.

Constructing hash functions is a hot topic. Specifically, it is desired to have hash functions whose design is based on a difficult mathematical problem and thus whose security follows rigorous mathematical proofs and formal reduction. Such functions are called provably secure hash functions and only a few examples of them were proposed in literature like SWIFFT [21], VSH [13] and ECHO [11].

Error-correcting codes. A linear code of length n and rank k is a linear subspace $\mathcal{C}$ with dimension k of the vector space $\mathbb{F}_q^n$ where $\mathbb{F}_q$ is the finite field with q elements. The elements of $\mathbb{F}_q^n$ (resp. $\mathcal{C}$) are called words (resp. codewords). The Hamming weight of a word x, denoted by $wt(x)$, is the number of its non-zero entries. A parity check matrix H of $\mathcal{C}$ is defined by $H \cdot x^T = 0, \forall x \in \mathcal{C}$. In this paper, we take $q = 2$.

Definition 2 (Regular word). *A regular word of length n and weight w is a codeword consisting of w blocks of length n/w, each has exactly one non-zero entry.*

Definition 3 (2-Regular word). *A 2-regular word is defined as a sum of two regular words. It is of length n and weight less that equal to $2w$.*

The security of code-based cryptosystems is based on the hardness of several coding theory problems. The most relevant in our context are stated in the following.

Definition 4 (Binary Syndrome Decoding (SD) problem). *Given a binary $s \times n$ matrix H, a binary vector $y \in \mathbb{F}_2^s$ and an integer $w > 0$, find a word $x \in \mathbb{F}_2^n$ of weight $wt(x) = w$, such that $H \cdot x^T = y$.*

This problem is proven NP-complete in [3]. In [1] two further problems related to SD have been shown to be NP-complete. They can be stated as follows.

Definition 5 (Regular Syndrome Decoding (RSD) problem). *Given a binary $s \times n$ matrix H, a binary vector $y \in \mathbb{F}_2^s$ and an integer $w > 0$, find a regular word $x \in \mathbb{F}_2^n$, $x \neq 0^n$, of weight $wt(x) = w$, such that $H \cdot x^T = y$.*

Definition 6 (2-Regular Null Syndrome Decoding (2-RNSD) problem). *Given a binary $s \times n$ matrix H and an integer $w > 0$, find a 2-regular word $x \in \mathbb{F}_2^n$ of weight $\leq 2w$, such that $H \cdot x^T = 0$.*

Throughout this paper, we will denote $SD(n, s, w)$ and $RSD(n, s, w)$ to indicate instances of the above problems with parameters (n, s, w).

3   Related Works

In this section, we briefly provide a description of the main ingredients that we need to design our family of hash functions: the FSB hash function [1] and the sponge construction [18].

FSB hash functions. The Fast Syndrome-Based Hash Functions (FSB) were first introduced in 2003 by Daniel Augot et al. [1] and improved in 2007 [16]. The FSB follows the iterative Merkle-Damgård design principle [22,15] based on the compression function $\mathcal{F}$ defined by

$$\mathcal{F} : \mathbb{F}_2^s \to \mathbb{F}_2^r$$
$$x \mapsto \mathcal{F}(x) = H \cdot \varphi_{n,w}(x)^T,$$

where H is a random binary matrix of size $r \times n$ and the mapping $x \mapsto \varphi_{n,w}(x)$, called a regular encoder, is an encoding algorithm, which takes an s-bit and returns a regular word of length n and weight w. In each round, the input of the compression function $\mathcal{F}$ consists of s-bit string, which is a concatenation of r bits taken from the output of the previous round and $s - r$ bits taken from the message to be hashed. The use of this encoder speeds up the computing of the vector-matrix multiplication, since this process is equivalent to XORing w columns of length r from the matrix H. In order to obtain a smaller hash size the whirlpool-hash function [2] is applied on the pre-final hash value.

Remark 1. Recently and just after finishing this work, we have come to know that a new construction based on the FSB hash family due to Bernstein et al. [8] has been proposed. Their proposal seems to be more efficient than the FSB SHA-3 proposal.

Sponge construction. This construction was presented by Bertoni et al. [18] in 2007. It represents a new way to build hash functions from a random transformation/permutation, denoted by $\mathcal{S}$, operating on states of length $s = r + c$ bits. The parameter r is called the rate, c the capacity, and s the width. The initial state is initialized to zero. The first r (resp. the last c bits) of a state is called the outer part (resp. the inner part (or inner state)) of the construction. Let x denote the message to be hashed. After padding x, the hashing process consists of two phases: the absorbing phase followed by the squeezing phase. During the absorbing phase, only the outer part of the state is combined with a r-bit message block using the bitwise XOR-operation. The result is then fed through $\mathcal{S}$. After processing all blocks of x the squeezing phase follows. In this phase only the outer parts are returned as intermediate hash values, interleaved with applications of $\mathcal{S}$. The number of hash blocks is chosen at will by the user.

4   Our Construction: S-FSB

In this section, we present a variant of the FSB hash function, called *Sponge Fast Syndrome-Based* hash function (in short S-FSB). We will use the same notations as in the previous section and define five positive integers n, w ,s, r and c such that the ratio n/w is a power of 2, and $s = r + c = w \log_2(n/w)$.

4.1   Description of S-FSB

The main idea behind our proposal is to use the sponge construction [18] of mode of operation rather than the Merkle-Damgard mode [22,15] of operation used in FSB. The S-FSB is based on the FSB transformation introduced in [19] to design the SYND stream cipher. This transformation, denoted here by $\mathcal{T}$, is defined by:

$$\mathcal{T} : \mathbb{F}_2^s \to \mathbb{F}_2^s$$
$$x \mapsto \mathcal{T}(x) = H \cdot \varphi_{n,w}(x)^T,$$

Where H is a random binary matrix of size $s \times n$ and the mapping $x \mapsto \varphi_{n,w}(x)$ is a regular encoding algorithm as in FSB For plugging this transformation into the sponge construction, we take s width, r the rate, and c the capacity (see section 3) such that $s = r + c$ (see section 3).

As illustrated in Figure 1, absorbing each r-bit message block m_i is performed as follows. The block m_i is first combined with the outer part of the current state (the previous output of $\mathcal{T}$) using the bitwise XOR operation. The result is then encoded into a regular word y of length n and weight w by applying the regular encoder $\varphi_{n,w}$. Finally, the multiplication of y by the transpose of H (denoted H^T) is performed to get the next state. When all message blocks are processed, the construction switches to the squeezing step as in the sponge construction to output the first r bits of the state as hash blocks. As in the sponge construction, those blocks form the pre-final hash value, which are extracted to get the final hash value of length l.

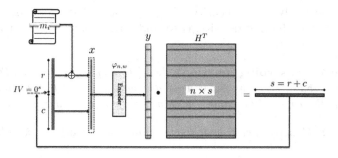

Fig. 1. Absorbing step of S-FSB hash function

The performance of our proposal depends directly on the number of bitwise XOR operations computed at each round to treat the r bits of one message block. That is, one needs first r XORs for the bitwise addition and then s XORs of w columns of the matrix H. This result to $r + sw$ binary XOR-operations. Since the number of bits of each message block is r, the number of expected binary XORs (denoted by $\mathcal{N}_{xor}$) in average for each message input bit is:

$$\mathcal{N}_{xor}(n, w, r, c) = \frac{r + (r + c)w}{r}.$$

where $r + c = s = w \log_2(n/w)$. This results to

$$\mathcal{N}_{xor}(n, w, r, c) = 1 + \frac{w^2 \log_2(n/w)}{r} \tag{1}$$

This quantity is the main measure to estimate the theoretical performance of our proposal.

5 Security Analysis

In this section, we consider the security of S-FSB. We will show how the security of S-FSB is reduced to the security of the syndrome decoding problem. More precisely, finding of pre-images (resp. collisions) is reduced to regular syndrome decoding problem (resp. 2-regular null syndrome decoding problem). Furthermore, we analyze the security in terms of current best known algorithms for solving these two problems.

5.1 Theoretical Security

In a cryptography environment, we require more properties of a hash function than just compressing the input value into a short bit string. In particular, there are three basic security requirements that a cryptographic hash function at least should fulfill. Namely, this is collision and (second) pre-image resistance. These requirements are defined in Definition 1.

In order to analyze the security of sponge-based hash functions, we need to introduce the following definitions to understand how generic attacks work against our proposal.

Definition 7 (Absorbing function). *Let S be a sponge function. The absorbing function $abs[\cdot]$, takes as input a padded message x of length multiple of r and returns the value of the state e obtained after absorbing x, i.e. $abs[x] = e$.*

Definition 8 (Path). *Let S be a sponge function. An input x is called a path to the state e if $abs[x] = e$.*

Definition 9 (Squeezing function). *Let S be a sponge function. The squeezing function, denoted by $sqz[\cdot]$, takes as input a state e given at the beginning of the squeezing step and returns an l-bit string Z_l the output truncated to l bits of S.*

We will denote by e_c the inner state of a state e. i.e. the last c bits of state e.

Definition 10 (Output binding). *Given an arbitrary string Z. Output binding is to find a state e such that $sqz[e] = Z$.*

Definition 11 (State Collision). *Let S be a sponge function. A state collision is a pair of two different paths $x, x' \in \mathbb{F}_2^*$ such that $abs[x] = abs[x']$.*

Definition 12 (Inner Collision). *Let S be a sponge function. An inner collision is a pair of two distinct paths $x, x' \in \mathbb{F}_2^*$ resulting in the same inner part, i.e. $abs[x]_c = abs[x']_c$.*

It is easy to check that a state collision is an inner collision, since any two distinct paths $x, x' \in \mathbb{F}_2^*$ such that $abs[x] = abs[x']$ leads to $abs[x]_c = abs[x']_c$. However, the converse does not hold.

Notions for Security. In order to prove collision resistance of our proposed hash function family S-FSB, we need to show that experiment $\mathsf{Col}_{\mathcal{A}}^{H}$ from Definition 1 evaluates to 1 only with negligible probability where $H : \{0,1\}^* \rightarrow \{0,1\}^l$ is the S-FSB hash family. Let $\mathsf{Adv}_{H,\lambda}^{Col}$ denote the maximum probability over any PPT algorithm $\mathcal{A}$ to compute a collision as defined in experiment $\mathsf{Col}_{\mathcal{A}}^{H}(\lambda)$, i.e. $\mathsf{Adv}_{H,\lambda}^{Col} = \max_{PPT\mathcal{A}}\{\mathrm{Prob}\left[\mathsf{Col}_{\mathcal{A}}^{H}(\lambda) = 1\right]\}$.

(Second) Pre-image resistance is defined analogously denoted by $\mathsf{Adv}_{H,\lambda}^{PreImg}$ (resp. $\mathsf{Adv}_{H,\lambda}^{SecPre}$). Furthermore, we reduce to security of our scheme to the syndrome problem (see Definition 4) which requires to specify its hardness. We denote $\mathsf{Adv}^{SD}(n, s, w)$ the maximum probability over any PPT algorithm $\mathcal{A}$ to solve the syndrome decoding problem with parameters (n, s, w).

5.1.1 Collision Resistance.

Security properties of hash functions build upon the sponge methodology are scrutinized against generic attacks assuming random transformation S. In terms of collision resistance the following statements are elaborated. An inner collision can easily (i.e. in polynomial time) transformed into a state collision. Assume x, x' are given inputs to a state collision, i.e. $\mathsf{abs}[x] = \mathsf{abs}[x']$. Then choose $p \in \{0, 1\}^*$ randomly and set $m := x||p$ and $m' := x'||p$. Obviously, m, m' lead to a collision in the output of the hash function since $\mathsf{sqz}[\mathsf{abs}[x||p]] = \mathsf{sqz}[\mathsf{abs}[x'||p]]$. Therefore, shown in [18], assuming a random sponge the workload of generating a collision in the output of the hash function is of the order $\min\{2^{(c+3)/2}, 2^{(l+3)/2}\}$.

Due to space limitations, we give here a short intuition how the security proof for collision resistance works and refer interested reader to the full version of this paper.

In order to produce collision for the S-FSB hash family where the sponge transformation is defined as $\mathcal{T} : \mathbb{F}_2^s \to \mathbb{F}_2^s; \; x \mapsto \mathcal{T}(x) = H \cdot \varphi_{n,w}(x)^T$ where H is a random binary matrix of size $s \times n$, we require to analyze the complexity of generating an inner collision. Since the capacity of a state is fixed (e.g. by $IV = 0$) in the beginning of the absorption phase, it suffices for an adversary to find two r bit values m, m' such that $\mathsf{abs}[m]_c = \mathsf{abs}[m']_c$. The complexity of generating collisions for transformation $\mathcal{T}$ is equivalent to $SD(n, s, 2w)$, shown in the security proof of FSB [16]. At the same time, for an inner collision, one needs to solve $SD(n_r, c, 2w_r)$ where $n = n_r + n_c$ and $w = w_r + w_c$ are the corresponding columns of H and weights of the input regular word belonging to the first r bits and the last c bits, respectively.

This leads to the following proposition.

Proposition 1 (Collision Resistance). *Let h be an S-FSB$_{(n,w,r,c)}$ hash function scheme instantiated with parameters (n, w, r, c) where $n = n_r + n_c$ and $w = w_r + w_c$. Then, we have*

$$\mathsf{Adv}_{h,(n,w,r,c)}^{Col} \leq \mathsf{Adv}^{SD}(n_r, c, 2w_r) + \mathsf{Adv}^{SD}(n, s, 2w) + 2^{-(c+3)/2} + 2^{-(l+3)/2}.$$

Proof. Proof is given in the full version.

5.1.2   (Second) Pre-image Resistance.

Unfortunately, due to space limitations, we only provide our results of (second) pre-image resistance and refer the reader to the full version of the paper for the corresponding proof.

Proposition 2 ((Second) Pre-Image Resistance). *Let h be an S-FSB$_{(n,w,r,c)}$ hash function scheme instantiated with parameters (n, w, r, c) where $n = n_r + n_c$ and $w = w_r + w_c$. Then, we have*

$$\mathsf{Adv}_{h,(n,w,r,c)}^{PreImg} \leq \mathsf{Adv}^{SD}(n_r, c, w_r) + \mathsf{Adv}^{SD}(n, l, w) + 2^{-l} + 2^{-(c-1)}$$

,and

$$\mathsf{Adv}_{h,(n,w,r,c)}^{SecPre} \leq m \cdot (\mathsf{Adv}^{SD}(n_r, c, w_r) + 2^{-c/2})$$

where m is the path length of a given pre-image.

Proof. Proof is given in the full version.

5.2   Practical Security

In practice, to assess the security of our scheme regarding the collision and (second) preimage resistance, we have to identify all known applicable attacks and to estimate the minimal complexities required to execute these attacks. As far as we know, there exist three kind of attacks: Information Set Decoding (ISD), Generalized Birthday Attack (GBA).

Information Set Decoding (ISD). ISD attacks are probabilistic algorithms for solving the SD problem. The main idea behind an ISD attack to find a valid set (information set) of $k = n - s$ (k is the dimension and n the length of the code) positions among the n positions. This set is valid if the SD problem has a solution whose support does not meet the chosen k positions. To check the validity of this set, one has to perform the Gaussian elimination of an $s \times s$ submatrix of the parity check matrix H of size $s \times n$, and thereby the whole complexity of this algorithm is expressed as $G(s)/P(n, s, w)$, where $G(s)$ is the cost of the Gaussian elimination and $P(n, s, w)$ the probability to find a valid information set.

Let $P_r(n, s, w)$ be the probability that a given information set is valid for one given solution of RSD. Let denote by $N_r(n, s, w)$ the expected number of solution of RSD. As stated in [1], the probability $P(n, s, w)$ can approximated by $P(n, s, w) = P_r(n, s, w) \times N_r(n, s, w)$. Since there exist $\left(\frac{n}{w}\right)^w$ regular words, then the average number of solutions of RSD is

$$N_r(n, s, w) = \frac{\left(\frac{n}{w}\right)^w}{2^s}.$$

In our setting, we have $s = w \log 2(n/w)$. This results in $N_r(n, s, w) = \frac{\left(\frac{n}{w}\right)^w}{\left(\frac{n}{w}\right)^w} = 1$. That means, we have only one solution to RSD, on average. Furthermore, as shown in [1], the $P_r(n, s, w)$ is given by

$$P_r(n, s, w) = \left(\frac{s}{n}\right)^w = \left(\frac{\log_2(n/w)}{n/w}\right)^w$$

If we set $\log_2(n/w) = \beta$, for some integers β, then the final probability of selecting a valid set to invert RSD equals to:

$$P(n, s, w) = P_r(n, s, w) \times N_r(n, s, w) = \left(\frac{\beta}{2^\beta}\right)^w \quad \text{with} \quad \beta = \log_2(n/w). \quad (2)$$

To estimate the cost of finding collisions, we have to evaluate the complexity of solving the 2-RNSD problem stated above. This can be done in the same way as in [1]. We compute the number of two-regulars words, then we multiply it by the probability of the validity, to get the total probability of choosing a valid set. This probability, denoted by P_I, is given by:

$$P_I(n, s, w) = \left(\frac{w}{n}\right)^w \left[\left(\frac{\log_2(n/w)}{2}\right) + 1\right]^w$$

For simplicity, we can assume that $\beta \geq 2$. So, we get an upper bound for this probability, denoted by P_C, which is equal to:

$$P_C(n, s, w) = \left(\frac{\beta^2}{2^{\beta+1}} \right)^w \text{ with } \beta = \log_2(n/w). \tag{3}$$

From the equation (3), we conclude that the probability for a random information set to be valid in case of collisions search is larger by a factor $(\frac{\beta}{2})^w$ compared to the probability for a random information set to be valid in case of finding preimages, where $\beta = \log_2(n/w)$.

In practice, there exists a lower bound for information set decoding attacks, presented in [6]. We will use these bounds to estimate the security of our scheme.

Generalized Birthday Attack (GBA). The GBA algorithm is due to Wagner [25] and was introduced to cryptanalyze the FSB hash function by Coron et al. [14].

We now describe the attack from Matthieu and Sendrier [17], which relies on the Generalized Birthday Problem introduced by Wagner [25]. The basic idea behind this algorithm is, for a given integer α, to find a set of indexes $\mathcal{I} = \{1, 2, \cdots, 2^\alpha\}$ verifying

$$\bigoplus_{i \in \mathcal{I}} H_i = 0.$$

To find this set $\mathcal{I}$, one has to compile 2^α lists of $2^{\frac{s}{\alpha+1}}$ elements containing distinct columns of the matrix H of size $s \times n$. These lists are then pairwise combined to get $2^{\alpha-1}$ lists of XORs of 2 columns of H. In the resulting lists, only 2 columns starting with $\frac{s}{\alpha+1}$ zeros are kept, instead of all the possible columns. Then, the new lists are pairwise merged to obtain $2^{\alpha-2}$ lists of XORs of 4 columns of H. Only 4 columns of H starting with $2\frac{s}{\alpha+1}$ zeros, are kept. This process will be continued, until only two lists are left. These two lists will contain $2^{\frac{s}{\alpha+1}}$ XORs of $2^{\alpha-1}$ columns of H having $(\alpha-1)\frac{s}{\alpha+1}$ zeros at the beginning. After that, the standard birthday algorithm can be applied to get one solution. Since all lists treated above, have the same size $\frac{s}{\alpha+1}$, the complexity of GBA is at least in $O\left(\frac{s}{\alpha+1} 2^{\frac{s}{\alpha+1}} \right)$.

As we can see in this algorithm, the number of XORed columns was a power of 2. However, this does not hold in general because the weight w can be any number. So if w is not a power of 2, one can modify the above algorithm such that one can back in the general case of GBA by imposing the following condition on α: $\frac{1}{2^\alpha} \left(\frac{n}{\frac{2w}{2^\alpha}} \right) \geq 2^{\frac{s-\alpha}{\alpha}}$ (see [17] for more details). This condition can be rewritten as:

$$\binom{2^\beta w}{2^{(1-\alpha)} w} \geq 2^{\beta w + \alpha(\alpha-1)} \tag{4}$$

where $\log_2(n/w) = \beta$. In this case, one gets a lower bound of the cost of solving an instance SD problem with parameters (n, s, w) as follows:

$$\left(\frac{w\beta}{\alpha} - 1\right) 2^{\frac{w\beta}{\alpha} - 1}. \tag{5}$$

As we can see, for fixed weight w, this complexity is an increasing function in n. So, to avoid the GBA attack, we have to choose large n.

Remarks:

- In [5] an implementation of GBA is presented against the compression function of FSB. This implementation includes two techniques introduced in [4] in order to mount GBA on computers, which do not have enough storage capacity to hold all list entries. However, the complexity of this attack is still exponential. Since our scheme is based on the FSB compression function, we claim that our proposal is secure against this implementation.
- It was shown in [20] that the sponge-based hash functions can be attacked by slide attacks. This kind of attacks was introduced in [10] by Biryukov et.al for cryptanalyzing iterative block ciphers. For attacking a sponge-like construction, the self-similarity issue can be exploited, meaning that all the blank rounds behave identically. As noted in [20], a simple defense against slide attacks consists in adding nonzero constant just before running the blank rounds. This can be achieved by a convenient padding such that the last block of the message is different from null vector. That is exactly, what we are used in our construction. Therefore, our proposal is secure against slide attacks.
- In [24], the so-called linearization attack (LA) was proposed against FSB to find collisions. The key idea is to reduce the problem of finding collisions to a linear algebra problem that can be solved in polynomial time, when the ratio s/w is up to 2. Furthermore, as shown in [24], this attack can still be applied if $s > w$. It can be extended even to $s > 2w$ with complexity $O(s^3 \left(\frac{3}{4}\right)^{s-2w})$. So, to avoid the LA attack, we have to choose $s > 2w$.
- Most recently a new variant of ISD algorithm [7] was presented for estimating the hardness of the 2-Regular Null Syndrome Decoding problem (2-RNSD). This algorithm runs faster than the lower bounds given in [17]. The parameters we propose in the next section are chosen to resist this attack as well.

6   Proposed Parameters

When selecting parameters for S-FSB, we have to look for parameters providing the desired security with least processing cost required to hash one bit of the message. As mentioned in Section 4, this cost can be measured using formula (1), which is expressed as a function depending on the parameters set (n, w, r, c). This function is defined by

$$\mathcal{N}_{xor}(n, w, r, c) = 1 + \frac{w^2 \log_2(n/w)}{r} = 1 + \frac{ws}{r} = 1 + \frac{w(r+c)}{r} = 1 + w\left(1 + \frac{c}{r}\right) \tag{6}$$

We observe that for increasing values of c, this function is an implicitly increasing quantity in w and n. So, if we want to have a good performance, then we have to choose small values of c (as small as possible) and select w and n such that the value of r are large. But from security point of view, we should choose s greater than $2w+1$ to withstand the linearization attack mentioned earlier. Furthermore, to avoid inner and outer collisions, the running time of solving instances of RSD and 2-RNSD with parameters (n, s, w) and (n_r, c, w_r) according the best known collision attack, must be larger than the desired security.

Starting from those conditions, we propose three parameter sets (n, s, w, c) that provide different security levels. Those sets of parameters are presented in Table 1 together with the corresponding numbers of XORs and the complexities of the ISD and GBA attack.

Table 1. Proposed paramaters for S-FSB

Hash size	n	s	w	c	$\mathcal{N}_{xor}$	Preimage GBA	Preimage ISD	Collision GBA	Collision ISD
160	$3 \cdot 2^{19}$	384	24	240	64.0	2^{130}	2^{99}	2^{86}	2^{91}
224	$17 \cdot 2^{17}$	544	34	336	88.9	2^{150}	2^{144}	2^{114}	2^{122}
256	$39 \cdot 2^{17}$	624	39	296	90.5	2^{246}	2^{172}	2^{129}	2^{148}

7 Performance Evaluation

S-FSB has been implemented on a 2.53 GHz Pentium Core2 Duo, running Linux (Ubuntu 10.04) 32 Bit with 6MB of cache and 4GB of RAM. The C compiler is GCC, version 4.4.3 with -O3 optimization. In our implementation, we used truncated quasi-cyclic codes as in FSB. We propose three versions of S-FSB of hash size 160, 224, and 256 bits. The performance of these versions is reported in Table 2. This performance was measured on a message of size 1000 MB. The file hash time in the third row was measured by repeated calls to the `clock()` function to get the current millisecond clock value and subtracted the stop time from the start time. The number of samples we performed is about one million. To get the speed expressed in cycles per bytes, we multiplied the measured hash time by the CPU frequency and divided the result by the file size in bytes.

In order to compare our results with those of FSB SHA-3 proposal[1], we ran the C-code of FSB on the same desktop and we obtained the results presented in Table 3. As we can see, the S-FSB is more efficient than FSB by a factor of 1.44 (30%). Despite this improvement, the S-FSB hash function remains slower than the existing hash functions like the SHA-2 family.

---

[1] http://www-rocq.inria.fr/secret/CBCrypto/index.php?pg=fsb

Table 2. Performance of S-FSB on a 2.53 GHz Core2 Duo processor

Hash size (bits)	File size (MB)	File hash time (s)	Speed (cpb)
160	1000	66.90	≈ 160
224	1000	84.48	≈ 201
256	1000	75.63	≈ 183

Table 3. Performance of FSB SHA-3 proposal on a 2.53 GHz Core2 Duo processor

Hash size (bits)	File size (MB)	File hash time (s)	Speed (cpb)
160	1000	87.76	≈ 212
224	1000	102.99	≈ 248
256	1000	109.38	≈ 264

References

1. Augot, D., Finiasz, M., Sendrier, N.: A Family of Fast Syndrome Based Cryptographic Hash Functions. In: Dawson, E., Vaudenay, S. (eds.) Mycrypt 2005. LNCS, vol. 3715, pp. 64–83. Springer, Heidelberg (2005)
2. Barreto, P.S.L.M., Rijmen, V.: Whirlpool. Seventh hash-function of ISO/IEC 10118-3:2004 (2004)
3. Berlekamp, E., McEliece, R., van Tilborg, H.: On the inherent intractability of certain coding problems. IEEE Transactions on Information Theory 24(2), 384–386 (1978)
4. Bernstein, D.J.: Better price-performance ratios for generalized birthday attacks (2007)
5. Bernstein, D.J., Lange, T., Niederhagen, R., Peters, C., Schwabe, P.: FSBDay: Implementing wagner's generalized birthday attack against the SHA-3 candidate FSB (2009)
6. Bernstein, D.J., Lange, T., Peters, C.: Ball-Collision Decoding. Cryptology ePrint Archive, Report 2010/585 (2010), http://eprint.iacr.org/
7. Bernstein, D.J., Lange, T., Peters, C., Schwabe, P.: Faster 2-regular information-set decoding (2011)
8. Bernstein, D.J., Lange, T., Peters, C., Schwabe, P.: Really fast syndrome-based hashing. Cryptology ePrint Archive, Report 2011/074 (2011), http://eprint.iacr.org/
9. Bertoni, G., Daemen, J., Peeters, M., Van Assche, G.: Keccak specifications. Submission to NIST, Round 2 (2009)
10. Biryukov, A., Wagner, D.: Slide attacks. In: Knudsen, L.R. (ed.) FSE 1999. LNCS, vol. 1636, pp. 245–259. Springer, Heidelberg (1999)
11. Brown, D.R.L., Antipa, A., Campagna, M., Struik, R.: Ecoh: the elliptic curve only hash. Submission to NIST (2008)

12. De Cannière, C., Rechberger, C.: Finding sha-1 characteristics: General results and applications. In: Lai, X., Chen, K. (eds.) ASIACRYPT 2006. LNCS, vol. 4284, pp. 1–20. Springer, Heidelberg (2006)

13. Contini, S., Lenstra, A.K., Steinfeld, R.: Vsh, an efficient and provable collision-resistant hash function. LNCS, pp. 165–182. Springer, Heidelberg (2006)

14. Coron, J.-S., Joux, A.: Cryptanalysis of a provably secure cryptographic hash function. Cryptology ePrint Archive, Report 2004/013 (2004), http://eprint.iacr.org/

15. Damgård, I.: A Design Principle for Hash Functions. In: Brassard, G. (ed.) CRYPTO 1989. LNCS, vol. 435, pp. 416–427. Springer, Heidelberg (1990)

16. Finiasz, M., Gaborit, P., Sendrier, N.: Improved fast syndrome based cryptographic hash functions. In: Rijmen, V. (ed.) ECRYPT Hash Workshop 2007 (2007)

17. Finiasz, M., Sendrier, N.: Security Bounds for the Design of Code-based Cryptosystems. In: Matsui, M. (ed.) ASIACRYPT 2009. LNCS, vol. 5912, pp. 88–105. Springer, Heidelberg (2009)

18. Peeters, M., Bertoni, G., Daemen, J., Van Assche, G.: Sponge Functions. In: ECRYPT Hash Workshop 2007 (2007)

19. Gaborit, P., Laudaroux, C., Sendrier, N.: Synd: a very fast code-based cipher stream with a security reduction. In: IEEE Conference, ISIT 2007, Nice, France, pp. 186–190 (July 2007)

20. Gorski, M., Lucks, S., Peyrin, T.: Slide attacks on a class of hash functions. In: Pieprzyk, J. (ed.) ASIACRYPT 2008. LNCS, vol. 5350, pp. 143–160. Springer, Heidelberg (2008)

21. Lyubashevsky, V., Micciancio, D., Peikert, C., Rosen, A.: Swifft: A modest proposal for fft hashing, pp. 54–72 (2008)

22. Merkle, R.C.: One Way Hash Functions and DES. In: Brassard, G. (ed.) CRYPTO 1989. LNCS, vol. 435, pp. 428–446. Springer, Heidelberg (1990)

23. National Institute of Standards and Technology (NIST). Secure Hash Standard (October 2008)

24. Saarinen, M.-J.O.: Linearization attacks against syndrome based hashes. In: Srinathan, K., Rangan, C.P., Yung, M. (eds.) INDOCRYPT 2007. LNCS, vol. 4859, pp. 1–9. Springer, Heidelberg (2007)

25. Wagner, D.: A generalized birthday problem. In: Yung, M. (ed.) CRYPTO 2002. LNCS, vol. 2442, p. 288. Springer, Heidelberg (2002)

26. Wang, X., Yin, Y.L., Yu, H.: Finding collisions in the full sha-1. In: Shoup, V. (ed.) CRYPTO 2005. LNCS, vol. 3621, pp. 17–36. Springer, Heidelberg (2005)

Improved Identity-Based Identification and Signature Schemes Using Quasi-Dyadic Goppa Codes

Sidi Mohamed El Yousfi Alaoui, Pierre-Louis Cayrel,
and Meziani Mohammed

CASED – Center for Advanced Security Research Darmstadt,
Mornewegstrasse 32, 64293 Darmstadt, Germany
{elyousfi,pierre-louis.cayrel,meziani}@cased.de

Abstract. In this paper, we present an improved version of an identity-based identification scheme based on error-correcting codes. Our scheme combines the Courtois-Finiasz-Sendrier signature scheme using quasi-dyadic codes (QD-CFS) proposed in [2] and the identification scheme by Stern [18]. Following the construction proposed in [5], we obtain an identity-based identification scheme which has the advantage to reduce a public data size, the communication complexity and the signature length.

Keywords: Error-Correcting codes, Identity-based Cryptography, Quasi-dyadic Goppa codes.

1 Introduction

In 1984, Shamir introduced the concept of identity-based Public Key Cryptography ID-PKC [17] in order to simplify the management of public keys used for the authentication of users. In ID-PKC, the public key of a user is obtained from his identity *id* which can be a concatenation of any publicly known information that singles out the user: a name, an e-mail, or a phone number. ID-PKC requires a trusted third part called Key Generation Center (KGC), the KGC is the owner of a system-wide secret, thus called the *master key*. After successfully verifying (by non-cryptographic means) the identity of the user, the KGC computes the corresponding user private key from the master key, the user identity *id* and a trapdoor function. The motivation behind identity-based systems is to create a cryptographic system resembling an ideal mail system. In this ideal system, a knowledge of a person's name alone suffices for confidential mailing to that person, and for signature verification that only that person could have produced. In such an ideal cryptographic system, we get the following advantages:

1. users need no exchange neither of symmetric keys nor of public keys;
2. public directories (databases containing public keys or certificates) need not be kept;
3. the services of a trusted authority are needed solely during a set-up phase (during which users acquire authentic public system parameters).

T.-h. Kim et al. (Eds.): ISA 2011, CCIS 200, pp. 146–155, 2011.

Coding theory is one of few alternatives supposed to be secure in a post quantum world. The most popular cryptosystems in coding theory are the McEliece [13] and Niederreiter [15] cryptosytems. The main advantage of these two public cryptosystems is the provision of a fast encryption and decryption (about 50 times faster for encryption and 100 times faster for decryption than RSA), but they have a major disadvantage as requiring very large keys and consequently, large memory size allocation.

In order to make use of the benefits of ID-based cryptography, the authors in [5] proposed the first identity-based identification (IBI) scheme based on coding theory. This scheme combines the signature scheme of Courtois, Finiasz and Sendrier (CFS) [7] and Stern identification scheme [18]. The basic idea of this construction is to start from a Niederreiter-like problem which can be inverted by using the CFS scheme. This permits to associate a secret to a random (public) value obtained from the identity of the user. The secret and public values are then used for the Stern zero-knowledge identification scheme.

An improvement of the CFS signature scheme using the quasi-dyadic (QD) structure was proposed in [2]. Using this improvement, we propose in this paper an identity based identification scheme built on quasi-dyadic codes.

The paper is organized as follows. In Section 2, we recall basic facts on code-based cryptography. Section 3 describes the first identity based on error correcting code proposed by Cayrel et. al. in [5]. Section 4 presents the improvement of the CFS signature scheme using the quasi-dyadic Goppa codes proposed in [2]. In Section 4, we introduce our improved identity based identification and the gain it offers in terms of performance. Finally, we conclude in Section 5.

2   Background of Coding Theory

Next, we provide some background for coding theory.

Let $\mathbb{F}_q$ to denote the finite field with q elements.

Let n and k be two integers such that $n \geq k$ and $\mathbb{F}_q^n$ be a finite field over $\mathbb{F}_q$. A code C is a k-dimensional subspace of the vector space $\mathbb{F}_q^n$.

Definition 1. (Minimum distance and Hamming weight)
The minimum distance is defined by $d := \inf_{x,y \in C} dist(x,y)$, where "dist" denotes the hamming distance.

Let x be a vector of $\mathbb{F}_q^n$, then we call $wt(x) := dist(x,0)$ the weight of x. It represents the number of non-zero entries.

$C = C[n,k,t]$ is a code with length n, dimension k and the ability of error-correcting in C is up to t errors (t is an integer).

Definition 2. (Generator, Parity Check Matrix and Syndrome)
A matrix $G \in \mathbb{F}_q^{k \times n}$ is called generator matrix of C, if the rows of G span C.

A matrix $H \in \mathbb{F}_q^{r \times n}$, where $r = n - k$, is called parity check matrix of C, if $Hx^{\mathsf{T}} = 0, \forall x \in C$.

The security of the most code-based cryptosystems relies on the difficulty of solving a syndrome decoding problem (SD), which is defined as follows:

Definition 3. (Syndrome Decoding (SD) Problem)
Input: A $r \times n$ random binary matrix H over $\mathbb{F}_q$, a target vector $y \in \mathbb{F}_q^r$ and an integer $t > 0$.
Problem: Find a vector $x \in \mathbb{F}_q^n$ with $wt(x) \leq t$, such that $Hx^{\mathsf{T}} = y$.

This problem is proven NP-complete in [3].

2.1   Quasi-Dyadic Codes

Since a large public matrix size is one of the drawbacks of code-based cryptography, there have been many attempts to reduce the matrix size. Miscozki and Barreto proposed in [14] the use of quasi-dyadic Goppa codes which admit a compact parity-check matrix and permit then to store it more efficiently.

In what follows we recall some definitions from [14] that we need in this paper, and we refer the reader to [14] for a detailed description of the quasi-dyadic codes construction.

Definition 4. Given a vector $h = (h_0, \ldots, h_{n-1}) \in \mathbb{F}_q^n$, where q is a power of 2. The dyadic matrix $\Delta(h) \in \mathbb{F}_q^{n \times n}$ is the symmetric matrix with components $\Delta_{ij} = h_{i \oplus j}$, where $\oplus$ stands for bitwise exclusive-or on the binary representations of the indices. The sequence h is called its signature. The set of dyadic $n \times n$ matrices over $\mathbb{F}_q$ is denoted $\Delta(\mathbb{F}_q^n)$.
Given $t > 0$, $\Delta(t, h)$ denotes $\Delta(h)$ truncated to its first t rows.
We call a matrix quasi-dyadic matrix if it is a block matrix whose component blocks are dyadic submatrices.

If n is a power of 2, then every $2^k \times 2^k$ dyadic matrix M can be recursively characterized as

$$M = \begin{bmatrix} A & B \\ B & A \end{bmatrix},$$

where A and B are $2^{k-1} \times 2^{k-1}$ dyadic matrices.

We can remark that the signature $h = (h_0, \ldots, h_{n-1})$ of a dyadic matrix coincides with its first row.

Definition 5. A quasi-dyadic (QD) code is a linear error-correcting code that admits a quasi-dyadic parity-check matrix.

Definition 6. Given two disjoint sequences $z = (z_0, \ldots, z_{t-1}) \in \mathbb{F}_q^t$ and $L = (L_0, \ldots, L_{n-1}) \in \mathbb{F}_q^n$ of distinct elements, the Cauchy matrix $C(z, L)$ is the $t \times n$ matrix with elements $C_{ij} = 1/(z_i - L_j)$, i.e.

$$C(z, L) = \begin{bmatrix} \dfrac{1}{z_0 - L_0} & \cdots & \dfrac{1}{z_0 - L_{n-1}} \\ \vdots & \ddots & \vdots \\ \dfrac{1}{z_{t-1} - L_0} & \cdots & \dfrac{1}{z_{t-1} - L_{n-1}} \end{bmatrix}.$$

Cauchy matrices have the property that all of their submatrices are nonsingular [16]. Notice that, Goppa codes admit a parity-check matrix in cauchy form under certain assumption [12]. Misoczki and Barreto showed in [14] Theorem 2 that the intersection of these two classes is non-empty if the code is defined over a field with characteristic 2.

This result was given in the following theorem.

Theorem 1 ([14]). *Let $H \in \mathbb{F}_q^{n \times n}$ with $n > 1$ be simultaneously a dyadic matrix $H = \Delta(h)$ for some $h \in \mathbb{F}_q^n$ and a Cauchy matrix $H = C(z, L)$ for two disjoint sequences $z \in \mathbb{F}_q^n$ and $L \in \mathbb{F}_q^n$ of distinct elements. Then $\mathbb{F}_q$ is a binary field, h satisfies*

$$\frac{1}{h_{i \oplus j}} = \frac{1}{h_i} + \frac{1}{h_j} + \frac{1}{h_0},$$ (1)

and $z_i = 1/h_i + \omega$, $L_j = 1/h_j + 1/h_0 + \omega$ for some $\omega \in \mathbb{F}_q$.

2.2 Usual Attacks

Any public-key cryptosystem primarily requires to be resistant to an adversary who manages either to extract the private data given only public data, or to invert the trapdoor encryption function given the ciphertexts of his choice (and public data). Against code-based cryptosystem there are two classes of attacks : structural attacks which try to recover the structure of the code and decoding attacks which try to decode directly a plaintext. The most threatening attacks are based on decoding algorithms for generic, but because we deal with Goppa codes, one has to take care as well of structural attacks.

3 Identity-Based Identification and Signature Scheme

Identity-based (IB) public key cryptography was introduced in 1984 by Shamir [17] in order to simplify public key management and to avoid the need for digital certificates. However, identity based PKC need a third party called Key Generation Center (KGC) or trusted, which generates user private keys corresponding to user identities (e.g., name, e-mail,...); the key generation requires a secret, called master key.

The first identity-based scheme based on error-correcting codes was proposed by Cayrel et. al in [5]. This scheme consists of two phases: the key generation part using the signature scheme of Courtois, Finiasz, and Sendrier (CFS) [7] and the interaction part, which uses the Stern identification scheme [18].

In this section, we recall the description of the CFS and Stern schemes, then we show how the authors in [5] combined them in order to construct an identity-based identification scheme.

3.1 Description of CFS Signature Scheme

In 2001, Courtois, Finiasz and Sendrier proposed in [7] the first practical signature scheme in coding theory, which is based on the Niederreiter cryptosystem.

Due to the fact that not all syndromes are decodable, the idea of CFS is to hash the message M, which has to be signed after a counter has been appended to it. If the resulting hash value is not decodable, it has to try successive counter values until a decodable syndrome is found. The actual signature on the message M consists of both the error pattern of weight t corresponding to the syndrome, and the value of the counter giving this syndrome.

Let $\mathcal{H} : \{0,1\}^* \times \mathbb{N} \to \mathbb{F}_q^k$ be a random oracle for a given vector space $\mathbb{F}_q^k$ over a finite field $\mathbb{F}_q$. Formally, the CFS signature scheme consists of the following algorithms:

- Keygen: For the desired security level expressed by suitable integers q, n, k, t, choose a linear t-error correcting $[n, k, t]$-code over $\mathbb{F}_q$ defined by a public parity-check matrix H with a private decoding trapdoor $\mathcal{T}$. The private-public key pair is $(\mathcal{T}, H)$.
- Sign: Let $M \in \{0,1\}^*$ be the message to sign. Find $i_0 \in \mathbb{N}$ (either sequentially or by random sampling) such that $x \leftarrow \mathcal{H}(M, i_0)$ is a decodable syndrome. Using the decoding trapdoor $\mathcal{T}$, find $s \in \mathbb{F}_q^n$ of weight $\mathsf{wt}(s) \leqslant t$ such that $Hs^\mathrm{T} = x^\mathrm{T}$. The signature is the pair (s, i_0).
- Verify: Let (s, i_0) be a purported signature of a message M. Compute $x \leftarrow \mathcal{H}(M, i_0)$, and accept iff $\mathsf{wt}(s) \leqslant t$ and $Hs^\mathrm{T} = x^\mathrm{T}$.

The authors of [7] used Goppa codes, which have a good proportion of decodable words, and choose parameters such that this proportion is reasonable. For a t-error correcting Goppa code $[n = 2^m, n - mt, t]$ (m integer), the number of decoding attempt required to get one signature will be approximately around $(t!)$. The security of this scheme can be reduced to the syndrome decoding (SD) problem.

3.2 Description of the Stern Identification Scheme

At CRYPTO'93, Stern proposed the first identification scheme based on error-correcting codes [18]. This construction is an interactive zero-knowledge protocol which enables a prover (P) to identify himself to a verifier (V).

Let H be a public random $(n - k) \times n$ binary matrix ($n \geq k$) and h a hash function returning a binary word n. Each prover P receives a n-bit secret key s_k of Hamming weight t ($t \geq n$) and computes a public identifier id_P such that $id_P = Hs_k^T$. This identifier is calculated once in the lifetime of H and can be used for several identifications.

We now describe this protocol:

- Commitment Step: P randomly chooses $y \in \mathbb{F}_2^n$ and a permutation σ of $\{1, 2, \ldots, n\}$. Then P sends to V the commitments c_1, c_2, and c_3 such that :

$$c_1 = h(\sigma \| Hy^T); \quad c_2 = h(\sigma(y)); \quad c_3 = h(\sigma(y \oplus s_k)),$$

where $h(a\|b)$ denotes the hash of the concatenation of the sequences a and b.

- Challenge Step: V sends $b \in \{0,1,2\}$ to P.
- Answer Step: The are three possibilities :
  - if $b = 0$: P reveals y and σ.
  - if $b = 1$: P reveals $(y \oplus s_k)$ and σ.
  - if $b = 2$: P reveals $\sigma(y)$ and $\sigma(s_k)$.
- Verification Step: There are three possibilities :
  - if $b = 0$: V verifies that c_1, c_2 are correct.
  - if $b = 1$: V verifies that c_1, c_3 are correct.
  - if $b = 2$: V verifies that c_2, c_3 are correct, and that the weight of $\sigma(s_k)$ is t.
- Soundness Amplification Step: Iterate the above steps until the expected security level is reached.

For the verification step and when b equals 1, it can be noticed that Hy^T derives directly from $H(y \oplus s_k)^T$ since we have: $Hy^T = H(y \oplus s_k)^T \oplus id_p = H(y \oplus s_k)^T \oplus Hs_k^T$. It is proven in [18] that this protocol verifies the zero-knowledge proof and for each iteration, the probability that a dishonest party succeeds in cheating is $(2/3)$. Therefore, to get a confidence level of β, the protocol must be iterated a number α of times with $(2/3)^\alpha \leq \beta$ holds.

3.3   Identity Based Identification (IBI) Protocol

The identity based identification protocol proposed in [5] is an interactive identification protocol between a prover and a verifier, consisting of two parts: the first one, called key deliverance, uses the CFS signature scheme to create the private key for the prover, while the Stern's protocol is used for the identification in the second part. We describe these two parts as follows:

- Key deliverance: Let h be a hash function with values in $\{0,1\}^{n-k}$ and let id_p be the prover's identifier identities. The goal of this part is to generate a prover's secret key by using the CFS signature. The prover receives a secret key s_k such that $Hs_k^T = h(id_p|i_0)$, where i_0 is the smallest value of i for which it is possible to decode $h(id_p|i_0)$. The secret key corresponding to the prover's identifier consists then of $\{s_k, i_0\}$.
- Prover and verifier's interaction: Each prover is associated now with the tuple $\{s, i_0\}$. In this case a prover P wishes to identify to a verifier V using the same matrix H and proving that he knows the secret key. This is achieved by Stern's protocol such that in the commitment step, the prover has to submit the counter i_0 together with other commitments c_1, c_2 and c_3. The knowledge of i_0 is needed for the verification step when b equals 1, since we have: $Hy^T = H(y \oplus s_k)^T \oplus h(id_v|i_0) = H(y \oplus s_k)^T \oplus Hs_k^T$.

By virtue of the so-called Fiat-Shamir Paradigm [9], it is possible to convert this identity based identification scheme into an identity based signature scheme, but the resulting signature size is long (about 1.5 Mbyte long for 2^{80} security).

A proof of security for this scheme in the random oracle model is given in [4], assuming the hardness of the two problems: Goppa Parametrized Bounded Decoding (GPBD) and Goppa Code Distinguishing (GD). However, due to the recently work proposed in [8] , the hardness of GD problem is no longer valid.

Suggested parameters. Because the IBI scheme uses CFS scheme in the first part of the protocol, its security relies on CFS parameters. The authors of IBI scheme in [4] suggest $t = 9$ and $m = 16$, which gives the following properties:

- Public Key: tm (180 Bits)
- Private Key: tm (180 Bits)
- Matrix size: $2^m tm$ (1 Mbyte)
- Communication cost for IBI $\approx 2^m \times \#rounds$ (500 Kbyte), where $\#rounds = 58$.
- Signature length for IBS $\approx 2^m \times \#rounds$ (2.2 Mbyte), where $\#rounds = 150$.

Due to Daniel Bleichenbacher attack's described in [11] are these suggested parameters not realistic for 2^{80} as security level, to ensure this security level, the authors of [11] suggested $t = 12$ and $m = 15$.

4   Identity-Based Identification Using Quasi-Dyadic Codes

In what follows, we give the main idea of the quasi-dyadic CFS signature construction, which consists of using a family of quasi-dyadic codes described in Section 2 instead of Goppa codes. The use of such family of codes allows to reduce the public key size by almost a factor of 4, but the number of signing attempts is increased by a factor of 2. For more detail, we refer the reader to [2].

4.1   Quasi-Dyadic Codes for CFS Signature

The strategy to get shorter keys is due to the fact that the CFS signature scheme needs only a very small t, so most rows of the parity matrix H are unused anyway when defining the code. Therefore, we can have some undefined entries in H, as long as the corresponding rows are not used to define the code. This leads to extend the code length to $2^m - t$.

Algorithm 1 picked from [2] describes this construction.

Parameter combinations proposed in [2] are put forward on Table 1.

Table 1. Suggested parameters for practical security levels

level	m	t	$n = \lfloor 2^{m-1/t} \rfloor$	$k = n - mt$	key size (Kbyte)
80	15	12	30924	30744	169
100	20	12	989724	989484	7248
120	25	12	31671168	31670868	289956

Implementation of QD-CFS signature scheme: To attract the attention of QD-CFS scheme, the authors in [1] proposed an GPU implementation of this scheme, it was demonstrated that signing a document using a QD-CFS can be performed in acceptable time (around 5 minutes). A GTX 295 running CUDA Version 3.0 has been used for the implementation process.

Algorithm 1. Constructing a purely dyadic, CFS-friendly code

INPUT: m, n, t.

OUTPUT: A dyadic signature h from which a CFS-friendly t-error correcting binary Goppa code of length n can be constructed from a code over $\mathbb{F}_{2^m}$, and the sequence b of all consistent blocks of columns (i.e. those that can be used to define the code support).

```
 1: q ← 2^m
 2: repeat
 3:     U ← 𝔽_q \ {0}
 4:     h_0 ⭠$ U, U ← U \ {h_0}
 5:     for s ← 0 to m − 1 do
 6:         i ← 2^s
 7:         h_i ⭠$ U, U ← U \ {h_i}
 8:         for j ← 1 to i − 1 do
 9:             if h_i ≠ 0 and h_j ≠ 0 and 1/h_i + 1/h_j + 1/h_0 ≠ 0 then
10:                 h_{i+j} ← 1/(1/h_i + 1/h_j + 1/h_0)
11:             else
12:                 h_{i+j} ← 0 ▷ undefined entry
13:             end if
14:             U ← U \ {h_{i+j}}
15:         end for
16:     end for
17:     c ← 0 also: U ← 𝔽_q
18:     if 0 ∉ {h_0, ..., h_{t−1}} then ▷ consistent root set
19:         b_0 ← 0, c ← 1 ▷ also: U ← U \ {1/h_i, 1/h_i + 1/h_0 | i = 0, ..., t − 1}
20:         for j ← 1 to ⌊q/t⌋ − 1 do
21:             if 0 ∉ {h_{jt}, ..., h_{(j+1)t−1}} then ▷ consistent support block
22:                 b_c ← j, c ← c+1 ▷ also: U ← U\{1/h_i+1/h_0 | i = jt, ..., (j+1)t−1}
23:             end if
24:         end for
25:     end if
26: until ct ⩾ n ▷ consistent roots and support
27: h ← (h_0, ..., h_{q−1}), b ← (b_0, ..., b_{c−1}) ▷ also: ω ⭠$ U
28: return h, b ▷ also: ω
```

4.2 Improved Identity-Based Identification and Signature Schemes Using Quasi-Dyadic Goppa Codes (QD-IBI)

The main advantage of the QD-CFS signature scheme presented in subsection 4.1 is to reduce the size of the public key. But, the drawback is the high signature cost, which originates in the elaborate key deliverance process of the IBI scheme. However, since the key deliverance is a one-time process, the long-term computational cost is reduced by the smaller parity check matrix. We extend this result by using quasi-dyadic codes in the identity based identification (IBI) scheme presented in subsection 3.3. The main idea consists in replacing the CFS signature scheme by the QD-CFS signature scheme during the key deliverance in the IBI-protocol. In second part of our IBI scheme, the prover can identify itself through Stern's protocol using the same matrix H and proving that he knows the private key s_k. The quasi-dyadic structure of the matrix used as public key permits to reach better performance compared to the original IBI scheme in [5]. We can mention, that the use of a quasi-dyadic matrix in Stern's protocol preserves the security against Simple Analysis (SPA) and Differential Power Analysis (DPA) attacks, this can be achieved by adapting the masking technique suggested in [6] for the case of quasi-cyclic codes.

By virtue of the so-called Fiat-Shamir Paradigm [9], it is possible to convert the identity based identification scheme using quasi-dyadic codes (QD-IBI) into an identity based signature scheme (QD-IBS).

Suggested parameters of the QD-IBI scheme. We suggest the same parameters suggested for the QD-CFS in subsection 4.1, i.e. $(m, t) = (15,12)$; these parameters are enough to ensure a security of more than 2^{80} binary operations against all currently known attacks.

In the following table, we compare the QD-IBI and QD-IBS schemes using the QD-CFS with the original IBI and IBS schemes for the parameters $m = 15$, $t = 12$.

Table 2. Comparison of IBI/IBS and IBI (QD-IBI/IBS)

	IBI/IBS	IBI (QD-IBI/IBS)
Private key size	180 Bit	180 Bit
Public key size	180 Bit	180 Bit
Matrix size	720 kByte	169 kByte
Communication cost	232 kByte	219 kByte
Signature length	600 kByte	560 kByte

Table 2 shows the advantage of QD-IBI and QD-IBS schemes concerning the size of public data, the signature size, and the communication overhead.

5   Conclusion

In this paper, we have proposed an improved identity based identification and signature scheme based on coding theory using quasi-dyadic codes. Our scheme has the advantage to reduce a public data size, the communication complexity and the signature length. For further improvements, we can imagine the use of Parallel-CFS proposed in [10]. Unfortunately, as often in code-based cryptography our improved scheme suffers from large system parameters, therefore we encourage the cryptography community to work in this area because a lot of proposals are needed to make code based schemes more practical and then to be a good alternative for the classic cryptography.

References

1. Barreto, P.S.L.M., Cayrel, P.-L., Hoffman, G., Misoczki, R.: GPU implementation of the quasi-dyadic CFS signature scheme (2010) (preprint)
2. Barreto, P.S.L.M., Cayrel, P.-L., Misoczki, R., Niebuhr, R.: Quasi-dyadic CFS signature. In: Inscrypt 2010 (2010)
3. Berlekamp, E., McEliece, R., van Tilborg, H.: On the inherent intractability of certain coding problems. IEEE Transactions on Information Theory 24(3), 384–386 (1978)
4. Cayrel, P.-L., Gaborit, P., Galindo, D., Girault, M.: Improved identity-based identification using correcting codes. CoRR, abs/0903.0069 (2009)
5. Cayrel, P.-L., Gaborit, P., Girault, M.: Identity-based identification and signature schemes using correcting codes. In: Augot, D., Sendrier, N., Tillich, J.-P. (eds.) International Workshop on Coding and Cryptography, WCC 2007, pp. 69–78 (2007)
6. Cayrel, P.-L., Gaborit, P., Prouff, E.: Secure implementation of the Stern authentication and signature schemes for low-resource devices. In: Grimaud, G., Standaert, F.-X. (eds.) CARDIS 2008. LNCS, vol. 5189, pp. 191–205. Springer, Heidelberg (2008)
7. Courtois, N., Finiasz, M., Sendrier, N.: How to achieve a McEliece-based digital signature scheme. In: Boyd, C. (ed.) ASIACRYPT 2001. LNCS, vol. 2248, pp. 157–174. Springer, Heidelberg (2001)
8. Faugére, J.-C., Otmani, A., Perret, L., Tillich, J.-P.: A distinguisher for high rate mceliece cryptosystem – extended abstract. In: Véron, P. (ed.) Yet Another Conference on Cryptography, YACC 2010, Toulon, pp. 1–4 (2010)
9. Fiat, A., Shamir, A.: How to prove yourself: Practical solutions to identification and signature problems. In: Odlyzko, A.M. (ed.) CRYPTO 1986. LNCS, vol. 263, pp. 186–194. Springer, Heidelberg (1987)
10. Finiasz, M.: Parallel-CFS, strengthening the CFS mceliece-based signature scheme. In: SAC 2010 (2010) (to appear)
11. Finiasz, M., Sendrier, N.: Security bounds for the design of code-based cryptosystems. In: Matsui, M. (ed.) ASIACRYPT 2009. LNCS, vol. 5912, pp. 88–105. Springer, Heidelberg (2009), http://eprint.iacr.org/2009/414.pdf
12. Macwilliams, F.J., Sloane, N.J.A.: The theory of error-correcting codes (1978)
13. McEliece, R.: A public-key cryptosystem based on algebraic coding theory. The Deep Space Network Progress Report, DSN PR 42–44 (1978), http://ipnpr.jpl.nasa.gov/progressreport2/42-44/44N.PDF
14. Misoczki, P.S.L.M., Barreto, P.S.L.M.: Compact McEliece keys from Goppa codes. In: Jacobson Jr., M.J., Rijmen, V., Safavi-Naini, R. (eds.) SAC 2009. LNCS, vol. 5867, pp. 376–392. Springer, Heidelberg (2009)
15. Niederreiter, H.: Knapsack-type cryptosystems and algebraic coding theory. Problems of Control and Information Theory 15(2), 159–166 (1986)
16. Schechter, S.: On the inversion of certain matrices. Mathematical Tables and Other Aids to Computation 13(66), 73–77 (1959), http://www.jstor.org/stable/2001955
17. Shamir, A.: Identity-based cryptosystems and signature schemes. In: Blakely, G.R., Chaum, D. (eds.) CRYPTO 1984. LNCS, vol. 196, pp. 47–53. Springer, Heidelberg (1985)
18. Stern, J.: A new identification scheme based on syndrome decoding. In: Stinson, D.R. (ed.) CRYPTO 1993. LNCS, vol. 773, pp. 13–21. Springer, Heidelberg (1994)

A Detrministic Factorization and Primality Testing Algorithm for Integers of the Form Z Mod 6 = -1

Noureldien Abdelrhman Noureldien, Mahmud Awadelkariem,
and DeiaEldien M. Ahmed

Faculty of Computer Science and Information Technology,
University of Science and Technology, Omdurman, Sudan
Noureldien@hotmail.com, {mah_awad,Diamahamed}@gmail.com

Abstract. Prime numbers are known to be in one of two series; P mod 6 = ±1. In this paper, we introduce the concept of Integer Absolute Position in prime series, and we use the concept to develop a structure for composite integer numbers in the prime series P mod 6 = -1.

We use the developed structure to state theorems and to develop a deterministic algorithm that can test simultaneously for primality and prime factors of integers of the form Z mod 6 = -1.

The developed algorithm is compared with some of the well known factorization algorithms. The results show that the developed algorithm performs well when the two factors are close to each other.

Although the current version of the algorithm is of complexity $((N/6^2)$ ½ /2), but the facts that, the algorithm has a parallel characteristics and its performance is dependent on a matrix search algorithm, makes the algorithm competent for achieving better performance.

Keywords: Factorization, Primality Testing; Prime Series; Absolute Position, Relative Position.

1 Introduction

Factoring numbers is a hard task, which means that any algorithm designed to factor will not run in polynomial time. In fact, most of the algorithms that exist today run on the order of e^n, where e is Euler's number [1]. Generally speaking, the most useful factoring algorithms fall into one of the following two main classes [2]:

A. The run time depends mainly on the size of N, the number being factored, and is not strongly dependent on the size of the factor found. Examples are: Lehman's algorithm [8] which has a rigorous worst-case run time bound $O(N^{1/3})$, . Shanks's SQUFOF algorithm [9], which has expected run time $O(N^{1/4})$. Shanks's Class Group algorithm [3,4] which has run time $O(N^{1/5+\epsilon})$ on the assumption of the Generalised Riemann Hypothesis.

The Continued Fraction algorithm [5] and the Multiple Polynomial Quadratic Sieve algorithm [6], which under plausible assumptions have expected run time $O(\exp(c(\log N \log \log N)^{1/2}))$, where c is a constant (depending on details of the algorithm).

T.-h. Kim et al. (Eds.): ISA 2011, CCIS 200, pp. 156–165, 2011.

B. The run time depends mainly on the size of f, the factor found. (We can assume that f ≤ N.) Examples are;– The trial division algorithm, which has run time O(f · (log N)^2). The Pollard "rho" algorithm [7] which under plausible assumptions has expected run time O(f$^{1/2}$·(logN)^2). Lenstra's "Elliptic Curve Method" (ECM) [10, 11] which under plausible assumptions has expected run time O(exp(c(log f log log f)$^{1/2}$. log(N)^2), where c is a constant.

In these examples, the term (log N)^2 is a generous allowance for the cost of performing arithmetic operations on numbers of size O(N) or O(N^2), and could theoretically be replaced by (log N)$^{1+\epsilon}$ for any ϵ > 0.

The fastest known general-purpose factoring algorithm is the General Number Field Sieve (GNFS), which in asymptotic notation takes S = O (exp((64/9 n)$^{1/3}$ (log n)$^{2/3}$)) steps to factor an integer with n decimal digits. The running time of the algorithm is bounded below by functions polynomial in n and bounded above by functions exponential in n [12].

The apparent difficulty of factoring large integers is the basis of some modern cryptographic algorithms. The RSA encryption algorithm [13], and the Blum-Blum Shub cryptographic pseudorandom number generator [14] both rely on the difficulty of factoring large integers. If it were possible to factor products of large prime numbers quickly, these algorithms would be insecure. The SSL encryption used for TCP/IP connections over the World Wide Web relies on the security of the RSA algorithm [15]. Hence if one could factor large integers quickly, "secured" Internet sites would no longer be secure. Finally, in computational complexity theory, it is unknown whether factoring is in the complexity class P. In technical terms, this means that there is no known algorithm for answering the question "Does integer *N* have a factor less than integer *s*?" in a number of steps that is less than O(*P(n)*) , where *n* is the number of digits in *N*, and *P(n)* is a polynomial function. Moreover, no one has proved that such an algorithm exists, or does not exist.

In this paper we present a new approach for developing a primality testing and factorization algorithms. The run time of this algorithm is mainly based on the distant between the two factors, more precisely on the distant between the square root of the integer and the smallest factor.

Although we only deal in this paper with integers of the form Z mod 6 =-1, but the same approach can be applied for integers of the form Z mod 6 = 1. Our proposed approach handles primality testing and prime factorization as one problem, and is based on looking for a prime factor for a given integer within a determined search space. If a factor is found within this space then the given integer is composite otherwise it is prime.

To define the searching space, we state the concept of absolute position for composite numbers of the form Z mod 6=-1, and we use this concept to define an infinite matrix space of absolute positions for composite numbers. In this structure or matrix space, a composite number is represented by its absolute position, and its location in the matrix space is defined by its prime factors. To determine the matrix space searching boundaries for a given integer we state and proof some theorems based on absolute position concept.

Based on the stated theory we present a deterministic primality testing and factorization algorithm by constructing a simple equation that   correlates the absolute position of the integer under testing and its prime factors.

This paper contributes to number theory efforts in introducing new concepts and approaches to develop algorithms that improve the complexity of primality testing and factorization algorithms.

This paper is organized as follows; in section 2 we define prime series and state the basic compositeness theorem for composite numbers of the form Z mod 6 =-1. In section 3 we develop and highlight a structure of those composites using the concept of absolute position. In section 4 we discuss the developed absolute positions structure. Based on this structure a preliminary algorithm for Primality testing and factorization was presented in section 5. Conclusions are given in section 6.

2   Prime Series

It is a well known fact that prime numbers falls either in R5={z: z mod 6 = 5, z $\in$ Z} or R1={z : z mod 6 =1, z $\in$ Z}. We call R5 and R1 prime series, where R5 and R1 represent integers of the for Z mod 6 =-1 and Z mod 6 =1 respectively. Thus R5 = {5, 11, 17, 23, 29, 35, 41, 47, .} and R1 = {1, 7, 13, 19, 25, 31, 37, 43, 49, ...}. To understand the nature of the composite numbers in R5, we state the following theorem.

Theorem (1)
For any integer Z $\in$ R5, then either Z is a prime or composite number. If Z is a composite number, then it either has the form Z= mn, where m $\in$ R5 and n $\in$ R1. Or Z has more than two factors, in which case, either Z has the form Z = $m_1 m_2 ..... m_i$, where $m_1, m_2, ..., m_i$ $\in$ R5 and i =3,5,7,,9 .., or it has the form Z= $m_1 m_2 ..... m_i . n_1 n_2 ...... n_j$, where $m_1, m_2, ..., m_i$ $\in$ R5 i=3,5,7,9,.., and $n_1, n_2, ..., n_j$ $\in$ R1 j=1,2,3,4,5....

Proof:
We only need to prove the theorem for compositeness.

(a) Suppose Z $\in$ R5 is a composite number that has two factors, then

$$Z=mn \rightarrow mn \ (mod \ 6) = 5 \rightarrow (((m \ mod \ 6) \ (n \ mod \ 6)) \ mod \ 6) =5 \qquad (1)$$

Since (m mod 6) and (n mod 6) is either 0,1,2,3,4 or 5,. (1) holds only if either (m mod 6) =5 and (n mod 6) =1 or (m mod 6) =1 and (n mod 6) =5. Therefore one factor (m or n) $\in$ R5 and the other factor $\in$ R1.

(b) If Z is a composite number with more than two factors, then Z can either be expressed as:

$$Z= m_1 m_2 ..... m_i, \text{ where } m_1, m2, ..., mi \in R5 \qquad (2)$$
$$Or$$
$$Z = m_1 m_2 ..... m_i . n_1 n_2 ...... n_j, \text{ where } m_1, m_2, ..., m_i \in R5 \text{ and } n_1, n_2, ..., n_j \in R1. \qquad (3)$$

Clearly (2) holds only when i=3,5,7,9,..., and (3) holds only when i=3,5,7,9,... and j=1,2,3,4,5,6,....

3 The Structure of Composite Numbers in R5

Based on theorem (1), each prime number in R5 generates a chain of composite numbers in R5 in arithmetic progression. The following Lemma defines chains generated by primes in R5.

Lemma (1)

If P is a prime in R5, then P generates the following chain of composites in R5:

$$Zp= \{ z = 6nP+P; n=1,2,3,4,...\} \tag{4}$$

Thus any composite number Z generated by P is given by:

$$Z = P(6n+1), \text{ where P is the prime generator, } n=1,2,3, \tag{5}$$

Table (1) shows part of the composite numbers matrix space generated by primes in R5.

Table 1. Matrix Space for Composite Numbers in R5

R5	5	11	17	23	29	35	41	...	R1
	35	77	119	161	203	245	287	...	7
	65	143	221	299	377	455	533	...	13
	95	209	323	437	551	665	779	...	19
	125	275	425	575	725	875	1025	...	25
	155	341	527	713	899	1085	1271	...	31
	:	:	:	:	:	:	:	:	:

Definition (1): We call the position of each number within the R5 series as an Absolute Position (AP) and for a given integer Z this position is calculated by the following equation:

$$AP(Z) = Z \text{ div } 6 \tag{6}$$

Thus AP (5) = 0.

Definition (2): We call the position of a composite number Z within its prime chain as a Relative Position (RP), and for a given number Z this position is calculated from (5) as:

$$AP(Z) = ((Z \text{ div } P) - 1) \text{ div } 6 \tag{7}$$

Obviously, all primes have RP=0. For example, to find the 15th composite number in chain 17, use (5) to calculate

$$Z= p (6n + 1) = 17 (6.15 + 1) = 17. 91 = 1547$$

Theorem (2)

The relationship between the Absolute Position (AP) and the Relative Position (RP) for a composite number Z generated by the prime P is given by:

$$AP(Z) = P * RP(Z) + (P \text{ div } 6) \qquad (8)$$

For example, using (8), the AP for the 15th composite number in chain 17 is:

$$AP = 15 * 17 + (17 \text{ div } 6) = 255 + 2 = 257$$

$$\text{Using (6), } AP = (1547 \text{ div } 6) = 257$$

4   The Structure of Absolute Positions for R5 Composite Numbers

The Absolute Positions for composite numbers in R5 are distributed along an infinite matrix space in a regular manner. Table (2) shows this matrix space.

Table 2. Distribution of Composite Number's Absolute Positions in R5

P	11	17	23	29	35	41	47	.	Q	A
AP	1	2	3	4	5	6	7	.		P
	12	19	26	33	40	47	54	.	7	1
	23	36	49	62	75	88	101	.	13	2
	34	53	72	91	110	129	148	.	19	3
	45	70	95	120	145	170	195	.	25	4
	56	87	118	149	180	211	242	.	31	5
	67	104	141	178	215	252	289	.	37	6
	78	121	164	207	250	293	336	.	43	7
	:	:	:	:	:	:	:	:	:	:

From the structure of Table (2), we note the following:

- The AP of the first composite number generated by prime P is given by : P + AP(P).
- The consecutive difference between adjacent column positions is P.
- The AP of the first composite number generated by prime Q is given by : Q + 5*AP(Q)
- The consecutive difference between adjacent row positions is Q.

The position of any entry in the matrix space can be denoted by X_{rc}, where r denotes the RP(X) row wise and c denotes the RP(X) column wise; For example X_{64} is the entry in row 6, column 4 of the absolute positions matrix, which is 141.

Now, if X is an AP in matrix space which is generated column wise by P and row wise by Q, then X satisfies the following two equations:

$$X = P * AP(Q) + AP(P) \qquad (9)$$

$$X = Q * AP(P) + 5\, AP(Q) \qquad (10)$$

For example the AP of the 7TH element generated by 17 which is the second element generated by 43 can be calculated from (9) as: $X = 17 * 7 + 2 = 119 + 2 = 121$, and calculated from (10) as: $X = 43 * 2 + 5*7 = 86 + 35 = 121$.

Now if we denote AP(P)=c and AP(Q)=r then (9) and (10) becomes respectively:

$$X = r (6c+5) + c \tag{11}$$

and

$$X = c(6r +1) + 5r \tag{12}$$

From (11) and (12) we get respectively:

$$(X- c) \bmod (6c + 5) = 0 \tag{13}$$

$$(X - 5r) \bmod (6r+1) = 0 \tag{14}$$

5   A Factorization and Primality Testing Algorithm

Given Z as an R5 integer, we can use (13) and (14) to scan the absolute positions matrix space vertically or/and horizontally, to verify whether AP(Z)=X is within the matrix space or not. To determine the search space limits we have to specify an initial value for c and r to represent the lower limit, and to use the fact that the first composite position generated by P (column wise) and Q (row wise) are P+AP(P)= (6c +5) + c and 5*AP(Q) = 5r respectively, as an upper limit.

Now if Z is composite, then its position in the matrix space is defined by the values of AP(P) =c and AP(Q)=r. And since one of the two factors for Z is more nearer to the initial value of c (the R5 factor) or r (the R1 factor), we need an algorithm to scan the search space vertically and horizontally. The following algorithm initialize c and r to 1, bounds the upper search limit to $((6c+5) + c < n)$ and scans the matrix space forwards vertically and horizontally simultaneously.

Algorithm

1.   Choose a number, Z *in R5*, you wish to factor
2.   Let n = Z div 6
3.   Is (n mod 5 = 0)
      - YES: Z is composite, the two factors are; f1= 5 and Z/f1.
      - NO? - continue to next step
4.   Let c= r = 1
5.   Let PrimalityFlag = 1.
6.   While $((6c+5) +c) < n)$
         a.   **Is $((n - c) \bmod (6*c + 5)) = 0$**
      - YES: Z is composite, the two factors are; f1=c * 6 +5 and Z/f1, PrimalityFlag=0, End.
      - NO: b.   **Is $(n - 5*r) \bmod (6*r + 1)) = 0$**
      - YES: Z is composite, the two factors are; f1=r * 6 +1 and Z/f, PrimalityFlag =0, End.
      - NO: increment c and r

7. Go back to step 6
8. Z is Prime.

The algorithm is a parallel algorithm since the searching space $[c=1, ((6c+5) + c)) < n)]$ can be divided to disjoint intervals as value of n is known.

5.1   Algorithm Performance

There are two major performance degradation problems in the above algorithm. The *first* problem is when the column and row variables c and r takes a value that they generates before as a composite absolute position, (for example, when c takes the values 5, 10, 15, 20, ...which are generated previously by c=0, or when c takes the values 12,23,34,45, ...which are values generated previously by c=1, and so on, or when r takes the values 10,23, 36, 49, ... which are values generated previously by r=2, and so on), which makes the algorithm repeat a non-significant tests.

The *second* problem is the low initial value for c and r when Z is a very large prime number, or a composite number with very large factors.

The first performance problem is due to the fact that each prime in R5 generates a chain of composite numbers in R5. Although it is known that the distance between the prime P and its offspring composite numbers is 6P (for example the composites generated by c=0 are c=5,10,15,.... and the composites generated by c=1 are c=12,23,34, ... and so on) generally c=i generates c= i + k (6i+5) , k=1,2,3,4,.....,

To make the algorithm recognizing all previous prime values the column generator variable P takes in order to avoid non significant tests, this will make the algorithm very complex in terms of storage and speed. Therefore for simplicity and hence performance wise it is better to omit this problem.

To deal with the second problem of low initial values for c and r, we state the following theorem.

Theorem (3)
Let Z be an R5 large composite number with AP (Z) =X. The suitable initial value for column and row variables c and r (most nearer values to the expected column or row value that generates Z) is c=r= sqrt(X/6).
Proof:
From (11) and (12) we have X= 6rc+5r +c. This implies that $X > 6rc$. Now if we assume c=r (i.e we will initialize c and r to the same value) then $X > 6 c^2$ → $X/6 > c^2$ → $c < sqrt (X/6)$.

Based on the above theorem it follows that one of Z factors will be generated by a c value greater than the c initial value while the second factor is generated by a c value less than the initial value.

Since the square root of any composite integer number Z leans towards the smallest factor, it is always more efficient to locate the smallest factor by scanning the absolute positions matrix space backwards rather than forwards. Also since the smallest factor may either be in R5 or R1, for a deterministic reliable algorithm, the scanning should be done simultaneously column and row wise.

Based on theorem (3), we introduce the following algorithm.

Deterministic Primality Testing and Factorization Algorithm

1. Choose a number, Z *in R5*, you wish to factor
2. Let n = Z div 6
3. Is (n mod 5 = 0)
    a. YES: Z is composite, the two factors are; f1= 5 and Z/f1.
    b. NO? - continue to next step
4. Let c= r = sqrt(n/6)
5. Let PrimalityFlag = 1.
6. While (c >0)
    a. **Is ((n - c) mod (6*c + 5)) = 0**
        o YES: Z is composite, the two factors are; f1=c * 6 +5 and Z/f1. PrimalityFlag=0, End.
        o NO:
    b. **Is (n - 5*r)mod (6*r + 1)) = 0**
        o YES: Z is composite, the two factors are; f1=r * 6 +1 and Z/f1. PrimalityFlag=0, End.
        o NO: decrement c and r
7. Go back to step 6
8. Z is Prime.

The above algorithm works backwards, which will performs poorly if one of the two factors is much smaller than the other, in such case the same algorithm with initial value of 1 for r and c and forwarding scanning will performs better.

5.1.1 Algorithm Complexity and Testing Results
The worst case of the algorithm is when N is prime, in such case the while loop is executed $((N/6^2)$ ½) times. The best case is when Z is composite with factors f1 and f2 are twins, in such case the while loop executed only once O(1). The average case is when Z is composite and f1 and f2 are not twins, is this case the while loop executed in average O $((N/6^2)$ ½ /2).

It is obvious that the performance of this algorithms depends on the distant (D) between the absolute positions of the prime generators of the composite factors f1 1nd f2. If we assume that f1 and f2 are generated by P and Q with AP(P)=c and AP(Q)=r respectively and f1 < f2 then   D= r –c. The exact no of iterations required to fix f1 is $(((N/6^2)$ ½) – c).

5.1.2 Testing
We test our algorithm against the well known factoring algorithms, Fermat, Pollard p-1, Pollard-Roh, and Shanks algorithm. All tests were run on an Intel Pentium 4 3.20 GHz processor with 1GB of RAM. Windows XP Service Pack 2 was the host operating system. Version 1.6.0_07 of the Java Runtime Environment was used. Test programs were executed using a command line invocation of the Java client virtual machine. Java Development Kit version 1.6.0_07 was used for compiling test code. Table (3) shows the testing results. The developed algorithm performs when the factors are too close.

Table 3. Comparison Between the Developed Algorithm and Known Algorithms

Length in bits	Number	Factors	Fermat	Shanks	Pollard p-1	Pollard rho	Developed Algorithm
32	2213186951	63709 34739	62	31	0	0	0
40	614278415189	1014131 605719	608	78	16	31	15
48	141053907833849	12746687 11065927	811	203	47	31	16
48	103566076470137	10304911 10050167	47	218	31	31	0
60	807759537987786023	784133621 1030129963	319707	1841	545923	218	26005
64	11002930366353704069	3267000013 3367900313	13790	7361	7004	592	11201
64	15273041663564843243	3990032597 3827798719	31216	9875	3759	718	17955
64	15920357810903658149	3990032597 3990032017	0	0	120385	702	0
95	31571389633921701333 404835491	167102507056669 188934266696639	Too large	Too large	266979	28505 9	Too large

6   Conclusion

The developed algorithm utilizes a new approach for developing primality testing and factorization algorithms that gives new sights to the factorization and primality testing problems. The parallel characteristic of the developed algorithm and its dependency on a matrix search algorithm makes it competent for a fast performance on refinements.

The major contributions of the developed theory and algorithm are simplicity and ease of implementation, parallelism, and high speed when integer factors are relatively close.

References

1. Diffie, W., Hellman, M.E.: New directions in cryptography. IEEE Trans. Inform. Theory 22(6), 644–654 (1976)
2. Brent, R.P.: Some parallel algorithms for integer factorization. In: Amestoy, P.R., Berger, P., Daydé, M., Duff, I.S., Frayssé, V., Giraud, L., Ruiz, D. (eds.) Euro-Par 1999. LNCS, vol. 1685, pp. 1–22. Springer, Heidelberg (1999)
3. Schoof, R.J.: Quadratic fields and factorization. In: van de Lune, J. (ed.) Studieweek Getaltheorie en Computers, Amsterdam. Math. Centrum, pp. 165–206 (1980)
4. Shanks, D.: Class number, a theory of factorization, and genera. In: Proc. Symp. Pure Math. 20, American Math. Soc., pp. 415–440 (1971)
5. Morrison, M.A., Brillhart, J.: A method of factorization and the factorization of F7. Mathematics of Computation 29, 183–205 (1975)

6. Pomerance, C.: Analysis and comparison of some integer factoring algorithms. In: Lenstra Jr., H.W., Tijdeman, R. (eds.) Computational Methods in Number Theory, Amsterdam. Math. Centrum Tract, vol. 154, pp. 89–139 (1982)
7. Pollard, J.M.: A Monte Carlo method for factorization. BIT 15, 331–334 (1975)
8. Lehman, R.S.: Factoring large integers. Mathematics of Computation 28, 637–646 (1974)
9. Voorhoeve, M.: Factorization. In: van de Lune, J. (ed.) Studieweek Getaltheorie en Computers, Amsterdam. Math. Centrum, pp. 61–68 (1980)
10. Junod, P.: Cryptographic Secure Pseudo-Random Bits Generation: The Blum-Blum-Shub Generator (August 1999), http://www.win.tue.nl/~henkvt/boneh-bbs.pdf
11. Lenstra Jr., H.W.: Factoring integers with elliptic curves. Ann. of Math. 126(2), 649–673 (1987)
12. General number field sieve. From Wikipedia, an online encyclopedia, http://en.wikipedia.org/wiki/GNFS
13. Wesstein, E.W.: RSA Encryption. From Mathworld, an online encyclopedia, http://mathworld.wolfram.com/RSAEncryption.html
14. Brent, R.P.: Some integer factorization algorithms using elliptic curves. Australian Computer Science Communications 8, 149–163 (1986)
15. Housley, et al.: RFC 2459: Internet X.509 Public Key Infrastructure Certificate and CRL Profile, http://www.faqs.org/rfcs/rfc2459.html

Non-interactive Deniable Authentication Protocol Using Generalized ECDSA Signature Scheme

Jayaprakash Kar

Internet & e-Security, Department of Information Technology,
Al Musanna College of Technology, Sultanate of Oman
jayaprakashkar@yahoo.com

Abstract. Deniable authentication protocol enables a receiver to identify the true source of a given message, but not to prove the identity of the sender to a third party. This property is very useful for providing secure negotiation over the Internet. This paper describes a secure non-interactive deniable authentication protocol using ECDSA signature scheme. The security of the protocol is based on difficulty of breaking Elliptic Curve Discrete Logarithm Problem. It can be implemented in low power and small processor mobile devices such as smart card, PDA etc which work in low power and small processor.

Keywords: deniable authentication, ECDLP, non-interactive, ECDSA.

1 Introduction

Nowadays, authentication had emerged to be an essential communication process. In fact, the aim of this process is to assure the receiver by verifying the digital identity of the sender, especially when communicating via an insecure electronic channel. Authentication can be realized by the use of digital signature in which the signature (signers private key) is tied to the signer as well as the message being signed. This digital signature can later be verified easily by using the signer's public key. Hence, the signer will not be able to deny his participation in this communication. Generally, this notion is known as non-repudiation. However, under certain circumstances such as electronic voting system, online shopping and negotiation over the Internet, the non-repudiation property is undesirable. It is important to note that in these applications, the sender's identity should be revealed only to the intended receiver. Therefore, a significant requirement for the protocol is to enable a receiver to identify the source of a given message, and at the same time, unable to convince to a third party on the identity of the sender even if the receiver reveal his own secret key to the third party. This protocol is known as deniable authentication protocol.

2 Background

In this section we brief overview of prime field, Elliptic Curve over that field and Elliptic Curve Discrete Logarithm Problem.

T.-h. Kim et al. (Eds.): ISA 2011, CCIS 200, pp. 166–176, 2011.

2.1   The Finite Field $\mathbb{F}_p$

Let p be a prime number. The finite field F_p is comprised of the set of integers $0, 1, 2, \ldots p - 1$ with the following arithmetic operations [12] [13] [14]:

- Addition: If $a, b \in \mathbb{F}_p$, then $a + b = r$, where r is the remainder when $a + b$ is divided by p and $0 \leq r \leq p - 1$. This is known as addition modulo p.
- Multiplication: If $a, b \in \mathbb{F}_p$, then $a.b = s$, where s is the remainder when $a.b$ is divided by p and $0 \leq s \leq p - 1$. This is known as multiplication modulo p.
- Inversion: If a is a non-zero element in $\mathbb{F}_p$, the inverse of a modulo p, denoted a^{-1}, is the unique integer $c \in \mathbb{F}_p$ for which $a.c = 1$.

2.2   Elliptic Curve over $\mathbb{F}_p$

Let $p \geq 3$ be a prime number. Let $a, b \in F_p$ be such that $4a^3 + 27b^2 \neq 0$ in $\mathbb{F}_p$. An elliptic curve E over $\mathbb{F}_p$ defined by the parameters a and b is the set of all solutions $(x, y), x, y \in \mathbb{F}_p$, to the equation $y^2 = x^3 + ax + b$, together with an extra point $\mathcal{O}$, the point at infinity. The set of points $E(\mathbb{F}_p)$ forms a Abelian group with the following addition rules [16]:

1. Identity : $P + \mathcal{O} = \mathcal{O} + \mathcal{P} = \mathcal{P}$, for all $P \in E(\mathbb{F}_p)$
2. Negative : if $P(x, y) \in E(\mathbb{F}_p)$ then $(x, y) + (x, -y) = \mathcal{O}$, The point $(x, -y)$ is dented as $-P$ called negative of P.
3. Point addition: Let $P((x_1, y_1), Q(x_2, y_2)) \in E(\mathbb{F}_p)$,then $P + Q = R \in E(\mathbb{F}_p)$ and coordinate $(x_3, y_3)$of R is given by $x_3 = \lambda^2 - x_1 - x_2$ and $y_3 = \lambda(x_1 - x_3) - y_1$ where $\lambda = \frac{y_2 - y_1}{x_2 - x_1}$
4. Point doubling : Let $P(x_1, y_1) \in E(\mathbb{F}_p)$ where $P \neq -P$ then $2P = (x_3, y_3)$ where $x_3 = (\frac{3x_1^2 + a}{2y_1})^2 - 2x_1$ and $y_3 = (\frac{3x_1^2 + a}{2y_1})(x_1 - x_3) - y_1$

2.3   Elliptic Curve Discrete Logarithm Problem (ECDLP)

In 1985, Neal Koblitz and Victor Miller independently proposed the concepts of ECC. It is based on the Discrete Logarithm Problem (DLP) in a group defined by points on Elliptic Curve over a finite field.

Definition 1. *Given an elliptic curve E defined over a finite field $\mathbb{F}_p$, a point $P \in E(\mathbb{F}_p)$ of order n, and a point $Q \in < P >$, find the integer $l \in [0, n - 1]$ such that $Q = lP$. The integer l is called discrete logarithm of Q to base P, denoted $l = log_p Q$.*

3   Elliptic Curve Digital Signature Algorithm

The Elliptic Curve Digital Signature Algorithm (ECDSA) is the elliptic curve analogue of the Digital Signature Algorithm (DSA), and is under consideration for standardization by the ANSI X9 committee. Unlike the normal discrete logarithm problem and the integer factorization problem, the elliptic curve discrete logarithm problem has no sub-exponential time algorithm. For this reason, the strength-per key-bit is substantially greater in an algorithm that uses elliptic curves.

3.1 ECDSA Signature Generation and Verification

This section describes the procedure for generating and verifying signature using the ECDSA. To sign a message m, an entity A having the key pair (d, Q) executes the following steps.

ECDSA Signature Generation

1. Select a random or pseudorandom integer $k \in [1, n - 1]$.
2. Compute $k \cdot P = (x_1, y_1)$ and convert x_1 to an integer $\bar{x}_1$.
3. Compute $r = x_1 \pmod{n}$. If $r = 0$ then go to step 1.
4. Compute $k^{-1} \pmod{n}$.
5. Compute SHA-1(m) and convert to the bit string e.
6. Compute $s = k^{-1}(e + dr) \pmod{n}$. If $s = 0$ then go to step 1.
7. A's signature for the message m is the pair (r, s).

ECDSA Signature Verification

1. Verify r and s are integers in the interval $[1, n - 1]$.
2. Compute SHA-1(m) and convert the bit string to an integer e.
3. Compute $\beta = s^{-1} \pmod{n}$.
4. Compute $u_1 = e\beta \pmod{n}$ and $u_2 = r\beta \pmod{n}$.
5. Compute $R = u_1 \cdot P + u_2 \cdot Q$.
6. If $R = \mathcal{O}$, then reject the signature. Otherwise, convert the x-coordinate x_1 of R to an integer $\bar{x}_1$, and compute $v = \bar{x}_1 \pmod{n}$
7. Accept the signature if and only if $v = r$.

4 Preliminaries

4.1 Notations

We first introduce common notations used in this paper as follows.

- p is the order of underlying finite field;
- $\mathbb{F}_p$ is the underlying finite field of order p
- E is an an elliptic curve defined on finite field $\mathbb{F}_p$ with large order.
- G is the group of elliptic curve points on E.
- P is a point in $E(\mathbb{F}_p)$ with order n , where n is a large prime number.
- $\mathcal{H}()$ is a secure one-way hash function which is collision resistant.
- $\|$ denotes concatenation operation between two bit stings.
- Let S denotes be the Sender.
- Let R denotes be the Receiver.
- Public and Private key pair of the Sender S is (d_s, Q_s), where $Q_s = d_s \cdot P$.
- Public and Private key pair of Receiver R is (d_r, Q_r), where $Q_r = d_r \cdot P$.

5   Relatated Works

In 1998, Dwork et al. [3] developed a notable deniable authentication protocol based on the concurrent zero-knowledge proof, however the protocol requires a timing constraint and the proof zero-knowledge is subject to a time delay in the authentication process. Auman and Rabin [17] proposed some other deniable authentication protocols based on the factoring problem. In 2001, Deng et al. [9] also proposed two deniable authentication protocols based on the factoring and the discrete logarithm problem respectively.

In the past several years, numerous deniable authentication protocols have been proposed but many of them have also been proven to be vulnerable to various cryptanalytic attacks [5] [10] [11] . The concept of deniable authentication protocol was initially introduced by Dwork et al. [3], which is based on the concurrent zero knowledge proof. However, this scheme requires a timing constraint. Not only that, the proof of knowledge is also time-consuming [7]. Another notable scheme which was developed by Aumann and Rabin [1] is based on the intractability of the factoring problem, in which a set of public data is needed to authenticate one bit of a given message. Few years later, Deng et al. [7] have proposed two deniable authentication schemes based on Aumaan and Rabins scheme. The proposed schemes are based on the intractability of the factoring problem and the logarithm problem. However, in 2006, Zhu et al. [11] have successfully demonstrated the Man-in-the-Middle attack against Aumann and Rabins scheme and this indirectly results in an insecure implementation of Deng et al.s schemes. In 2003, Boyd and Mao [2]have proposed another two deniable authenticated key establishment for Internet protocols based on elliptic curve cryptography. These schemes are believed to be able to solute the complexity of computation and appear to be more efficient than others but their vulnerability to Key Compromise Impersonation (KCI) attack has been exploited by Chou et al. [4] in 2005. Besides that, Fan et al.have proposed a simple deniable authentication protocol based on Diffie-Hellman key distribution protocol in 2002. Unfortunately, in 2005, Yoon et al. [10] have pointed out that their protocol suffers from the intruder masquerading attack and subsequently proposed their enhanced deniable authentication protocol based on Fan et al.s scheme.

6   Model of Deniable Authentication Protocol

A deniable authentication protocol (DAP) consists of the following four algorithms: **Setup, Extract, Send** and **Receive**. We describe the functions of each as follows [6].

- **Setup:** On input of the security parameter 1^k the PKG (Private Key Generator) uses this algorithm to produce a pair $(params, master - key)$, where *params* are the global public parameters for the system and master-key is the master secret key kept secretly by PKG. We assume that *params* are publicly known so that we do not need to explicitly provide them as input to other algorithms.

- **Extract:** On input of an identity i and the master secret key master-key, the PKG uses this algorithm to compute a public-secret key pair (pk_i, sk_i) corresponding to i.
- **Send:** The sender S uses this algorithm with input (m, sk_S, pk_R) to output a deniable authentication message $\tilde{m}$, where pk_R is the public key of the receiver R.
- **Receive:** The receiver R uses this algorithm with input $(\tilde{m}, m, pk_S, pk_R)$ to output 1 if the deniable authentication message $\tilde{m}$ is valid or 0 otherwise. The above algorithms must have the following consistency requirement. If

$$\tilde{m} \leftarrow \textbf{Send}(m, sk_S, pk_R)$$

then we must have $1 \leftarrow \textbf{Receive}(\tilde{m}, m, pk_S, pk_R)$.

7   Security Model

Security Notions In this subsection describes about security notions of deniable authentication protocol. We first recall the usual security notion: the unforgeability against chosen message attacks (Goldwasser et al., 1988), then we consider another security notion: the deniablity of deniable authentication protocol.

Player. Let $P = \{\mathcal{P}_0, \mathcal{P}_1, \dots \mathcal{P}_n\}$ be a set of players who may be included in the system. Each player $\mathcal{P}_i \in P$ get his public-secret key pair (pk_i, sk_i) by providing his identity i to the **Extract** algorithm. A player $\mathcal{P}_i \in P$ is said to be fresh if $\mathcal{P}_i$'s secret key sk_i has not been revealed by an adversary; while if $\mathcal{P}_i$s secret key sk_i has been revealed, $\mathcal{P}_i$ is then said to be corrupted. With regard of the unforgeability against chosen-message attacks, we define the security notion via the following game played by a challenger and an adversary.

[**Game 1**]

- Initial: The challenger runs Setup to produce a pair $(params, master-key)$, gives the resulting $params$ to the adversary and keeps the master-key secretly.
- Probing: The challenger is probed by the adversary who makes the following queries.
- Extract: The challenger first sets $\mathcal{P}_0, \mathcal{P}_1$ to be fresh players, which means that the adversary is not allowed to make Extract query on $\mathcal{P}_0$ or $\mathcal{P}_1$. Then, when the adversary submits an identity i of player $\mathcal{P}_i, (i = 0, 1)$, to the challenger. The challenger responds with the public-secret key pair (pk_i, sk_i) corresponding to i to the adversary.
- Send: The adversary submits the requests of deniable authentication messages between $\mathcal{P}_0$ and $\mathcal{P}_0$. The challenger responds with deniable authentication messages with respect to $\mathcal{P}_0$ (resp. $\mathcal{P}_1$) to $\mathcal{P}_1$ (resp $\mathcal{P}_0$).
- Forging: Eventually, the adversary outputs a valid forgery $\tilde{m}$ between $\mathcal{P}_0$ and $\mathcal{P}_1$. If the valid forgery $\tilde{m}$ was not the output of a Send query made during the game, we say the adversary wins the game.

Definition 2. (Unforgeability). *Let A denote an adversary that plays the game above. If the quantity $Adv_{DAP}^{UF}[A] = Pr[Awins]$ is negligible we say that the deniable authentication protocol in question is existentially unforgeable against adaptive chosen-message attacks.*

To capture the property of deniablity of deniable authentication protocol, we consider the following game run by a challenger.

[Game 2]

- Initial: Let $\mathcal{P}_0$ and $\mathcal{P}_1$ be two honest players that follow the deniable authentication protocol, and let $\mathcal{D}$ be the distinguisher that is involved in the game with $\mathcal{P}_0$ and $\mathcal{P}_0$.
- Challenging: The distinguisher $\mathcal{D}$ submits a message $m \in \{0,1\}^*$ to the challenger. The challenger first randomly chooses a bit $b' \in \{0,1\}^*$, then invokes the player P_b to make a deniable authentication message $\tilde{m}$ on m between $\mathcal{P}_0$ and $\mathcal{P}_1$. In the end, the challenger returns $\tilde{m}$ to the distinguisher $\mathcal{D}$.
- Guessing: The distinguisher $\mathcal{D}$ returns a bit $b \in \{0,1\}^*$. We say that the distinguisher $\mathcal{D}$ wins the game if $b = b'$.

Definition 3. (Deniablity). *Let D denote the distinguisher that is involved the game above. If the quantity $Adv_{DAP}^{DN}[D] = |Pr[b = b'] - \frac{1}{2}|$ is negligible we say that deniable authentication protocol in question is deniable.*

8 Proposed Protocol

Security of the proposed is based on the difficulty of breaking of ECDLP problem. This will be achieving the following security properties.

- **Deniable authentication:** The intended receiver can identify the source of a given message, but cannot prove the source to any third party.
- **Authentication:** During the protocol execution, the sender and the intended receiver can authentication each other.
- **Confidentiality:** Any outside adversary has no ability to gain the deniable authentication message from the transmitted transcripts.
- **Completeness:** If a sender and a receiver follows the protocol to negotiate with each other, the receiver can identify the source of message.

The protocol involves two entities : a sender S and a intended receiver R. It follows the followings steps.

- **Setup** Let $\mathcal{H} : \{0,1\}^* \to \{0,1\}^l$ be a secure cryptographic hash function which is of collision free. Let E be the elliptic curve define over the prime field $\mathbb{F}_p$. The key pair of both Sender S and receiver are (d_s, Q_s) and (d_r, Q_r) respectively.
- **Extract** Here S executes the the following steps
  - Choose a random integer $k \in [1, n-1]$

- Computes

$$U = k \cdot P \tag{1}$$

$$r = x_1 \bmod n \tag{2}$$

where $x_1 = (U)_x$, x- coordinate of the point $U \in E(\mathbb{F}_p)$

$$\gamma = \mathcal{H}(M)d_s + rk \tag{3}$$

$$\alpha_1 = \gamma \cdot Q_r \tag{4}$$

$$MAC = \mathcal{H}(\alpha_1 \| M) \tag{5}$$

Authentication message is $\psi = (U, MAC, M)$
- **Send** $\psi = (U, MAC, M)$ to R
- **Receive** in this phase R executes the following steps.
  - Computes

$$r = x_1 \bmod n, \text{ Where } x_1 = (U)_x$$

$$\alpha_2 = \{\mathcal{H}(M) \cdot Q_s + r \cdot U\} \cdot d_r \tag{6}$$

  - Verify whether $\mathcal{H}(\alpha_2 \| M) = MAC$. If valid, accepts M otherwise reject.

The protocol is illustrated in the following fig.

Sender S	Receiver R
Select random number $d_s \in [1, n-1]$ Computes $Q_s = d_s \cdot P$ Select $k \in [1, n-1]$ Computes the following $U = k \cdot P$ $r = x_1 \bmod n$ $\gamma = \mathcal{H}(M)d_s + rk$ $\alpha_1 = \gamma \cdot Q_r$ $MAC = \mathcal{H}(\alpha_1 \| M)$	
$\xrightarrow{\quad \psi \quad}$	
	Select random number $d_r \in [1, n-1]$ $Q_r = d_r \cdot P$ Compute $\alpha_2 = \{\mathcal{H}(M) \cdot Q_s + r \cdot U\} \cdot d_r$ Verify whether $\mathcal{H}(\alpha_2 \| M) = MAC$ accept M otherwise reject

9   Correctness

Theorem 1. *If $\psi = (U, MAC, M)$ is a authentication message produced by the Sender S honestly, then the recipient R will always accept it.*

Proof: The proposed protocol satisfies the property of correctness. In effect, if the deniable authentication message ψ is correctly generated, then $\alpha_1 = \alpha_2$

$$\alpha_2 = \{\mathcal{H}(M) \cdot Q_s + r \cdot U\} \cdot d_r$$
$$= \{\mathcal{H}(M)d_s \cdot P + rk \cdot P\}d_r$$
$$= \mathcal{H}(M)d_s \cdot Pd_r + rd_r k \cdot P$$
$$= \mathcal{H}(M)d_s \cdot Q_r + rkQ_r$$
$$= \{\mathcal{H}(M)d_s + rk\} \cdot Q_r$$
$$= \gamma \cdot Q_r = \alpha_1$$

10   Security Analysis

In this section, we analyze the security of our proposed deniable authentication protocol . The security of our protocol is based on the difficulty of breaking of Elliptic Curve Discrete Logarithms. The security of the proposed protocol is analyzed and illustrated a model for the protocol.

Theorem 2. *The proposed Protocol achieves the authentication between the sender and the intended receiver.*

Proof : In our proposed protocol, if the receiver accepts the authentication message ψ, receiver R can always identify the source of the message. If an adversary wants impersonate the sender S, he has to construct the α_2. If the adversary tries to compute α_2 he has to know the sender's private key d_s for that it needs to solve ECDLP.   □

Definition 4. *Informally, a deniable authentication protocol is said to achieve the property of confidentiality, if there is no polynomial time algorithm that can distinguish the transcripts of two distinct messages.*

Theorem 3. *The proposed protocol achieves the property of confidentiality provided that the ECDLP is hard in $E(\mathbb{F}_p)$.*

Proof : $MAC = (\alpha_1 \| M)$ is actually a hashed cipher text [18]. Hashed based encryption is semantically secure in the random oracle model provided ECDLPis hard. As a result, the proposed protocol can achieves the confidentiality.   □

Theorem 4. *The proposed protocol also achieves the property of deniability.*

Proof : To prove that the proposed protocol has deniable property, first we should prove that it enables an intended receiver R to identify the source of the given message M and can not able to prove the source of message to the third party.

Relationship between U and MAC for a given message M can be verified only by knowing α_1. When M and R are given, α_1 can be derived from Eq.(4)

or (6). Therefore, both the sender with the knowledge of d_s and the receiver with knowledge of d_r have the same ability to generate (U, MAC) for a given message M. Obviously, it is difficult to verify whether the message was send by the sender or forged by the receiver, so the receiver can only identify the source of message but can not prove the source of message to the third party.   □

Also we can prove considering the security model describe in section-5. Let us consider a distinguisher $\mathcal{D}$ and two honest players $\mathcal{P}_0$ and $\mathcal{P}_1$ involved in **Game 2**. The distinguisher $\mathcal{D}$ first submits a message $m \in \{0,1\}^*$ to the challenger. Then, the challenger chooses a bit $b \in \{0,1\}$ uniformly at random, and invokes the player $\mathcal{P}_b$ to make a deniable authentication message (U_b, MAC_b) on M between $\mathcal{P}_0$ and $\mathcal{P}_1$. In the end, the challenger returns $\psi = (U_b, MAC_b, M)$ to the distinguisher $\mathcal{D}$. Since both $\mathcal{P}_0$ and $\mathcal{P}_1$ can generate a valid deniable authentication message $\psi = (U, MAC, M)$, which can pass the verification equation, in an indistinguishable way, when $\mathcal{D}$ returns the guessed value b, we can sure that the probability $\Pr[b = b']$ is $\frac{1}{2}$, and the quantity $Adv_{DAP}^{DN}[D] = |Pr[b = b'] - \frac{1}{2}| = |\frac{1}{2} - \frac{1}{2}| = 0$ Based upon the analysis above, we can conclude that the proposed protocol can achieve the deniable authentication.   □

Theorem 5. *The Protocol authenticates the source of the message.*

Proof: If someone proves MAC to R, he must be S. Since from Eq.(5), to computes MAC, he has to calculate $\alpha_1 = \gamma \cdot Q_r$, for that he needs to find γ i.e nothing but solving of ECDLP problem. If an adversary gets all the information Q_r in **Extract** phase, he can not compute the session key α_1. Hence the protocol authenticates the sources of message.   □

Definition 5. Secure against Man-in-the-middle *An authentication protocol is secure against an Man-in-the-middle, if Man-in-the-middle can not establish any session key with either the sender or the receiver. This is also called forgery attack.*

Theorem 6. *The proposed protocol is secure with respect to the man-in-the-middle (MIA) attack.*

Proof: Since the session key $\alpha_2 = \{\mathcal{H}(M) \cdot Q_s + r \cdot U\} \cdot d_r = \gamma \cdot Q_r = \alpha_1$, only an attacker who has the ability to create γ can forge valid deniable authentication message. However γ can be computed by Eq.(3). No one can forge γ without knowing the private key of S i.e d_s. Therefore it is resistant against forgery attack.   □

Theorem 7. *(Completeness).If a sender and a receiver follows the protocol to negotiate with each other, the receiver can identify the source of message.*

Proof : From Theorem 1, it can be seen that the sender and the receiver share the same session secret key $\alpha_1 = \alpha_2$. Hence the receiver can identify the source of message M according to $\mathcal{H}(\alpha_1 \| M) = \mathcal{H}(\alpha_2 \| M)$.   □

Theorem 8. *A compromised session secret does not affect the security of the proposed protocol.*

Proof: The session secret can be derived from Since the session key $\alpha_2 = \{\mathcal{H}(M)\cdot Q_s + r\cdot U\}\cdot d_r = \gamma\cdot Q_r = \alpha_1$, where a random number k is chosen independently for each session. If an attacker wants to forge the deniable information with the forged message $\tilde{M}$ by using the compromised session secret α_1, the receiver will derive a different session secret from the forged information. This is because the message and its corresponding session secret are interdependent. To solve this problem, the session secret for each round must be independent. This has been realized in our protocol which as well guarantees the underlying signature scheme as shown in Eq. (3). Therefore, a compromised session secret does not affect the security of other sessions. □

11   Conclusion

The proposed protocol is an non-interactive protocol where ECDSA signature scheme has been used. The security of the proposed protocol is based on difficulty of breaking the Elliptic Curve Discrete Logarithm Problem. It archives deniable authentication confidentiality and completeness. Also it is resistant against Man-in-Middle attack. It can be easy to implemented in mobile devices such as PDA, smart card etc. Since the protocol is based on the elliptic curve cryptography (ECC) and thus it has high security complexity with short key size.

References

1. Aumann, Y., Rabin, M.O.: Efficient Deniable Authentication of Long Messages. In: Int. Conf. on Theoretical Computer Science in Honour of Professor Manuel Blum's 60th Birthday (1998), http://www.cs.cityu.edu.hk/dept/video.html
2. Boyd, C., Mao, W., Paterson, K.G.: Deniable authenticated key establishment for Internet protocols. In: 11th International Workshop on Security Protocols, Cambridge (UK) (April 2003)
3. Dwork, C., Naor, M., Sahai, A.: Concurrent zero-knowledge. In: Proc. 30th ACM STOC 1998, Dallas TX, USA, pp. 409–418 (1998)
4. Chou, J.S., Chen, Y.L., Huang, J.C.: A ID-Based Deniable Authentication Protocol on pairings. Cryptology ePrint Archive: Report (335) (2006)
5. Chou, J.S., Chen, Y.L., Yang, M.D.: Weaknesses of the Boyd-Mao Deniable Authenticated key Establishment for Internet Protocols. Cryptology ePrint Archive: Report (451) (2005)
6. Kar, J.P., Majhi, B.: A Novel Deniable Authentication Protocol based on Diffie-Hellman Algorithm using Pairing techniques. In: ACM International Conference on Communication, Computing and Security (ICCCS 2011), India, pp. 493–498 (2011)
7. Deng, X., Lee, Lee, C.H., Zhu, H.: Deniable authentication protocols. IEEE Proc. Comput. Digit. Tech. 148(2), 101–104 (2001)
8. Dwork, C., Naor, M., Sahai, A.: Concurrent zero-knowledge. In: Proc. 30th ACM STOC 1998, Dallas TX, USA, pp. 409–418 (1998)
9. Deng, X., Lee, C.H., Zhu, H.: Deniable authentication protocols. IEE Proceedings. Computers and Digital Techniques 148, 101–104 (2001)

10. Yoon, E.J., Ryu, E.K., Yoo, K.Y.: Improvement of Fan et al.'s Deniable Authentication Protocol based on Diffie-Hellman Algorithm. Applied Mathematics and Computation 167(1), 274–280 (2005)
11. Zhu, R.W., Wong, D.S., Lee, C.H.: Cryptanalysis of a Suite of Deniable Authentication Protocols. IEEE Communication Letter 10(6), 504–506 (2006)
12. Koblitz, N.: A course in Number Theory and Cryptography, 2nd edn. Springer, Heidelberg (1994)
13. Rosen, K.H.: Elementary Number Theory in Science and Communication, 2nd edn. Springer, Berlin (1986)
14. Menezes, A., Van Oorschot, P.C., Vanstone, S.A.: Handbook of applied cryptography. CRC Press, Boca Raton (1997)
15. Hankerson, D., Menezes, A., Vanstone, S.: Guide to Elliptic Curve Cryptography. Springer, Heidelberg (2004)
16. Certicom ECC Challenge and The Elliptic Curve Cryptosystem, http://www.certicom.com/index.php
17. Aumann, Y., Rabin, M.: Authentication, enhanced security and error correcting codes. In: Krawczyk, H. (ed.) CRYPTO 1998. LNCS, vol. 1462, pp. 299–303. Springer, Heidelberg (1998)
18. Shoup, V.: Sequences of games: a tool for taming complexity in security proofs. In: Cryptology ePrint Archive: Report 2004/332, http://eprint.iacr.org/2004/332

Lower Bounds for Interpolating Polynomials for Square Roots of the Elliptic Curve Discrete Logarithm*

Gerasimos C. Meletiou[1], Yannis C. Stamatiou[2,3], and Apostolos Tsiakalos[2]

[1] A.T.E.I. of Epirus, P.O. Box 110, GR 47100, Arta, Greece
gmelet@teiep.gr
[2] Department of Mathematics, University of Ioannina, GR 45110, Ioannina, Greece
istamat@cc.uoi.gr, aptsiakalos@hotmail.com
[3] Research Academic Computer Technology Institute, University of Patras,
N. Kazantzaki, Rio, Patras, GR 26504, Greece

Abstract. In this paper we derive lower bounds for the degree of polynomials that approximate the square root of the discrete logarithm for Elliptic Curves with orders of various specific types. These bounds can serve as evidence for the difficulty in the computation of the square root of discrete logarithms for such elliptic curves, with properly chosen parameters that result in the curve having order of any of types studied in this paper. The techniques are potentially applicable to elliptic curves of order of any specific, allowable (by Hasse's bounds), order type that is of interest for the application in hand.

1 Introduction

Elliptic Curve (EC) cryptography has proven to be an attractive alternative for building fast and secure public key cryptosystems. Elliptic curves give rise to algebraic structures that offer a number of distinct advantages (smaller key sizes and highest strength per bit) over more customary algebraic structures used in various cryptographic applications (e.g., RSA). The use of smaller parameters for a given level of cryptographic strength make them suitable for implementations on hardware devices of limited resources (e.g., memory, computing speed, bandwidth, etc).

One of the fundamental problems in EC cryptography is the generation of "good", i.e. cryptographically secure, ECs over (mainly) prime fields, suitable for use in various cryptographic applications. A typical requirement of all such applications is that the *order* of the EC (number of elements in the algebraic structure induced by the EC) possesses certain properties (e.g., robustness against known attacks [4], small prime factors [1], etc). These properties are, dynamically, changing and are formulated taking into account the currently known cryptanalysis methods.

---

* This work was partially supported by the European Union project ABC4Trust (Attribute-based Credentials for Trust) funded within the context of the 7th Research Framework Program (FP7).

T.-h. Kim et al. (Eds.): ISA 2011, CCIS 200, pp. 177–187, 2011.

One technique that has been employed as evidence to the hardness of various cryptography related problems on finite groups is that of proving *lower bounds* on the degree of approximating polynomials that are assumed to solve the problem on a subset of the possible instances. More specifically, in [23] techniques are described that show that polynomials that approximate the discrete logarithm problem in the prime field $\mathbb{F}_p$ cannot have degree below a certain lower bound that depends on the cardinality of the subset of the instances on which the polynomial gives the correct answer (i.e. the discrete logarithm of the instances). Fortunately, it is possible to construct Elliptic Curves with predetermined order. One such method is the *Complex Multiplication* (CM) method (see [1,17]). In the case of prime fields, the CM method takes as input a given prime (the field's order) and determines a specific parameter, called the *CM discriminant D* of the EC. The EC of the desirable order is generated by constructing certain class field polynomials based on D and finding their roots.

In this paper we study approximations to the square root of the Elliptic Curve Discrete Logarithm Problem, in analogy with the problem of computing k-th roots of the discrete logarithm problem in the field $\mathbb{F}_p$ (see [20]) and the problem of computing the double discrete logarithm (see [21]). Our results extend results obtained in [20], with regard to approximations with interpolation polynomials, based on the possibility of generating elliptic curves with known order, possessing certain desirable properties, using the complex multiplication method (see, e.g., [17,3,22,13,14,15]).

Briefly, let E be an elliptic curve over the finite field $\mathbb{F}_p$ (See Section 2 for more detailed definitions). Let P be a point different than the zero element. Then given a point Q such that $Q = kP$ the Elliptic Curve Discrete Logarithm Problem (ECDLP) consists in determining k. This value is called *the discrete logarithm of Q to the base P*. An lth root of the discrete logarithm of Q to the base P is an integer k such that $Q = k^l P$. In this paper we consider the computation of square roots, i.e. the case $l = 2$, and derive lower bounds for the degree of polynomials that approximate the square root of the discrete logarithm for Elliptic Curves of orders of specific types frequently encountered in cryptographic applications. More specifically, we consider ECs over $\mathbb{F}_p$, p a prime larger than 3, of orders r, rq, and rq^2, with r, q primes, and prove lower bounds to polynomials that approximate the square root of the ECDL for curves with such orders. We consider ECs with these orders since they are frequently encountered in practice for multiplicative finite fields. For instance, in [5,11,19] the group order m is an RSA modulus $m = rq$, with r, q primes. Since in all such applications the factorization of m is not known, the computation of lth roots is computationally intractable. In [27] the problem of taking lth roots was studied for groups with order $m = q^2 r$.

Our view is that proving lower bounds to approximating polynomials can be employed to define sets of possible Elliptic Curve orders for which the degree of the polynomials is high, thus providing concrete evidence of the difficulty of the target problem (e.g. root of the ECDLP) for the curves possessing these orders.

2   A Brief Overview of Elliptic Curve Theory

This section contains a brief introduction to elliptic curve theory, to the Complex Multiplication method for generating prime order elliptic curves and to the Hilbert class field polynomials. The interested reader is referred to [4,8,25,26] for details not given here.

Definition 1. *An* elliptic curve *defined over a finite field* $\mathbb{F}_p$, $p > 3$ *and prime, is denoted by* $E(\mathbb{F}_p)$ *and contains the points* $(x, y) \in \mathbb{F}_p \times \mathbb{F}_p$ *(in affine coordinates) that satisfy the equation (in* $\mathbb{F}_p$*)* $y^2 = x^3 + ax + b$ *with* $a, b \in \mathbb{F}_p$ *satisfying* $4a^3 + 27b^2 \neq 0$.

The set of these points equipped with a properly defined point addition operation and a special point, denoted by $\mathcal{O}$ and called *point at infinity* (zero element for the addition operation), forms an Abelian group. This is the *Elliptic Curve group* and the point $\mathcal{O}$ is its identity element (see [4,24] for more details on this group). The *order*, denoted by m, is the number of points that belong in $E(\mathbb{F}_p)$. The numbers m and p are related by the *Frobenius trace* $t = p + 1 - m$. Hasse's theorem (see e.g., [4,24]) implies that $|t| \leq 2\sqrt{p}$. Given a point $P \in E(\mathbb{F}_p)$, its *order* is the smallest positive integer n such that $nP = \mathcal{O}$. By Langrange's theorem, the order of a point $P \in E(\mathbb{F}_p)$ divides the order m of the group $E(\mathbb{F}_p)$.

   Two of the most important quantities of an elliptic curve $E(\mathbb{F}_p)$ defined through Eq. (1) are the *curve discriminant* Δ and the *j-invariant*: $\Delta = -16(4a^3 + 27b^2)$ and $j = -1728(4a)^3/\Delta$. Given $j_0 \in \mathbb{F}_p$ ($j_0 \neq 0, 1728$), two ECs of j-invariant j_0 can be easily constructed. If $k = j_0/(1728 - j_0) \bmod p$, one of these curves is given by Eq. (1) by setting $a = 3k \bmod p$ and $b = 2k \bmod p$. The second curve (the *twist* of the first) is given by the equation $y^2 = x^3 + ac^2x + bc^3$ with c any quadratic non-residue of $\mathbb{F}_p$. If m_1 and m_2 denote the orders of an elliptic curve and its twist respectively, then $m_1 + m_2 = 2p + 2$ which implies that if one of the curves has order $p + 1 - t$, then its twist has order $p + 1 + t$, or vice versa (see [4, Lemma VIII.3]). These definitions generalize easily for elliptic curves defined over any finite field. For an *elliptic curve* defined over the finite field $\mathbb{F}_{p^k}$, $p > 3$ and prime the following holds (also by Hasse):

Theorem 1. *For the order* m *of* $E(\mathbb{F}_{p^k})$ *it holds* $|m - (p^k + 1)| \leq 2\sqrt{p^k}$.

In the same context, the following theorem of Deuring from [9] established the fact that any integer in the interval $(p + 1 - 2\sqrt{p}, p + 1 + 2\sqrt{p})$ can be the order of an elliptic curve:

Theorem 2. *For any integer* $m \in (p + 1 - 2\sqrt{p}, p + 1 + 2\sqrt{p})$, *there exists some pair* (a, b) *in the set* $\{(a, b) : a, b \in \mathbb{F}_p, 4a^3 + 27b^2 \neq 0\}$ *such that the order of* $E(\mathbb{F}_p)$ *is equal to* m.

Finally, in this paper we will employ the *division polynomials*, which are defined as follows (see, e.g., [4]).

Definition 2. *For an elliptic curve defined as in Definition 1, the division poly-nomials* $\psi_v(X,Y) \in \mathbb{F}_p[X,Y]/(Y^2 - X^3 - aX - b), v \geq 0$, *are recursively defined as follows:*

$\psi_0 = 0, \psi_1 = 1, \psi_2 = 2Y, \psi_3 = 3X^4 + 6aX^2 + 12bX - a^2,$

$\psi_4 = 4Y(X^6 + 5aX^4 + 20bX^3 - 5a^2X^2 - 4abX - 8b^2 - a^3),$

$\psi_{2k+1} = \psi_{k+2}\psi_k^3 - \psi_{k+1}^3\psi_{k-1}, k \geq 2, \psi_{2k} = \psi_k(\psi_{k+2}\psi_{k-1}^2 - \psi_{k-2}\psi_{k+1}^2)/(2Y), k \geq 3.$

The division polynomials can be used to determine multiples of a given point, which is of central importance in proving the lower bounds. Let $P = (x,y) \neq \mathcal{O}$. Then the first coordinate of the point vP is given by $\frac{\theta_v(x)}{\psi_v^2(x)}$ where $\theta_v(X) = X\psi_v^2(X) - \psi_{v-1}\psi_{v+1}(X)$.

3   The Complex Multiplication Method

As stated in the previous section, given a j-invariant one may readily construct an EC. Finding a suitable j-invariant for a curve that has a given order m can be accomplished through the theory of *Complex Multiplication* (CM) of elliptic curves over the rationals. This method is called the *CM method* and in what follows we will give a brief account of it.

By Hasse's theorem, $Z = 4p - (p+1-m)^2$ must be positive and, thus, there is a unique factorization $Z = Dv^2$, with D a square free positive integer. Therefore $4p = u^2 + Dv^2$ for some integer u that satisfies the equation $m = p + 1 \pm u$. The negative parameter $-D$ is called a *CM discriminant for the prime p*. For convenience throughout the paper, we will use (the positive integer) D to refer to the CM discriminant. The CM method uses D to determine a j-invariant. This j-invariant in turn, will lead to the construction of an EC of order $p+1-u$ or $p+1+u$. In general, the CM method requires as input a prime p (for defining the field $\mathbb{F}_p$). Then the smallest D is chosen that along with integers u, v satisfy the equation $4p = u^2 + Dv^2$. The next step is to check whether $p + 1 - u$ and/or $p + 1 + u$ is a suitable order (which will be denoted by m). If none of them is suitable, then the whole process is repeated with another prime p as input. If one, however, is found to be suitable, then the Hilbert polynomial is constructed and its roots (modulo p) are computed. A root of the Hilbert polynomial is the j-invariant we are seeking. Then, the EC and its twist are constructed. Since only one of these ECs has the required suitable order, it can be found using Lagrange's theorem by picking random points P in each EC until a point is found in some curve for which $mP \neq \mathcal{O}$. Then, the other curve is the one we are seeking (see [17,3,22,12,13,14,15], among others, for complex multiplication based Elliptic Curve construction approaches as well as the P1363 standardization document [10] for algorithms related to the Elliptic Curve manipulation and Complex Multiplication).

There are four commonly employed methods for the computation of u and v. The first is to use the modified Cornacchia's algorithm [6,7] as in [13]. The second is to generate them at random as it is done in [22]. The third method was proposed in [2, p. 68] and uses some clever heuristic in order to speed up the discovery of a suitable prime p.

4   Cardinalities of Elliptic Curve Classes with Order of a Specific Form

In this section we will provide estimates for the number of elliptic curves with orders of the types covered by the lower bounds for the interpolating polynomials stated in Section 5.

4.1   Randomly Generated Elliptic Curves

One way to generate an elliptic curve is to select, at random, the three defining parameters: the prime p and the curve coefficients a, b from within $\mathbb{F}_p$. The following was proved in [18]:

Theorem 3 (Lenstra). *Let $p > 3$ be a prime. Let S be a set of integers within the interval $(p+1-2\sqrt{p}, p+1+2\sqrt{p})$ (S is a set of possible elliptic curve orders). Then if by $N_1(S)$ we denote the number of pairs $(a, b) \in \mathbb{F}_p^2$ with $4a^3 + 27b^2 \neq 0$ such that the elliptic curve $E(\mathbb{F}_p)$ has order $m \in S$, the following holds for an effectively computable positive constant c: $N_1(S) > \frac{c|S|p^{3/2}}{\ln p}$.*

Given p, we will now consider orders within $(p + 1 - 2\sqrt{p}, p + 1 + 2\sqrt{p})$ of the form $m = rq^2$, with r, q primes. We prove the following:

Theorem 4. *The number of possible orders of the form rq^2, with r, q primes, for elliptic curves defined over $\mathbb{F}_p$ is, asymptotically, bounded from below by $p^{\frac{7}{4}+\epsilon} \frac{1}{(\ln p)^3}$.*

Proof. Let q be a prime such that $2 \leq q \leq p^{1/4-\epsilon}$ with $0 < \epsilon < 1/4$. Given such a q, a range for r can be defined as follows, based on Hasse's bounds: $\frac{p+1-2\sqrt{p}}{q^2} < r < \frac{p+1+2\sqrt{p}}{q^2}$. Then it follows that $p+1-2\sqrt{p} < rq^2 < p+1+2\sqrt{p}$. We will now count the number of possible (r, q) pairs, with r, p primes, for which the Hasse inequality holds.

With regard to q, it may be any prime within the interval $[2, p^{1/4-\epsilon}]$. From the Prime Number Theorem, the number of such q as well as the number of their corresponding squares q^2, is approximately

$$\frac{p^{1/4-\epsilon}}{\ln(p^{1/4-\epsilon})}. \tag{1}$$

With regard to the possible values of r, they are exactly the prime numbers in the interval $\frac{p+1-2\sqrt{p}}{q^2} < r < \frac{p+1+2\sqrt{p}}{q^2}$. Let $\Delta = (\frac{p+1+2\sqrt{p}}{q^2}) - (\frac{p+1-2\sqrt{p}}{q^2}) = \frac{4\sqrt{p}}{q^2}$ be the interval length. From the Prime Number Theorem, again, this number is approximately equal to

$$\frac{\Delta}{\ln(\frac{p+1-2\sqrt{p}}{q^2})} = \frac{\frac{4\sqrt{p}}{q^2}}{\ln(\frac{p+1-2\sqrt{p}}{q^2})} > \frac{\frac{4\sqrt{p}}{(p^{\frac{1}{4}-\epsilon})^2}}{\ln(p+1-2\sqrt{p})} = \frac{4p^{2\epsilon}}{\ln(p+1-2\sqrt{p})}. \tag{2}$$

From (1) and (2) we conclude the the size of the set S of elliptic curve orders of the form rq^2, with r, q primes, has cardinality $|S|$ bounded, from below, as follows:

$$|S| \geq \frac{p^{1/4-\epsilon}}{\ln(p^{1/4-\epsilon})} \cdot \frac{4p^{2\epsilon}}{\ln(p+1-2\sqrt{p})}. \tag{3}$$

From Theorem 3 and (3) we conclude that

$$N(S) \geq \frac{c|S|p^{1.5}}{\ln p} \geq \frac{p^{1/4-\epsilon}}{\ln(p^{1/4-\epsilon})} \cdot \frac{4p^{2\epsilon}}{\ln(p+1-2\sqrt{p})} \frac{cp^{1.5}}{\ln p} =$$

$$p^{\frac{7}{4}+\epsilon} \frac{4c}{\ln(p^{1/4-\epsilon})\ln(p+1-2\sqrt{p})\ln p}. \tag{4}$$

This lower bound can be approximated, asymptotically with p, by the quantity $p^{\frac{7}{4}+\epsilon}\frac{1}{(\ln p)^3}$, completing the proof of the theorem.   □

Thus, for randomly chosen a, b from within $\mathbb{F}_p$, the probability of choosing a pair $(a, b) \in \mathbb{F}_p^2$ giving an elliptic curve with order of the form rq^2, with r, q primes, is

$$\frac{N(S)}{p^2} > \frac{\frac{p^{\frac{7}{4}+\epsilon}}{(\ln p)^3}}{p^2} = \frac{1}{p^{\frac{1}{4}-\epsilon}(\ln p)^3}. \tag{5}$$

Given p, we will now consider orders within $(p+1-2\sqrt{p}, p+1+2\sqrt{p})$ of the form $m = rq$, with r, q primes. It can be proved, along the lines of the proof of Theorem 4, the following:

Theorem 5. *The number of possible orders of the form rq, with r, q primes, for elliptic curves defined over $\mathbb{F}_p$ is, asymptotically, bounded from below by $p^2 \frac{1}{(\ln p)^3}$.*

Finally, given p, we will consider orders within $(p+1-2\sqrt{p}, p+1+2\sqrt{p})$ of the form $m = r$, with r prime. Te following can be proved:

Theorem 6. *The number of possible orders of the form r, with r prime, for elliptic curves defined over $\mathbb{F}_p$ is, asymptotically, bounded from below by $p^2 \frac{1}{(\ln p)^2}$.*

5   Interpolation of the Square Root of the Discrete Logarithm for Elliptic Curves of Orders of Different Types

The square root of the elliptic curve discrete logarithm is used as a one way function (see, e.g., [5]). We show that there are no low degree polynomials representing the function for a large set of given data. The multiplicative group of the ring Z_M of integers modulo M will be denoted by Z_M^* (all invertible elements). Obviously $|Z_M^*| = \phi(M)$, where ϕ is the Euler phi function. The set of all quadratic residues (QR) modulo M will be denoted by QR_M. QR_M is a subgroup of Z_M^*.

Theorem 7. *Let p be a large prime, E an elliptic curve over $\mathbb{F}_p$ and P a point of E of prime order t, $t \equiv 3 \mod 4$. For $k : 1 \leq k \leq t - 1$ the first coordinate of kP is denoted by X_k. Let $S \subseteq \{1, \cdots, \frac{t-1}{2}\}$, $|S| = \frac{t-1}{2} - s$. Let $F \in \mathbb{F}_p[X]$ be a polynomial of degree d satisfying $F(X_{k^2}) = k$, $k^2 P = (X_{k^2}, Y_{k^2})$, for all $k \in S$. Then $\deg(F) \geq \frac{t-1-4s}{64}$.*

Proof. According to the *Hasse-Weil* theorem (see, e.g., [4]) $t < p + 1 + 2\sqrt{p} \implies \frac{t+1}{2} < p$. Consider the point $k^2 P = (X_{k^2}, Y_{k^2})$. At most two points of E have the same first coordinate, namely $k^2 P$ and $-k^2 P$. The condition $t \equiv 3 \mod 4$ implies that $-k^2$ is not a quadratic residue modulo t. Therefore $X_{k_1^2} = X_{k_2^2} \implies k_1 = k_2$ for all $k_1, k_2 \in S$. Then S becomes a disjoint union $R_1 \bigcup R_2 \bigcup W_1 \bigcup W_2$, where

$$R_1 = \{k : k \in S, 2k \in S\}, W_1 = \{k : k \in S, 2k \notin S, 2k \in \{1, \cdots, \frac{t-1}{2}\}$$

$$R_2 = \{k : k \in S, 2k \in \{\frac{t-1}{2} + 1, \cdots, t-1\}, t - 2k \in S\}$$

$$W_2 = \{k : k \in S, 2k \in \{\frac{t-1}{2} + 1, \cdots, t-1\}, t - 2k \notin S\}.$$

The set $W_1 \bigcup W_2$ has at most s element. Therefore the set $R_1 \bigcup R_2$ has at least $|S| - s = \frac{t-1}{2} - 2s$ elements.

Assume $k^2 P = (X_{k^2}, Y_{k^2})$, $4k^2 P = (X_{(2k)^2}, Y_{(2k)^2})$. Using the polynomials ψ_v^2, θ_v we get $X_{4k^2} = X_{(2k)^2} = \frac{\theta_4(X_k)}{\psi_4^2(X_k)}$. For all $k \in R_1$ we obtain $F(X_{4k^2}) = 2k = 2F(X_k)$. For all $k \in R_2$ we obtain $F(X_{4k^2}) = t - 2k = t - 2F(X_k)$. Set $z = X_{k^2}$, assume $k \in R_1 \bigcup R_2 = R$. Consider the polynomials:

$$H_1(z) = \psi_4^{2d}(z)[F(\frac{\theta_4(z)}{\psi_4^2(z)})] - 2F(z)], k \in R_1$$

$$H_2(z) = \psi_4^{2d}(z)[F(\frac{\theta_4(z)}{\psi_4^2(z)})] + 2F(z) - t], k \in R_2.$$

Let $a \in \overline{\mathbb{F}}_p$ be a zero of $\psi_4^2(z)$. Then $\theta_4(a) \neq 0$. It is easy to verify that $H_i(a) = f_d \theta_4(a) \neq 0$ where f_d is the leading coefficient of the polynomial $F(z)$. H_i is not identical to zero and $\deg(H_i) \leq 4^2 d$. At least one of the polynomials H_i has at least $\frac{|R|}{2}$ roots. We get $4^2 d \geq \deg(H_i) \geq \frac{|R|}{2} \geq \frac{1}{2}[(\frac{t-1}{2} - 2s)] \geq \implies d \geq \frac{t-1-4s}{64}$. $\square$

We, now, address the question: can the square F^2 of the polynomial mentioned in Theorem 7 represent the discrete logarithm over a set of given data?

Claim. We keep the same assumptions as in Theorem 7. Consider the polynomial $[F(x)]^2$. Then F^2 interpolates the (elliptic curve) discrete logarithm only in the cases $t = p$ or $k^2 < p$.

Proof. By $Q = (U, V)$ we denote $k^2 P$, that is $Q = (U, V) = (X_{k^2}, Y_{k^2}) = k^2 \cdot (X, Y) = k^2 P$, k is the square root of the discrete logarithm of Q, $1 \leq k \leq \frac{t-1}{2}$.

We apply the polynomial F^2 and calculate $[F(U)]^2 = w$. Obviously, $k^2 = w + jp$, $1 \leq w < p$, $j \geq 0$. It follows that $k^2 P = wP + (jp)P$. The assertion that

w is the discrete logarithm of Q, i.e. $Q = wP$ implies that $jp \cdot P = \mathbf{O}$. The point P generates a cyclic group of order t, therefore $t/(jp)$. This implies that either t/p of t/j.

Assume that t/p. Both t and p are primes and, thus, $t = p$. Assume that $t/j, j = 0$. Then $k^2 = w < p$. Assume that $t/j, j > 0$. Then $j \geq t$. Since $p \geq \frac{t-1}{2}$ (from the proof of Theorem 7) it is evident that $k^2 = w + jp \geq \frac{t(t-1)}{2}$. However $k \leq \frac{t-1}{2}$ or $k^2 \leq \left(\frac{t-1}{2}\right)^2$, a contradiction. $\square$

Remark 1. Note that by the Hasse-Weil theorem we have $p + 1 + \sqrt{p} \leq t$. The case $k^2 < p$ implies that $(k-1)^2 < t$ or $k < \sqrt{t} + 1$. Since t is a large prime, $\sqrt{t} \ll \frac{t-1}{2}$. Only at most $O(\sqrt{t}$ function values of the square root of the discrete logarithm can be used for the computation of the discrete logarithm.

Remark 2. Note that $\deg(F^2) = 2 \deg(F)$. It is evident that when F^2 represents the discrete logarithm over a given set of integers better lower bounds can be obtained (see [16]).

Now we state some corollaries of Theorem 7.

Corollary 1. *Theorem 7 can be generalized for the case $t = mq$, where m is a "small" integer, q is a prime (i.e. t is "nearly prime"), $q \equiv 3 \mod 4$ and (of course) $\gcd(m, q) = 1$.*

This corollary easily follows with the use of the Chinese Remainder Theorem. Concerning cryptographic applications see [10].

Corollary 2. *Theorem 7 can be generalized for the case $t = q^e$, a prime power, with $q \equiv 3 \mod 4$.*

Observe that b is a QR modulo q^e iff it is a QR modulo q. Every QR of $Z_{q^e}^*$ admits two square roots. One from the set $Z_{q^e}^* \cap \{1, 2, \ldots, \frac{t-1}{2}\}$ and one from the set $Z_{q^e}^* \cap \{\frac{t+1}{2}, \ldots, t-1\}$. In most of the applications (see [5,11,19]) t, the order of the group, is not a prime power but an RSA modulus, i.e. $t = N = pq$, where p and q are large primes and the factorization of N is unknown. In [27], $t = N = p^2 q$, where p and q are large primes. In Theorem 8 the RSA modulus case is addressed. In Corollary 3 the general case $t = N = p^a q^b$ is handled.

Theorem 8. *Let r be a large prime, E an elliptic curve over $\mathbb{F}_r$, P a point of E order N, $N = pq$ an RSA modulus. In addition we assume $p \equiv q \equiv 3 \mod 4$. Consider the subset $S \subseteq QR_N \subseteq Z_N^*$.*

$$|S| = \tfrac{1}{4}\phi(N) - [(N-1) - min(N-1, r-1)] - s =$$
$$min(N, r) - N + \tfrac{1}{4}\phi(N) - s.$$

Let $F \in \mathbb{F}_r[x]$ be a polynomial of degree d satisfying $F(X_k^2) = k$, $k \in S$ (X_m denotes the first coordinate of $mP = (X_m, Y_m), 0 \leq m \leq N - 1$). Let v be the smallest quadratic residue $\mod N$, $v \in \{2, 3, 4\}$. Then $\deg(F) \geq \frac{1}{v^5}[min(N, r) - N + \tfrac{1}{4}\phi(N) - 2s]$.

Proof. The assumption $p \equiv q \equiv 3 \mod 4$ implies that all quadratic residues in Z_N^* have exactly one square root which is also a quadratic residue ($\mod N$), that is the square root function becomes a bijection. Set $R = \{k : k \in S, vk \in S\}$. If is obvious that $v \in Z_N^*$. Also $|R| \geq |S| - s$. For all $k \in S$ it is true that $F(X_{(vk)^2}) = vk - jN, j = 0, 1, \ldots, v - 1$ and $F(X_{v^2k^2}) = vF(X_{k^2}) - jN$. Set $z = X_{k^2}$. Then $X_{u^2k^2} = \frac{\theta_{v^2}(z)}{\psi_{v^2}^2(z)}$ (division polynomials). We get $F\left(\frac{\theta_{v^2}(z)}{\psi_{v^2}^2(z)}\right) = vF(z) - jN$ for some $j = 0, \cdots, v - 1$. Consider the polynomials

$$H_j(z) = \psi_{v^2}^{2d}\left[F\left(\frac{\theta_{v^2}(z)}{\psi_{v^2}^2(z)}\right) - vF(z) - jN\right] \quad j = 0, \cdots, v - 1.$$

It is easy to verify that they are not identically zero and that $\deg H_j \leq v^4 d$. At least one of the H_j polynomials has at least $\frac{|R|}{v}$ zeros. Thus

$$v^4 d \geq \deg(H_j) \geq \frac{|R|}{v} \geq \frac{|S|-s}{v} \implies d \geq \frac{|S|-s}{v^5} = \frac{1}{v^5}[\min(N,r) - N + \tfrac{1}{4}\phi(N) - 2s],$$

completing the proof of the theorem. $\qquad\square$

We will now show that the quantity $min(N,r) - N + \frac{1}{4}\phi(N)$ in the statement of Theorem 8 is larger than 0 and, asymptotically, it is $\Omega(N)$. Thus, the quantity is positive always and larger than the constant s, for any value it may assume in the proof of the theorem.

Claim. The assumption $r > (14)^2$ implies that $min(N,r) - N + \frac{1}{4}\phi(N) > 0$ and, asymptotically, this quantity is $\Omega(N)$.

Proof. It suffices to handle the case $\min(N,r) = r$. We first prove that that $8r > 7(N-1)$. From the Hasse-Weil theorem follows that $N < r + 2\sqrt{r} + 1 \implies 7(N-1) < 7r + 14\sqrt{r}$. Assume, on the contrary, that $8r \leq 7(N-1)$. Then $8r < 7(N-1) < 7r + 14\sqrt{r} \implies r < 14\sqrt{r} \implies r < (14)^2$, contrary to the assumption that $r > (14)^2$.

In the sequence we compute: $\min(N,r) - N + \frac{1}{4}\phi(N) = r - N + \frac{1}{4}\phi(N) = r - pq + \frac{1}{4}(p-1)(q-1) = \frac{8r-6pq-2p-2q+2}{8}$. However, $8r - 6pq = 8r - 6N > N - 7 = pq - 7$. Thus $\frac{8r-6pq-2p-2q+2}{8} > \frac{pq-7-2p-2q+2}{8} = \frac{pq-2p-2q-5}{8}$ which is larger than 0 and $\Omega(N)$. $\qquad\square$

Corollary 3. *Theorem 8 can be generalized for the case* $t = N = p^a q^b$, *with* p, q *primes such that* $p \equiv q \equiv 3 \mod 4$, *and* $a, b > 1$.

Observe that $Z_N^* \approx Z_{p^a}^* \times Z_{q^b}^*$. Every QR of Z_N^* admits four square roots and exactly one of them is also a QR. The corollary then follows, by proving the analogous of Claim 5:

Claim. With the same assumptions of Theorem 8, except that $N = p^a q^b$, with a, b integers larger than 1, and p, q primes such that $p \equiv q \equiv 3 \mod 4$ primes, it holds that $\min(N,r) - N + \frac{1}{4}\phi(N) > 0$ and, asymptotically, this quantity is $\Omega(N)$.

Proof. We first observe that, again, $8r > 7(N-1)$ for $r > (14)^2$. Then the following holds:

$$r - N - \frac{1}{4}\phi(N) = r - p^a q^b - \frac{1}{4}(p^a - p^{a-1})(q^b - q^{b-1}) = \frac{8r - 6p^a q^b - 2p^a - 2q^b + 2}{8}.$$

Since $8r - 6N > N - 7$

$$\frac{1}{8}(8r - 6N - 2p^a - 2q^b + 2) > \frac{1}{8}(p^a q^b - 7 - 2p^a q^{b-1} - 2p^{a-1}q^b + 2p^{a-1}q^{b-1}) =$$

$$\frac{1}{8}\left[p^{a-1}q^{b-1}(pq - 2p - 2q + 2) - 7\right]$$

which is larger than 0 and $\Omega(N)$. $\square$

References

1. Atkin, A.O.L., Morain, F.: Elliptic curves and primality proving. Mathematics of Computation 61, 29–67 (1993)
2. Baier, H.: Efficient Algorithms for Generating Elliptic Curves over Finite Fields Suitable for Use in Cryptography, PhD Thesis, Dept. of Computer Science, Technical Univ. of Darmstadt (May 2002)
3. Buchmann, J., Baier, H.: Efficient construction of cryptographically strong elliptic curves. In: Roy, B., Okamoto, E. (eds.) INDOCRYPT 2000. LNCS, vol. 1977, pp. 191–202. Springer, Heidelberg (2000)
4. Blake, I., Seroussi, G., Smart, N.: Elliptic curves in cryptography. London Mathematical Society Lecture Note Series, vol. 265. Cambridge University Press, Cambridge (1999)
5. Camenisch, J., Stadler, M.: Efficient Group Signature Schemes for Large Groups (Extended Abstract). In: Kaliski Jr., B.S. (ed.) CRYPTO 1997. LNCS, vol. 1294, pp. 410–424. Springer, Heidelberg (1997)
6. Cohen, H.: A Course in Computational Algebraic Number Theory. Graduate Texts in Mathematics, vol. 138. Springer, Berlin (1993)
7. Cornacchia, G.: Su di un metodo per la risoluzione in numeri interi dell' equazione $\sum_{h=0}^{n} C_h x^{n-h} y^h = P$. Giornale di Matematiche di Battaglini 46, 33–90 (1908)
8. Cox, D.A.: Primes of the form $x^2 + ny^2$. John Wiley and Sons, New York (1989)
9. Deuring, M.: Die Typen der Multiplikatorenringe elliptischer Funktionenkörper. Abh. Math. Sem. Hansischen Univ. 14, 197–272 (1941)
10. IEEE P1363/D13, Standard Specifications for Public-Key Cryptography (1999), http://grouper.ieee.org/groups/1363/tradPK/draft.html
11. Konoma, C., Mambo, M., Shizuya, H.: The Computational Difficulty of Solving Cryptographic Primitive Problems Related to the Discrete Logarithm Problem. IEICE Transactions 88-A(1), 81–88 (2005)
12. Konstantinou, E., Stamatiou, Y., Zaroliagis, C.: A Software Library for Elliptic Curve Cryptography. In: Möhring, R.H., Raman, R. (eds.) ESA 2002. LNCS, vol. 2461, pp. 625–637. Springer, Heidelberg (2002)
13. Konstantinou, E., Stamatiou, Y., Zaroliagis, C.: On the Efficient Generation of Elliptic Curves over Prime Fields. In: Kaliski Jr., B.S., Koç, Ç.K., Paar, C. (eds.) CHES 2002. LNCS, vol. 2523, pp. 333–348. Springer, Heidelberg (2003)

14. Konstantinou, E., Stamatiou, Y.C., Zaroliagis, C.: On the Construction of Prime Order Elliptic Curves. In: Johansson, T., Maitra, S. (eds.) INDOCRYPT 2003. LNCS, vol. 2904, pp. 309–322. Springer, Heidelberg (2003)
15. Konstantinou, E., Kontogeorgis, A., Stamatiou, Y., Zaroliagis, C.: Generating Prime Order Elliptic Curves: Difficulties and Efficiency Considerations. In: Park, C.-s., Chee, S. (eds.) ICISC 2004. LNCS, vol. 3506, pp. 261–278. Springer, Heidelberg (2005)
16. Lange, T., Winterhof, A.: Polynomial Interpolation of the Elliptic Curve and XTR Discrete Logarithm. In: Ibarra, O.H., Zhang, L. (eds.) COCOON 2002. LNCS, vol. 2387, pp. 137–143. Springer, Heidelberg (2002)
17. Lay, G.J., Zimmer, H.: Constructing Elliptic Curves with Given Group Order over Large Finite Fields. In: Huang, M.-D.A., Adleman, L.M. (eds.) ANTS 1994. LNCS, vol. 877, pp. 250–263. Springer, Heidelberg (1994)
18. Lenstra Jr., H.: Factoring integers with elliptic curves. Ann. of Math. 2, 649–673 (1987)
19. Lysyanskaya, A., Ramzan, Z.: Group Blind Digital Signatures: A Scalable Solution to Electronic Cash. In: Hirschfeld, R. (ed.) FC 1998. LNCS, vol. 1465, pp. 184–197. Springer, Heidelberg (1998)
20. Meletiou, G.C.: Polynomial Interpolation of the k-th Root of the Discrete Logarithm. In: Bozapalidis, S., Rahonis, G. (eds.) CAI 2009. LNCS, vol. 5725, pp. 318–323. Springer, Heidelberg (2009)
21. Meletiou, G.C., Winterhof, A.: Interpolation of the Double Discrete Logarithm. In: von zur Gathen, J., Imaña, J.L., Koç, Ç.K. (eds.) WAIFI 2008. LNCS, vol. 5130, pp. 1–10. Springer, Heidelberg (2008)
22. Savaş, E., Schmidt, T.A., Koç, Ç.K.: Generating Elliptic Curves of Prime Order. In: Koç, Ç.K., Naccache, D., Paar, C. (eds.) CHES 2001. LNCS, vol. 2162, pp. 142–161. Springer, Heidelberg (2001)
23. Shparlinski, I.E.: Number Theoretic Methods in Cryptography: Complexity Lower Bounds. In: Progress in Computer Science and Applied Logic (PCS). Birkhäuser, Basel (1999)
24. Silverman, J.H.: The Arithmetic of Elliptic Curves. GTM 106 (1986)
25. Stewart, I.: Galois Theory, 3rd edn. Chapman & Hall/CRC, Boca Raton, FL (2004)
26. Stewart, I., Tall, D.: Algebraic Number Theory, 2nd edn. Chapman & Hall, London (1987)
27. Traoré, J.: Group Signatures and Their Relevance to Privacy-Protecting Off-Line Electronic Cash Systems. In: Pieprzyk, J.P., Safavi-Naini, R., Seberry, J. (eds.) ACISP 1999. LNCS, vol. 1587, pp. 228–243. Springer, Heidelberg (1999)

Towards Next Generation System Architecture for Emergency Services

Jari Veijalainen and Veikko Hara

Faculty of Information Technology,
FI-40014 University of Jyväskylä
Finland
{jari.veijalainen,veikko.hara}@jyu.fi

Abstract. European Union has decided that all emergencies can be reported to authorities by European citizens by calling 112 or sending a text message to 112. Distributing warnings and alerts of authorities to citizens currently happens through national TV and radio channels, but telecom networks are also used now in some countries for this purpose. During the last ten years there have been attempts to develop new system architectures for various emergency service provision phases. Some of them are already deployed in special cases, like in ambulance services. Multimedia emergency alert messages can be delivered to citizens over fixed and mobile telecom networks and commercial systems are already in operation. Emergency service delivery has been computer supported for long time at emergency centers. In this paper we will review the current situation primarily in Europe and discuss what issues a novel architecture design for the emergency calls/messages and emergency warnings and alerts should address. The issue is mainly how to utilize better accurate positioning and wireless networks for these tasks. The usability of global social media applications for emergency service provisioning is also considered.

Keywords: Emergency Service Provisioning, Mobile Emergency Services, Emergency Alerts, Public Safety Answering Point

1 Introduction

Societies have experienced various kinds of life or property threatening incidents during their existence on the Earth. The nature or humans are the root cause for these. In the modern world one speaks about emergency situation or emergency. The exact definition of an emergency varies, but if one of the conditions below is met, one or several simultaneous incidents are usually considered an emergency: a) Incident(s) is (are) immediately threatening to life, health, property or environment; b) it/they have already caused loss of life, health detriments, property damage or environmental damage; c) it/they have a high probability of escalating to cause immediate danger to life, health, property or environment (cf. [40]).

The incident could be caused by erroneous or deliberate actions of human beings, animals, micro-organisms or physical forces of the nature (wind, flood, fire, radiation, and earthquake). The root cause can also be a failure of the technical infrastructure,

T.-h. Kim et al. (Eds.): ISA 2011, CCIS 200, pp. 188–202, 2011.
© Springer-Verlag Berlin Heidelberg 2011

such as nuclear plant or power grid failure that then cause economic or social hazard. The emergencies can be further classified in different ways into categories. One dimension is the scale of the emergency, measured by the number of people, the value of the property, or both, in hazard. Large scale incidents are sometimes called *disasters*. Typically these are large scale forest or other fires, heavy earthquakes, hurricanes etc. They might also be caused by a large scale military operation or terrorist attack (cf. 911 attack).

Most emergencies are fortunately small scale ones, where one or at most a few persons or relatively small property values are in danger. In the modern world the responsibility for dealing with emergencies is mainly on public authorities of the nation states. Citizens are in some cases required to take part in these activities. Based on the scale and type of the hazard, the authorities can determine what kind of resources, how much, and how fast, are needed to be deployed in a particular emergency case. E.g. medical emergencies can be classified into four or five classes based on the threat to the patient's life. Various countries also have usually plans for disaster recovery. The magnitude 9.0 earthquake on March 11, 2011 in Japan, the tsunami caused by it, and the recovery actions taken so far by the Japanese authorities are an example of an extreme case in this sense.

The overall scenario for emergency services can be viewed to consist of several consecutive phases:

1)   The emergency situation detection and reporting to authorities; this is done by individuals or sensors – in some cases the authorities determine the situation by modeling (weather warnings). If an individual reports a situation to authorities, this is called *emergency call*, although also other digital communication services can be used than voice call.

2)   Categorization of the emergency situation and determining which actions to take; this is done by certain persons in limited cases (fire alarm in a building), but in most cases by authorities (e.g. PSAP personnel) often together with the individual reporting the incident

3)   Dispatching suitable rescue resources (fire brigade, ambulance, police, and social worker) to the incident scene; this is performed by the PSAP and rescue personnel

4)   If deemed necessary, issuing *emergency announcements* or *alerts* to the public in targeted area(s); this is also done by PSAP or other authority (cf. below)

The process can stop in phase 2), if the authorities consider that the "emergency" situation described by the individual does not require actions. Phase 4) is also often omitted, if the emergency does not influence the lives or property of the wider population. The new ubiquitous technology can be used in all phases above. One can also consider, whether in some scenarios the authorities could be left out of the loop.

In this paper we will describe the current situation in Europe and ponder how to use emerging technologies mainly in the phases 1) and 3)-4) above. The rest of the paper is organized as follows. Section 2 discusses the current emergency service provision in the European Union. Section 3 discusses new techniques that could be deployed for emergency calls. Section 4 discusses emerging technologies that could be used to warn and alert population and some systems to be used emergency service provision. Section 5 draws conclusions.

2 Emergency Legislation and 112 Emergency Number in Europe

2.1 Emergency Service Provision in Europe

In most countries there are four different major organizations that take care of emergencies: police, medical organizations, fire departments, and military forces. The core military forces are only used in disaster relief operations in stable countries, though. For operations at sea there are often separate rescue organizations such as coast guard or maritime rescue associations. In various countries there can also exist special private associations or semi-official organizations that take care of particular emergencies. An example is the Mountain Rescue Association in USA [27], or voluntary roadside assistance; ADAC in Germany [5], AAA in USA [2], etc.

We are in the sequel concentrating on those emergency services that are provided by the PSAPs (Public Safety Answering Point), together with police, medical organizations, and fire departments. As in some sense dangerous incident happens, a citizen or sensor-based system must inform the emergency service providers by issuing an emergency call. A recent legislation change e.g. in Finland, following from EU legislation, allows also SMS to be used for this purpose ([7,37,§5]). Automatic fire sensors connected to fire brigade premises have been in use for long time in buildings and the planned eCall functionality in cars (see 3.1) will implement a somewhat similar idea in the traffic accident situations.

In each EU country emergency calls can be made using the emergency number 112 [1] and they are first received at a suitable PSAP. In the enhanced scheme (E112), mobile and fixed telecom networks must provide the location information of the caller to the PSAP. Those working at PSAP then assess what kind of resources is needed, when and where, and contact a suitable emergency service provider (local police, fire department, ambulance, social worker). The emergency service provision at PSAP consists of gathering as much as possible accurate information from the caller, and possibly from other sources, in order to determine the needed resources - but also to guide the caller to act properly in the situation. Based on this information phase 3) is entered or the case is considered closed.

Phase 4) is to issue *emergency announcements* or *alerts* to people in danger due to the incident. This can be done by PSAP, an actual emergency service provider (police, medical emergency service provider), or other authorities that have the right to issue such announcements (meteorological centre, border guard, air traffic control, vehicle safety centre, etc.). In serious large scale emergencies, especially if a disaster occurs, authorities can declare a state of emergency for a certain area or for the entire country. This usually means that special emergency legislation enters into force and some rights of the citizens are restricted, resources such as fuel or water might be rationed, etc. In this context we do not discuss these most severe situations.

The current practice assumes that the TV and radio stations and telecom networks are the main channels to issue emergency alerts [37]. TV, radio, and telecom operators are mentioned e.g. in the Finnish law [35,§35a]. According to the legislation, these operators must distribute – in a reasonable time - a *targeted official announcement*, if it is issued by a PSAP, Maritime Rescue Coordination Center, or Areal Maritime Rescue Center. Further, police, boarder guard, various safety authorities (fire departments, health monitoring, PSAPs. etc.), Radiation and Nuclear

Safety Authority (STUK), and the Finnish Meteorological Institute can issue *targeted emergency alerts*. These must be forwarded by the above operators without delay and without altering the contents. The source of the announcements and alerts must be authenticated towards operators. Faxes or voice calls from certain authorized fixed numbers are reliable enough. Another way would be to use digitally signed emails.

2.2 The Status of the 112 and E112 Service in Europe

The Universal Service Directive 22/2002/EC mandates that 112 will be the common emergency number in all EU countries and this is confirmed also in the New Regulatory Framework issued in 2009 [7,16]. It can be called free of charge from any fixed or mobile phone. The directive also mandates the operators to make the callers location known to authorities providing emergency services. The number must function also while roaming. Detailed analysis and recommendations concerning 112 service were given in [17]. The report divides the network service providers into four categories:

1. A service where E.164 numbers (specified by ITU) are not provided and from which there is no access to or from the PSTN.

2. Outbound voice. A service where there is outgoing access to the PSTN only and E.164 numbers are not provided.

3. Inbound voice. A service where there is incoming access from the PSTN, mobile networks or via IP and E.164 numbers are provided. A Service belonging to this category does not provide outbound calls (whether to the PSTN, mobile or otherwise).

4. Voice telephony. A service where there is incoming and outgoing access to the PSTN, mobile network, and E.164 numbers are provided. This category includes traditional 'PATS' (Public Access Telephone Service), other services which can generally be regarded as a substitute for 'PATS' (like most VoB offers) and ECS VoIP (Voice-over-IP) services.

In the most recent meeting of EU CoCom Expert Group on Emergency Access (EU CoCom EGEA) on March 11, 2011 the Commission presented results of the survey addressed to the MS and EEA states [15,34]. The survey was made in order to get an accurate picture of what is the level of access to 112, what is the call handling performance, how is the callers location information obtained, and what its accuracy is. The survey was done in 2010. According to the results, PATS providers (i.e. those providing voice services perhaps among other telecom services, cat. 4 above) have a legal obligation to provide 112 access in 25 MS and in Norway. Non-PATS providers must inform customers if 112 access does not function (cf. VoIP). In two countries also these must provide 112 access. Caller's location is obtained in 19 MS both for mobile and fixed telephone service and in 22 countries for PATS with fixed access. Caller's registered subscription address is provided to the PSAP in 14 MS and in Norway for mobile 112 calls. 112 works for roaming subscribers in 26 MS and in Norway and 112 can be called without SIM card in 20 MS and Norway. In 7 MS the PSAP can be accessed by SMS, in 4 MS by fax and in 2 MS by chat or text relay. The time to pick a 112 call was from 0.05 to 11 seconds in average in 19 MS. Measurements are still scarce.

According to [17] caller's location/address can be obtained by PSAP by pulling it from a special database or from the telecom provider. In the pull scheme the clerk at PSAP asks the network to locate the caller. Thus, the callers of 112 are located, if deemed necessary. Telecom operator can also push the location data to the PSAP whenever a 112 call takes place, i.e. all 112 callers are located automatically in this scheme and the coordinates and possible address provided for all 112 calls. Callers location was found using the push method almost instantly in 10(13) MSs, and for pull method 11 MS reported under 5 s response time to report the address of the fixe-line subscriber. 7 MS reported to remain below 15 seconds average access time for the location information for mobile phones for the pull method. The ERG recommended push method in [17] and this recommendation has been followed to some extent.

Article 26/5 in the above directive [7] mandates the National Regulatory Authorities (NRA) to specify the required accuracy in each country. Minimum location accuracy requirement for 112 calls originating from mobile phones is cell-id/sector id(CI). In the scheme, the position of the mobile station is approximated by the position of the base transceiver station (BTS) or access point, perhaps restricted to a specific sector served by the BTS. The actual accuracy depends in this basic scheme on the cell diameter that varies from tens of meters (dense city area) to kilometers (rural areas). Improved accuracy can be gained e.g. by triangulation or trilateration [38]. Various enhancements to gain better location accuracy for 112 calls were reported by 8 MS and Norway.

If the position accuracy of 112 call is low, the area from where the incident is reported might be several square kilometers. Some field tests suggest that even the enhanced network positioning methods [38] do not provide much better accuracy than CI. A problem related with the low positioning accuracy is that some PSAP support systems might show only one point on the map, not the most probable area where the call is coming from. Further, in city environments buildings can be high and network positioning methods are incapable of providing the floor information, unless the building happens to have BTS in different floors. Thus, the caller must provide it.

23 MS and Norway report international roaming support (i.e. 112 calls while abroad), but national roaming still has gaps. The problem arises if the "own" operator is not accessible, and the caller cannot use the network of another domestic operator to issue a 112 call. 16 MS and Norway report that national roaming is possible.

Another issue connected to roaming is the question whether foreign languages can be used when making emergency calls abroad. According to [34] English is offered by 23 MS, French by 13 MS, and German by 12 MS while receiving a 112 call.

A considerable percentage of the population cannot use normal voice calls to report emergencies. The idea of "total conversation" was developed by ITU. 3GPP and IETF have standardized it as well [30]. Shortly, the goal is to support simultaneous video, voice and text messaging during a call. Thus also sign language can be used during an emergency call. Reach 112 project [30] will improve access to emergency services for people with hearing or speech impairments or people with serious injuries. It will provide alternative ways of communication as compared to traditional voice telephony in the spirit of total conversation.

In the UK, a pilot project [31] implements a national video, voice and text infrastructure that can be used by people with various hearing, speech and vision defects for free. UK residents can download the needed software from http://www.myfriendcentral.com/. In 2011 the project will offer a video relay service that translates the signed language to speech and vice versa. This can then be used e.g. in communication with the PSAP in emergency cases.

In Sweden, trials of SMS-based 112 emergency services for deaf people and those with speech problems continue since 2006 [14]. Positioning of the person in need does now take place by automatic means, similarly to the voice calls. The service requires pre-registration, because a lot of misuse was observed during the trials. It has been observed that handling an emergency message exchange takes 14 minutes in average, as compared to 2 minutes handling time in the case of an incoming voice emergency call. There are ca. 20000 potential users of the service in Sweden, out of which ca. 10 % were registered mid 2010. The 112 text message service in Sweden functions if the operator has not barred the SMS service of the subscriber.

In Finland, regional emergency centers (that take care of the PSAP activity in a specific area) have a special (GSM) number for incoming emergency text messages. The plan is to provide a national emergency text message service using 112 as the recipient number in 2012. Usage of the current service requires pre-registration and the same would hold for the national service [26].

In the above CEC survey [34] some additional issues are also addressed. Prioritization of calls must in general happen. One issue is SIM-less calls for which the caller's identity cannot be determined although the position can be determined. Another problem is filtering silent calls; quite often the number 112 is randomly generated by phone if the keyboard is not locked and thus a non-intended call happens – often without even the knowledge of the phone user. Another problem area is people who call 112 for no real reason or in order to cause confusion, etc. The numbers of such persons can be blacklisted, or the mobile phone can be e.g. deactivated. Also warnings and legal sanctions are issued in some cases towards malicious persons.

The ERG report [17] records recommendations for the cases where non-PATS infrastructure is used for emergency calls (using e.g. Skype). In the UK, the systems architecture for positioning emergency calls originating from computers or other devices not using fixed or mobile telecom networks has been standardized [28]. The architecture addresses practically all scenarios, including ones, where a DSL connection, Cable (TV), Enterprise network, Wi-Fi and GPRS/HSPA are used as primary access network when an emergency call is made. The assumptions are that neither user nor device is trusted for location information and that (phase 1) PSAPs do not have direct VoIP (i.e. packet) access, only TDM functionality. The industrial uptake of the standard is currently unclear.

2.3 Current Warning and Alerting Systems in Europe

These are needed to mediate warnings or emergency alerts to a certain area or certain people. A typical example is a poisonous gas leakage, smoke from fire, or explosion hazard. TV and radio announcements and analog sirens or loud speakers are currently commonly used for warning and alerting. The sirens have a few signaling patterns with different meanings that should be correctly understood by people. This requires deliberate education of the people. Loudspeakers are sometimes installed in cities and buildings. The alerts and warnings can then be issued in natural language using them. A challenge in hotels and in other places with a lot of tourists is to use the right languages in announcements and educate them to understand the siren and other alert signals correctly.

Whereas sirens and loudspeaker alerts can be usually targeted well to those concerned, national TV and radio channels cannot be targeted areas smaller than one TV or radio station coverage area (10-200 km in diameter). Further, most of the people do not follow TV or radio programs continuously and thus do not receive the alerts instantly. A further problem is that in some cases the issued warnings attract people to the area for which the warning (such as a bear in a city area) has been issued. Telecom networks can be better used for targeted alerts.

3 New Emergency Call/Reporting Systems

The most notable developments in this field are social media applications and special vehicle applications. We discuss them shortly below.

3.1 eCall System in Europe

The (Ericsson) patent [23] contains the idea of emergency short messages with positioning information included. The pan-European eCall system is designed for vehicles [10,12]. It utilizes E112 voice call and E112 SMS. An eCall can be started manually or by in-vehicle sensors when a severe accident occurs. The mandatory minimum data sent by the call includes: a time stamp, the precise location of the vehicle, the vehicle id, the service provider id, and an eCall qualifier (manual/automatic launch) [10,12].

The foreseen benefits of the system would be an immediate reporting of accidents with accurate location data provided by satellite positioning. This would save in Europe up to 2,500 lives every year and reduce by 10-15% the severity of injuries of the victims. The estimated savings are in billions of euro per year. Additional benefits would be less congestion on roads caused by accidents, and more efficient traffic-incident management by authorities. Further, the system could be used for other useful services – electronic tolling, tracking hazardous goods, advanced insurance models, etc. Finally, the car and telecoms industries would be able to provide new services on an in-vehicle system with satellite navigation, data processing and communication capabilities. Obviously, such a system requires proper standardization in order to be usable. There are seven eCall related ETSI standards, three CEN standards, and one ISO standard [13].

There is currently a formal support from 21 member states of the eCall MoU [10,11]. In addition, Iceland, Norway, Croatia, and Switzerland have signed it. Interestingly, UK and France have not signed and they seem to be reluctant to do so [11]. UK states that it is not sure about the cost/benefit relationship of the eCall and declines the mandatory implementation. France refers to a recent directive about intelligent transport system [6] that defines the role of eCall.

HeeRo project [21] is currently piloting the system in 8 MS and in Russia. Deployment of the system should start in 2014 or later in all member states. Currently 15 MS and 3 EEA states have agreed to implement the system [11].

3.2   Social Media in Emergency Reporting and Management

One of the first cases where authorities miserably failed to provide much assistance or correct information was the earthquake under the ocean and tsunami in the countries around the Indian Ocean on Dec. 26, 2004. Ordinary people could fast organize web sites that gathered information about dead and survivors and the help they needed. The information flowed from the catastrophe area and back mainly in short messages.

The volcano eruption in Iceland in 2010 caused a chaos in the European and North-Atlantic air traffic. Many people were using social media sites to organize their further travel and share viable information with others. There are also cases, where a person has reported an emergency to Twitter (www.twitter.com) or Facebook (www.facebook.com) and authorities have noticed it directly or somebody else has drawn their attention to the case on time. Because of the wide use and global accessibility of many of these sites one should carefully consider in which phases of the emergency service provisioning they could be reasonably used.

Community-based local emergency services are also developed. An example is [24].

4   New Alerting and Service Provisioning Systems

In principle, both citizens and authorities could issue warnings or even alerts. In a small scale people of course warn each other by simply shouting, waving, calling, or communicating with various other technical means. This is also the only possibility if the time window to issue an alert and react to it is in seconds or tens of seconds. Analog systems are still in use e.g. for fire or gas alerts in buildings. The decision to start a siren is usually made by specially trained people in buildings. In larger outdoor areas sirens are operated by responsible authorities.

Xu [41] lists different issues that have to be considered while issuing warnings or alerts; When should the alert be sent, i.e. correct timing; what should be the geographic target area of the warning or alert; who are the ones that need to be warned or alerted; what is the purpose of the warning or alert; which are the components, form and content of the warning or alert; what are the methods and channels used for delivering warning or alert to the people concerned.

Technically it would be possible to base warnings and alerts on P2P architecture and the location of the personal devices. One could e.g. broadcast an alert message in a Wi-Fi cell (if this was technically achievable through simple means), or send an email to the distribution list of the working place. Social media sites could be used for this; e.g. a person could "tweet" in Twitter about a hazard and those who follow his or her tweets would get this information – if they happen to read the alert tweet.

Although the pulling scenarios might be reasonable in some warnings, they are bad for alerts, because getting the alert and reacting to it depends on whether the persons affected happen to read it in the time during which reaction is required. The same holds for emails, because even if they often arrive fast into the terminal, if the mail client is actively receiving mail, they are not necessarily read immediately by the people. So, push scenarios where the attention of the affected people is gotten with high probability are better for the alert messages that require immediate attention and reaction.

Another issue closely related especially with alerts is who should estimate the severity of the possible danger and the people affected? For dangers requiring actions in seconds the authorities cannot of course be involved in the loop (cf. V2V scenarios below). If the reasonable reaction time is in minutes or hours, then there is a time window for authorities to react. In this case authorities can be integrated into the decision loop. Clerk at PSAP or some other responsible authority or person can then decide upon the severity and can design and issue warnings or alerts to be distributed to the population in danger.

If ordinary people would issue severe alerts with consequences for others, they might be false or even malicious. This kind of approach might cause great confusion (consider e.g. anybody be able launch a common radiation or poisonous gas alert) and undermine the trust of people on alerts. So the authorities or persons responsible must always assess the severity of hazards and issuance of warnings or alerts to the common public. The responsibility to report possible dangers to authorities must still be everyone's duty, because authorities have only a limited possibility to detect them. These considerations also affect the system architecture choices that are possible to deploy in real life.

4.1 Alerting Population through Cell Broadcast (CB) and Multimedia Broadcast and Multicast Service (MBMS) in Mobile Networks

As discussed above, the targeted announcements should be limited to those people that are in jeopardy. The cells of telecom or Wi-Fi networks are rather small and thus the alert messages can be targeted much better to those people that are concerned than with TV or radio networks. Second, mobile devices are very often carried with people or at least kept in their proximity and people react to the messages often immediately. Especially, when they see that the message comes from authorities. Third, mobile wireless devices can also form ad-hoc networks in a limited area and transmit the emergency messages directly to other users or retransmit the alert messages from authorities to others. With the current high penetration rate mobile devices are an interesting option to provide warning and alerts.

When the GSM system was designed, Cell Broadcast (CB) was also standardized by ETSI. 3GPP adopted it to be part of UMTS [9]. The technology makes it possible to broadcast a bulk message to all subscribers in a cell, in several cells or in the entire telecom network. A "page" can be max. 82 octets (i.e. 93 7-bit characters) long and up to 15 such "pages" can be chained to form a single message. Thus, a rather extensive textual information can be distributed in one message. The same message can be sent several times and the BTS that will broadcast the message can be individually specified by the Cell Broadcast Centre of the operator. In the basic mode a page can be sent every 1,833 seconds in a cell. Thus, the longest message takes ca. 30 seconds to receive. Based on the sequence number included into every page the mobile station can drop copies of the same message. [39].

The major operators in EU have cell broadcast in use in their networks [39]. Most current 2G/3G handsets sold in Europe also support this functionality, but the feature is by default not on, because it consumes energy while in use. It must be switched on from menus of the phone. This is a problem if we think of using this technology in emergency alerts. Those who do not have the feature on cannot receive alerts. In Finland the technology is not even deployed.

As stated in [22] MBMS has been specified by 3GPP as an add-on feature to existing cellular network technologies, including GSM/EDGE and UMTS. Existing transport and physical radio channels of those systems were reused to a large extent in order to keep the implementation effort low. In the ongoing standardization of Long Term Evolution (LTE) very efficient support of MBMS is taken into account from the start as a main requirement.

MBMS relies on IP packets and offers two basic transmission modes, broadcast and multicast, for delivering IP packets. The service is intended to deliver mobile TV streaming and emergency alerts. The MBMS Broadcast mode can be used to deliver IP packets to all terminals in certain cells or in the whole network, as long as the service is running. This feature could be used in the similar way as CB for targeted alerts. In the broadcast mode MBMS does not use uplink communication.

Users can also "join" multicast IP streams. In this case the radio access network and core network receives a request from a terminal. Delivering the requested steam can be started to it. If enough terminals in a cell will receive the same multicast stream, it can be broadcasted in that cell.

The problems of using this technology or non-cellular mobile TV (e.g. using DVB/H) for alerting people are similar to CB.

4.2 Alerting Population Based on Location Information

A mobile 2G/3G telecom network keeps track of the mobile stations (i.e. mobile handsets) that have reported to be accessible in the network, i.e. are "on". If there is not incoming or outgoing traffic from the mobile station, the network keeps track of the Location Area (LA) where the MS resides. A LA usually covers several cells. If the mobile station communicates using a BTS, the MSC stores the cell-id(s) through which the voice call, data connection, or short message was sent or received. The information is kept at Mobile Switching Center (MSC) of that network that currently serves the mobile station. If the mobile station is roaming, the LA information is also updated to the HLR of the home network. When the mobile station leaves a particular LA, the new LA (identifier) of that mobile station is updated to the MSC. If the terminal is switched off or does not interact with the network for several hours, its LA entry is purged from the MSC database (and from the HLR).

For the above reasons the LA information is too inaccurate to be used to target alert messages to individual handsets. The last active cell id is better, but only if it is fresh, because a mobile station in a car can move 30 m/s or faster.

The LA information could still be used in principle to select those mobile stations that are in the dangerous area. The decision support system must form a union of the cells of those LAs that have an intersection with the dangerous area. Subsequently, all mobile stations in this union will get the alert messages. This method still addresses usually too many mobile stations in order to be well targeted.

A commercial solution UMS-PAS [36] is built based, among other, on the above LA information in HLR/VLR. It seems to collect the LA information and last active cell information for all mobile stations in a particular network from the SS7 traffic between MSC and BSCs. It stores this information into a separate data base of its own. Thus, it is possible to answer a query "how many mobile subscribers are in the designated area now?"; or how many French persons are in the designated area now?" etc., without accessing the actual fixed or mobile network. The latter query can be answered, because any mobile network maintains a VLR that contains the current visitor information, including the LA and the last active cell for each mobile station. The nationality of the operator is encoded into the first 3 digits of the International Mobile Subscriber Identity (IMSI) stored into VLR. IMSI is evidently copied to the UMS-PAS database. The above system can send both voice and text messages to the individual fixed-line phones and mobile stations in a designated area. Thus, the messages can be issued in the right language. The provider claims to guarantee that the used network is not overloaded. This should happen by monitoring the target network load in real time and by automatically controlling the generated call/message load based on this information.

Because the HLR very often contains roaming information (i.e. which subscriber is in which foreign network in which LA), the above system can also be used to send alerts and announcements to the citizens currently abroad or in a specific country or even in a specific area. This might be an interesting option for warnings and alerts.

4.3 Vehicle-to-vehicle Alert Systems

There is an emerging WAVE standard (IEEE 1609 family) based on IEEE 802.11p [25] that is supporting wireless ad-hoc communication between vehicles. The standard can be used also in emergency cases, e.g. in accidents on the highway. The vehicles can send warnings to other vehicles approaching accident site. In the simulations [19] it was shown that the high-priority, high-power CCH channel has 3 Mbps rate for 2.5 km range and 27 Mbps for 1 km range. A low-priority channel has a max range of 750 meters and a smaller throughput. Thus, the cars in a specific area can exchange data already while 500-1000 meters apart. The transmission delay remains under 100 ms up to 60 nodes sharing the same radio spectrum for CCH. The transmission rate drops drastically with the increasing number of mobile nodes in the same area. For two nodes the throughput of CCH is 900 kbps, but for 15 nodes only ca. 100 kbps. Other channels only reach 10 -15 kbps transmission rates when 15 nodes share the usable bandwidth.

If one considers accidents, an alert message to other vehicles could be triggered by similar mechanism as an emergency eCall or e.g. from acceleration sensors of those cars that break heavily in order to avoid a collision. Various scenarios with transmission rates in the 0.1-0.4 Mbps range were simulated in [42]. The authors discovered that the rear-end collisions could be reacted to by the drivers and avoided, assuming that the distances between the cars are large enough for a driver to react and the message delay is reasonable. The needed maneuvering time is about 2 s, including the reaction time of the driver and the time it takes to break/avoid the collision with a vehicle ahead. The message transmission delays remain under the critical 100 ms limit in all scenarios where at most 10 vehicles are in the communication range and also in some further scenarios.

Evidently, a larger number of collisions could be avoided, if all cars started automatically breaking immediately after having received an alert message and observed the cars ahead breaking. This requires, however, additional technology in the cars, such as radars and sophisticated decision systems, because breaking cannot be controlled by alert messages only. Message relaying to further cars approaching the dangerous section also helps to avoid further problems. These are for further study, as is the connection between eCall and V2V alerting systems.

4.4 Other System Proposals and Deployed Systems

There are many systems that researchers have proposed to be used in various phases in emergency service provision. One of them is WIPER [32,33]. The idea is to equip mobile handsets with further sensors and collect this information continuously into a database. This is used for simulations that make use of real-time data streams as well [34]. Based on the information gathered it should be possible to infer what kind of emergency situation has occurred or is evolving. This information could then help authorities to find a proper course of actions in a shorter time or detect emergency without anybody specifically reporting it. In [18] a next generation support system for PSAP is investigated. The main idea is to use SOA approach.

ADAMO project [4] addresses mainly the problem of wireless communication support of the rescue teams, e.g. for the fire fighters in burning buildings. This is because the TETRA technology used commonly by rescue personnel has a poor indoor coverage in Belgium. The authors also discuss the information needs of the persons in various roles in a rescue effort.

The authors of [29] suggest a telematic system architecture for emergency medical services. For these there are already deployed systems that use extensively GPS positioning and mobile technologies during service provisioning. In [8] there is a short overview on these efforts, including the real case from Australia [3] and Malaysia [20]. The paper also contains a proposal for a very advanced ambulance emergency provision system that retrieves patient data to the ambulance while it is driving towards the hospital and upload information about the injuries and/or status to the hospital in advance so that appropriate precautions can be taken.

5 Conclusions

We have discussed in this paper emergency situations and provision of them in various cases. The analysis shows that new mobile, wireless and positioning technologies could be involved more heavily in many places of the emergency service provisioning. The current 112 service in Europe could be improved as concerns the positioning of the calls coming from mobile networks. It might be wise to rely more on satellite positioning mechanisms than on network positioning, because the accuracy is better and soon also the low-end handsets will probably have a satellite chip. This makes especially sense after GALILEO system will become operational. In some emergencies, like car failures, special smart phone emergency "call" applications with GPS positioning have already been deployed. Thus, the service provider gets accurate information on where to provide help. It is important to evaluate experiences gained from these kind of less critical services and design next generation 112 service where satellite positioning and perhaps also indoor positioning are included. SMS access to 112 service should also be possible with coordinates included into the emergency message. An emerging challenge is non-PATS providers that do not provide location information with the call. There is a system architecture developed by NICC in UK that addresses several scenarios, where data connection is primarily used to carry 112 (VoIP) call and that provides either address or coordinate to the PSAP.

The more accurate positioning could also be used in alerting scenarios. Now the targeting accuracy is on the level of location areas for mobile users. Satellite positioning could be used in a clever way to keep track of the mobile terminals position. This might work quite well, if the positioning data streams are used to provide other location-based services. Users would then more probably allow their generation.

Acknowledgments. This research was done as part of the SCOPE project at Univ. of Jyväskylä. The project is funded in part by the Finnish Funding Agency for Technology and Innovation (TEKES) and private companies.

References

1. 112- Single European emergency number, `http://ec.europa.eu/information_society/activities/112/glossary/index_en.htm` (accessed on June 8, 2011)
2. American Automobile Association, `http://www.aaa.com` (accessed on June 8, 2011)
3. Ambulance Victoria, `http://www.ambulance.vic.gov.au/Ambulance-Victoria.html` (accessed on June 10, 2011)
4. Bergs, J., Naudts, D., Van den Wijngaert, N., Blondia, C., Moerman, I., Demeester, P., Paquay, J., De Reymaeker, F., Baekelmans, J.: The ADAMO project: Architecture to support communication for emergency services. In: Proc. of 8th IEEE International Conference on Pervasive Computing and Communications; Workshops, pp. 382–387 (2010), doi:10.1109/PERCOMW.2010.547063
5. Der Allgemeine Deutsche Automobil-Club e.V, `http://www.adac.de` (accessed on June 8, 2011)
6. Directive 2010/40/EU OF THE EUROPEAN PARLIAMENT AND OF THE COUNCIL of 7 July 2010 on the framework for the deployment of Intelligent Transport Systems in the field of road transport and for interfaces with other modes of transport. Official Journal of the European Union, en L207/1, August 6 (2010)
7. Directive 2009/136/EC OF THE EUROPEAN PARLIAMENT AND OF THE COUNCIL of 25 November 2009 amending Directive 2002/22/EC on universal service and.. Official Journal of the European Union, en L 337/11, December 18 (2009)
8. El-Mashi, S., Saddik, B.: Mobile Emergency System and Integration. In: Proc. of 12th IEEE Conference on Mobile Data Management (MDM 2011), vol. 2, pp. 67–72 (2011); Accessible through IEEE XPlore
9. ETSI/3GPP Standards for Cell Broadcast (TS 23.041, TS 44.012, TS 45.002, TS 48.049), `http://www.3gpp.org/ftp/Specs/html-info/23041.htm` (accessed on June 10, 2011)

10. European Union, Factsheet 49: eCall - saving lives through in-vehicle communication technology (July 2010),
    `http://ec.europa.eu/information_society/newsroom/cf/`
    `itemdetail.cfm?item_id=2842` (accessed on December 15, 2010)
11. European Union, eCall consultation,
    `http://ec.europa.eu/information_society/activities/esafety/`
    `ecall/index_en.htm#eCall_consultation` (accessed on June 8, 2011)
12. European Union, eSafety Forum: eCall Driving Group Memorandum of Understanding for Realisation of Interoperable In-Vehicle eCall, May 28 (2004),
    `http://ec.europa.eu/information_society/activities/esafety/`
    `ecall/index_en.htm#Memorandum_of_UnderstandingInteroperable`
    (accessed on December 15, 2010)
13. European Union, eCall-related standards,
    `http://ec.europa.eu/information_society/activities/esafety/`
    `ecallstandards/index_en.htm` (accessed on December 15, 2010)
14. European Union, 8th EU EGEA meeting materials, May 31 (2010),
    `http://circa.europa.eu/Public/irc/infso/egea/library?l=/`
    `egea_meeting_2010&vm=detailed&sb=Title` (accessed on December 14, 2010)
15. European Union 9th EGEA meeting materials, March 11 (2011),
    `http://circa.europa.eu/Public/irc/infso/egea/library?l=/`
    `egea_presentations/` (accessed on June 8, 2011)
16. European Union, ICT regulation toolkit, Section 4.5.1,
    `http://www.ictregulationtoolkit.org/en/section.2110.html`
    (accessed on June 8, 2011)
17. European Union, Eureopan Regulator Group, ERG common position on VoIP, final (December 2007), `http://www.erg.eu.int/doc/publications/`
    `erg_07_56rev2_cp_voip_final.pdf` (accessed on June 9, 2011)
18. Feng, Y.-I., Lee, C.J.: Exploring Development of Service-Oriented Architecture for Next Generation Emergency Management System. In: Proc. of IEEE 24th International Conference on Advanced Information Networking and Applications Workshops (WAINA), pp. 557–561 (2010), doi:10.1109/WAINA.2010.198
19. Gräfling, S., Mähönen, P., Riihijärvi, J.: Performance Evaluation of IEEE 1609 WAVE and IEEE 802.11p for Vehicular Communications. In: Proc. of ICUFN 2010, pp. 344–348 (2010), doi:10.1109/ICUFN, 5547184
20. Hameed, S.A., Miho, V., AlKhateeb, W., Hassan, A.: Medical Emergency and Healthcare Model Enhancement with SMS and MMS Facilities. In: Proc. of International Conference on Computer and Communication Engineering (ICCCE 2010), pp. 1–6 (2010), doi:10.1109/ICCCE.2010.5556798 (accessed on June 9, 2011 through IEEE Xplore)
21. Harmonised eCall European Pilot Project (HeeRo),
    `http://ec.europa.eu/information_society/activities/esafety/ec`
    `all/index_en.htm#eCall_consultation` (accessed on June 8, 2011)
22. Hartung, F., Horn, U., Huschke, J., Kampmann, M., Lohmar, T.: MBMS – IP Multicast/Broadcast in 3G Networks. International Journal of Digital Multimedia Broadcasting (2009), doi:10.1155/2009/597848
23. Hoirup, C., Frank, M.: Features for Emergency Calling and Short Messaging System. US Patent Nr. 6397054 B1, May 28 (2002)
24. Hwang, Z., Uhm, Y., Lee, M., Kim, G., Park, S.: A Context-Aware System Architecture for Dealing with the Emergency by the Community Service in Apartment. Future Generation Communication and Networking (FGCN) 1, 402–407, doi:10.1109/FGCN.2007.5

25. IEEE 802.11p-2010 - IEEE Standard for Local and Metropolitan Area Networks - Specific requirements Part 11: Wireless LAN Medium Access Control (MAC) and Physical Layer (PHY) Specifications Amendment 6: Wireless Access in Vehicular Environments
26. Ministry of Transport and Communications, 112-emergency text messages to be launched in 2012 (in Finnish), http://www.lvm.fi/web/fi/tiedote/view/1225393 (accessed on June 11, 2010)
27. Mountain Rescue Association, http://www.mra.org/drupal2 (accessed on June 8, 2011)
28. NICC Standard Ltd, VOIP - Location for Emergency Calls (Architecture). NICC ND 1638 Issue 1.1.2 (2010-3) (January 2010), http://www.niccstandards.org.uk/files/current/ND1638%20V1.1.2.pdf?type=pdf (accessed on December 15, 2010)
29. Protogerakis, M., Gramatke, A., Henning, K.: A System Architecture for a Telematic Support System in Emergency Medical Services. In: Proc. of 3rd International Conference on Bioinformatics and Biomedical Engineering (ICBBE 2009), pp. 1–4 (2009), doi:10.1109/ICBBE.2009.5162255
30. REACH112 - REsponding to All Citizens needing Help,http://www.reach112.eu/view/en/index.html (accessed on December 14, 2010)
31. REACH112 -UK Pilot Project, http://www.reach112.co.uk/press/ (accessed on December 15, 2010)
32. Schoenharl, T., Bravo, R., Madey, G.: WIPER: Leveraging the Cell Phone Network for Emergency Response. International Journal of Intelligent Control and Systems 11(4) (2006)
33. Schoenharl, T., Zhai, Z., McCune, R., Pawling, A., Madey, G.: Design And Implementation of An Agent-Based Simulation For Emergency Response And Crisis Management. In: Proceeding SpringSim 2009, Proceedings of the 2009 Spring Simulation Multiconference (2009), http://www.acm.org/DL (accessed on June 10, 2011)
34. Stantchev, B.: 112 Questionnaire – Best Practice State of play: A set of transparencies (2010), http://circa.europa.eu/Public/irc/infso/egea/library?l=/egea_presentations/ (accessed on June 8, 2011)
35. Sähköisen viestinnän tietosuojalaki, 516/2004, http://www.finlex.fi (accessed on June 8, 2011)
36. UMS Population Alert System, http://www.ums.no/wip4/ums-population-alert-system/d.epl?id=447437 (accessed on June 10, 2011)
37. Viestintämarkkinalaki 23.5.2003/393, http://www.finlex.fi (accessed on June 9, 2011)
38. Wang, S., Min, J., Yi, B.K.: Location-Based Services Mobiles: Technologies and Standards. Tutorial given at IEEE ICC 2008, Beijing, http://sites.google.com/site/toswang/ICC2008LBSforMobilessimplifiedR2.pdf?attredirects=0 (accessed on June 10, 2011)
39. Wikipedia: Cell Broadcast, http://www.wikipedia.org/Cell_Broadcast (accessed on June 10, 2011)
40. Wikipedia: Emergency, http://www.wikipedia.org/ Emergency (accessed on June 8, 2011)
41. Xu, Z., Yuan, Y.: A Decision Analysis Framework for Emergency Notification. In: Proc. of 41st HICSS, pp. 1–9 (2008)
42. Ye, H., Adams, M., Roy, S.: V2V Wireless Communication Protocol for Rear-End Collision Avoidance on Highways. In: Proc. of IEEE International Conference on Communications (IEEE ICC, Workshops) (2008), doi:10.1109/ICCW, 77 (accessed on June 9, 2011)

Securing Communication between SCADA Master Station and Mobile Remote Components

Rosslin John Robles and Gil-Cheol Park[*]

Multimedia Engineering Department, Hannam University,
Daejeon, Korea
rosslin_john@yahoo.com, gcpark@hnu.kr

Abstract. Conventional SCADA communications has been fixed Point-to-Multipoint serial communications over lease line or private radio systems. Mobility of Remote Components can widen the coverage and can make SCADA more powerful and more efficient. Instead of a steady sensor which can only gather limited information, the mobile sensor can cover larger space and gather more specific information. In this paper, we discussed the architecture of a traditional SCADA system, its evolution, the web SCADA and presented a new setup which utilizes remote components. We also suggested the use of Symmetric-Key Encryption to secure the communication between these components.

Keywords: SCADA, Control Systems, Communication, Encryption, Security.

1 Introduction

A SCADA System collects data from various sensors at a factory, plant or in other remote locations and then sends this data to a central computer which then manages and controls the data. SCADA and other Control Systems have been so important since it control most of our commodities. Conventional SCADA communications has been Point-to-Multipoint serial communications over lease line or private radio systems. With the advent of Internet Protocol (IP), IP Technology has seen increasing use in SCADA communications.

The connectivity of can give SCADA more scale which enables it to provide access to real-time data display, alarming, trending, and reporting from remote equipment. SCADA Communication is a core component of a SCADA Monitoring System. Common misconception regarding SCADA security was SCADA networks were isolated from all other networks and so attackers could not access the system. As the industry grows, the demand for more connectivity also increased. From a small range network, SCADA systems are sometimes connected to other networks like the internet. The open standards also make it very easy for attackers to gain in-depth knowledge about the working of these SCADA networks.

Mobility of Remote Components can widen the coverage and can make SCADA more powerful and more efficient. Instead of a steady sensor which can only gather

---

[*] Corresponding author.

T.-h. Kim et al. (Eds.): ISA 2011, CCIS 200, pp. 203–210, 2011.
© Springer-Verlag Berlin Heidelberg 2011

limited information, the mobile sensor can cover larger space and gather more specific information. In the next sections, we discussed the architecture of a traditional SCADA system, its evolution, the web SCADA and presented a new setup which utilizes remote components. We also suggested the use of Symmetric-Key Encryption to secure the communication between these components.

2 Supervisory Control and Data Acquisition (SCADA)

Supervisory Control and Data Acquisition (SCADA) existed long time ago when control systems were introduced. SCADA systems that time use data acquisition by using strip chart recorders, panels of meters, and lights. Not similar to modern SCADA systems, there is an operator which manually operates various control knobs exercised supervisory control. These devices are still used to do supervisory control and data acquisition on power generating facilities, plants and factories. [1][2]

Telemetry is automatic transmission and measurement of data from remote sources by wire or radio or other means. It is also used to send commands, programs and receives monitoring information from these remote locations. SCADA is the combination of telemetry and data acquisition. Supervisory Control and Data Acquisition system is compose of collecting of the information, transferring it to the central site, carrying out any necessary analysis and control and then displaying that information on the operator screens. The required control actions are then passed back to the process. [3]

Typical SCADA systems include the following components: [4]

1. Operating equipment such as pumps, valves, conveyors and substation breakers that can be controlled by energizing actuators or relays.
2. Local processors that communicate with the site's instruments and operating equipment.
3. Instruments in the field or in a facility that sense conditions such as pH, temperature, pressure, power level and flow rate.
4. Short range communications between the local processors and the instruments and operating equipment.
5. Long range communications between the local processors and host computers.
6. Host computers that act as the central point of monitoring and control.

The measurement and control system of SCADA has one master terminal unit (MTU) which could be called the brain of the system and one or more remote terminal units (RTU). The RTUs gather the data locally and send them to the MTU which then issues suitable commands to be executed on site. A system of either standard or customized software is used to collate, interpret and manage the data. Supervisory Control and Data Acquisition (SCADA) is conventionally set upped in a private network not connected to the internet. This is done for the purpose of isolating the confidential information as well as the control to the system itself. [2]

Because of the distance, processing of reports and the emerging technologies, SCADA can now be connected to the internet. This can bring a lot of advantages and disadvantages which will be discussed in the sections. Conventionally, relay logic was used to control production and plant systems. With the discovery of the CPU and other electronic devices, manufacturers incorporated digital electronics into relay logic equipment. Programmable logic controllers or PLC's are still the most widely used control systems in industry. As need to monitor and control more devices in the plant grew, the PLCs were distributed and the systems became more intelligent and smaller in size. PLCs (Programmable logic controllers) and DCS (distributed control systems) are used as shown in the next Figure.

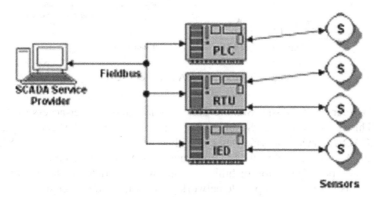

Fig. 1. Conventional SCADA Architecture

Data acquisition begins at the RTU or PLC level and includes meter readings and equipment status reports that are communicated to SCADA as required. Data is then compiled and formatted in such a way that a control room operator using the HMI can make supervisory decisions to adjust or override normal RTU (PLC) controls. Data may also be fed to a Historian, often built on a commodity Database Management System, to allow trending and other analytical auditing. [2]

SCADA systems typically implement a distributed database, commonly referred to as a tag database, which contains data elements called tags or points. A point represents a single input or output value monitored or controlled by the system. Points can be either "hard" or "soft". A hard point represents an actual input or output within the system, while a soft point results from logic and math operations applied to other points. Points are normally stored as value-timestamp pairs: a value, and the timestamp when it was recorded or calculated. A series of value-timestamp pairs gives the history of that point. It's also common to store additional metadata with tags, such as the path to a field device or PLC register, design time comments, and alarm information. [2]

3 Internet SCADA Technology

Conventional SCADA only have 4 components: the master station, plc/rtu, fieldbus and sensors. Internet SCADA replaces or extends the fieldbus to the internet. This means that the Master Station can be on a different network or location.

In the next Figure, you can see the architecture of SCADA which is connected through the internet. Like a normal SCADA, it has RTUs/PLCs/IEDs, The SCADA

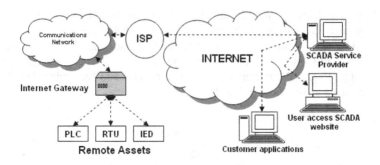

Fig. 2. Internet SCADA Architecture [6]

Service Provider or the Master Station. This also includes the user-access to SCADA website. This is for the smaller SCADA operators that can avail the services provided by the SCADA service provider. It can either be a company that uses SCADA exclusively. Another component of the internet SCADA is the Customer Application which allows report generation or billing. Along with the fieldbus, the internet is an extension. This is setup like a private network so that only the master station can have access to the remote assets. The master also has an extension that acts as a web server so that the SCADA users and customers can access the data through the SCADA provider website. [5]

AS the system evolves, SCADA systems are coming in line with standard networking technologies. Ethernet and TCP/IP based protocols are replacing the older proprietary standards. Although certain characteristics of frame-based network communication technology (determinism, synchronization, protocol selection, environment suitability) have restricted the adoption of Ethernet in a few specialized applications, the vast majority of markets have accepted Ethernet networks for HMI/SCADA.

A few vendors have begun offering application specific SCADA systems hosted on remote platforms over the Internet. This removes the need to install and commission systems at the end-user's facility and takes advantage of security features already available in Internet technology, VPNs and SSL. Some concerns include security, [6] Internet connection reliability, and latency.

4   Remote Mobile Components

Mobility is in demand in many IT systems. In this section, the architecture of SCADA in the web with remote sensors is discussed. We believe that having mobile components can improve the performance and it can provide larger operational coverage for SCADA systems. [8] This solution is designed to increase the coverage and flexibility of SCADA systems. It may not appear to be a security solution, but it some cases this could discourage attackers to attack the system. [9]

This architecture is based on web SCADA and the functionality is patterned on mobile IPv6. The parts are still similar to a typical SCADA system. It has a master station, remote terminals like the PLC and the RTU and the sensors will act as the fieldbus. [8] The main difference of this system is that the sensors are mobile. It is not attached to a specific place. So instead of having a specific remote terminal to control the sensors, all the remote terminals will have the capability of controlling and gathering information from the sensors. The function of the master station is still the same but master station will be able to redirect the commands to the specific RTU in which mobile sensor is presently connected. [8][9]

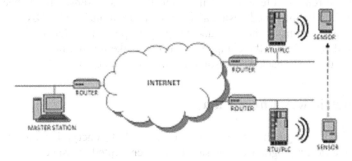

Fig. 3. SCADA with mobile components

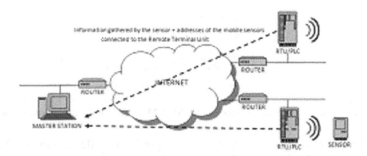

Fig. 4. The remote terminal periodically transmits the information from the sensors and the addresses of the sensors

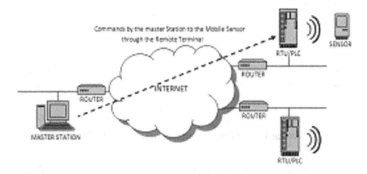

Fig. 5. The master station sends a command to the mobile sensors which transferred to another terminal

As the function of the typical remote terminal, it periodically transmits information gathered by the sensors. In this architecture, the remote terminal also periodically transmits the addresses of all mobile sensors connected to it as shown in Figure 6. Whenever mobile sensor moves to another terminal, the remote terminal sends its address to the master station. In this case, the master station knows all the whereabouts of the remote Sensor. As shown in Figure 5, it can send commands through the current remote terminal in which the remote sensor is connected. This Architecture can be improved, tested and implemented to many SCADA systems. The main advantage of this is the cost and the larger space in which it will cover. [9] Because of the mobility of the components, it will make it difficult for attackers to set their hacking device to hack or control a specific SCADA component.

5   Symmetric Key Encryption

In Symmetric cryptography, same key is used for both encryption and decryption. Using symmetric cryptography, it is safe to send encrypted messages without fear of interception. This means only the SCADA master and the remote assets can communicate with each other because of the said key.

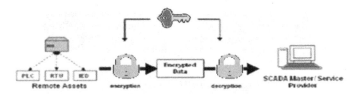

Fig. 6. Symmetric cryptography between SCADA Master Station and Remote Components

WEP was included as the privacy of the original IEEE 802.11 standard. WEP uses the stream cipher RC4 for confidentiality, and the CRC-32 checksum for integrity. It can be implemented to wireless SCADA as it is implemented to other wireless systems. Messages between remote RTU's can be converted to ciphertext by utilizing this mechanism. The next Figure shows how this is done. [10]

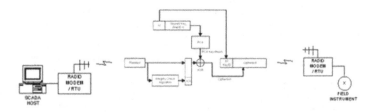

Fig. 7. Standard WEP Encryption in Wireless SCADA environment

The use of symmetric key encryption specifically the RC4 cipher was also is applicable in a wireless Web-SCADA. It can provide security to the data that is transmitted from the SCADA master and the mobile remote assets and also communication between mobile remote RTU's. Once a system is connected to the internet especially wirelessly, it is not impossible for other internet users to have access to the system that is why encryption should be implemented. Data and report generation is also in demand so the internet SCADA is designed to have a web based report generation system through http. And to cut off the budget for communication lines, SCADA operators utilize the wireless based SCADA. [10]

To test the usability of this scheme, it was tested using the web base Symmetric-key Encryption simulator. Since there are many kinds of Symmetric-key Encryption, in this simulator, RC4 is used. The simulator uses the following javascript function to encrypt the command:

```
function rc4encrypt() {
document.rc4.text.value=textToBase64(rc4(document.rc4.key
.value,document.rc4.text.value))
}
```

And the following javascript function is used to decrypt the command:

```
function rc4decrypt() {
document.rc4.text.value=(rc4(document.rc4.key.value,base6
4ToText(document.rc4.text.value)))
}
```

In the next table, results of encrypted commands are depicted. The first column shows the command; the second column shows the key which is used for encryption; the third column shows the encrypted data and the last column shows the actual command. It reflects the encrypted data in which will be difficult for the attackers to crack. These scheme will improve the security of communication between the master station and the remote mobile components.

Table 1. Symmetric-key Encryption of SCADA commands

Command	Key 1	Encrypted data	Decrypted data
command 1	10001	JqMgRYo7ca	turn on
command 2	10001	JqMgRYo7kig	turn off
command 3	10001	04NbRMk4ya	connect
command 4	10001	ZG3gMoA7ce2dCb	disconnect
command 5	10001	4ewdRYE9nGMgnb	open valve
command 6	10001	003b2M6OAugaEXa	close valve
command 7	10001	"ahbJYo7CeMa	half open
command 8	10001	"ahbJYo4aS2hnb	half close

6 Conclusion

SCADA (Supervisory Control and Data Acquisition) communication can take place in a number of ways. SCADA Communication is a core component of a SCADA Monitoring System. Early SCADA communication took place over radio, modem, or dedicated serial lines. The process of communication over a SCADA system involves several different SCADA system components. These include the sensors and control relays, Remote Terminal Units (RTUs), SCADA master units, and the overall communication network. Conventional SCADA communications has been fixed Point-to-Multipoint serial communications over lease line or private radio systems.

Mobility of Remote Components can widen the coverage and can make SCADA more powerful and more efficient. Instead of a steady sensor which can only gather limited information, the mobile sensor can cover larger space and gather more specific information. We believe that having mobile components can improve the performance and it can provide larger operational coverage for SCADA systems. In this paper, we discussed the architecture of a traditional SCADA system, its evolution, the web SCADA and presented a new setup which utilizes remote components. We also suggested the use of Symmetric-Key Encryption to secure the communication between these components.

Acknowledgement. This work was supported by the Security Engineering Research Center, granted by the Korea Ministry of Knowledge Economy.

References

1. Reed, T.: At the Abyss: An Insider's History of the Cold War. Presidio Press (March 2004)
2. Kim, T.-h.: Weather Condition Double Checking in Internet SCADA Environment. WSEAS Transactions on Systems and Control 5(8), 623 (2010) ISSN: 1991-8763
3. Bailey, D., Wright, E.: Practical SCADA for Industry (2003)
4. Hildick-Smith, A.: Security for Critical Infrastructure SCADA Systems (2005)
5. Robles, R.J., Seo, K.-T., Kim, T.-h.: Security solution for internet SCADA. In: Korean Institute of Information Technology, IT Convergence Technology - Summer Workshops and Conference Proceedings, vol. 5, pp. 461–463 (2010)
6. Wallace, D.: Control Engineering. How to put SCADA on the Internet (2003), http://www.controleng.com/article/CA321065.html (accessed: January 2010)
7. McClanahan, R.H.: SCADA AND IP: Is Network Convergence Really Here? IEEE Industry Applications Magazine (March/April 2003)
8. Choi, M.-k., Robles, R.J., Cho, E.-s., Park, B.-j., Kim, S.-s., Park, G.-c., Kim, T.-h.: A Proposed Architecture for SCADA System with Mobile Sensors. Journal of Korean Institute of Information Technology 8(5), 13–20 (2010) ISSN: 1598-8619
9. Kim, T.-h.: SCADA Architecture with Mobile Remote Components. WSEAS Transactions on Systems and Control 5(8) (August 2010) ISSN: 1991-8763
10. Robles, R.J., Choi, M.-K.: Symmetric-Key Encryption for Wireless Internet SCADA. In: Security Technology. CCIS, vol. 58, pp. 289–297 (1865) ISSN: 1865-0929

Retrofit to CAIN of IP-Based Supervisory Control and Data Acquisition System

Maricel O. Balitanas, Seung-Hwan Jeon, and Tai-hoon Kim[*]

Multimedia Engineering Department,
Hannam University
133 Ojeong-dong, Daeduk-gu,
Daejeon, Korea
maricel1@hotmail.com,
jeoninoldenburg@hanmail.net,
taihoonn@hnu.kr

Abstract. SCADA historically is responsible for monitoring and controlling critical infrastructures and manufacturing processes in an isolated environment. But with the requirement of a timely access of information for making decisions, large and modern companies being in a geographically diverse location take advantage of the internet as an important communication channel to allow the exchange of data. However, with SCADA being in the internet raise the issue of security. With the posted threats and listed vulnerabilities in this study, a retrofit for these threats through the crossed cipher scheme is presented. To get the best of both types of cipher symmetric using AES (Advanced Encryption Standard) and the asymmetric ECC (Elliptic Curve Cryptography) to address the Confidentiality, Authentication, Integrity and Non-repudiation issues in SCADA system.

Keywords: SCADA, Cryptography, Asymmetric, Symmetric.

1 Introduction

Major concern about cyber attack stems from the notion that the SCADA network is no longer an isolated network which prohibits outsiders from entering the network, nor is the specialized network based on private platforms and protocols, allowing only technical staffs with special knowledge to access to the resources. The reasons of claiming that the SCADA network is not a protected closed network is twofold. First, the communication architecture is more relying on the open standard communication protocols. The use of the open communication protocols renders the system more vulnerable to cyber attacks in many applications. Second, the SCADA network is moving toward being connected to corporate networks for convenience and other business reasons. Thus the SCADA network may open its doors to outsiders who can enter the corporate networks maliciously.

Historically, the industrial control and SCADA systems that are responsible for monitoring and controlling our critical infrastructures and manufacturing processes

---

[*] Corresponding author.

T.-h. Kim et al. (Eds.): ISA 2011, CCIS 200, pp. 211–218, 2011.
© Springer-Verlag Berlin Heidelberg 2011

have operated in isolated environments. These control systems and devices communicated with each other almost exclusively, and rarely shared information with systems outside their environment. As more components of control systems become interconnected with the outside world using IP-based standards, the probability and impact of a cyber attack will heighten. In fact, there is increasing concern among both government officials and control systems experts about potential cyber threats to the control systems that govern critical infrastructures. Even the flaws in SCADA specific technologies have become general knowledge

For the past several years a few of researches have been done on the SCADA security issues. Along with the works in the research community, the international standard bodies also have worked to derive the standard documents for the SCADA security. The purpose of this study is not only to define the challenges for a known isolated SCADA system, but also to organize the results that these isolated case is no longer isolated but is now vulnerable to cyber attack threats. The current results on these challenges will be summarized from the efforts of the international organization as well as research communities.

2   The SCADA Infrastructure Process

2.1   SCADA over the Internet

There are several different Web-based architectures currently on offer for an Internet based SCADA system. The systems are quite different in design and functionality. Each has its own set of advantages and disadvantages. In general, Internet and Web-based SCADA systems have advantages over traditional SCADA systems for reasons of [4, 5].

A Web Server does all the data processing and returns the HMI graphics to the user across the web as a Java/Web graphical Interface. This interface is again accessed using a standard web browser. Figure 1 shows both local and remote clients using the SSP server to access the plant.

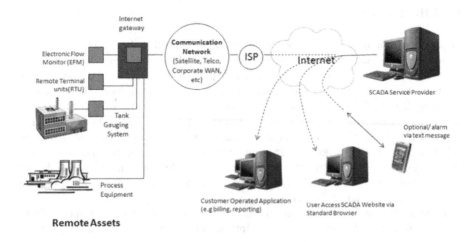

Fig. 1. Remote Access via a SCADA Service Provider [4]

The main advantage of this system is that it removes some of the cost associated with a traditional large scale SCADA system. The need for in house expertise to provide support and maintenance for the system is removed as this is all done by the SCADA Service Provider [4].

3   The Problem

The complexity of modern SCADA systems leaves many vulnerabilities as well as vectors for attack. Attacks can come from many places, including indirectly through the corporate network, virtual private networks (VPN), wireless networks, and dial-up modems. Possible attack vectors on an SCADA system include:

- Backdoors and holes in network perimeter.
- Vulnerabilities in common protocols.
- Database attacks.
- Communications hijacking and 'man-in-the-middle' attacks.

3.1   Known Attacks

2000 and 1982: Gas Pipelines in Russia (and the former Soviet Union). In 2000, the Interior Ministry of Russia reported that hackers seized temporary control of the system regulating gas flows in natural gas pipelines, although it is not publicly known if there was physical damage [6]. The former Soviet Union was victim of an attack to their gas pipeline infrastructure in 1982 when a logic bomb caused an explosion in Siberia [7].

January 2000: Maroochy Shire Sewage Spill [10]. The most well-known attack upon a SCADA system was the attack on the Maroochy Shire Council's sewage control system in Queensland, Australia. On January 2000, almost immediately after the control system for the sewage plant was installed by a contractor company, the plant experienced a series of problems. Pumps failed to start or stop when specified. Alarms failed to be reported. There were intermittent loss of communications between the control center and the pumping stations. At the beginning, the sewage system operators thought there was a leak in the pipes. Then they observed that valves were opening without being months of logging that they discovered that spoofed controllers were activating the valves. It took several more months to find the culprit: a disgruntled ex-employee of the contractor company that had installed the control system originally. The ex-employee was trying to convince the water treatment company to hire him to solve the problems he was creating.

The effect of the attacks was the flooding of the grounds of a nearby hotel, park, and river with approximately 264,000 gallons of raw sewage. In analyzing this attack, one of the insights was that cyber attacks may be unusually hard to detect (compared to physical attacks). The response to this attack was very slow; the attacker managed to launch 46 documented attacks before he was caught.

August 2005: Automobile plants and the Zotob Worm [9]. Zotob is a worm that spreads by exploiting the Microsoft Windows Plug and Play Buffer Overflow Vulnerability4. In August 2005, Zotob crashed thirteen of DaimlerChrysler's U.S.

automobile manufacturing plants forcing them to remain offline for almost an hour. Plants in Illinois, Indiana, Wisconsin, Ohio, Delaware, and Michigan were also forced down. Zotob affected computers by slowing them down and causing them to continually crash and reboot. Infected Windows 2000 computers were potentially left exposed to more malicious attacks, while infected Windows XP computers can only continue to spread the worms. While the Zotob worm itself did not have a destructive payload, it left an open backdoor control channel that could allow attackers to commandeer the infected machine. The worm also added several lines of code into a machine to prevent it from accessing certain antivirus websites. Zotob and its variations also caused computer outages at heavy-equipment maker Caterpillar Inc., aircraft-maker Boeing, and several large U.S. news organizations.

4   The Scheme for CAIN Threats

4.1   Integration of Cryptography

Cryptography is the science of writing in secret code and is an ancient art; the first documented use of cryptography in writing dates back to circa 1900 B.C. when an Egyptian scribe used non-standard hieroglyphs in an inscription. Some experts argue that cryptography appeared spontaneously sometime after writing was invented, with applications ranging from diplomatic missives to war-time battle plans. It is no surprise, then, that new forms of cryptography came soon after the widespread development of computer communications. In data and telecommunications, cryptography is necessary when communicating over any untrusted medium, which includes just about any network, particularly the Internet.

A cryptosystem consists of three algorithms: one for key generation, one for encryption, and one for decryption. Their application to industrial control systems may present design and operational challenges. This primer provides assistance to control systems security professionals to identify appropriate encryption techniques and determine whether to deploy a cryptosystem solution as a security feature in their specific control systems environment. This primer also presents examples of cryptosystem deployment solutions to assist users in identifying appropriate application for their specific system.

Cryptosystems have four intended goals:

• Confidentiality
• Authentication
• Integrity
• Non-repudiation

Symmetric and asymmetric ciphers each have their own advantages and disadvantages. Symmetric ciphers are significantly faster than asymmetric ciphers, but require all parties to somehow share a secret (the key). The asymmetric algorithms allow public key infrastructures and key exchange systems, but at the cost of speed. So, in this study a combination of the best features of both symmetric and asymmetric encryption techniques is presented in the form of a cryptography scheme presented in the next figure. It depicts the Chain of operation.

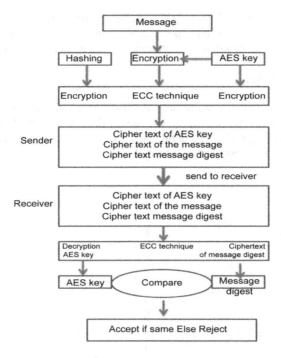

Fig. 2. Cryptography Scheme Chain of operation

4.2   Implementation

The implementation was done using out in J2SE (Java 2, Standard Edition) v 1.4.0. J2SE has the built-in classes for AES, and MD5 Hashing. The code uses these packages

Fig. 3. Cipher emulator

and the header files have the following header. Using Java a method has been developed for elliptic curve generation, base point generation, keys (both public and private) generation and encryption and decryption. Below is the emulator used for this study. [9]

4.3   Testing the Scheme

Testing the cipher scheme on a test data of various sizes, Table 1 provides details on the time taken for encryption; decryption and calculation of MD5 message digest process. The following table depicts information on Encryption & Decryption of 128 bit AES key and MD5 message digest using ECC.

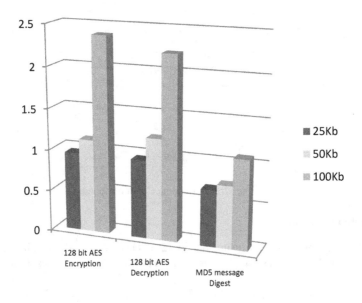

Fig. 4. Graphical analysis of AES and MD5

Table 1. Encryption & Decryption of AES key and MD5 message digest using ECC

	Encryption	**Decryption**
128 bit AES key	32	36
MD5 Hashing of Ciphertext	33	38

Since the ECC key sizes are so much shorter than comparable RSA keys, the length of the public key and private key is much shorter in elliptic curve cryptosystems. This results into faster processing times, and lower demands on memory and bandwidth. With any cryptographic system dealing with 128 bit key, the total number of combination is 2128. The time required to check all possible combinations at the rate of 50 billion keys/second is approximately 5 x 1021 years. Computational complexity for breaking the elliptic-curve cryptosystem for an elliptic curve key size of 150 bits is 3.8 x 1010 MIPS (Million Instructions Per Second years) [10]. While ECC may be relatively difficult to understand for the layman, it is nevertheless an important technology that has great potential to prosper in the future. The challenging and somewhat complicated nature of elliptic curve groups makes it harder to crack the ECC discrete logarithm problem. With less bits required to give the same security, ECC has fared favorably compared to RSA.

5   Conclusion

The design and implementation of the scheme was done in Java combining the best of both symmetric (AES) and asymmetric (ECC) cryptography and to ensure integrity of the data, the MD5 hash algorithm was adopted. The design and strength of all key lengths of the AES algorithm (i.e., 128, 192 and 256) are sufficient to protect classified information up to the SECRET level. TOP SECRET information will require use of either the 192 or 256 key lengths. This symmetric cryptography AES was used along with ECC asymmetric cryptography. An important feature of these curves is that their points can be interpreted as part of a mathematical group and the challenging and somewhat complicated nature of elliptic curve groups makes it harder to crack the ECC discrete logarithm problem. With less bits required by ECC to give the same security compared to other existing asymmetric cryptography, ECC is indeed a reliable cryptographic scheme that will be important in the near future.

Acknowledgement. This work was supported by the Security Engineering Research Center, granted by the Korea Ministry of Knowledge Economy.

References

1. Ryu, D., Balitanas, M.: Security Management for Distributed Denial of Service Attack. Journal of Security Engineering 7(2) (April 2010) ISSN: 1738-7531
2. McClanahan, R.H.: SCADA AND IP: Is Network Convergence Really Here? IEEE Industry Applications Magazine (March/April 2003)
3. GAO-04-628T. Critical infrastructure protection: challenges and efforts to secure control systems. Testimony Before the Subcommittee on Technology Information Policy, Intergovernmental Relations and the Census, House Committee on Government Reform. March 30 (2004), http://www.gao.gov/new.items/d04628t.pdf
4. e-scada.com (2002), http://www.e-scada.com/why.html (viewed on October 15, 2005)
5. Bentek Systems (n.d.), Internet and Web-based SCADA, http://www.scadalink.com/technotesIP.htm (viewed on October 15, 2005)

6. Quinn-Judge, P.: Cracks in the system. TIME Magazine (January 9, 2002)
7. Reed, T.: At the Abyss: An Insider's History of the Cold War. Presidio Press (March 2004)
8. Balitanas, M., Robles, R.J., Kim, N., Kim, T.: Crossed Crypto-scheme in WPA PSK Mode. In: BLISS 2009, IEEE CS, Edinburgh (August 2009) ISBN 978-0-7695-3754-5
9. Roberts, P.: Zotob, PnP Worms Slam 13 DaimlerChrysler Plants, eweek.com, August 18 (2005), http://www.eweek.com/c/a/Security/Zotob-PnP-Worms-Slam-13-DaimlerChrysler-Plants/
10. Stallings, W.: Cryptography and Network Security, 2nd edn. Prentice Hall, Upper Saddle River

Application Program Interface as Back-Up Data Source for SCADA Systems

Rosslin John Robles and Tai-hoon Kim[*]

Multimedia Engineering Department, Hannam University,
Daejeon, Korea
rosslin_john@yahoo.com, taihoonn@hnu.kr

Abstract. Internet SCADA was developed to widen the coverage span of the SCADA system. In this section, a double checking scheme for Internet SCADA Environment is analyzed. This is to improve the accuracy of data and to improve the performance of SCADA Systems. This scheme uses data from weather API Providers. Many API Provider such as Google, Yahoo, etc have Weather API's. Weather API's can give weather condition and forecast about a specific place.

Keywords: SCADA, Control Systems, Communication, API.

1 Introduction

A SCADA System collects data from various sensors at a factory, plant or in other remote locations and then sends this data to a central computer which then manages and controls the data. SCADA and other Control Systems have been so important since it control most of our commodities. Conventional SCADA communications has been Point-to-Multipoint serial communications over lease line or private radio systems. With the advent of Internet Protocol (IP), IP Technology has seen increasing use in SCADA communications.

The connectivity of can give SCADA more scale which enables it to provide access to real-time data display, alarming, trending, and reporting from remote equipment. SCADA Communication is a core component of a SCADA Monitoring System. Common misconception regarding SCADA security was SCADA networks were isolated from all other networks and so attackers could not access the system. As the industry grows, the demand for more connectivity also increased. From a small range network, SCADA systems are sometimes connected to other networks like the internet. The open standards also make it very easy for attackers to gain in-depth knowledge about the working of these SCADA networks.

Mobility of Remote Components can widen the coverage and can make SCADA more powerful and more efficient. Instead of a steady sensor which can only gather limited information, the mobile sensor can cover larger space and gather more specific information. In the next sections, we discussed the architecture of a traditional SCADA system, its evolution, the web SCADA and presented a new setup

---

[*] Corresponding author.

T.-h. Kim et al. (Eds.): ISA 2011, CCIS 200, pp. 219–226, 2011.
© Springer-Verlag Berlin Heidelberg 2011

which utilizes remote components. We also suggested the use of Symmetric-Key Encryption to secure the communication between these components.

2   Supervisory Control and Data Acquisition (SCADA)

Supervisory Control and Data Acquisition (SCADA) existed long time ago when control systems were introduced. SCADA systems that time use data acquisition by using strip chart recorders, panels of meters, and lights. Not similar to modern SCADA systems, there is an operator which manually operates various control knobs exercised supervisory control. These devices are still used to do supervisory control and data acquisition on power generating facilities, plants and factories. [1][2]

Telemetry is automatic transmission and measurement of data from remote sources by wire or radio or other means. It is also used to send commands, programs and receives monitoring information from these remote locations. SCADA is the combination of telemetry and data acquisition. Supervisory Control and Data Acquisition system is compose of collecting of the information, transferring it to the central site, carrying out any necessary analysis and control and then displaying that information on the operator screens. The required control actions are then passed back to the process. [3]

Typical SCADA systems include the following components: [4]

1. Operating equipment such as pumps, valves, conveyors and substation breakers that can be controlled by energizing actuators or relays.
2. Local processors that communicate with the site's instruments and operating equipment.
3. Instruments in the field or in a facility that sense conditions such as pH, temperature, pressure, power level and flow rate.
4. Short range communications between the local processors and the instruments and operating equipment.
5. Long range communications between the local processors and host computers.
6. Host computers that act as the central point of monitoring and control.

The measurement and control system of SCADA has one master terminal unit (MTU) which could be called the brain of the system and one or more remote terminal units (RTU). The RTUs gather the data locally and send them to the MTU which then issues suitable commands to be executed on site. A system of either standard or customized software is used to collate, interpret and manage the data. Supervisory Control and Data Acquisition (SCADA) is conventionally set upped in a private network not connected to the internet. This is done for the purpose of isolating the confidential information as well as the control to the system itself. [2]

Because of the distance, processing of reports and the emerging technologies, SCADA can now be connected to the internet. This can bring a lot of advantages and disadvantages which will be discussed in the sections. Conventionally, relay logic was used to control production and plant systems. With the discovery of the CPU and other electronic devices, manufacturers incorporated digital electronics into relay logic equipment. Programmable logic controllers or PLC's are still the most widely used control systems in industry. As need to monitor and control more devices in the plant grew, the PLCs were distributed and the systems became more intelligent and smaller in size. PLCs (Programmable logic controllers) and DCS (distributed control systems) are used as shown in the next Figure.

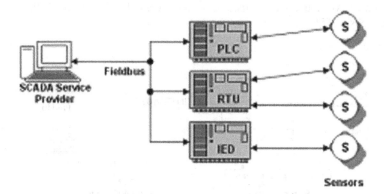

Fig. 1. Conventional SCADA Architecture

Data acquisition begins at the RTU or PLC level and includes meter readings and equipment status reports that are communicated to SCADA as required. Data is then compiled and formatted in such a way that a control room operator using the HMI can make supervisory decisions to adjust or override normal RTU (PLC) controls. Data may also be fed to a Historian, often built on a commodity Database Management System, to allow trending and other analytical auditing. [2]

SCADA systems typically implement a distributed database, commonly referred to as a tag database, which contains data elements called tags or points. A point represents a single input or output value monitored or controlled by the system. Points can be either "hard" or "soft". A hard point represents an actual input or output within the system, while a soft point results from logic and math operations applied to other points. Points are normally stored as value-timestamp pairs: a value, and the timestamp when it was recorded or calculated. A series of value-timestamp pairs gives the history of that point. It's also common to store additional metadata with tags, such as the path to a field device or PLC register, design time comments, and alarm information. [2]

3 Internet SCADA Technology

Conventional SCADA only have 4 components: the master station, plc/rtu, fieldbus and sensors. Internet SCADA replaces or extends the fieldbus to the internet. This means that the Master Station can be on a different network or location.

In the next Figure, you can see the architecture of SCADA which is connected through the internet. Like a normal SCADA, it has RTUs/PLCs/IEDs, The SCADA Service Provider or the Master Station. This also includes the user-access to SCADA website. This is for the smaller SCADA operators that can avail the services provided by the SCADA service provider. It can either be a company that uses SCADA exclusively. Another component of the internet SCADA is the Customer Application which allows report generation or billing. Along with the fieldbus, the internet is an extension. This is setup like a private network so that only the master station can have access to the remote assets. The master also has an extension that acts as a web server so that the SCADA users and customers can access the data through the SCADA provider website. [5]

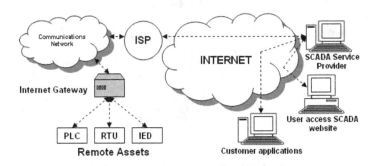

Fig. 2. Internet SCADA Architecture [6]

AS the system evolves, SCADA systems are coming in line with standard networking technologies. Ethernet and TCP/IP based protocols are replacing the older proprietary standards. Although certain characteristics of frame-based network communication technology (determinism, synchronization, protocol selection, environment suitability) have restricted the adoption of Ethernet in a few specialized applications, the vast majority of markets have accepted Ethernet networks for HMI/SCADA.

A few vendors have begun offering application specific SCADA systems hosted on remote platforms over the Internet. This removes the need to install and commission systems at the end-user's facility and takes advantage of security features already available in Internet technology, VPNs and SSL. Some concerns include security, [6] Internet connection reliability, and latency.

4 API

API's or application program interface, are set of routines, protocols, and tools for building software applications. A good API makes it easier to develop a program by providing all the building blocks. A programmer then puts the blocks together. [8]

Most operating environments, such as MS-Windows, provide an API so that programmers can write applications consistent with the operating environment. Although APIs are designed for programmers, they are ultimately good for users because they guarantee that all programs using a common API will have similar interfaces. This makes it easier for users to learn new programs. [8] Many API Provider such as Google, Yahoo, etc have Weather API's. Weather API's can give weather condition and forecast about a specific place. [7]

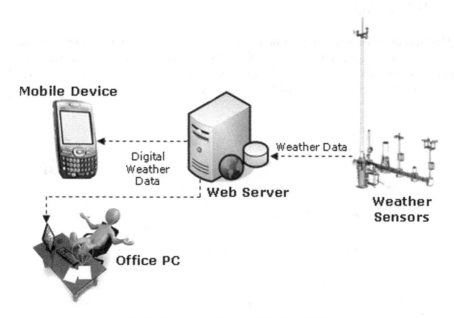

Fig. 3. Data transmission of Weather API's

We developed a program that was use in gathering the weather information from Google Web API. [9] This program was created in Visual Basic 6 and was designed to gather weather data. And to show that it is possible to acquire real time data from these API's.

The result of application can be found in the next figure. This application has the function of gathering weather information such as temperature, Humidity, Wind direction, etc. [9]

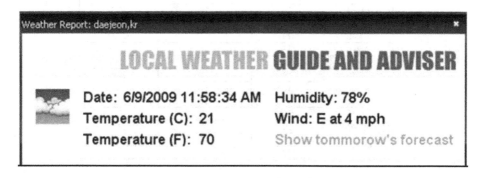

Fig. 4. Interface of an application that we created to gather weather information of a specific place from an API source

5   Integrating API to SCADA

This Scheme is designed to provide more data integrity to SCADA Systems. Weather API's can be integration to Internet SCADA systems to double check the weather condition. Weather sensors of SCADA systems may not gather correct data. This is very crucial and integration of API's can improve the data gathered. [7]

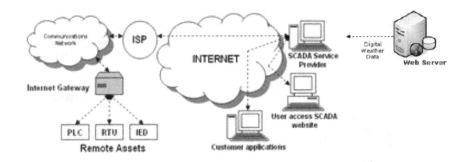

Fig. 5. SCADA Service Provider getting information from API service server

Table 1. Comparison of Gathered Weather Data

Time	Sensor Data	API Data	Average
06:10	26	27	26.5
06:13	24	27	25.5
06:16	26	27	26.5
06:19	23	24	23.5
06:22	24	24	24
06:25	25	24	24.5
06:28	26	24	25
06:31	21	22	21.5
06:34	20	19	19.5
06:37	19	18	18.5
06:40	23	20	21.5
06:43	18	19	18.5
06:46	17	16	16.5
06:49	15	14	14.5
06:52	12	12	12
06:55	16	15	15.5
06:58	18	17	17.5
07:01	20	19	19.5
07:04	23	22	22.5
07:07	22	24	23

SCADA controller or SCADA master station can get both data from the sensor (x) and the data from the Weather API (y). Usually, the controller only bases the commands on the sensor data. Since we integrate the Weather API to the system, we

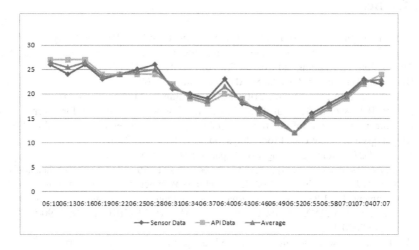

Fig. 6. Comparison of Gathered Sensor Data, API Data and the Average

can also gather its data and we propose to get the average between the Sensor data and the API's data to get the base data (z) in which the commands will be based. [7]

$$z = (x + y) / 2 \tag{1}$$

Formula *(1)* will be the bases of the SCADA Controller in executing commands to the remote terminals. In Figure 4-10, we can see the comparison between the gathered Sensor data, API data and the average data. We will notice that there's sometimes a difference between the Sensor data and API data. [7]

If an attacker attacks or alter the data in SCADA, because of the double checking Scheme, the operator may notice a large disparity between the sensor data and API data. This could help prevent large damages in SCADA systems and Infrastructures.

6   Conclusion

The security of SCADA systems is important because compromise or destruction of these systems would impact multiple areas of society far removed from the original compromise. The data that is gathered by the system is very important. The system reacts to the data it gets. Imagine what will happen if the data is not accurate. It can damage the society. To improve the accuracy of data and to improve the performance of SCADA systems, a double checking scheme for Weather Condition in Internet SCADA Environment was designed. This scheme uses data from weather API Providers. Many API Provider such as Google, Yahoo, etc have Weather API's. Weather API's can give weather condition. [7]

References

1. Reed, T.: At the Abyss: An Insider's History of the Cold War. Presidio Press (March 2004)
2. Kim, T.-h.: Weather Condition Double Checking in Internet SCADA Environment. WSEAS Transactions on Systems and Control 5(8), 623 (2010) ISSN: 1991-8763
3. Bailey, D., Wright, E.: Practical SCADA for Industry (2003)
4. Hildick-Smith, A.: Security for Critical Infrastructure SCADA Systems (2005)
5. Robles, R.J., Seo, K.-T., Kim, T.-h.: Communication Security solution for internet SCADA. In: Korean Institute of Information Technology 2010 IT Convergence Technology - Summer workshops and Conference Proceedings, pp. 461–463 (May 2010)
6. Wallace, D.: Control Engineering. How to put SCADA on the Internet (2003), http://www.controleng.com/article/CA321065.html (accessed: January 2010)
7. Robles, R.J., Kim, T.-H.: Double Checking Weather Condition in Internet SCADA Environment. In: 12th WSEAS International Conference on Automatic Control, Modelling & Simulation (ACMOS 2010), Catania, Italy, May 29-31 (2010) ISSN: 1790-5117, ISBN: 978-954-92600-1-4
8. What is API? A word definition from the Webopedia Computer Dictionary, http://www.webopedia.com/TERM/A/API.html (accessed: April 2010)
9. Ozdemir, E., Karacor, M.: Mobile phone based SCADA for industrial automation. ISA Trans. 45(1), 67–75 (2006)

Supervisory Control and Data Acquisition
System CAIN Issues

Maricel O. Balitanas and Tai-hoon Kim[*]

Multimedia Engineering Department,
Hannam University
133 Ojeong-dong, Daeduk-gu,
Daejeon, Korea
maricel@hotmail.com,
taihoonn@hnu.kr

Abstract. The industrial control and SCADA systems that are responsible for monitoring and controlling our critical infrastructures and manufacturing processes historically have operated in isolated environments. These control systems and devices communicated with each other almost exclusively, and rarely shared information with systems outside their environment. As more components of control systems become interconnected with the outside world using IP-based standards, the probability and impact of a cyber attack will heighten. There is an increasing concern among both government officials and control systems experts about potential cyber threats to the control systems that govern critical infrastructures. With the posted threats and listed vulnerabilities, a retrofit for these threats through the crossed cipher scheme is the main contribution of this study. To get the best of both types of cipher (symmetric and asymmetric) to address the Confidentiality, Authentication, Integrity and Non-repudiation issues in SCADA system.

Keywords: SCADA, Cryptography, Asymmetric, Symmetric.

1 Introduction

Historically, the industrial control and SCADA systems that are responsible for monitoring and controlling our critical infrastructures and manufacturing processes have operated in isolated environments. These control systems and devices communicated with each other almost exclusively, and rarely shared information with systems outside their environment. As more components of control systems become interconnected with the outside world using IP-based standards, the probability and impact of a cyber attack will heighten. In fact, there is increasing concern among both government officials and control systems experts about potential cyber threats to the control systems that govern critical infrastructures.

Major concern about cyber attack stems from the notion that the SCADA network is no longer an isolated network which prohibits outsiders from entering the network,

---

[*] Corresponding author.

T.-h. Kim et al. (Eds.): ISA 2011, CCIS 200, pp. 227–235, 2011.

nor is the specialized network based on private platforms and protocols, allowing only technical staffs with special knowledge to access to the resources. The reasons of claiming that the SCADA network is not a protected closed network is twofold. First, the communication architecture is more relying on the open standard communication protocols. The use of the open communication protocols renders the system more vulnerable to cyber attacks in many applications. Second, the SCADA network is moving toward being connected to corporate networks for convenience and other business reasons. Thus the SCADA network may open its doors to outsiders who can enter the corporate networks maliciously.

For the past several years a few of researches have been done on the SCADA security issues. Along with the works in the research community, the international standard bodies also have worked to derive the standard documents for the SCADA security. The purpose of this study is not only to define the challenges for a known isolated SCADA system, but also to organize the results that these isolated case is no longer isolated but is now vulnerable to cyber attack threats. The current results on these challenges will be summarized from the efforts of the international organization as well as research communities.

2   The SCADA Infrastructure Process

The evolution of SCADA system has been through 3 generations. [11]

2.1   Monolithic: First Generation

Computing in the first generation was done with the help of Mainframe systems. When the SCADA was developed networks did not exist. Therefore the SCADA systems were without any connectivity to any other system hence were independent systems. Later on RTU vendors designed the Wide Area Networks which helped in communication with RTU. The usage of communication protocols at that time was proprietary. If the main mainframe system failed a back-up mainframe existed which was connected at the bus level hence the SCADA system of the first generation was considered redundant.[11]

2.2   Distributed: Second Generation

The information between multiple stations was shared in real time through LAN and the processing was distributed between various multiple stations. The cost and size of the stations used reduced in comparison to the ones used in first generation as responsibility for a task was assigned to one station. The protocols used for the networks were still proprietary, which caused many security issues for a SCADA system that came under the eye of the hacker. Due to the proprietary nature of the protocols, the number of people who knew how secure the SCADA installation was apart from the hackers and developers is very few. Due to vested interest in keeping the issues of security quite, the security of the SCADA installation is overestimated, if security is ever under consideration.[11]

2.3   Networked: Third Generation

The SCADA system used today belong to this generation, these systems instead of using a proprietary environment which is vendor controlled these systems use the open architecture system. For distributing functionality across the WAN instead of the LAN this system uses open protocols and standards. By using the open system architecture the connectivity of any peripheral device to the system like tape drives, printers, disk drives etc is very easy. The communication between the communication system and the master station is done by the WAN protocols like the Internet Protocols (IP). Since the standard protocols used and the networked SCADA systems can be accessed through the internet, the vulnerability of the system for cyber attacks increases. But by using security techniques and standard protocols it is assumed that the SCADA system receive timely updates and maintenance meaning that the standard security improvements are applicable to SCADA system [11].   Below, is a Remote Access via SCADA Service Provider.

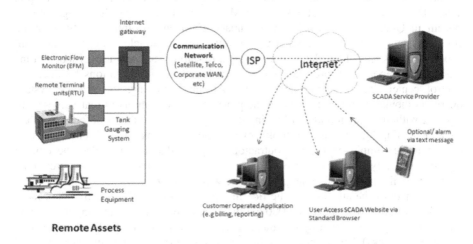

Fig. 1. Remote Access via a SCADA Service Provider [4]

The main advantage of this system is that it removes some of the cost associated with a traditional large scale SCADA system. The need for in house expertise to provide support and maintenance for the system is removed as this is all done by the SCADA Service Provider [12].

3 The Problem

The complexity of modern SCADA systems leaves many vulnerabilities as well as vectors for attack. Attacks can come from many places, including indirectly through the corporate network, virtual private networks (VPN), wireless networks, and dial-up modems. Possible attack vectors on an SCADA system include:

- Backdoors and holes in network perimeter.
- Vulnerabilities in common protocols.
- Database attacks.
- Communications hijacking and 'man-in-the-middle' attacks.

3.1 Known Attacks

2000 and 1982: Gas Pipelines in Russia (and the former Soviet Union). In 2000, the Interior Ministry of Russia reported that hackers seized temporary control of the system regulating gas flows in natural gas pipelines, although it is not publicly known if there was physical damage [6]. The former Soviet Union was victim of an attack to their gas pipeline infrastructure in 1982 when a logic bomb caused an explosion in Siberia [7].

January 2000: Maroochy Shire Sewage Spill [10]. The most well-known attack upon a SCADA system was the attack on the Maroochy Shire Council's sewage control system in Queensland, Australia. On January 2000, almost immediately after the control system for the sewage plant was installed by a contractor company, the plant experienced a series of problems. Pumps failed to start or stop when specified. Alarms failed to be reported. There were intermittent loss of communications between the control center and the pumping stations. At the beginning, the sewage system operators thought there was a leak in the pipes. Then they observed that valves were opening without being months of logging that they discovered that spoofed controllers were activating the valves. It took several more months to find the culprit: a disgruntled ex-employee of the contractor company that had installed the control system originally. The ex-employee was trying to convince the water treatment company to hire him to solve the problems he was creating.

The effect of the attacks was the flooding of the grounds of a nearby hotel, park, and river with approximately 264,000 gallons of raw sewage. In analyzing this attack, one of the insights was that cyber attacks may be unusually hard to detect (compared to physical attacks). The response to this attack was very slow; the attacker managed to launch 46 documented attacks before he was caught.

August 2005: Automobile plants and the Zotob Worm [9]. Zotob is a worm that spreads by exploiting the Microsoft Windows Plug and Play Buffer Overflow Vulnerability4. In August 2005, Zotob crashed thirteen of DaimlerChrysler's U.S. automobile manufacturing plants forcing them to remain offline for almost an hour. Plants in Illinois, Indiana, Wisconsin, Ohio, Delaware, and Michigan were also forced down. Zotob affected computers by slowing them down and causing them to continually crash and reboot. Infected Windows 2000 computers were potentially left exposed to more malicious attacks, while infected Windows XP computers can only continue to spread the worms. While the Zotob worm itself did not have a destructive payload, it left an open backdoor control channel that could allow attackers to commandeer the infected machine. The worm also added several lines of code into a machine to prevent it from accessing certain antivirus websites. Zotob and its variations also caused computer outages at heavy-equipment maker Caterpillar Inc., aircraft-maker Boeing, and several large U.S. news organizations.

4   The Scheme for CAIN Threats

4.1   Integration of Cryptography

Cryptography is the science of writing in secret code and is an ancient art; the first documented use of cryptography in writing dates back to circa 1900 B.C. when an Egyptian scribe used non-standard hieroglyphs in an inscription. Some experts argue that cryptography appeared spontaneously sometime after writing was invented, with applications ranging from diplomatic missives to war-time battle plans. It is no surprise, then, that new forms of cryptography came soon after the widespread development of computer communications. In data and telecommunications, cryptography is necessary when communicating over any untrusted medium, which includes just about any network, particularly the Internet.

A cryptosystem consists of three algorithms: one for key generation, one for encryption, and one for decryption. Their application to industrial control systems may present design and operational challenges. This primer provides assistance to control systems security professionals to identify appropriate encryption techniques and determine whether to deploy a cryptosystem solution as a security feature in their specific control systems environment. This primer also presents examples of cryptosystem deployment solutions to assist users in identifying appropriate application for their specific system.

Cryptosystems have four intended goals:

• Confidentiality
• Authentication
• Integrity
• Non-repudiation

Symmetric and asymmetric ciphers each have their own advantages and disadvantages. Symmetric ciphers are significantly faster than asymmetric ciphers, but require all parties to somehow share a secret (the key). The asymmetric algorithms allow public key infrastructures and key exchange systems, but at the cost of speed. So, in this study a combination of the best features of both symmetric and asymmetric encryption techniques is presented in the form of a cryptography scheme presented in the next figure. It depicts the Chain of operation.

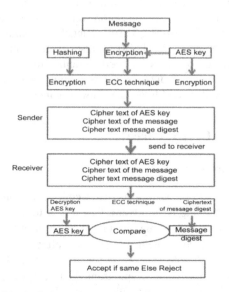

Fig. 2. Cryptography Scheme Chain of operation

4.2   Implementation

The implementation was done using out in J2SE (Java 2, Standard Edition) v 1.4.0. J2SE has the built-in classes for AES, and MD5 Hashing. The code uses these packages and the header files have the following header. Using Java a method has been developed for elliptic curve generation, base point generation, keys (both public and private) generation and encryption and decryption. Below is the emulator used for this study. [9]

Fig. 3. Cipher emulator

4.3   Testing the Scheme

Testing the cipher scheme on a test data of various sizes, Figure 5 provides details on the time taken for encryption; decryption and calculation of MD5 message digest process. The following table depicts information on Encryption & Decryption of 128 bit AES key and MD5 message digest using ECC.

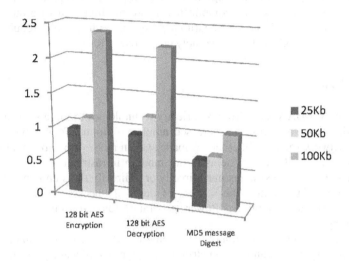

Fig. 4. graphical analysis of AES and MD5

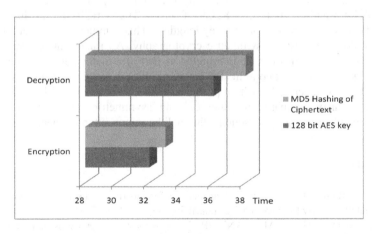

Fig. 5. Graphical analysis of Encryption & Decryption of AES key and MD5 message digest using ECC

Since the ECC key sizes are so much shorter than comparable RSA keys, the length of the public key and private key is much shorter in elliptic curve cryptosystems. This results into faster processing times, and lower demands on memory and bandwidth. With any cryptographic system dealing with 128 bit key, the total number of combination is 2128. The time required to check all possible combinations at the rate of 50 billion keys/second is approximately 5 x 1021 years. Computational complexity for breaking the elliptic-curve cryptosystem for an elliptic curve key size of 150 bits is 3.8 x 1010 MIPS (Million Instructions Per Second years) [10] . While ECC may be relatively difficult to understand for the layman, it is nevertheless an important technology that has great potential to prosper in the future. The challenging and somewhat complicated nature of elliptic curve groups makes it harder to crack the ECC discrete logarithm problem. With less bits required to give the same security, ECC has fared favorably compared to RSA.

5   Conclusion

The move of SCADA system from proprietary technologies to more standardized and open solutions together with the increased number of connections between systems and office networks and the Internet has made system more vulnerable to attacks. The reliable function of SCADA systems in our modern infrastructure may be crucial to people. Attacks on these systems may directly or indirectly threaten public health and safety since SCADA control the sources of our daily necessities such as Oil and Gas, Air traffic and railways, Power generation and transmission, water and manufacturing.

The design and implementation of the scheme was done in Java combining the best of both symmetric (AES) and asymmetric (ECC) cryptography and to ensure integrity of the data, the MD5 hash algorithm was adopted. The design and strength of all key lengths of the AES algorithm (i.e., 128, 192 and 256) are sufficient to protect classified information up to the SECRET level. TOP SECRET information will require use of either the 192 or 256 key lengths. This symmetric cryptography AES was used along with ECC asymmetric cryptography. An important feature of these curves is that their points can be interpreted as part of a mathematical group and the challenging and somewhat complicated nature of elliptic curve groups makes it harder to crack the ECC discrete logarithm problem. With less bits required by ECC to give the same security compared to other existing asymmetric cryptography, ECC is indeed a reliable cryptographic scheme that will be important in the near future.

References

1. Ryu, D., Balitanas, M.: Security Management for Distributed Denial of Service Attack. Journal of Security Engineering 7(2) (April 2010) ISSN: 1738-7531
2. McClanahan, R.H.: SCADA AND IP: Is Network Convergence Really Here? IEEE Industry Applications Magazine (March/April 2003)
3. GAO-04-628T. Critical infrastructure protection: challenges and efforts to secure control systems. Testimony Before the Subcommittee on Technology Information Policy, Intergovernmental Relations and the Census, House Committee on Government Reform, March 30 (2004), http://www.gao.gov/new.items/d04628t.pdf
4. e-scada.com (2002), http://hwww.e-scada.com/why.html (viewed on October 15, 2005)

5. Bentek Systems (n.d.), Internet and Web-based SCADA,
   `http://www.scadalink.com/technotesIP.htm` (viewed on October 15, 2005)
6. Quinn-Judge, P.: Cracks in the system. TIME Magazine (January 9, 2002)
7. Reed, T.: At the Abyss: An Insider's History of the Cold War. Presidio Press (March 2004)
8. Balitanas, M., Robles, R.J., Kim, N., Kim, T.: Crossed Crypto-scheme in WPA PSK Mode. In: BLISS 2009. IEEE CS, Edinburgh (2009) ISBN 978-0-7695-3754-5
9. Roberts, P.: Zotob, PnP Worms Slam 13 DaimlerChrysler Plants, eweek.com, August 18 (2005), `http://www.eweek.com/c/a/Security/Zotob-PnP-Worms-Slam-13-DaimlerChrysler-Plants/`
10. Stallings, W.: Cryptography and Network Security, 2nd edn. Prentice Hall, Upper Saddle River
11. `http://www.scadasystems.net/`
12. e-scada.com (2002), `http://www.e-scada.com/why.html` (viewed on October 15, 2005)

RFID Implementation and Security Issues

Young B. Choi[1], Tae Hwan Oh[2], and Rajath Chouta[2]

[1] Department of Natural Science, Mathematics and Technology,
School of Undergraduate Studies, RH 464,
Regent University,
Virginia Beach, VA 23464-98
ychoi@regent.edu
[2] Department of Networking,
Security and Systems Administration,
Golisano College of Computing and Information Sciences,
Rochester Institute of Technology,
52 Lomb Memorial Drive,
Rochester, NY 14623
{tom.oh,rsc5726}@rit.edu

Abstract. Radio Frequency Identification (RFID) is a technology that uses electronic tags to store data which in turn can be accessed in real time wirelessly. There is great potential for RFID technology in our society. RFID tags can be used for supply chain management, inventory systems, animal tracking, instant payments or even human implantation. Standards in the RFID industry are examined with an emphasis place on global standardizing bodies. With the growing use of RFID devices in supply chain management and global shipping, several shipping standards including EPC and ASN are examined. Security has become a major concern with several threats to RFID technology recently exposed. Several solutions are presented for firms wishing to implement RFID technology and minimize the risk to sensitive information and company systems.

Keywords: Radio Frequency Identification Security Issues, RFID Security Issues, RFID problems.

1 Introduction

Radio Frequency Identification (RFID) Devices are a silent part of everyone's day to day lives. When you pass through a toll, waive your badge to get into your office or purchase gas with a "Speed Pass" from Exxon you are engaging in the RFID revolution. RFID has become standard instrument in global shipping, credit cards, passport identification and even theft protection. Since its introduction in the 1940's, RFID technology has a topic of controversy in the privacy and security fields. Security flaws are only now becoming realized and solutions are scarce and often unrealistic.

T.-h. Kim et al. (Eds.): ISA 2011, CCIS 200, pp. 236–249, 2011.

1.1 History

A Scottish physicist, Alexander Watson-Watt, discovered how to use radio waves to detect objects. This discovery led to the invention of radars in 1935. During World War II, radars were heavily used to detect incoming planes. The ground base station would send out pulses of radio energy and if it hits an object, the pulses would echo back indicating it detects something. The one main problem with this was that the base could not tell if the plane was an ally or an enemy. [24]

The Germans solved this problem by having their planes spiral towards the base. When the pulses hit the spiraling plane, a different signal would reflect back. This was the first active RFID method to be used. The British developed a more advanced method. Under the lead of Watson-Watt, the British developed a system called Identify Friend or Foe (IFF). With this system each plane would have a transmitter attached to it. When the ground radar sends a signal to the plane and if it was a British plane, the transmitter placed on it would send a friendly signal back [24].

1.2 How It Works

Radio Frequency Identification (RFID) is an automatic wireless-based identification method that evolved from radio technology. RFID tags are wireless computer chips that can be placed as a label, or attached or embedded to anything, such as a product or wireless keys. The RFID tag is composed of 3 components, a coil, a silicon chip and material onto which the coil and chip are implanted. The coil acts as an antenna. The silicon chip includes a processor that contains all the information about the product as well as the radio transceiver [3]. The chip can hold as much as 2 kilobytes of data.

In order to retrieve the information from the RFID tag, an RFID reader must be used. The reader generates a radio frequency field around it and when the tags are within the range of the reader, depending on the type of reader, it will be able to capture and transmit the data. The frequency field emits and receives radio waves from and to the tags. The RFID reader is attached to a network that receives the information to a central computer.

There are two types of RFID tags, active and passive. Active tags have an on-board power source that makes the tags bigger and more expensive. It can deliver its own signals over long distance to the reader. The range can be anywhere from 60 feet to 300 feet. There are two types of active tags, transponders and beacons. Transponders are tags that would be awaken when a signal from the receiver is sent to it. This type of tag would conserve energy because it is active only when the signal sent by the receiver is within range of the reader. Beacon tags are more real-time and emit a unique identity signal at certain intervals which could be every few seconds or once a day. The reader would pick up the signal sent by the beacon tag. Active tags are more expensive depending on amount of memory, battery life and other features such as on-board temperature sensor. Passive tags do not require a battery source because they use the RFID readers' own magnetic field to power the microchip's circuits and antenna which enables the chip to transmit information. This also means that the distance of the range between the reader and the RFID tag must be shorter. These tags are very inexpensive and the life of the tag does not expire [23].

2 Current Usages

RFID tags can be embedded in clothing seams, molded into plastic, integrated into packages, embedded into the skin and can be printed in ink. A more widely used method of the RFID system is the E-ZPass. This is an active transponder type RFID tag that is attached to the windshield of a vehicle. When the vehicle is in range, the reader sends a signal to the active tag to wake it up and access the information of the account. ExxonMobil developed what is known as Speedpass which is an RFID system that allow users to pay for gas electronically without using a credit card. This is similar to the E-ZPass. The RFID Speedpass transponder can be attached to a keychain, see Figure 1, wave the transponder to the reader at the pump. The reader would then access the associated account to pay for the gas.

Fig. 1. ExxonMobil Speedpass [16]

RFID tags are also being used in toys to make them interact. In 1999, Hasbro embedded Star Wars: Episode I - The Phantom Menace actions figures with RFID tags to be interactive when the figures were close to a base station. RFID tags are also placed in passports issued from the government (RFID Consumer Applications and Benefits n.d.). The tag would contain information about the owner of the passport and their records of travel. In a sense, it would be an electronic passport. The tags are used in inventory tracking and Wal-Mart already has implemented it. Wal-Mart required their top 100 suppliers to place RFID tags on cases and pallets (RFID Consumer Applications and Benefits n.d.). Along with tracking inventory, RFID tags are used to track animals. Some libraries use the RFID system to replace their current system. The automation advantage of RFID eases the process checkouts and check-ins of books much faster. These are just some of the usages for RFID. We research more in depth about some of them and introduce other usages of RFID.

RFID is also used in financial sectors since 2009. RFID technology has been developed to enable individuals to use their cell phones as sources of payment. A Texas based company, DeviceFidelity, has made a microSD size RFID card that can work as a passive tag as well as a RFID reader. By clubbing it with bank accounts of the end user, a cell phone can effectively be used for payment purposes. Some of the companies that have started using these cards for the purposes of payments include companies like Dairy Queen and 7-Eleven. These companies have made it possible for their patrons to use their cell phones as a means of loyalty rewards program.

RFID is also used all over the world as a means of using the public transportation. Owing to its ease of implementation and relevance for the application, all major countries across the world are now making use of this technology as a way for people to use their mass transit systems. While countries in Europe lead the way in implementation, major countries in other parts of the world are now using smart RFID cards that can be rewritten and used multiple numbers of times.

Asset management with RFID is also possible, when used in conjunction with mobile computing devices. By clubbing suitable software with RFID tags, it is possible to obtain data regarding attendance, identification as well as other necessary parameters that are a part of asset tracking. When combined with the Internet, it is possible to update and monitor data on the go. Passive RFID is used for wide scale asset tracking, especially since cost of implementation has dropped significantly. Companies like Bank of America and the US State Department tag all their assets by means of passive RFID [18].

Logistics as well as transportation are other major areas that play well when it comes to RFID technology. Aspects like shipping, freight distribution as well as yard management serve as potential areas that can make use of RFID technology. The same is applicable for airlines as well, with certain carriers like Qantas using RFID tags to expedite the check in process. Cargos tagged with RFID technology are also being put to use now, with countries like the Netherlands actively testing out the technology and ensuring that the cargo container can be tracked regardless of where it is.

Animal tracking is another area that can take advantage of RFID technologies. Similar to asset tracking, these RFID tags provide a lot of information about the animal and helps in real time tracking of the animals through the Web. Although this is actually a passive RFID tag, it might also be called as a "chip" on the animal.

Hospitals can take advantage of RFID in order to improve patient care and ensure that monitoring is done with more details readily available. ClearCount Medical introduced the first of such systems [25] in 2008 to improve patient safety as well as the efficiency of the operating room. By implementing the system, the hospital hopes to eliminate surgical errors caused by introduction of foreign objects in the patient. By tagging all items entering and leaving the OR, the chances of an error occurring are significantly reduced.

3 Potential Usages and Benefits

Once the RFID system has been refined and fully implemented, it can help revolutionize tracking in real time. Now, it is restricted only to tracking on a smaller scale. However, you might be able to do more, like tracking animals and humans on a more refined basis. RFID might not be able to transmit as much data as Wireless LAN networks, but will nevertheless be a valuable addition to sensor networks. Asset tracking, although currently being used with RFID, can be extended to other things like memorabilia and other goods that are of historical significance. The RFID system could lead to smart appliances that can read everything in the pantry or determines how to wash certain pieces of clothing while in the washer. Products with RFID technology enable products can be checkout quickly due to scanning all the objects in the cart at once. Theft can be reduced with the tracking system of the RFID tags. Repetitive strain injuries can be prevented with the automated process of the RFID system.

4   Implementation Issues of RFID

4.1 E-passports

A passport is an identification method issued by national governments to identify their citizens [13]. First used in Malaysia in 1999, and implemented by the United States as of 2006, e-passports combine the traditional document based passport with electronic identification. E-passports are now being used because of the increase in security measures which support passport inspection and strengthen border control systems. One of the major issues surrounding RFID technology is standardization. E-passport standardization is defined by the International Civil Aviation Organization (ICAO). Currently the ICAO uses the ISO 14443 RFID specification for e-passports According to the U.S. State Department e-passports store:

- A biometric identifier in the form of a digital image of the passport photograph, which will facilitate the use of face recognition technology at ports-of-entry;
- The same data visually displayed on the data page of the passport;
- The unique chip identification number; and
- A digital signature to protect the stored data from alteration.

Fig. 2. E-passport RFID Tags [26] & [27]

E-passports have been under scrutiny due to privacy and security issues. While the new passports do in fact better protect against unwanted individuals entering countries, they do have issues that are of concern. The four major concerns about RFID tags in passports as stated by the U.S. State Department are skimming, eavesdropping, tracking and cloning. The State Department has taken steps to prevent each of these concerns from transforming into serious threats. Since RFID tag information is possible to intercept, e-passports pose a serious threat to personal privacy. Skimming is "the act of obtaining data from an unknowing end user who is not willingly submitting the sample at that time, while eavesdropping is defined as "the interception of information as it moves electronically between the chip and the chip reader" [13]. To protect against skimming and eavesdropping the State Department uses imbedded metallic components, which block an unopened passports data transmission, and basic access control (BAC) in e-passports. BAC requires that an initial interaction between the RFID tag and the reader include protocols for secure communications. Tracking is usually done through the obtaining of a passport's unique identifier (UID). To protect against tracking, random UIDs are used changing the UID after ever use. Cloning is the act of substituting a fake chip with a real chip or altering the information on the RFID chip. This threat is being deterred through the use of public key infrastructure (PKI) technology. PKI technology prevents the information on the chip from being altered and provides authentication of data.

A final concern that is associated with e-passports is that they could be turned into a weapon. The issue is that terrorists could devise a method of inserting some sort of explosive device into the tags. While this is an unlikely scenario, it is a theoretical possibility.

4.2 Human Implantation

The implantation of humans with RFID tags is a promising innovation that has numerous potential uses but also has some serious privacy issues. RFID tags could be used for things such as tracking felons, knowing the whereabouts of children or employees, or even allowing for instant digital payments. An example of uses for RFID implantation can be seen in the movie "Minority Reports." In the movies' near future, citizens are imbedded with chips that not only use current RFID innovations, but also include their personal tastes and habits. This allows for marketing and relative information to be transmitted directly to individuals.

While there is great potential for this use of RFID technology, there are concerns that need to be addressed. Identity theft has become an increasing threat as the use of technology has expanded. RFID implants would be susceptible to a man-in-the-middle-attack where an attacker could steal the identity of a person in real-time. In regards to the tracking of individuals, some proponents of RFID implants claim, the use of RFID tags in humans could lead to a totalitarian state such as "Big Brother" in George Orwell's' Nineteen Eighty-Four. A government with the ability to watch over and track is a serious threat to personal liberties and privacy. The widespread use of RFID implants would allow governments to easily conduct widespread invasion of privacy. Two final concerns of implantation are religious objections and cancer risks.

4.3 Religious Objection

Religion is thought of as a set of practices, beliefs and values often associated with supernatural and moral claims. These beliefs and values sometimes come into conflict with emerging technology. RFID is one such technology that has become a concern among numerous religious leaders. The most basic of these objections arise from the aspect of human implantation of RFID tags. Various religions and religious sects throughout the world deem that the body is a sanctuary and view any alteration of the human body as a sin. The implanting of RFID tags, which commonly placed somewhere on the individuals hand, is a direct violation of this belief and has caused a concern against implantation.

Another religious objection to RFID is found within the Book of Revelation. In the manuscript it is stated that prior to the end of the world humans will be compelled "to receive a mark on their right hand or on their foreheads."

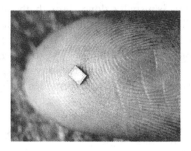

Fig. 3. RFID Chip [28]

As stated earlier many of the implanted RFID tags are located on an individual's hand, and this has led to claims that RFID tags are the mark foretold by Revelations. Katherine Albrecht, founder of the Consumers Against Supermarket Privacy Invasion and Numbering (CASPIAN) advocates to Christians that "radio frequency identification may evolve to become the "mark of the beast" [3]. Another passage from the manuscript states that "a foul and loathsome sore came upon the men who had the mark of the beast and those who worshiped his image." According to research and conducted studies an implanted RFID tag could potentially lead to such a sore as described the Revelations. Whether or not RFID tags are the mark of the beast foretold by the Book of Revelations is yet to be seen, but one thing to keep in mind is that new technologies often trigger religious objections.

4.4 Cancer Risk

According to the Wikipedia "veterinary and toxicology studies spanning the last ten years surfaced indicating that RFID chips induced malignant tumors in laboratory animals [16]." The number of subjects that developed tumors from RFID implants in these studies ranged from 1% to 10%. It has been suggested that just because these studies have shown tumors developed in laboratory animals, it does not necessarily mean that the result will be the same in humans. Also, according to Wikipedia the studies were limited in scope, did not test large animals and lacked control groups. Verichip, one of the largest makers of human RFID implants, and the Food and Drug Administration (FDA) maintain that the implants are in fact safe [16]. Over the past decade the rate at which human implants has increased and only time will tell whether RFID implants will in fact lead to cancer in humans [16].

4.5 Privacy

Justice William O. Douglas once said "The right to be let alone is indeed the beginning of all freedom." Privacy is one of the most fundamental needs of all people, but in a time when technology and environmental occurrences, for example 9/11 and War on Terror, have given way to the ability and the government's desire to invade privacy, this right is being threatened. Radio frequency identification technology is fast becoming a major risk for basic human privacy. RFID technology allows for everything from items and products to animals and humans to be tracked. "Civil liberties advocates point out that the ability to track people, products, vehicles, and even currency would create an Orwellian world" [11]. RFID technology could easily create such a world, where the government and even corporations could profile individuals or even monitor and survey them in real time. However, it is not the technology itself that poses a threat. "Privacy breaches occur when RFID, like any technology, is deployed in a way that is not consistent with responsible information management practices that foster sound privacy protection" [6]. A primary reason that privacy issues are such a major concern is because security and privacy features are often built into RFID tags after their initial design. This method leads to RFID technology that is not focused on privacy but on working efficiency. Another concern relating to privacy is since RFID tags are so small, it is possible to place tags on items without the knowledge of individuals. The concept of consumer transparency, where there are no secret RFID tags or readers, should be at the forefront of RFID laws and standardization. All new technologies have had concerns initially in regards to privacy. RFID technology may have been around for over half a century, but its widespread use is just coming to light. Before this technology is widely accepted, lawmakers and standardization organizations will have to address the privacy issues surrounding RFID.

5 Standardization

RFID tags are designed to be extremely mobile and flexible. The small size and inexpensive characteristics of RFID tags make them ideal for a large range of uses. To keep costs low, mass production of RFID devices will be necessary. Given the portability of RFID devices, tags must be able to be read by a multitude of different readers and these readers must have the ability to read tags from different producers. This interoperability of RFID hardware and software producers can only be accomplished through RFID standards.

There are two primary types of standards in the RFID industry. Tag standards define how data is stored on RFID tags as well as how they interact via wireless interface with compatible readers. There are also a number of industry specific standards that detail how RFID tags are tracked as they move from location to location [4]. Security standards will play an important role in protecting privacy and the integrity of RFID devices and is discussed further.

5.1 Tag Standards

Mass production is essential in the future RFID devices. The ability for RFID tags to be mass produced at an extremely low cost is related to the size of the devices [1]. The smaller the device, the easier it will be to mass produce at a relatively low cost. Many of the standards, including MIT's Auto-ID Center are focusing on making basic devices that that store as little information as possible which can then be linked to an external database with more detailed information about the tag [1]. The Auto-ID Center has classified RFID tags into 5 major classes ranging from Class I, which are passive devices that can only be read, to Class V, which are extremely active tags that can even read other Class V tags [15]. The classification of devices is important for understanding the potential uses of each device. Companies interested in implementing this technology should first select which type of class is most effective given the requirements for use. Class identification will simplify the comparison of different tags produced by a magnitude of suppliers.

One of the leading developers of RFID standards is the International Organization for Standardization (ISO). ISO has worked in conjunction with the International Electrotechnical Commission (IEC) to publish standards for both data read/write and air transmission [4]. These standards are available to all developers of RFID technology to make their technology more compatible. The ISO/IEC 18000 series consists of 7 protocol parts which establish standards for air communications at varying frequencies [4]. The use of standard air transmission protocols is complicated when considering the international market. RFID devices that operate on unlicensed frequencies in the US may operate on licensed cellular frequencies used in Europe and Asia [14]. These inconsistencies highlight the need for global standards and are the driving forces behind many of the international organizations such as ISO.

5.2 Shipping Standards

It has been observed that the RFID industry has become very specialized in the development of new technology. "As the RFID market expands, we'll see the continued proliferation of RFID tags built for highly specialized vertical markets, which means greater variety and the consequent need to ensure interoperability" [14]. One such vertical market is the shipping industry. Standards play a large role in the shipping industry because tags are constantly moving from location to location between firms who may utilize different RFID vendors. To support RFID technology in the tracking of packages several, international standards and industry applications are available.

To facilitate the tracking of objects, the Electronic Product Code (EPC) was created by the Auto-ID Center. The EPC network consists of 96-bit product codes, identification systems, middleware, Object Naming System (ONS) and an XML based markup language for displaying product information [12]. Much like a UPC that can be found on a variety of consumer items, an EPC is a unique identifier given to individual objects. The EPC consists of a header with structure information, a manager number for identifying the company the number is assigned to, an object class identifying the object and finally a serial number to identify the instance of the object [14].

An EPC is simply a number that does not tell the user much about the actual item the tag is attached to. An EPC global network was designed to link tags with supplier databases containing information on the objects. Once an EPC is obtained from a tag that code is sent to the ONS which points the user to the supplier's database [14]. EPC is ideal for supply chain management, but can fall short when dealing with global shipping and tracking.

The Advanced Shipping Notice (ASN) is a more suitable RFID solution when shipping items from one location to another. ASN can be viewed as an electronic shipping slip that identifies a package's information including its contents and where it came from [14]. Once shortfall of this system is that the information on the RFID tag is useless without the associated electronic file. This electronic file is created by the shipper and sent to the receiver [14]. EPC uses RFID tags similar to ASN, but EPC offers specific item identification and can follow an individual object as it travels through all steps of the supply chain.

6   RFID Threats

RFID technology can greatly benefit firms when implemented correctly but can create numerous unique security risks that expose the vulnerabilities and shortcomings of RFID devices. When deciding to implement RFID solutions, firms should examine their risk in each of the threats listed below to determine the amount of vulnerability and risk they are willing to take on.

6.1   Unauthorized Reads

The simplest RFID threat comes from unauthorized users gaining access to the information on the tag. Basic RFID tags do not discriminate against users; they were developed to respond to a read request by any device [20-23]. When sensitive information including Personally Identifiable Information (PII) is included on tags, the risk of that the information being obtained by an unauthorized user increases. A hacker using the open source program called RFDump can read virtually any RFID tag and obtain its information [29]. The software was developed to work on almost all RFID protocols [30]. RFDump highlights the vulnerability of RFID tags to hackers. Because of this threat, firms should not place sensitive information on RFID devices; EPC and ASN numbers probably are not sensitive information, but an individual's PII certainly is.

6.2   Cloning

The opposite of the unauthorized read threat is cloning. Cloning is when an attacker "mimic[s] authentic RFID tags by writing appropriately formatted data on blank RFID tags" [20-23]. By cloning the tag, a hacker is able to trick the RFID reader into believing it is an authentic tag thereby granting the hacker unauthorized access.

Researchers at John's Hopkins University demonstrated that by cloning an authentic RFID credit card, a hacker can purchase items without the original tag [20-23]. Unlike with traditional credit cards, it would be virtually impossible to determine if a hacker has stolen an RFID credit card because it can be done wirelessly without the owner noticing. Cloning is particularly important when considering the potential of RFID viruses and malware.

6.3 Viruses and Malware

Researchers at the University of Amsterdam successfully demonstrated that RFID devices could be used to transmit malicious viruses and malware. Through SQL injections on RFID tags they were able to exploit vulnerabilities in the backend software that supported the RFID devices [20-23]. This vulnerability is not a threat to the RFID tag itself, but with the middleware. Research showed an average of 6 – 16 bugs per 1,000 lines of code in the middleware used to support RFID devices [20]. These problems are easily corrected through careful coding. Hopefully, now that researchers have highlighted the possibility of viruses in RFID devices, programmers will be more conscious and place safeguards in the code.

The second threat to RFID technology the researchers found was the potential for buffer overflow attack [20-23]. In a buffer overflow attack, a hacker sends more data than is expected to the software. The software cannot handle the excess of data and crashes. In RFID devices, buffer overflow attacks can be accomplished through cloning authentic tags and replacing the data with malicious code [20].

6.4 Kill Command

When a password known as a kill command is sent to a tag, it renders the tag permanently useless and prevents it from responding to any readers [17]. This command can be useful when a tag owner wants to prevent unauthorized access once the need for the device has ended. If a hacker obtains the kill command for devices they could wreak havoc on a firm's RFID infrastructure. The problem becomes more serious given that many manufactures order large numbers of tags all with the same kill command password [14]. With one kill command any hacker could disable all of the RFID devices in the area.

7 RFID Security Measures

Given the plethora of threats to RFID technology, several security measures can be implemented to protect a company's system. The purpose of security measures are to ensure authenticity in tags and readers and to prevent unauthorized readers from accessing any sensitive information on the device. Companies must effectively balance security and protection over cost savings and efficiency [14]. The level and amount of security should be decided based on the sensitivity of the information contained on the RFID devices as well as the importance of RFID systems in the company's overall business process.

7.1 Software Based Security

Successful implementation of software based security should be standard in all middleware packages sold on the market. As mentioned previously, simple coding protections can guard against SQL injections and buffer overflow, which is not difficult to implement. Access controls on supporting networks should be coupled with sound programming [15]. RFID devices must be viewed as another potential entry point for hackers and treated as such in network designs. Also, sensitive information about RFID devices such as kill commands, passwords and data structure should be guarded to further protect the integrity of RFID infrastructures.

7.2 Encryption

Encryption is a simple security measure with several obstacles. Encryption involves writing data to an RFID tag that is useless when read without a proper decryption key. This method of security is ideal when RFID tags contain sensitive data because it prevents hackers using software such as RFDump from interpreting the information it obtains. The difficulty with implementing encryption is that it requires more powerful and complex tags which often greatly increase the cost and decrease the efficiency of RFID technology [15]. Encryption technology also does nothing to prevent hackers from obtaining the data on the tag.

7.3 Signal Jamming and Blocking

RFID devices use radio waves to wireless transmit information and are susceptible to interception. Active jamming and signal blocking are two ways to prevent unauthorized users from intercepting RFID signals [31]. Jamming uses reverse anti-collision protocols to cause interference in signals rendering RFID reading nearly impossible [12]. This technology can be effective; however, it does not discriminate between legitimate and illegitimate reads. This implementation method is only useful in situations where no reading of RFID tags should occur. Shielding can be effective by allowing a device to be read only when unblocked. If shielding is implemented around a building, it will prevent rouge users from intercepting a signal while allowing legitimate users inside of the building to operate normally.

7.4 Authentication and Challenge Response

Authentication and challenge response allow both the reader and tag to verify that they are communicating with legitimate users. A password on RFID tags can prevent unauthorized readers from gaining access to the stored information [31]. Once the user has been authorized to gain access, the tag transmits back the stored information. The drawback to authentication is that an interception of the authentication message or password would allow a user to have unlimited access to the tag.

A challenge response can solve the problem of authentication interception. With challenge response, the tag or reader sends a random message which is decrypted using a key in the receiving device and returned for verification [20-23]. This method of security protects against unauthorized access and cloning. Authentication and challenge response does not prevent unauthorized users from intercepting the signal during transmission. The best approach to prevent unauthorized access is combining authentication with encryption. As with all RFID security, price increases greatly with added features.

8 Conclusion

Since the introduction of RFID technology, the industry has changed drastically. It can only be assumed that new uses for RFID will be thought up as the industry continues to evolve. For the evolution of RFID to occur many improvements are needed. A balance of cost and efficiency of the tags with security and privacy concerns would need to be address in order for the widespread use of RFID tags. During production, RFID tags defects need to decrease. There are currently some security protections in place but there needs to be more protection measures because anyone can get a reader and scan for information. Methods of encryption and authentication would need to evolve into a more powerful protective tool against privacy concerns. RFID can be the future of tomorrow and only time can tell.

References

1. Asahi, T., Yamato, J.: MIT Auto-ID Center Advances the Standardization of RFID Tags. Global Standardization Activities 1, 95–97 (2003)
2. Baard, M.: RFID: Sign of the (End) Times? (2006),
   http://www.wired.com/science/discoveries/news/2006/06/70308
3. Bhatt, H., Glover, B.: RFID Essentials. O'Reilly Media, Inc., Sebastopol (2006)
4. Brown, M., Sabella, R., Zeisel, E.: RFID + Exam Cram. Que Publishing, Indiana (2006)
5. Campbell, A., Das, A., Haines, B., Kleinschmidt, J., Thornton, F.: RFID Security. Syngress Publishing, Canada (2006)
6. CDT Working Group on RFID: Privacy Best Practices for Deployment of RFID Technology,
   http://www.cdt.org/privacy/20060501rfid-best-practices.php
7. EPCglobal Inc. - The EPCglobal Architecture Framework (2007),
   http://www.epcglobalinc.org/standards/architecture/
   architecture_1_2-framework-20070910.pdf
8. Gralla, P.: How Personal & Internet Security Work. Que Publishing, Indiana (2006)
9. Grunwald, L.: What is RFDump (2002),
   http://www.rf-dump.org/about.shtml
10. Juels, A.: RFID Security and Privacy: A Research Survey. IEEE Journal on Selected Areas in Communications 24(2), 381–394 (2006)
11. Kim, J.: RFID Technology and Private Issues. KSEA Letters 36(2), 45–51 (2008)
12. Knospe, H., Pobl, H.: RFID Security. Information Security Technical Report 9, 39–49 (2004)
13. Passports (n.d),
    http://travel.state.gov/passport/passport_1738.html
14. Phillips, T., Karygiannis, T., Huhn, R.: Security Standards for the RFID Market. IEEE Security and Privacy 3, 85–89 (2005)
15. So, S.C.K., Lui, J.J.: Securing RFID Applications: Issues, Methods, and Controls. Information Security Journal: A Global Perspective 15(4), 43–50 (2006)
16. Radio-frequency identification (n.d), http://en.wikipedia.org/wiki/RFID
17. Radio Frequency Identification (RFID) Systems,
    http://epic.org/privacy/rfid/

18. RFID Business Applications,
    http://www.rfidjournal.com/article/articleview/1334/1/129/
19. RFID Consumer Applications and Benefits,
    http://www.rfidjournal.com/article/articleview/1332/1/129/
20. Rieback, M.R., Crispo, B., Tanenbaum, A.S.: The Evolution of RFID Security. Pervasive Computing 5(1), 62–69 (2006)
21. Reiback, M., Crispo, B., Tanenbaum, A.: The Evolution of RFID Security. IEEE Pervasive Computing 5, 62–69 (2006)
22. Reiback, M., Crispo, B., Tanenbaum, A.: RFID Malware: Truth vs. Myth. IEEE Security and Privacy 4, 70–72 (2006)
23. The Basics of RFID Technology,
    http://www.rfidjournal.com/article/articleview/1337/1/129/
24. The History of RFID Technology,
    http://www.rfidjournal.com/article/articleview/1338/2/129/
25. RFID: Improved Patient Safety,
    http://clearcount.com/rfid-improved-patient-safety
26. Fuqua, M.: Is RFID Getting Primed To Change Digital Marketing?,
    http://fifthgearanalytics.com/2010/11/is-rfid-getting-primed-to-change-digital-marketing/
27. Cho, N.: New US High Tech E-passport,
    http://www.mydigitallife.info/new-us-high-tech-e-passport/
28. Jukes, I.: Phones, Paper 'Chips' May Fight Disease,
    http://www.committedsardine.com/blogpost.cfm?blogID=914
29. Phillips, T., Karygiannis, T., Kuhn, R.: Security Standards for the RFID Market. IEEE Security & Privacy 3(6) (November/December 2005)
30. Grunwald, L.: RFDump can hack RFID tags,
    http://www.rfidgazette.org/2004/07/lukas_grunwalds.html
31. So, S.C.K., Liu, J.J.: Securing RFID Applications: Issues, Methods, and Controls. Information Systems Security, 43–50 (2006)

Vehicle Tracking Based on Kalman Filter in Tunnel

Gyuyeong Kim[1], Hyuntae Kim[2], Jangsik Park[3], and Yunsik Yu[1]

[1] Convergence of IT Devices Institute Busan,
Gaya-dong, San 24, Busanjin-ku, Busan, 614-714, Korea
{nz90nz,ysyu}@deu.ac.kr
[2] Department of Multimedia Engineering, Dongeui University,
Gaya-dong, San 24, Busanjin-ku, Busan, 614-714, Korea
htaekim@deu.ac.kr
[3] Department of Electronics Engineering, Kyungsung University,
Daeyeon3-dong, 110-1, Nam-gu, Busan, 608-736, Korea
jsipark@ks.ac.kr

Abstract. The image recognition system using CCTV camera has been introduced to minimize not only loss of life and property but also traffic jam in the tunnel. In this paper, object detection algorithm is proposed to track vehicles. The proposed algorithm is to detect cars based on Adaboost and to track vehicles to use Kalman filtering. As results of simulations, it is shown that proposed algorithm is useful for tracking vehicles.

Keywords: Adaboost Algorithm, Kalman Filter, Object Tracking.

1   Introduction

In countries around world, it has mountainous terrain characteristic. In this reason, the construction of tunnel is essential to avoid traffic congestion and to make be traffic flow smoothly. The rate of construction tunnel has shown an increase of 3.4 times since last 10 years. The long tunnel usually has been built. Accordingly, the risk of an accident in the tunnel has been increased. Usually, speeding, lane change, a traffic accident for carelessness of driving or deficiency of vehicle causes accident in the tunnel and huge accident such as fire in it may occur serious human, material damage. Therefore, it is becoming more and more important that image recognition systems can detect these elements being the cause of accident in the tunnel using CCTV in advance and can early prevent it as an accident occurs.

Most detecting approach works Adaboost [1, 2] for visual class detection are using Haar-like features. It is to build a strong classifier, assembling weighted weak classifiers, those being obtained iteratively by making use of weighting in the training set. We also make use of Adaboost algorithm in this paper.

The previous approaches of object tracking algorithm address optical flow [3], template matching [4], and Kamlam Filter [5]. Optical flow estimation has much computational costs that computation is done in every pixels of the frame. It is not very roubust against noise and illumination and hard if objects with large homogeneous area in motion. Template Matching method has been used for simple implementation and quick detection. But it is difficult to track as resizing problem of

T.-h. Kim et al. (Eds.): ISA 2011, CCIS 200, pp. 250–256, 2011.
© Springer-Verlag Berlin Heidelberg 2011

between template image and detected image. Also if many cars appear in video stream, a lot of complexity will increase.

Therefore, It is proposed that object tracking based on Kalman filter, is efficient enough to be implemented in real time and has robustness. It is dependent on reliable feature detection algorithm (Adaboost) and optimal parameter estimation of itself.

In the next section we will give an explanation of the proposed algorithm and the previous approaches. In section 3, we show experimental results which demonstrate excellence of our approach.

2   Proposed Algorithm

The block diagram of the proposed vehicle detection and tracking system is shown in fig. 1. The proposed system consists of two steps. The first step consists of detecting vehicles make use of Adaboost algorithm. And second step consists of tracking vehicles using Kalman filter.

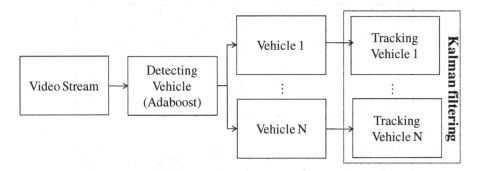

Fig. 1. Block diagram of the proposed vehicle detection and tracking system

2.1   Vehicle Detection Algorithm: Adaboost

In this paper, to detect object using input video stream, Adaboost algorithm is used. Adaboost algorithm makes strong classifier, combined by weak one linearly, which has high detection performance. A Weak classifier to create a strong classifier is generated by the Haar-like features shown in equation (1), an indication of characteristic of the vehicle.

$$h_j(x) = \begin{cases} 1, & if \ \ p_j f_j(x) < p_j \theta_j \\ 0, & otherwise \end{cases} \tag{1}$$

In equation (1), subscript j is number of specific group, f_j is detected feature value, θ_j is a threshold value, p_j is the sign determination parity. Each stage classifier was trained using the Adaboost algorithm. The idea of boosting is selecting and ensemble a set of weak learners to form a strong classifier by repeatedly learning processing over the training examples.

(a) non vehicle images

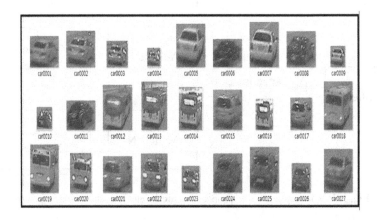

(b) vehicle images

Fig. 2. Training images of haar classifier for Adaboost

In t stage, T numbers of weak classifiers $h_t(x)$ and ensemble weights α_t are yielded by learning. Then a stage strong classifier $h_j(x)$ is shown i n equation (2). In this paper, we trained the classifier using haar classfier which build a boosted rejection cascade. We do this with OpenCV "*haartraining*" application, which creates a classifier given a training set (372 vehicle images and 1000 non-vehicle images). The figure 2 is shown in training images set.

$$h_j(x) = \begin{cases} 1, & \sum_{t=1}^{T} \alpha_t h_t(x) \geq \frac{1}{2}\sum_{t=1}^{T} \alpha_t \\ 0, & otherwise \end{cases} \tag{2}$$

2.2   Vehicles Tracking Algorithm

It has been proposed many algorithms for object tracking. First of all, we explain template matching, one of them to understand the previous approach. Then it is explains that object tracking based on Kalman filter, is efficient enough to be implemented in real time and has robustness.

2.2.1   Template Matching

Template matching is a technique to judge the degree of similarity between the two object and decide the fact that two objects are same or not. Among the method to find the similarity of template matching SAD (Sum of Absolute Differences) which is fast and has relatively low computational complexity was applied [4]. The SAD selected the same area given the values with the minimum cost in calculating the similarity.

$$SAD = \sum_{i=0}^{M-1}\sum_{i=0}^{N-1}\left|I_{i,j}-T_{i,j}\right| \tag{3}$$

In equation (3), using templates T and I in MxN pixels, the similarity of two templates are calculated.

Fig. 3. Normalization of image size for template matching

As shown in Figure 3, the detected vehicle images to apply the template matching are normalized to 16x16 pixels.

It is shown in Figure4, applied template matching method. First, calculated the SAD from comparing vehicle in the current frame and previous frame, second, if SAD is below a certain threshold, it will be judged the same vehicle and track. The threshold was determined through experiments. The size of detected vehicle using Adaboost algorithm is not constant.

It is difficult to track as resizing problem of between template image and detected image. Also if many cars appear in video stream, a lot of complexity will increase.

t frame

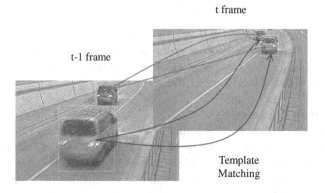

t-1 frame

Template
Matching

Fig. 4. Template matching results

2.2.2   Kalman Filtering

The Kalman filter instead recursively conditions the current estimate on all of the past measurements. Figure 5 offers a complete picture of the operation of the filter. It consists of two phases. In the first phase, typically called the prediction phase, we use information learned in the past to further refine tracking model for what the next location of vehicles will be. In the correction phase, we make a measurement and then reconcile that measurement with the predictions based on previous measurements.

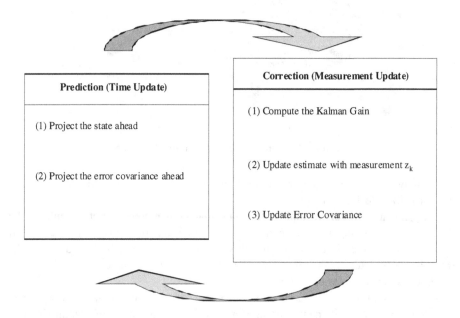

Fig. 5. The operation of the Kalman filter

After detecting by Adaboost, the next step is to track vehicle's motion. In order to do this, we consider the x and y coordinates of the center of the cars. Our state variables are the x and y coordinates of the center of the detected vehicles. We assume that the vehicle is moving with a constant velocity to implement [6].

3 Experimental Results

In order to implement the proposed algorithm, we used Visual Studio 2010 tool and open source library OpenCV. This algorithm is running the Multiprocessor PC having a 2.5 GHz Intel Core2 Quad Processor with 2 GB of RAM and Windows 7 as the operating system. The experiment showed that detection rate is about 98% and the tracking rate is about 95 % in total 1200 frames with 640x480 sizes. The noise which affects the measurements is smoothed to a great extent by the Kalman filter. Figure 6 shows correct tracking object and miss tracking by Kalman filter in simulation results. The figure 6. (b) was generated by detection error is that the filter predicts the next estimate to be along a linear path.

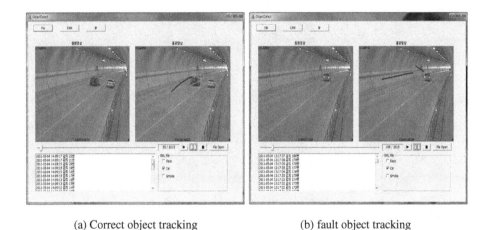

(a) Correct object tracking   (b) fault object tracking

Fig. 6. The examples of vehicle tracking

4 Conclusions

In this paper, the vehicles were detected and tracked by Adaboost and Kalman filter in the video frames. It is difficult to track in the tunnel because of noise, reflection of lights and a lot of motion. So, the Kalman filter tracking algorithm will be important application of vehicle tracking in the tunnel increasingly. We solved these problems to use Adaboost algorithm and Kalman filter. The experimental results showed relatively fast run time and accurate tracking.

Acknowledgement. This work was supported in part by MKE(NIPA), Busan Metropolitan City and Dong-Eui University.(08-GIBAN-13, Convergence of IT Devices Institute Busan).

References

1. Freund, Y., Schapire, R.E.: A short introduction to boosting. Journal of Japanese Society for Artificial Intelligence 14(5), 771–780 (1999)
2. Viola, P., Jones, M.: Rapid object detection using a boosted cascade of simple features. In: Proceedings IEEE Conf. on Computer Vision and Pattern Recognition (2001)
3. Barron, J.L., et al.: Systems and Experiment In: Performance of optical flow techniques. International Journal of Computer Vision 12(1), 43–77 (1994)
4. Watman, C., Austin, D.: Fast sum of absolute differences visual landmark detector. In: Proceedings IEEE Conf. on Robotics and Automation (2004)
5. Welch, G., Bishop, G.: An introduction to the Kalman filter. UNC-Chapel Hill, TR 95-041, July 24 (2006)
6. Rad, R., Jamzad, M.: Real time classification and tracking of multiple vehicles in highways. ELSEVIER 26, 1597–1607 (2005)

The Contents Based Music Retrieval Method Using Audio Feature Analysis against Polyphonic Music

Chai-Jong Song[1], Seok-Pil Lee[1], and Hochong Park[2]

[1] Digital Media Research Center, KETI,
#1599, Sangam-dong, Mapo-gu,
Seoul, South Korea
{jcsong,lspbio}@keti.re.kr
[2] Department of Electronics Engineering,
Kwangwoon University,
Seoul, Republic of Korea
hcpark@kw.ac.kr

Abstract. This paper describes the way of Music Retrieval Method based on audio feature analysis techniques which is proposed with three major new algorithms to improve performance of conventional way and implements the whole system including client and server side prototype. The first one of the major algorithms is to extract the high level melody feature from polyphonic music using harmonic structure attribute. The second one is to extract the feature and suppress the noise from user humming signal. The last one is fusing the way of methods with Dynamic Time Warp (DTW), Linear Scaling (LS) and Quantized Binary Code (QBCode). This has focused on targeting of commercial services such as music portal services, fixed stand-alone devices, mobile devices, and so on.

Keywords: Melody extraction, Pitch estimation, Matching engine, Query by Singing and Humming.

1 Introduction

With the recent proliferation of digital contents, there are increasing demands for efficient management of the large digital contents' databases, and the tag based retrievals have been used widely so far and it will be as it have been unless the new way which replaces the tagged method is not emerged. But, the way of tagging with metadata is a laborious and time-consuming work. Music Information Retrieval (MIR) techniques are considered rapidly as complementary way to manage music database rather than faster as we thought: [1]. For responding to the trends of these way early on we make sure building up the music retrieval method against huge polyphonic music database is very important and propose three advanced algorithms to realize it. The system architecture is organized as followed description. At the client side device, recording user humming signal with background noise for 10 seconds and then suppressing noise and extracting melody from this signal and finally it transmits the query data formatted with MP-QF international standard through the

T.-h. Kim et al. (Eds.): ISA 2011, CCIS 200, pp. 257–263, 2011.

network to the server waiting for request as you expect. The noise suppression block can be switched turning on and off by depending on the background noise circumstance. The server parses the received data and calculates the similarity score between queried data and feature vectors stored in database, and then recommends top 20 items getting highest similarity score to client vice versa. The overall system block diagram is shown as Figure 1.

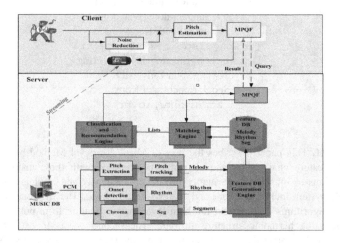

Fig. 1. Overall system diagram

This system is built up with three different databases at each step to set up the prototype version with MIDI sources and to verify inter-stage form of real music sources and then to maximize improving the performance. At the setup stage we starts with Roger Jang's corpus DB which is marked with the manuscript pitch vectors represented by semitones at every 32ms to build up the system of prototype. It has 2,789 humming clips which are sampled at 8 kHz of 8 bits per sample and 48 main melody MIDI files including its' pitch vectors and wave files. At this stage, we develop the noise suppression algorithm for humming data with Aurora2 dataset which has stationary and non-stationary background noise including several categories of car, airport, subway, babble, restaurant, train, exhibition and street on the real circumstance. The noise level is tuned to 10dB which is similar to real world humming situation. At the next stage, the database is changed to main melody from MIDI and 1,200 humming clips recorded against 100 songs of Korean pop music consisted of several genres. We measure the possibility of the proposed algorithms. At the last one, it is focused on improving the performance of algorithms with the final destination database which is the melody vectors extracted from polyphonic music file like MP3 and estimated pitch vector from real time humming signal. This paper describes two main parts as the implementation of system and the three proposed algorithms. This paper is organized as followed sections: In chapter 2, describes proposed pitch estimation algorithm and the following chapter 3 covers the harmonic structure based melody extraction algorithm. Chapter 4 covers fusion method matching engine and the next chapter shows the experiments of above algorithms, the last chapter describes conclusion.

2   Pitch Estimation Algorithm

The autocorrelation is the most well-known method for finding pitch from periodic signal and robust against noise too. That is the powerful tool but it is the obvious fact that it has the critical problem for pitch estimation. It has the pitch doubling problem at the low frequency in time domain otherwise the pitch halving is at the high frequency in spectral one: [2]. The proposed way is merging temporal and spectral one to overcome those problems. This way is like merged by Eq. 1 and it leads the limitation of resolution to represent pitch and fundamental frequency because it is inversely proportional relation. It can be free from led trouble by taking interpolation of the spectral ones which is near field indexes against the pitch ones at time domain before merging them. In addition, we can take advantage with the calculation efficiency by reducing FFT length. $R_t(\tau)$ and $R_w(\tau)$ which is temporal and spectral one respectively is merged with different ratio after normalized by each energy. Merged one depends on the weighting factor β setup at 0.5 through the various experiments. It shows the result that β is better less than 0.5 for woman, vice versa for man. Merging method of each autocorrelation is like Eq. (1).

$$R_{tf}(\sigma) = \beta R_t(\sigma) + (1 - \beta)R_w(\sigma) \tag{1}$$

Some pitch candidates are estimated with peak indexes of temporal autocorrelation, and take linear interpolation at nearby spectral ones in contiguity with candidate pitches of time domain. Before this, the formant structure is flattened by whitening spectrum to void the harmonic structure blurring at the high frequency. In order to suppress the noise, it takes the spectral magnitude of the noisy humming signal through the FFT analysis, and estimates the noise using Minimum Statistics (MS) which assumes that the tainted frames have the minimum power from the noisy signal and Improved Minima Controlled Recursive Averaging (IMCRA) which uses SNR of the statistic ratio between the voiced region and the unvoiced region: [3]. Noise suppressed signal is calculated by taking IFFT. At the post-processing stage, the pitches as assumed shot noise are eliminated with median filter.

3   Melody Extraction

Multiple fundamental frequencies as called multi-F0 have to be calculated before extracting main melody from polyphonic music signal which has main vocal melody over the various instrument sources. It is the main trend that the accompaniment is more stronger than the main vocal in the modern popular song, especially it is outstanding at some genres like dance, rock, heavy metal, and so on: [4],[5],[6],[7]. Keeping that in mind, the method is proposed to track the main melody from the multi-F0 with the harmonic structure which is very important fact of vocal signal as well as almost of all musical instruments except percussive one. Figure 2 depicts the flow of proposed method. The vocal region is detected with the zero crossing rates, frame energy and the deviation of spectral peaks. It assures that F0 does not exist unless it is judged to voiced frame otherwise doing harmonic analysis. Multi-F0 is estimated through three processing module like peak picking, F0 detection and harmonic structure grouping. F0 has some peak combinations because polyphonic signal is mixed with several musical instrument sources. Average energy is different between two bands for the music signal in general. 2 kHz makes the point to split into two bands. F0 range is limited from 150 Hz to 1 kHz with considering of human vocal aspect. If all of the F0 satisfy the ideal harmonic structure, real frequency peak will be at the harmonic peak as they must be. Average Harmonic Structure (AHS) determine F0 significant degree by calculating the average energy of harmonic peaks. Vocal melody is tracking estimated F0 candidates of each frame.

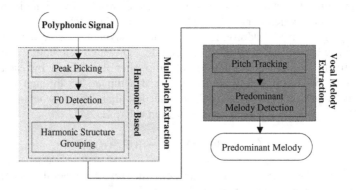

Fig. 2. Melody extraction flow gram

4   Fusion Method Matching Engine

The matching engine measures the similarity between pitch contour estimated from humming signal and melody contour extracted from music signal. It returns a list of top 20 candidates ranked from highest score from evaluating the similarity of two vectors using fusion matching method which is proposed in this paper. This proposed method as shown Fig. 3 is fused with three kinds of algorithms called DTW, LS and QBcode: [8]. It is starting with eliminating the silent duration on pitch and melody contour since it does not have any information for measuring the similarity but becomes more complex to calculate scores. After that it normalizes two vectors as test and reference through Mean-shift, Median-Average and Min-max scaling. After normalizing, three matchers evaluate the similarity simultaneously and get different scores that are combined with each weighting factor into single fusion score that is the main one of building a list of candidates. The most important one of three matchers is Asymmetric DTW advanced from conventional DTW having the several important constraints like start and end point alignment, local region constraint, and so on. It introduces log scale to measure the distance between two vectors in order to choose the vector having smaller distance in case the distance is same with Euclidian distance. Removing start and end point alignment is critical one since user can make humming at any point of music duration as well as we figure out it increasing the flexibility of matching process. That is why we called it Asymmetric DTW. Those two techniques make performance improved stiffly. The second matcher is QBcode matcher which has the 4 section of normalized vector and different binary codes assigned to each section as '000', '001', '011' and '111'. The distance is measured with hamming distance (HD) between two vectors. The third one is LS matcher which is the simplest one but it is quite effective one. The main idea of that is rescaling test vector into several different lengths against reference vector. Especially humming length depends on who is humming. So, humming data should be compressed or stretched to match with reference data. In this paper test vector is rescaled by scale factor from x1.0 to x2.0 with x0.2 scale of 5 steps. The distance is measured by log scale with same reason of DTW. The three scores from the above different matching algorithms are merged into one fusion score with the PRODUCT rule which multiply scores. Basically, Asymmetric DTW carries out the most important role on matching stage with assistant from LS and QBCode.

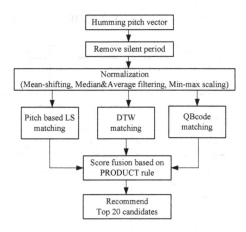

Fig. 3. Matching engine flow gram

5   Experiments

The reference dataset contains 2,000 pairs of MP3 and MIDI referred to Korean music chart. That covers 7 different genres including ballad, dance, children song, carol, rhythm and blues (R&B), rock, trot and well-known American pop. Test set is consisted of 1,200 humming clips of 12 second duration from 100 songs which are among reference dataset. The humming clips have almost same ratio of singing and humming and that is recorded from 29 persons. Three persons among them have the experience related music study at university but others not. That is classified into 3 groups as beginning, climax part and others based on hummed location of songs' duration. The beginning, climax and other part is about 60%, 30% and 10%

respectively. It is very interesting point to us that the ratio of beginning part is almost twice of climax one. The first one of three evaluations is the matching one as shown Table 1. The condition is as followed: 1,200 humming clips as test vector, 2,000 polyphonic songs with around 5 or 6 minutes duration as reference vector, Intel i7 973 with 8MB memory.

Table 1. Evaluation of matching engine

	Top1	Top10	top20	MRR	Time(sec)
32ms	74.90%	89.20%	92.20%	0.793	12.4
64ms	71.10%	80.10%	83.70%	0.738	4.7

The next one is the performance of proposed pitch estimation against well-known G.729 and YIN as shown left of Table 2: [2],[9]. The last one is the melody extraction as shown right of Table 2 with ADC 2004 dataset for evaluating the algorithm because the Korean dataset we build does not have the groudtruth: [10].

Table 2. (left) Evaluation of Pitch estimation, (Right) MIREX 2009 melody extraction result

Environmental Conditions		G.729	YIN	Proposed
		acc	acc	acc
clean		94.7	97.3	97.7
babble	30dB	94.4	97.2	97.5
	20dB	91.9	96.3	96.2
	10dB	80	81.4	86.9
	0dB	45.7	53	54.8
volvo	30dB	94.7	97.3	97.7
	20dB	94.6	97.2	97.8
	10dB	93.6	95.7	97.4
	0dB	83.3	80.1	91.2
white	30dB	94.6	97.3	97.6
	20dB	94	96.8	97.3
	10dB	87.7	85.9	95.8
	0dB	60.7	53.3	85.2
total average		85.4	86.8	91.8

Participant	RPA(%)	RCA(%)
Cao and Li	85.625	86.205
Durrieu & Richard	86.96	87.398
Hsu, Jang & Chen	63.11	74.101
Joo, Jo & Yoo	81.959	85.798
Dressler	85.969	86.424
Wendelboe	83.135	86.593
Cancela	86.962	87.545
Rao and Rao	81.446	88.038
Tachibana, Ono, Ono & Sagayama	59.768	72.129
Proposed Method	90.418	92.27

References

1. Orio, N.: Music Information Retrieval: A turorial and review. Found. Trends. Inf. Retr. 1, 1–90 (2006)
2. ITU-T, Recommendation G.729: Coding of speech at 8 kbit/s using CS-ACELP (March 1996)
3. Kamath, S., Loizou, P.: A multi-band spectral subtraction method for enhancing speech corrupted by colored noise. In: IEEE ICASSP (2002)
4. Poliner, G., Ellis, D.P., Ehamann, A.F., Gomez, E., Streich, S., Ong, B.: Melody Transcription from Music Audio: Approaches and Evaluation. IEEE Trans. Audio, Speech and Language Process. 15(4), 1066–1074 (2007)
5. Eggink, J., Broown, G.J.: Extracting melody lines from complex audio. ISMIR (2004)

6. Klapuri, A.: Multiple Fundamental Frequency Estimation by Summing Harmonic Amplitude. IEEE Trans. Speech and Audio Processing 8(6) (2003)
7. Goto, M.: A real-time music scene description system: Predominant-F0 estimation for detecting melody and bass lines in real-world audio signals. Speech Communication 43(4), 311–329 (2004)
8. Jang, J.-S.R., Lee, H.-R.: A General Framework of Progressive Filtering and Its Application to Query by Singing/Humming. IEEE Trans. Speech, Audio and Language 2(16), 250–258 (2008)
9. de Cheveigne, A., Kawahara, H.: YIN, a fundamental frequency estimator for speech and music. Journal ASA 111 (2002)

A Noise Robust Echo Canceller with Post-processing Using Liner Predictor and Wiener filter

Hyuntae Kim[1], Daehyun Ryu [2], and Jangsik Park[3]

[1] Department of Multimedia Engineering,
Dongeui University, Gaya-dong, San 24, Busanjin-ku, Busan, 614-714, Korea
htaekim@deu.ac.kr
[2] Faculty of Information Technology, Hansei University,
Dangjung-dong, 604-5, Kunpo city, Kyunggi Province, 435-742, Korea
dhryu@hansei.ac.kr
[3] Department of Electronics Engineering, Kyungsung University,
Daeyeon3-dong, 110-1, Nam-gu, Busan, 608-736, Korea
jsipark@ks.ac.kr

Abstract. When we talk with hands-free in a car or noisy lobby, the performance of the echo canceller degrade because background noise added to echo
caused by the distance from mouth to microphone is relatively long. It gives a
reason for necessity of noise-robust and high convergence speed adaptive algorithm. And if acoustic echo canceller operated not perfectly, residual signal going through the echo canceller to far-end speaker remains residual echo, which
degrade quality of talk. To solve this problem, post-processing needed to remove residual echo ones more. In this paper, we propose a new acoustic echo
canceller, which has noise robust and high convergence speed adaptive estimating echo path algorithm, linked with linear predictor and Wiener filter as a post-
processor. By computer simulation, it is confirmed that the proposed algorithm
shows better performance from acoustic interference cancellation (AIC) view-
point.

Keywords: Noise Robust Algorithm, Post-Processing, Linear Prediction Error
Filter, Wiener filter.

1   Introduction

NLMS family algorithms are simple and numerically robust. But these algorithms
have drawback of converging slowly, especially when input signal is colored. On the
other hand, RLS algorithm exhibits fast convergence in colored or strongly correlated
input signal, but it has heavy computational burdens. To solve these problems, affine
projection (AP) algorithm was suggested [1].

The AP algorithm is a generalization of the NLMS algorithm. This algorithm lies
somewhere between NLMS algorithm and RLS algorithm from a performance and
computational complexity point of view. But, when a projection is performed, noise
amplification problem arises and this phenomenon degrades the performances of the
AP algorithm [2][3].

T.-h. Kim et al. (Eds.): ISA 2011, CCIS 200, pp. 264–274, 2011.

And when the source of the acoustic echo signal is speech it is difficult to remove residual echo perfectly, because residual signal come from the output of the echo canceller has the same character of the speech signal [4].

In this paper, we propose a new modified AP algorithm for echo path modeling to reduce noise amplification problem of AP algorithm. And it is linked with linear predictor and Wiener filter as a post-processor, which whitens residual speech characteristics.

2   Proposed Echo Canceller

The block diagram of the proposed echo canceller is shown in fig. 1. The proposed system consists of two stages. The first stage consists of adaptive echo path modeling. And second stage consists of linear prediction error filter and Wiener filter, as a post-processor, which whitens residual speech characteristics and reduces the power of residual echo to background noise level respectively.

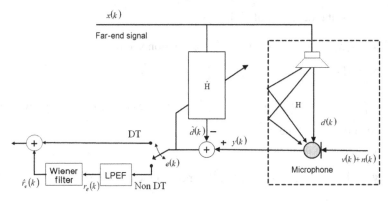

Fig. 1. Block diagram of the proposed echo cancellation system

2.1   Adaptive Echo Path Estimation Algorithm

A modified AP algorithm is proposed to estimate echo path for solving noise amplification problem of the AP algorithm in noisy circumstance. This algorithm normalizes the update equation to reduce noise amplification of AP algorithm, by adding the multiplication of error power and projection order to auto-covariance matrix of input signal. The proposed modified AP algorithm, in general form, is summarized by Table 1.

2.2   Double-Talk Detector

An important characteristic of a good echo canceller is a double-talk detector. But in some applications, near-end noise may be continuously present and then the use of a double-talk detector becomes futile. Robustness to double-talk may be established by taking into account the near-end signal characteristics [5].

In proposed system, normalized cross correlation (NCR) algorithm [6] as a double-talk detector, is based on a comparison of the variances of the estimated and measured microphone signals $\hat{y}(t)$ and $y(t)$. In its standard form, the NCR algorithm is computationally infeasible, but fortunately one may form a computationally cheap version of the algorithm by assuming that the adaptive filter has converged to the true echo path. Here, we use the forgetting factor version of the cheap NCR algorithm, forming the decision variable [7].

Table 1. Summary of the modified AP algorithm

$$\mathbf{e}_n = \mathbf{d}_n - \mathbf{X}_n^t \mathbf{w}_n \tag{1}$$

$$\mathbf{w}_{n+1} = \mathbf{w}_n + \mu \mathbf{X}_n \left[\mathbf{X}_n^t \mathbf{X}_n + P \cdot L \cdot \sigma_{e,n}^2 \mathbf{I} \right]^{-1} \mathbf{e}_n \tag{2}$$

where L is the adaptive filter length, P is the projection order of modified AP algorithm, and the following definitions are made:

x_n : excitation signal of nth instant

$$\mathbf{x}_n = \begin{bmatrix} x_n & x_{n-1} & \cdots & x_{n-L+1} \end{bmatrix}^t \text{ : excitation vector} \tag{3}$$

$$\mathbf{X}_n = \begin{bmatrix} \mathbf{x}_n & \mathbf{x}_{n-1} & \cdots & \mathbf{x}_{n-P+1} \end{bmatrix} \text{ : } P \text{ excitation matrix} \tag{4}$$

$$\mathbf{w}_n = \begin{bmatrix} w_{0,n} & w_{1,n} & \cdots & w_{L-1,n} \end{bmatrix}^t \text{ : adaptive coefficient vector, } w_{i,n} : \text{i}^{th}$$

adaptive coefficient at time n (5)

y_n : measurement noise signal.

$$\mathbf{y}_n = \begin{bmatrix} y_n & y_{n-1} & \cdots & y_{n-P+1} \end{bmatrix}^t \text{ : measurement noise vector} \tag{6}$$

$$\mathbf{d}_n = \begin{bmatrix} d_n & d_{n-1} & \cdots & d_{n-P+1} \end{bmatrix}^t \text{ : system output vector} \tag{7}$$

$$e_n = d_n - \mathbf{x}_n^t \mathbf{w}_n \text{ : } a \text{ priori error signal} \tag{8}$$

$$\mathbf{e}_n = \begin{bmatrix} e_n & e_{n-1} & \cdots & e_{n-P+1} \end{bmatrix}^t \text{ : } a \text{ priori error vector} \tag{9}$$

μ : step size parameter

$$\sigma_{e,n}^2 = \beta \sigma_{e,n-1}^2 + (1 - \beta) e_n^2 \text{ : running power estimate of } a \text{ priori error} \tag{10}$$

$$d_{CN}(k) = \sqrt{\frac{1}{\sigma_y^2} \hat{\mathbf{f}}_{xy}^T(k) \hat{\mathbf{H}}(k)} \tag{11}$$

where, $\hat{\mathbf{f}}_{xy}^T(k) = \lambda \hat{\mathbf{f}}_{xy}^T(k-1) + (1-\lambda) \mathbf{x}(k) y(k) \tag{12}$

$$\hat{\sigma}_y^2(k) = \lambda \hat{\sigma}_y^2(k-1) + (1-\lambda) y^2(k) \tag{13}$$

with λ denoting a forgetting factor. Double-talk is deemed to occur when $d_{CN}(k)$ is below some predetermined threshold, T, i.e.,

$$Decision = \begin{cases} d_{CN} \geq T, & DT \ not \ present. \\ d_{CN} < T, & DT \ present. \end{cases}$$

(14)

2.3   Linear Prediction Error Filter

The residual echo signal is whitened by using linear prediction error filter with P^{th} order. During non-double-talk states, estimated error signal $e(k)$ in adaptive filter includes residual echo $r(k)$ and background noise $n(k)$. Residual echo $r(k)$ which has speech characteristics removed by whitening process using P^{th} order linear prediction error filter, just like (15).

$$r_e(k) = e(k) - \sum_{i=1}^{P} a_i(k) e(k-i)$$

(15)

In equation (15) $a_i(k)$ and $r_e(k)$ denote coefficients of linear predictor and error signal from whitened acoustic echo canceller respectively. The coefficient of the linear predictor calculated from the solution of Wiener-Hopf equation, which is earned from Levinson-Durbin algorithm [8]. Input signal of the linear prediction error filter is $e(k) = r(k) + n(k)$. And output signals are linear prediction error $r_e(k)$, and linear predicted signal $r_s(k)$ for residual echo $r(k)$. Because background noise $n(k)$ is uncorrelated with residual echo $r(k)$, linear predictor can predict only residual echo component [9].

2.4   Wiener Filter

Also residual echo component still remain in linear prediction error $r_e(k)$. By using Wiener filter consisted of average powers of the linear predicted signal $r_s(k)$ and whitened prediction error $r_e(k)$, the power of residual echo reduced to background noise level. Proposed Wiener filter is shown in equation (16). And a detailed diagram of the proposed post-processing is shown in Fig. 2.

$$\hat{r}_e(k) = \left(\frac{E\left\{ r_e^2(k) \right\}}{E\left\{ r_e^2(k) \right\} + E\left\{ r_s^2(k) \right\}} \right) r_e(k)$$

(16)

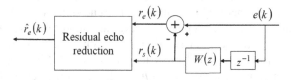

Fig. 2. A detailed diagram of the post-processing consisted of a linear prediction error filter and a Wiener filter

3   Computer Simulation and Results

3.1   Steady-State Echo Gain

First, we calculate steady-state echo gain with the proposed adaptive algorithm and AP by computer simulation [10]. In the simulation, step-size, $\mu = 0.2$, NFR(near- to far-end signal power ratio) are ranged from 10^{-3} to 10^{3}, and   projection order are 2, 6, 10 in AP and proposed algorithm, respectively.

From the Fig. 1, the echo gain of the AP algorithm increases linearly with target power and projection order. This is a serious shortcoming of the AP algorithm. In comparison, the proposed algorithm provides substantially improved steady-state performance at high NFR.

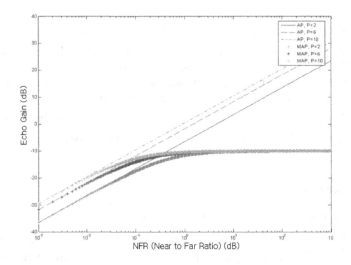

Fig. 3. Steady-state echo gain as a function of NFR

3.2   AIC (Acoustic Interference Cancellation) in Acoustic Echo Canceller

We apply to acoustic echo canceller with the proposed algorithm in hands-free envi-ronments. Far-end signal recorded with 8 kHz sampling rate, 16 bits quantization-level, and 10 second-long man and woman alternate pronounced English sentences. For considering double-talk situation, near-end signal recorded with 2 second-long man pronounced the other English sentences. Far-end signal to background noise ratio set to 30 dB and 20dB by assuming low level and high level white-Gaussian back-ground noise, respectively. And acoustic echo path impulse response measured in small size office room with 512th order lengths. Adaptive filter has the same length, step-size, $\mu = 0.125$ and projection order $P = 2$. For performance evaluation with pro-posed algorithm, AIC (acoustic interference cancellation) were used [4].

$$AIC(k) = 10 \log_{10} \frac{E\{y^2(k)\}}{E\{\hat{z}^2(k)\}} \tag{17}$$

$$= 10 \log_{10} \frac{E\{y^2(k)\}}{E\{y^2(k) - \hat{i}^2(k)\}} \quad [dB]$$

where, $\hat{i}(k) = \hat{d}(k) + \hat{n}(k)$ means estimated interference signal including estimated echo and background noise. Equation (17) means power ratio of microphone input signal $y(k)$ (including acoustic echo and background noise) and transmitted signal $\hat{z}(k)$ (or residual error signal). Therefore as acoustical echo is eliminated more by acoustic echo canceller, AIC has larger value.

The results at relatively high SNR, based on AIC with NLMS, AP, proposed modified AP with post-processing and proposed modified AP without post-processing are shown in Fig. 4. From the Fig. 4, it is impossible to distinguish performance of the AP algorithm from the proposed algorithm in relatively low background noise power. And the proposed algorithm has about 3 dB gain over the without post-processing method at relatively high SNR.

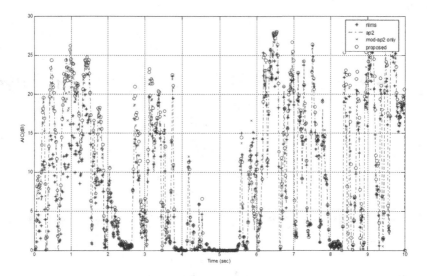

Fig. 4. AIC comparison with 30dB white Gaussian noise (NLMS, AP, proposed modified AP without post-processing, and proposed system)

Fig. 5 ~ 9 show the results for relatively low SNR, 20dB including double-talk intervals. In Fig. 5 ~ 9 (a), red color signal means near-end signal for double-talk intervals. As shown in Fig. 9 (c), the echo and residual signal well removed by the proposed adaptive filter before and after double-talk intervals at relatively low SNR.

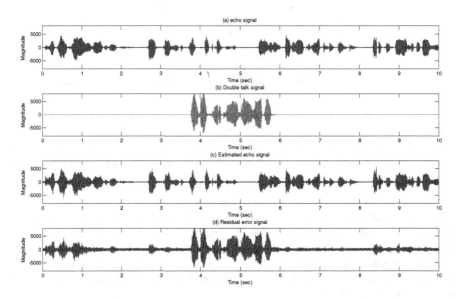

Fig. 5. A comparison of the echoes before and after cancellation (NLMS, 20dB white Gaussian noise)

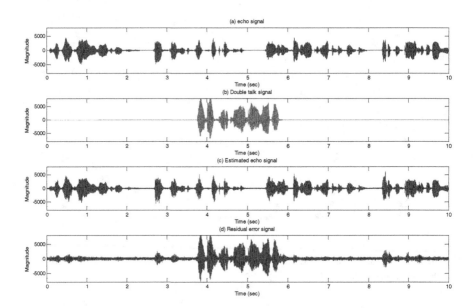

Fig. 6. A comparison of the echoes before and after cancellation (AP (P=2), 20dB white Gaussian noise)

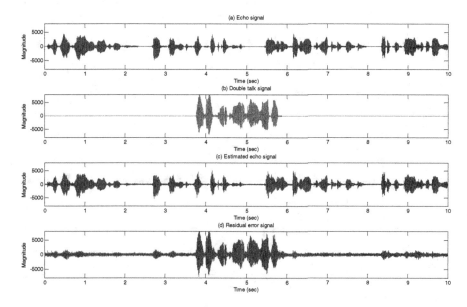

Fig. 7. A comparison of the echoes before and after cancellation (Proposed modified AP (P=2) without post-processing, 20dB white Gaussian noise)

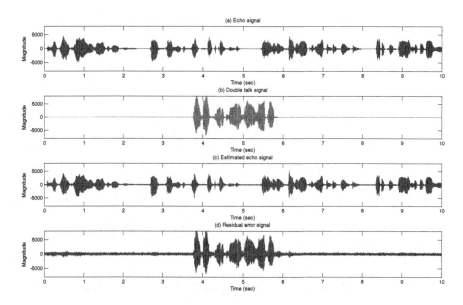

Fig. 8. A comparison of the echoes before and after cancellation (Proposed modified AP (P=2) with post-processing(LPEF only), 20dB white Gaussian noise)

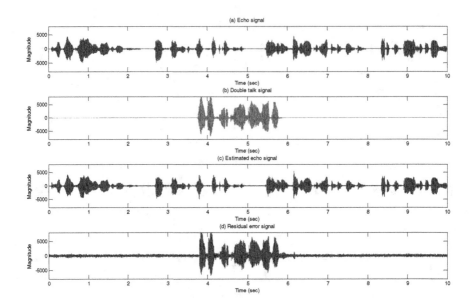

Fig. 9. A comparison of the echoes before and after cancellation (Proposed modified AP (P=2) with post-processing(LPEF + Wiener), 20dB white Gaussian noise)

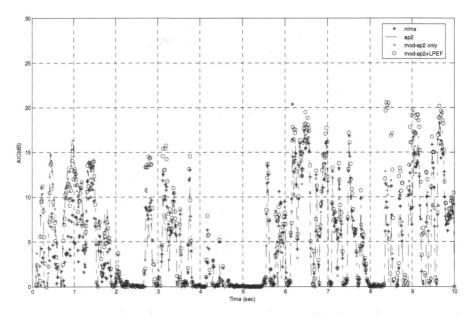

Fig. 10. AIC comparison with 20dB white Gaussian noise (NLMS, AP, proposed modified AP without post-processing, and proposed system with post-processing(LPEF only))

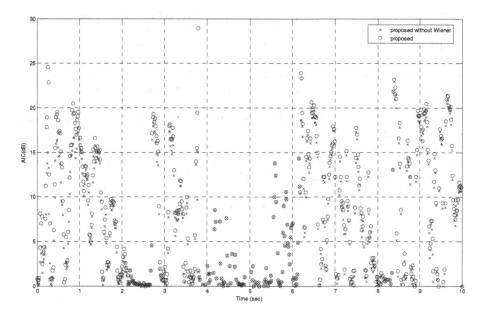

Fig. 11. AIC comparison with 20dB white Gaussian noise (proposed system with post-processing(LPEF only) and (LPEF + Wiener))

The results at relatively low SNR, based on AIC with NLMS, AP, proposed modified AP with post-processing(LPEF only) and proposed modified AP without post-processing are shown in Fig. 10. The Proposed algorithm has more than 3 ~ 5dB gain over the existing method at relatively low SNR. And proposed modified AP with post-processing(LPEF only) and proposed modified AP with post-processing(LPEF + Wiener) are shown in Fig. 11 specially. From the Fig. 11, Wiener filter is effective to reduce the residual noise.

4 Conclusions

By computer simulation, the proposed algorithm has better performance over the existing method at relatively low SNR. Consequently, the proposed algorithm is more efficient to large background noise and residual echo.

References

1. Gay, S.L.: A fast converging, low complexity adaptive filtering algorithm. In: Final Program and Paper Summaries. 1993 IEEE Workshop on App. of Signal Processing to Audio and Acoustics (1993)
2. Ferrer, M., Gonzalez, A.: Fast affine projection algorithms for filtered-x multichannel active noise control. IEEE Trans. on Audio, Speech, & Language Processing 16(8) (2008)
3. Ding, H.: Fast affine projection adaptation algorithms with stable and robust symmetric linear system solvers. IEEE Trans. on Signal Processing 55(5) (2007)

4. Park, Joon, S., Cho, Gun, C., Lee, Yong, C., Youn, Hee, D.: Park, Seon Joon, Cho, Chom Gun, Lee, Chungyong, Youn, Dae Hee: Integrated echo and noise canceler for hands-free applications. IEEE Trans. Analog and Digital Signal Processing 49(3), 188–195 (2002)
5. Waterschoot, T., Rombouts, G.: Double-talk-robust prediction error identification algorithms for acoustic echo cancellation. IEEE Trans. on Signal Processing 55(3) (2007)
6. Benesty, J., Morgan, D.R.: A new class of doubletalk detectors based on cross-correlation. IEEE Trans. Speech Audio Processing 8(2), 168–172 (2000)
7. Ahgren, P.: On system identification and acoustic echo cancellation. Ph.D. thesis, Uppsala University (2004)
8. Haykin, S.: Adaptive Filter Theory. Prentice Hall, N.J. (1995)
9. Kawamura, A., Fujii, K., Itoh, Y., Fukui, Y.: A noise reduction method based on linear prediction analysis. IEICE Trans. A 185-A, 415–423 (2002)
10. Hyuntae, K., Jangsik, P.: Convergence analysis of noise robust modified AP(affine projection) algorithm. International Journal of KIMICS 8(1) (2010)

Implementation Fire Detection Algorithm Using Fixed Point Digital Signal Processor

Jangsik Park[1], Hyuntae Kim[2], and Yunsik Yu[3]

[1] Department of Electronics Engineering, Kyungsung University,
Daeyeon3-dong, 110-1, Nam-gu, Busan, 608-736, Korea
jsipark@ks.ac.kr
[2] Department of Multimedia Engineering, Dongeui University,
Gaya-dong, San 24, Busanjin-ku, Busan, 614-714, Korea
htaekim@deu.ac.kr
[3] Convergence of IT Devices Institute Busan,
Gaya-dong, San 24, Busanjin-ku, Busan, 614-714, Korea
ysyu@deu.ac.kr

Abstract. In this paper, a fire detection algorithm based on video processing is proposed. Probability feature of smoke and flame is model by Gaussian mixture model. The whole process is divided into three parts, candidate flame or smoke selection, Gaussian mixture model calculation, and flame or smoke decision. The algorithm was implemented with fixed point DSP. As results of experiments, it is shown that the proposed algorithm and implemented video processing board effectively detects smokes and flames.

Keywords: Fire Detection, Gaussian Mixture Model, fixed-point DSP.

1 Introduction

Fires cause many environmental disasters, creating economical damage as well as endangering lives[1]. To early detect and prevent diffusion of fire, various sensing devices are developed and applied. Conventional fire detection systems with infra red and smoke sensors, have been used to detect indoor fires. These methods prove useless in outdoor settings, because of detection distance limitations. In order to detect fires early, previous workers have been researching methods using video processing techniques. The strength of using video in fire detection makes it possible to serve large and open spaces[2]. In addition, closed circuit television(CCTV) surveillance systems are currently installed in various public places monitoring indoors and outdoors.

Image and video content understanding and analysis methods have been studied by many researchers[3]. Content based understanding methods have to be designed according to the specific application. Fire detection in video is such an application that needs specific methods. There are several video based fire and flame detection algorithms in the papers. Healey et al. use only color clues for flame detection[4]. Phillips et al. use pixel colors and their temporal variations[5]. Chen et al. utilize a change detection scheme to detect flicker in fire regions[6].

T.-h. Kim et al. (Eds.): ISA 2011, CCIS 200, pp. 275–281, 2011.
© Springer-Verlag Berlin Heidelberg 2011

However, detection errors occurred in some situations despite various studies. In this paper, we propose a fire detection algorithm to detect fire early and to reduce errors based on GMM(Gaussian mixture model)[7] of smoke and flame. The proposed algorithm is implemented with high performance DSP. Developed smart video system is robust to artificial lights.

2   Fire Detection Algorithm and Smart Video Processing Board

Configuration of general fire detection system based on video is illustrated in Fig. 1. The input processing stage filters noise and converts color coordinates. Fire detection is performed in the detection processing stage using various algorithms developed by others. And then upon detection of a fire, an alarm message is propagated by devices such as lights or speakers.

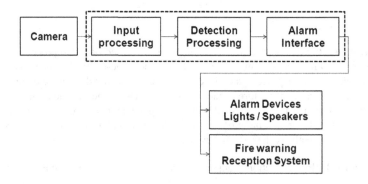

Fig. 1. Configurations of general fire detection system

Flame and smoke are clues of the existence of fire and they have specific colors and random motions. The frequency range is 6 to 10Hz. In contrast to specific objects, fire detection is difficult because of the variability of such things as fire density, lighting and diverse backgrounds. Furthermore, primitive image features such as intensity, motions, edge and obscuration do not characterize flames and smoke well. So, visual pattern of flame and smoke is difficult to model. And then detection errors occurred in various situations.

An approach using probability distributions is developed to reduce detection errors. The characteristic of flame and smoke are defined as a GMM. Flames and smoke are modeled as three clusters of Gaussian model with mean and variance as parameters for each Gaussian cluster. By comparing cluster parameters, fires can be distinguished from other situations because the cluster distributions of flame and smoke are different from causes of error. Meaning this approach is more robust to changes of lighting environments.

Parameters such as mean, variance and mixture weight are obtained by equation (1), (2) and (3) respectively. Parameters are calculated by an EM algorithm.

$$\mu_j = \frac{\sum_{n=1}^{N} P(\omega_j \,|X_n, \theta) X_n}{\sum_{n=1}^{N} P(\omega_j \,|X_n, \theta)} \tag{1}$$

$$\hat{\sigma}_j^2 = \frac{1}{d} \frac{\sum_{n=1}^{N} P(\omega_j \,|X_n) \left\| X_n - \hat{\mu}_j \right\|^2}{\sum_{n=1}^{N} P(\omega_j \,|X_n)} \tag{2}$$

$$\hat{\alpha}_j = \hat{P}(\omega_j) = \frac{1}{N} \sum_{n=1}^{N} P(\omega_j \,|X_n) \tag{3}$$

μ_j, $\hat{\sigma}_j^2$ and $\hat{\alpha}_j$ are mean, variance and mixture weight of j-th cluster. Relation of each probability is

$$P(\omega_i \,|\, x) = \frac{P(x\,|\,\omega_i)P(\omega_i)}{\sum_{k=1}^{M} P(x\,|\,\omega_k) \cdot P(\omega_k)} = \frac{P(x\,|\,\omega_i)P(\omega_i)}{P(X)} \tag{4}$$

The block diagram of the proposed fire detection algorithm is shown in Fig. 2. The algorithm is based on previous background. The whole fire detection process is divided into three parts, candidate flame or smoke selection, Gaussian mixture model calculation, and flame or smoke decision. The candidate flame or smoke selection stage finds moving regions based on background estimation. Moving regions are found from differences between estimated background and the current frame. The background estimation usually uses Gaussian running estimation.

The Gaussian mixture model calculation stage obtains Gaussian parameters, such as mean and variance of moving regions by EM algorithm. And finally, flames and smoke decision rules are performed in the flame or smoke decision stage by comparing Gaussian parameters with thresholds.

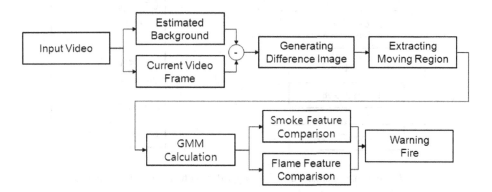

Fig. 2. Block diagram of the proposed fire detection algorithm

As mentioned earlier, Gaussian running estimation[8] is used to get a background estimate using equation (5).

$$B_n(x, y) = \begin{cases} aB_{n-1}(x, y) + (1-a)I_n(x, y) & \text{if } I_n(x, y) \text{ is non-moving.} \\ B_n(x, y) & \text{if } I_n(x, y) \text{ is moving.} \end{cases} \quad (5)$$

$B_n(x, y)$ is the background estimate, $I_n(x, y)$ is the current image. A candidate region is determined by equation (6) or (7).

$$|I_n(x, y) - I_{n-1}(x, y)| > T_I \quad (6)$$

$$|I_n(x, y) - B_n(x, y)| > T_B \quad (7)$$

2.1 Smoke and Flame Detection Algorithm

A detail smoke detection algorithm is illustrated in this flow chart. A GMM parameter is obtained. Gaussian clusters are aligned by intensity. The mean intensity of the candidate region is compared with threshold. And then, color differences are compared with thresholds. If intensity and color differences are in the specific range, the moving candidate is considered a smoke region. The flame detection algorithm is similar to the smoke detection one. The value of the threshold is slightly different.

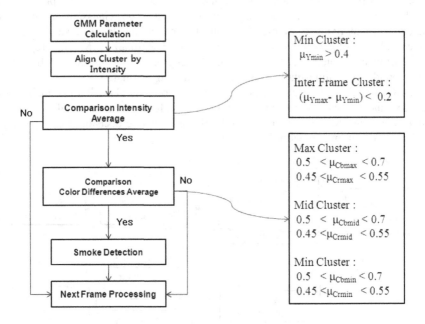

Fig. 3. Flow char of smoke detection algorithm with Gaussian mixture model

2.2 Smart Video Processing Board

The developed fire detection algorithm was implemented on a smart video processing board using fixed point DSP(Digital Signal Processing). A TMS320DM642 operating at 600MHz was used to implement smart video processing board.

Fig. 4. Smart video processing board with DSP including fire detection algorithm

3 Experimental Results

Smoke detection results in doors are illustrated in Fig. 5. Detected smoke regions are marked as black box. Ceiling reflects fluorescent light. These areas are detected as smoke by conventional algorithm. It shows that developed method performs well without errors.

Fig. 5. Smoke detection results in indoors. Detected regions are marked by black box.

Flame detection results are depicted in Fig. 6. Yellow boxes are sometimes detected as flames with conventional algorithms. Detection errors are dramatically decreased by developed algorithm and smart video system.

Fig. 7 shows experimental result of outdoor smoke detection. Captured images are experimental results of smoke detection in outdoors. Detected regions are marked as black box. An experiment is performed at the orchards. Another experiment is performed at conservation house as Korean style. It is good example developed video based fire detection system can be used as protection old house from fires.

Fig. 6. Flame detection results in indoors. Detected regions are marked by black box

Fig. 7. Smoke detection results in outdoors. Detected regions are marked by black box.

4   Conclusions

In this paper, flame and smoke detection algorithm are proposed to early detect fire using Gaussian mixture model of flame and smoke. As results of computer simulation and experiments, it is shown that the proposed algorithms are effective to detect fire. Flame and smoke detection algorithms are implemented with DSP(TMS320DM642) and some experiments are performed in interior and outside. Further studies are required to increase speed of processing.

Acknowledgement. This work was supported in part by MKE(NIPA), Busan Metropolitan City and Dong-Eui University.(08-GIBAN-13, Convergence of IT Devices Institute Busan).

References

1. Arrue, B.C., Ollero, A., Dios, J.R.M.: An intelligent system for false alarm reduction in infrared forest-fire detection. IEEE Intelligent Systems, 64–73 (2000)
2. Toreyin, B.U., Dedeoglu, Y., Gudukbay, U., Cetin, A.E.: Computer vision based method for real-time fire and flame detection. Pattern Recognition Letters, 1–10 (2005)
3. Healey, G., Slater, D., Lin, T., Drda, B., Goedeke, A.D.: A system for real-time fire detection. In: Proc. IEEE Computer Vision and Pattern Recognition Conference, pp. 605–606 (1993)
4. Javed, O., Shah, M.: Tracking and object classification for automated surveillance. In: Proc. European Conf. on Computer Vision, pp. 343–357 (2002)
5. Phillips III, W., Shah, M., Lobo, N.V.: Flame recognition in video. Pattern Recognition Letters 23(1-3), 319–327 (2002)
6. Chen, T., Wu, P., Chiou, Y.: An early fire-detection method based on image processing. In: Proc. IEEE International Conference on Image Processing, ICIP 2004, pp. 1707–1710 (2004)
7. Bilmes, J.: A gentle tutorial on the algorithm and its application to parameter estimation for Gaussian mixture and hidden Markov models. Technical Report ICSI-TR-97-021, International Computer Science Institute (ICSI), Berkeley. CA (1997)
8. Collins, R.T., Lipton, A.J., Kanade, T.: A system for video surveillance and monitoring. In: Proc. American Nuclear Society (ANS) 8th International Topical Meeting on Robotics and Remote System (1999)

An Efficient Private Registry Management System Using DHT Based on FIPA Agent Platform

Seung-Hyun Lee[1], Kyung-Soo Jang[2], Kee-Hyun Choi[1],
Choon-Sung Nam[1], and Dong-Ryeol Shin[1]

[1] School of Information & Communication, Sungkyunkwan University, Korea
{lshyun0,gyunee,namgun99,drshin}@ece.skku.ac.kr
[2] Dept. of Video Broadcasting & Information, Kyungin Women's College, Korea
ksjang@kic.ac.kr

Abstract. In this paper, we have redesigned the conception of SOA (Service oriented Architecture) by extension to existing service registry, and based on this definition; proposed a FIPA agent platform capable of capturing SOA components. According to the FIPA specification and reference model, we adopt several new Web service components called AgWebs in the FIPA agent system. They are designed the service management mechanism in private registry which agents are possible to lookup/register/de-register services using DHT algorithm with the DM module. Also, we can create a overlay network in the service registries on top of the existing physical network infrastructure, as using DHT based FIPA Agent platform. As it will be demonstrated, we develop an efficient private registry management system in FIPA agent platform.

Keywords: Web service, private registry management, DHT, FIPA agent, AgWebs.

1 Introduction

In recent years, internet computing trends are changed from a monolithic web application towards the SOA and a web environment. Especially, trend of SOA is changed to advanced Web service features by e-business models called the Enterprise Application Integration (EAI) [1]. In the primary stage of development, Web service discovery is the process of locating, discovering, and publishing as one or more related document which is composed to the specific services using the Web service standard technologies.

However, Web service provides only a simple, weakly structure and service than existing internet environment. Also, many researchers are currently working on integration between Agent platform and Web service. Standardization of integration will be scheduled to an official argument by several researchers and committees. But, the objective of using agents to integrate Web service composition has been increasingly, evidenced by a number of other publications. For example, The Web Services Integration Gateway (WSIG) [2] uses a Gateway agent to control the gateway into container of a JADE. Interaction among agents on different platforms is achieved through the Agent Communication Channel (ACC). Whenever a JADE

T.-h. Kim et al. (Eds.): ISA 2011, CCIS 200, pp. 282–291, 2011.
© Springer-Verlag Berlin Heidelberg 2011

agent sends a message and the receiver lives on a different agent platform, a Message Transport Protocol (MTP) is used to implement lower level message delivery procedures. But, WSIG does not considered the number of services between DF repository and UDDI repository. Also, it may be very huge to the gateway agent by a number of various services. Besides, WS2JADE [3] is proxy based on WS2JADE toolkit for integrating Web Service and Jade agent platform that allows Jade agents to offer Web service as their own services at runtime.

Formalized DHT has characteristic of a distributed system that forms a structured overlay allowing more efficient routing than the underlying network. We introduce the details in the related works.

FIPA-agent technologies for ubiquitous environments are becoming increasingly attractive for deployment. Agent is autonomous, intelligent, goal-oriented, and cognize user`s intention and environment. The Foundation for Intelligent Physical Agents (FIPA) establishes multi-agent system standards for the promotion of agent-based technology and interoperability of these standards [4]. Agents in the FIPA-compliant agent system can provide services to others, and store these services in the Directory Facilitator (DF) of the multi-agent system. Users can search for specific services through the DF, which maintains a database of service descriptions. The Java Agent Development Framework (JADE) is a popular multi-agent system for supporting the DF. We applied to JADE agent platform as agent environment in this paper [5].

In this paper, our goal is that Web service architecture can be composed to have the similar features like a structured P2P (peer-to-peer) overlay networks by using the centralized registries such as a private UDDI. In case of a private registry, can implement all the UDDI APIs (inquiry and publish) as defined by jUDDI [6]. These private UDDI will allow to high weight of application in real business environments.

This paper consists of the followings; In the Section 2, we addresses related works and background technologies. Section 3 describes the incorporation between the service registries for the environment. In section 4 presents proposed the system architecture. Section 5 shows the performance evaluation. Finally, this paper is concluded in section 6.

2   Related Work

In this section, we introduce related works and background technology such as FIPA agent platform, Web service architecture, and DHT.

2.1   FIPA Agent Platform

The FIPA (The Foundation for Intelligent Physical Agents) committee is the most promising standard organization in the agent technology. FIPA specification presents agent life cycle references of the creation, registration/deregistration, migration, retirement, and inter/outer-communication for each agent. The FIPA standard do not attempt to prescribe the internal architecture of agents nor how they should be implemented, but it specifies the interface necessary to support interoperability between agents. The FIPA specifications suggest the following mandatory component or normative agent. Also, the FIPA agent framework can support a large scale networks such as ad-hoc, mobile, and distributed networks [7][8].

- The **Directory facilitator** (DF) provides the functionality which is "yellow pages" services to other agents. Agents may register their services with the DF or query the DF for information on other agents. An agent platform can have multiple DF's thus providing the possibility of creating communities or domains of agents. DF's can register with each other forming a federation of domains.
- The **Agent Management System** (AMS) provides agent name services ("white pages"), and maintains an index of all agents which are registered with an agent platform. AMS exerts supervisory control over access to and the use of an AP. This normative agent is responsible for creation, deletion, and migration of the agents.
- The **Agent Communication Channel** (ACC) is the message transport system which controls all the exchanges of messages within the platform, as well as message to/from remote platforms.

2.2   Web Service Architecture

Since the advent of the internet, it has been cleared that the prevailing mode of human-to-machine interaction would be supplied and extended by technology designed to support direct machine-to-machine interaction, sometimes driven by human and in a completely autonomic web environment.

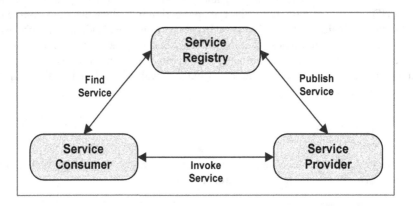

Fig. 1. Web Service Architecture

Web service promises to integrate business operations, reduce the time and cost of web application development and maintenance as well as promote reuse of code over the internet. Web service has simply some kind of service which is accessible over the network. Web service is the abstract set of functionality, which is provided by a component which is accessible over the network through the standard XML (eXtensible Markup Language) messaging. Web service represents a distributed system which is built on the architectural principles of the internet trying to tie up to its success [9].

As above fig 1, architecture of Web service has the some roles. Web service document is created and offered by service-provider, who registers the service in a service registry. (Generally, we call that UDDI which includes functionality of yellow pages, white pages, and green pages) and provides a description of it. The description of WSDL contains information about the functionality and location of the service. Service-consumer can find the service in the service registry, bind to the service and invoke to help from the service description.

2.3   DHT

DHT (Distributed Hash Table) is a set of decentralized distributed environment that provide a lookup service similar to a hash table: (name, value) pairs are stored in the distributed environment such as P2P (peer-to-peer) system [10][11]. Some participating node can efficiently retrieve the value associated with a given key. Also, it guarantees to scale to extremely large numbers of nodes and to handle continual node arrivals, departures, and failures [12]. Most DHTs (e.g. CAN, Chord, Pasty, Tapestry, and so on.) use some variant of consistent hashing scheme to map keys to nodes [13]. In practice, users look up resources stored in peer-to-peer systems often have only partial information for identifying these resources and tend to submit broad queries. However, The formalized DHT doesn't consider that a flexible and adaptive mechanism supporting keys which are useful to the several properties.

Table 1. The pseudo code of DHT

```
SDH(Keyword K){
    PR_Sname[] ⇐ discovery(K)
        {Retrieve from the keyword using Private Registry}
            PR_keys[][]
                for i = 0 to PR_Sname.length do
                        {Obtain DHT key for each PR Service_Name}
                        for j = 0 to NUMBER REPLICAS do
                                {one concept key has several replicas for fault-
                        tolerance}
                                PR keys[i][j] ⇐ Hash(PR [i] + j)
                        end for
                end for
        return PR keys
```

We considered that multiple keys present values of hash of several keywords from a service name or description, and so on. To solve these problems, we used grade up version of SDH algorithm as adopted agent system. The following presents that the pseudo code of service registry based on the Driven Hash algorithm [19].

3   System Architecture

Our goal proposes that how to support DHT mechanism can be leveraged to support the reliability and scalability for private registry in FIPA agent environment.

To satisfy them, we are organized to Web service registry and UDDI to solve the reliability problems in private Web service environment; there is a way to provide the services using service matching method in UDDI [14]. Also, there is a way to provide extended DHT (distributed hash table) mechanism in agent execution environment. Above all things, we consider that how to manage and discover more efficient the service in the distributed heterogeneous environment which is composing a peculiar service property [15].

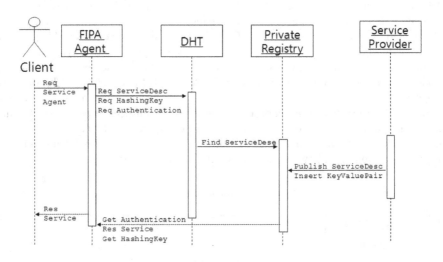

Fig. 2. Sequence Diagram

In our proposed system, distributed registries are composed to a private registry in fig 3. We assume that the registry does not leave and join, before it has been initiated between registries. After joined, registry is continually moving in and out of the network; we reconfigure the local routing table when each node configuration is changed. While the routing tables of the DM do need to be reconfigured, the nodes in the vicinity of the DM may join and leave at any time. The hash routing table is split into the unique value whose endpoints are the node identifiers. It means an each service registry.

The Agent Discovery Service (ADS) uses the existing discovery protocols in FIPA agent. It is performed that the functionality of ADS is similar to the DF. The ADS maintains one or more DHT modules, each of which provides services according to dynamic networks. Also, DHT module performs an available service that provides susceptible to move from domain to domain. Also, our proposed system presents architecture that is to build a service registry on top of a DHT infrastructure by using each service name and DHT to consider property, as mentioned in fig 3.

We can configure the overlay network only once in a while, because the DM is mandatory registry in each domain, and the agent who manages the DM can reconfigure the table whenever necessary. After the value is expired, they delete the entry from local routing table.

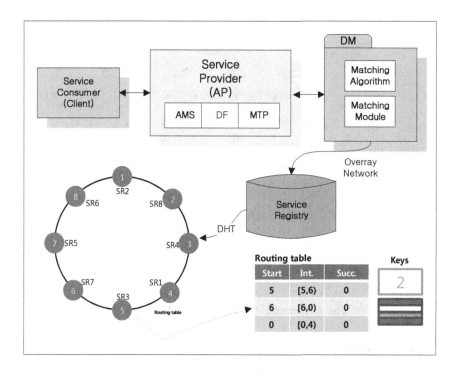

Fig. 3. System Architecture

3.1   Service Matchmaker

The results provided by the DM are forwarded to the Service Matchmaker in the Service Matching Module. The Service Matching Module consists of Service Matchmaker, Policy Manager, Category Classifier and two databases. When requests regarding registration or search `of the service are received, the Service Matchmaker accesses the AP through information created by the Policy Manager and Category Classifier [16]. Also, we consider five match relations between a query Q and a service S: [17]

- **Exact**: S is an exact match of Q.
- **Subsumes**: Q contains S. In this case S could be used under the condition that Q satisfies some additional runtime constraints such that it is specific enough for S.
- **PlugIn**: S is a plug-in match for Q, if S could be always used instead of Q.
- **Overlap**: Q and S have a given intersection. In this case, runtime constraints both over Q and S have to be taken into authtoken.
- **Fail**: In case of S not existing or Q is not exactly is failed.

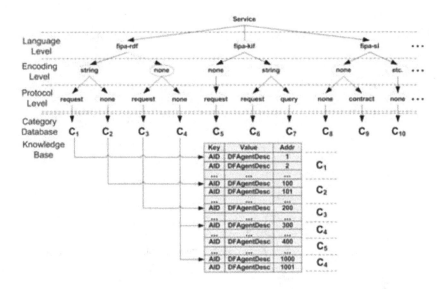

Fig. 4. Hierarchical Layer in Service Matchmaker

4   Implementation

We called as the AgWebs which uses to a project name for development in the S.H Lee at al [18]. The initial AgWebs exists type of a service registry. AgWebs is continuously developing version up for communication of and service registry. Through the AgWebs, user can request several service registries with other parameters, and achieves service information by the AgWebs using DHT.

Also, the AgWebs can be discovered for service description in private registries. The AgWebs as User Agent in JADE agent platform is running to local container. The client of AgWebs supports the entire service registry API for managing registries, including the whole query API set, and create/update/delete support for all entities in service registry. The client of AgWebs could be discovered information in several registries. It is implemented as Java language using the Swing libraries. The service registry configuration can be accessed by selecting the "Manage" menu and by selecting the "Find..." menu item, or by selecting the "Search" toolbar button. Businesses, services and tModels can be searched as fig 5.

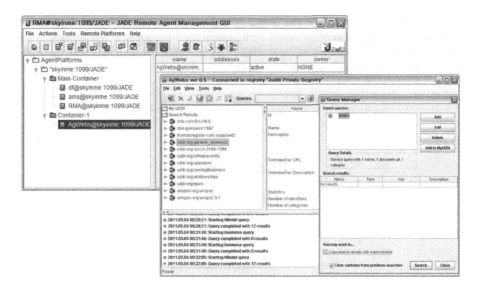

Fig. 5. The AgWebs Screenshot

5   Performance Evaluation

In this section, we measured performance with parameters in point of user's view. We constructed a testbed using AgWebs environment. Our testbed is a 100 Mbps Ethernet connected 2 PCs(server/client), each with Pentium core duo E7400 2.8 GHz and 3.25GB RAM, running Windows XP, Tomcat 5.5, mysql, and jUDDI. Basically, we use to Apache JMeter v. 2.4 [19] to measure the performance of the web parameters like response time, throughput, etc.

Table 2. HTTP Request Evaluation

Label	Sample	Avg.	Min	Max	Std. Dev	Through put	KB/ Sec	Avg. Bytes
HTTP Request	226	2	1	51	3.70	30.3/min	4.99	10125.0
HTTP Request	1000	5	1	557	30.79	1.0/Sec	9.89	10125.0

The Spline Visualizer (SV) provides a view of all sample times from the start of the test till the end, regardless of how many samples have been taken. The fig 6 shows each representing 10% of the samples each 226 and 1000 users. It connected using spline logic to show a single continuous line.

To quantify, the fig 6 shows accomplished the output by the Apache jmeter. In case of 1000 users than 226 users, the initial value is a small quantify. But, they could be produced by the output would be caused by overlapped server overhead and a number of a requested message. Also, this output would improve performance as long as the time spent in sending the code would be less than the time spent to the latency of the network during the request-response phase. As a result, we can see that there are obvious improvements brought by a number of users.

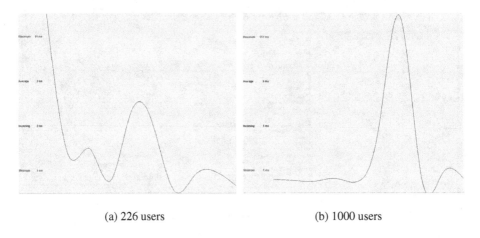

(a) 226 users   (b) 1000 users

Fig. 6. HTTP Req. in SV

6   Conclusion and Future Work

In this paper, we describe an efficient private registry management model using DHT in FIPA agent platform. Although this architecture follows the FIPA specification to discover agents/services in other domains by using the existing discovery protocols, there are still some problems which need to be resolved.

Also, private registry has a number of limited mechanisms. The respective problems describe two crucial disadvantages as the followings: Firstly, it has limited searching mechanism and secure service. There is made a registry without the specify data retrieval mechanism, because it provides an interface which progresses the searching process by means of keyword and taxonomy. Secondly, service registry is the usage of XML to describe its data model. They are not only guarantees syntactic interoperability, but bring about fail which provides a description of its content. Hence, XML's lack of explicit expression proves to be an additional barrier to the service registry discovery mechanism. For this reason, discovery mechanism of the existing can be found short enough for automated discovery, then. After all, these a number of service registries can lead to serious bottleneck of system performance and support of QoS.

We are trying to solve these several problems. Currently, we are working on an evaluation model of DHT for interoperability and awareness of services in the dynamic network environment.

References

1. Shen, W., Hao, Q., Wang, S., Li, Y., Hamada, Ghenniwa: A Multi-Agent-Based Service-Oriented Architecture for Inter-Enterprise Cooperation System. Robotics and Computer-Intergrated Manufacturing 23, 315–325 (2007)
2. Greenwood, D., Buhler, P., Reitbauer, A.: Web Service Discovery and Composition using the Web Service Integration Gateway. In: e-Technology, e-Commerce and e-Service, EEE 2005, 29 March-1 April, pp. 789–790 (2005)
3. Nguyen, X.T., Kowalczyk, R.: AAMAS 2007, SOCASE 2007 conference, pp. 147–159 (2007)
4. FIPA (The Foundation for Intelligent Physical Agents), http://www.fipa.org
5. JADE Homepage, http://www.jade.org, http://www.jade.org
6. jUDDI Homepage, http://juddi.apache.org
7. Choi, K.H., Shin, H.J., Shin, D.R.: D2HT:Directory Federation Using DHT to Support Open Scalability in Ubiquitoous Network. In: Proceedings of the Third IEEE International Conference on Pervasive Computing and Communications Workshops, pp. 253–257 (2005)
8. Choi, K.-H., Shin, H.-J., Shin, D.R.: Service Discovery Supporting Open Scalability Using FIPA-Compliant Agent Platform for Ubiquitous Networks. ICCSA (3), 99–108 (2005)
9. Web service Architecture, http://w3.org/TR/ws-arch/
10. Erdur, R.C., Dikenelli, O., Seylan, I., Gürcan, Ö.: An Infrastructure for the Integration of FIPA Compliant Agent Platforms. Autonomous Agent and Multiagent Systems, 1316–1317 (2005)
11. Aguilera, U., Abaitua, J., Diaz, J., Bujan, D., de Ipina, D.L.: A Matching Algorithm for Discovery in UDDI. In: International Conference on Computing (ICSC 2007), pp. 751–758 (2007)
12. Sangpachatanaruk, C., Znati, T.: Driven Hashing (SDH): An Ontology-Based Search Search Sheme for the Aware Network. In: Proceedings of the Fourth International Conference on Peer-to-Peer Computing, pp. 270–271 (2004)
13. Lua, K., Crowcroft, J., Pias, M., Sharma, R., Lim, S.: A survey and comparison of peer-to-peer overlay network schemes. IEEE Communications Surveys & Tutorials, 72–93 (2005)
14. UDDI Specification, http://www.serviceregisrty.org
15. Celik, D., Elqi, A.: A search agent approach:finding appropriate Web services based on user request term(s). Information and Communication Technology, 675–687 (December 2005)
16. Lee, G.H., Lee, S.H., Choi, K.H., Shin, D.R.: Design of Directory Facilitator for Agent-Based Service Discovery in Ubiquitous Computing Environments. In: IWSCA 2008, pp. 139–144 (2008)
17. Zhang, L.-J., Jeckle, M.: A Directory for Web Service Integration Supporting Custom Query Pruning and Ranking. In (LJ) Zhang, L.-J., Jeckle, M. (eds.) ECOWS 2004. LNCS, vol. 3250, pp. 87–101. Springer, Heidelberg (2004)
18. Lee, S.-H., Choi, K.-H., Shin, H.-J., Shin, D.-R.: AgWebs: Web Services based on Intelligent Agent Platform. In: ICACT 2007, February 12-14, pp. 353–356 (2007)
19. Jmeter Homepage, http://jakarta.apache.org/jmeter/

A Study for Method of Construct Encryption Scheme for Supporting Range Query Based on Bucket ID Transformation about Sensor Applications

You-Jin Song[1], Jae-Sang Cha[2], and Jang-Mook Kang[3],*

[1] Department of Information Management,
Dongguk University, 707 Seokjang-dong,
Gyeongju, Gyeongsangbuk-do, 780-714, Korea
song@dongguk.ac.kr
[2] Department of Media Engineering,
Seoul National University of Science and Technology,
Seoul, Korea
chajs@seoultech.ac.kr
[3] Electronic Commerce Research Institute,
Dongguk University, 707 Seokjang-dong,
Gyeongju, Gyeongsangbuk-do, 780-714, Korea
mooknc@gmail.com

Abstract. Encryption is a well established technology for protecting sensitive data. Unfortunately, the integration of existing encryption techniques with database systems causes undesirable performance degradation. We propose the bucket ID transformation that supports range queries without exposing the order of plaintext. The Bucket ID Transformation is performed by modulo arithmetic or pseudo-random number generation. This method is more powerful than the previous order-preserving methods and is expected to handle data more efficiently than other methods including auxiliary B+-tree. Experiment results show that our scheme outperforms other method in encryption and query speed.

Keywords: Bucket ID Transformation, Encryption, Database, Inference Attack, AES, Range Query.

1 Introduction

When the encryption algorithms are applied to the database, efficiency degradation occurs because the orders of cipher text and plaintext are not the same. To solve this problem, many solutions were proposed: Hacigümüs et al.[6] proposed the first method to query encrypted data, which is based on the definition of a number of buckets on the attribute domain. One of the main disadvantages of bucket-based indexing method is that it exposes data to inference. Order-preserving encryption

---

* Corresponding author.

T.-h. Kim et al. (Eds.): ISA 2011, CCIS 200, pp. 292–305, 2011.
© Springer-Verlag Berlin Heidelberg 2011

schemes that support the range queries over the encrypted data without decryption were proposed by Sun[8], and Agrawal[1]. But, the order of plaintext is exposed due to the encrypted data based on order-preserving encryption scheme. Therefore, existing proposed schemes cannot provide the security against ordinary-based inference attack and cannot universally be applied to the ordinal scale. Damiani[3] proposed the hash-based indexing method that can prevent frequency-based inference attack. The use of collision hash function for protecting inference attack is encouraged in the method. But, overhead problem exists because index collisions produce redundant tuples in the result of equality queries. In the same paper, Damiani also proposed the auxiliary B+ tree method. Auxiliary B+-tree method in which each tuple has different whole-tuple-encrypted data can provide the range query over the encrypted data and it may prevent frequency-based inference attack. It does not produce redundant tuples when executing a query, but rather evaluation of conditions is much more expensive. In order to support range queries for the encrypted data, it is very efficient way to preserve the order of plaintext. But we fall into a dilemma that it cannot prevent the order-based inference attack. It needs to harmonize with the problem between efficiency and inference attack. We propose the bucket ID transformation that supports range queries without exposing the order of plaintext. The Bucket ID Transformation is performed by modulo arithmetic or pseudo-random number generation. One of the many advantages of our method is that it makes possible to protect the order-based inference attack. Another advantage is that times of queries are greatly reduced in compared to the B+-tree method without disclosing the order of plaintext.

2   Paper Preparation

2.1   Figures

Notations used in this section are as follows:

m: Plaintext
r: Residue of plaintext
IB: Bucket ID
SB: Bucket size
K: Key of symmetric encryption algorithm
s: Seed for pseudo-random number generation
E(x) K: Encryption for x (= IB or r)
D(x) K: Decryption for x (= IB or r)

2.2   Overview of Our Scheme

In our scheme, transformation and inverse transformation procedures consist of two stages.

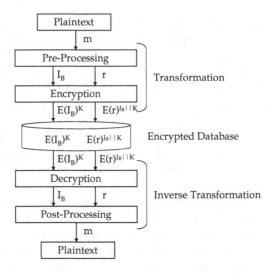

Fig. 1. Pre-Processing: Extracting two integers from plaintext m, Encryption: Encrypting integer IB and r which cannot be solved by attacker, Decryption: Decrypting IB and r from each set of $E(I_B)^K$ and $E(r)^{I_B\|K}$, Post-Processing: Calculating plaintext m based on IB and r

2.3   Transformation Process

2.3.1   Pre-processing
(1) Equi-Width Bucket Splitting by Modulo Arithmetic

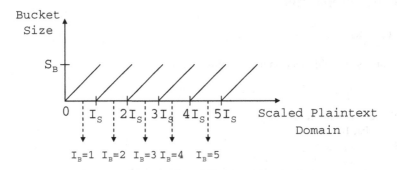

Fig. 2. Relation of IB and r in equi-width : As the m in the x-axis increases, I_B increases. The value r is less than the value S_B because r is created by modulo arithmetic. We consider I_B as bucket ID which has bucket size S_B because the plaintext m is segmented by S_B.

All integers have quotient IB and residue r through dividing arbitrary given SB. Computational procedure are as follows :
   r (Residue value) and IB (Bucket ID)   is calculated by next expression.

$$r \equiv m \bmod S_B, \quad I_B = \frac{m - r}{S_B}$$

Fig. 2 shows the relation of IB and r. ($0 \leq r < SB$).

(2) Coarse-Width Bucket Splitting by Pseudorandom Number Generation

Blum-Blum-Shub(BBS)[5] proposed a pseudorandom number generator which are used for coarse-width bucket splitting in our scheme. BBS takes the form :

$$x_{n+1} = (x_n)^2 \bmod n$$

where n=pq is the product of two large primes p and q. At each step of the algorithm, some output is derived from x_n;

I_B and r is calculated as Fig. 3. Seed s is given beforehand.

```
Input : m, s, prime number p,q
Output : I_B, r
x_0:=s
S_B:=p*q
    While (m>sum)
        x_0:=x_0^2 mod  S_B
        sum:=sum+x_0
        I_B:= I_B+1
    Endwhile
r:=m-(sum-x_0)
Return I_B,r
    End.
```

Fig. 3. Calculation of IB and r

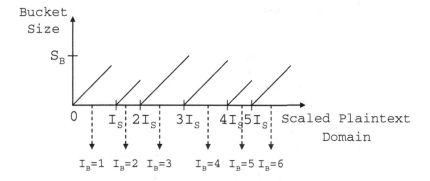

Fig. 4. Relation of IB and r in coarse-width

2.3.2 Encryption

(1) Encryption

In encryption process, $E(I_B)^K$ and $E(r)^{I_B\|K}$ are calculated by encryption algorithm, for example AES. Here, K is a symmetric key and must be kept secret.

(2) Transformation key Concatenated from IB and K

In the process of encryption of r, the key is IB ‖K. This means, if two r values are located within same bucket, transformation keys are identical. But since same r values in different buckets have different keys, the decryption results of same r values are different.

It can be denoted by $E(r)^{I_B\|K}$. Different key assignment in each bucket can protect inference for SB. That is, if every r have equal key, $E(r)^{I_B\|K}$ can be repeated by SB cycle. If an attacker attempts known-plaintext attack, he can guess range of r which has an identical bucket ID. This problem can be solved by different key assignment for each bucket.

Whoever knows K can decrypt original plaintext m. $E(I_B)^K$ and $E(r)^{I_B\|K}$ do not preserve the order of plaintext. Our scheme can provide robust and reliable protection from order-based inference attack.

2.4   Inverse Transformation Process

(1) Decryption

Input values of decryption are $E(I_B)^K$ and $E(r)^{I_B\|K}$. Then, IB and r can be obtained from the traditional decryption algorithm. Note that Inverse key is substituted by IB ‖K when decrypting r.

(2) Post-Processing

In case of equi-width, plaintext calculated from IB and r is m = IBSB+r. This m can be obtained by Fig. 5.

```
Input : I_B, r, s, prime number p,q
Output : plaintext m
  x_0:=s
  S_B:=p*q
    For i=1 to i= I_B
        x_0:=x_0^2 mod  S_B;
        sum:=sum+x_0;
    Endfor
  m:= sum+r
Return  m
    End.
```

Fig. 5. Calculation of plaintext m

2.5 Example

Suppose plaintext is 4835 and a key is 624. m is equal to the plaintext 4835 because original plaintext is integer. In the case of modular arithmetic, if SB is 100, 4835 mod 100 is equal to 35. That is, the value of r is 35. The value IB is calculated by $\frac{4832-35}{100}=48$.

In encryption stage, E(48)624 and E(35)48||624 are calculated by traditional encryption algorithms.

Then, database manager can get encrypted results that are $E(I_B)^K$ = YwaVIQ + XW7Q3w4LKV7 + go + E9Rms and $E(r)^{I_B||K}$ = Iai6yp4lQ3nMyjhiyAyz1jhjru4.

Now, the database contains these encrypted values. Therefore, the attacker cannot inference the original plaintext from encrypted data $E(I_B)^K$ and $E(r)^{I_B||K}$ because the encrypted values just look like insignificant values.

Encrypted data { $E(I_B)^K, E(r)^{I_B||K}$ } of example is presented in Fig. 6.

Name	Salary
Bob	4830
James	3527
Alice	7723

Name	$E(I_B)^K$	$E(r)^{IB||K}$
Bob	YwaVIQ+XW7Q3w4LK+E9Rms	Iai6yp4lQ3nMyjhiyAyz1jhjru4
James	+Lo7YRIktiicR1nXTzfLD6TnjQo	FWeAid+ewLO/xncEJSDfcDkoQ
Alice	gtS0izJW9Xngir5CJ6ZkkehIMi0	VCpg8E/wPszmO4NWGSblC6Bw

Fig. 6. Transformed Data

Then, whoever knows K can decrypt original plaintext m. $E(I_B)^K$ and $E(r)^{I_B||K}$ do not preserve the order of plaintext. Our mechanism can provide robust and reliable protection from ordinary-based inference attack.

3   Comparison with Related Works

3.1 Anti-Tamper Open-Form Encryption[8]

A simple scheme has been proposed in [8] that computes the encrypted value c of integer p as

$$c = \sum_{i=0}^{p} R_j$$
,

where R_j is the jth value generated by a secure pseudo-random number generator R. Unfortunately, the cost of making p calls to R for encrypting or decrypting c can be prohibitive for large values of p.

```
Encryption:
E_K(1) := 1 + z_1
E_K(n+1) := E_K(n) + 1 + z_{n+1}

Decryption:
Input: Y
Output: D_K(Y)
Begin
i := 0; W := Y;
    while W > i do
    begin i := i + 1; W := W + z_i
    endwhile
    if  W  =  i  then  return  D_K(Y) := i  else  output
"Failure'";
End.
```

Fig. 7. The encryption scheme of Anti-Tamper

The encryption scheme of Anti-Tamper is performed by summation of a set of pseudo-random numbers. It is very hard to prove the security of pseudo-random number. And since the nature of the plaintext distribution can be inferred from the encrypted values, it has the vulnerability to inference attack.

On the other hand, the encryption time increases exponentially if plaintext value is big. For example, if the plaintext is 1,000,000 and average of random sequence is 10,000, then encrypted value E(p) may reach to 1,000,000 * 1000 + 1,010,000,000 = 50,000,050,000.

In this case, the attacker can easily attempt the inference attack because pseudo-random number is less excessively than plaintext value.

Appearance extent is limited as many as SB in our scheme. For example, if the plaintext is 123456, encryption procedure of Anti-Tamper mechanism requires 123456 times pseudo-random number generation. Our scheme needs just 123+456 = 579 times pseudo random number generation and two times traditional encryption algorithm.

3.2   Order-Preserving Encryption(OPES)[1]

For numeric data, it may be a serious problem, if the attacker can get a value close to plaintext p corresponding to encrypted text c, though he doesn't know p exactly. In other words, in ordinary Order-Preserving Mechanism, if the distribution is known, the plaintext can be inferred.

Since this paper considers the ciphertext only attack only, the proposed mechanism is secure from estimation exposure.

However, when using this method, the order is exposed due to the nature of Order-Preserving. The p value can be inferred by designating a certain location.

The order of data encrypted using OPES scheme is identical with the order of plaintext. This characteristic causes some problems. Firstly, if plaintext is organized in ordinal scale such as grade of student, the encrypted data is very vulnerable to inference attack. Secondly, numeric ciphertext can cause precision error. For example, if an encrypted value is $1/3 = 0.333...$, it may be that the plaintext cannot be decrypted exactly. Our scheme is suitable for encryption of ordinal scale because it does not expose order information. Besides, precision error does not occur because the encryption of plaintext depends on bucket ID transformation.

The fact that order is kept means consequently that the order is known and this means that some of information is exposed. Therefore this paper proposes an encryption mechanism that allows range query without keeping the order.

3.3   Bucketization[6]

Hacigümüs et al.[6] proposed the technique that queries encrypted data. This is based on the definition of the number of buckets in the attribute area.

Let's assume that ri is the plaintext relation with schema Ri(Ai1, Ai2,..., Ain) and rki is the corresponding encrypted relation in Rki(Counter, Etuple). When a plaintext attribute Aij exists in RI where a domain is Dij, the bucket-based indexing technique can divide Dij without overlapping it. This is called "bucket". A bucket has a continuous value.

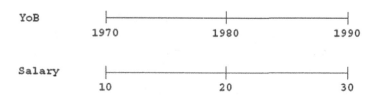

Fig. 8. An example of bucketization

This procedure called "bucketing". The buckets are always created with same size. Each bucket is connected with a unique value and this value is a domain for connection between Ij and Aij. If a plaintext tuple t is given in ri, the value of attribute Aij for t should belong to a bucket. This is very important in keeping data confidentiality.

In bucketization, special management for Bucket ID that has unique value, is essential. If Bucket ID is known to an attacker, order information can be exposed too. Moreover, it is not possible to perform aggregation queries(MIN, MAX, COUNT) without decrypting ciphertext.

Our scheme calculates the arithmetic $r \equiv m \bmod SB$ in pre-processing stage. And r is encrypted into $E(r)^{I_n \| K}$ in encryption stage. Therefore, it can support MIN,MAX,COUNT queries from encrypted data by using $E(r)^{I_n \| K}$. Besides, our scheme can prevent inference attack because the transformation keys of each bucket for transforming r are different.

3.4   B+-Trees Index[2][3]

An untrusted DMBS can find encrypted data only and any B+-Tree defined on the index doesn't reflect the order of plaint text. This, in effect, makes the range search impossible. To overcome this problem, we can entrust a trusted front-end with the decision on B+-Tree information. This paper proposes encrypting the whole B+-Tree node. The original B+-Tree is represented as two attributes (Node ID and encrypted value) in an untrusted DBMS. The Fig. 2 shows the plaintext representation and encrypted portion from B+-Tree table.

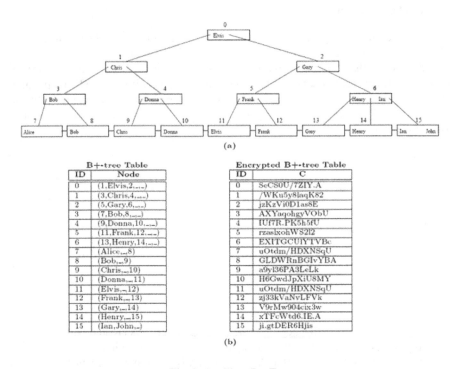

Fig. 9. Auxiliary B+-Tree

The advantage of this method is that the content of B+-Tree node is not seen in an untrusted DBMS. The disadvantage is that B+-Tree traversal can be executed only by a trusted front-end. By intuition, To execute an interval query, the front-end must execute quires needed to go down the tree node. Once reached a leaf, the node ID within the leaf can be used to compose tuple.

For example, to use B+-Tree to organize all customers whose names begins with DF, the front-end creates several queries to access the sequence node 0,1,4 and 10 and then other queries can be used to 10, 11 and 12 nodes (needed to search for other leaf).

However, this method requires reproductively of B+-Tree for data insertion, modification and deletion and has a security problem as it needs decryption of a whole encrypted text. In addition, since, unlikely tables, the index is not included in the portion that users can modify, delete or enter, it cannot be used with universal database and a separate DBMS that supports those functions must be built.

To restore K pieces of data, SQL queries as many as K+N are required (N: number of nodes). This process is one of factors that lower efficiency of database.

B+-Trees index can support range queries, but it requires many times SQL executions even one range query. That is, if the number of data within a range is 100, it executes SQL queries more than 100 times. For that reason, this method causes very much overhead. Moreover, it needs to decrypt entire data and reconstruct B+-Trees index if user or data manager perform many times insert, delete and update queries. As a result, it brings very high overhead and can't perform update queries without decryption.

3.5   Hash Based Index[2][3]

Hash based index can prevent inference attack. However, it does not support range query and has burden of re-filtering. Our scheme easily support range queries by modulo arithmetic and pseudorandom number generation.

Table 1. Comparison Table

Factor / Scheme	Eq uality Sea rch	Ra nge Sea rch	Updat ing	Preve nt of Order Expos ure
Bucketization[6]	○	□	○	□
B+-Tree[2]	○	○	□	○
Hash Based[2]	○	×	○	○
OPES[1]	○	○	○	×
Anti-Tamper[8]	○	○	○	×
Our Scheme	○	○	○	○

○ : Supported
□ : Semi-supported
× : Not supported

(1) Our Scheme.

Proposed scheme can prevent frequency based attack as well as order based inference attack because this mechanism does not preserve order. In addition, our mechanism supports range queries and aggregation queries (MIN,MAX,COUNT) over encrypted data. Even if insert or update transactions are performed somewhat repeatedly, decryption is not needed. In case of range query, execution times are greatly reduced compared to the B+-Tree index. A comparison table is presented in Table 1.

4   Analysis and Experiment

4.1 Example for Range Query

We will investigate operation for querying range for encrypted data splitted with coarse width bucket. Here, bucket size which is initially set is variable [Fig. 10].

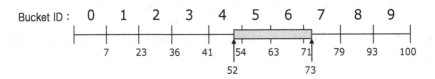

Fig. 10. Initial bucket size

- SQL querying
Assume that search the score between 52 and 73. In this case, the corresponding SQL query from client is shown below [Fig. 11].

select score from StudentScore where (score > 52) and (score < 73);

Fig. 11. SQL query from client

Consider the SQL query in [Fig. 12] when bucket ID number is 4, 5, 6. In case of ID number 5, client get the whole value with corresponding ID number. And the

select   *   from   StudentScore   where
(bucketid=$E_K(4)$ and   (score=$E_K(11)$ or
score=$E_K(12)$)   or   bucketid=$E_K(5)$ or
bucketid=$E_K(6)$ or   (bucketid=$E_K(7)$ and
(score=$E_K(0)$ or score=$E_K(1)$))

Fig. 12. Translated SQL

modified SQL query including query condition with all available value r of beginning bucket 4 and ending bucket 6 may be used in DBMS.

Namely, range [50~70] is corresponding to ID number 4, 5, 6 through preprocessing. In this case, value r becomes 11, 12 that are bigger than 10 because of bucket size with ID number 4 is 13. Similarly, the value r for ID number 6 becomes 0, 1. It is not necessary for ID number 5 to compute value r. Because it enables to get the whole value with corresponding bucket ID within beginning and ending bucket. If first query is SQL in [Fig. 11], the result and SQL query finally translated is shown as [Fig. 13].

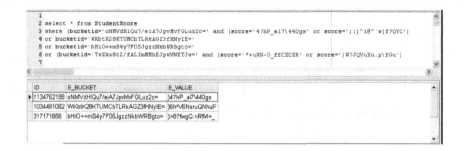

Fig. 13. SQL query result

Through above SQL query execution, we can get a row value encrypted. Finally, we get plaintext 57, 62, 65 by performing the decryption and postprocessing for result value.

4.2 Experiment

We have conducted experiment to show the validity and effectiveness of scheme proposed in this paper.

The experiments were conducted on IBM Intel-based PC with Pentium IV 3.0Ghz processors with 1G RAM. Relevant software components used were Oracle 9i standard and Microsoft Windows XP as the operating system. To encrypt the rows of the relations, we used the AES algorithm implemented in .NET.

We conducted the test for measuring speed of the encryption and decryption with increasing value of plaintext. Fig. 14 and 15 show the test results in case of equi-width and coarse-width bucket splitting in pre-processing. The graphs show the elapsed time of encrypting and decrypting 1,000 to 30,000 of plaintext. Each shows that our scheme is faster than random number based open-form encryption[8]. In case of open-form encryption, encryption cost significantly increases with increasing value of plaintext.

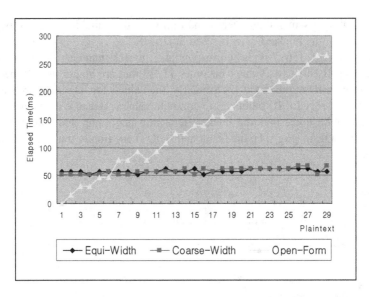

Fig. 14. Time per plaintext size (in milliseconds) required to encrypt plaintext.

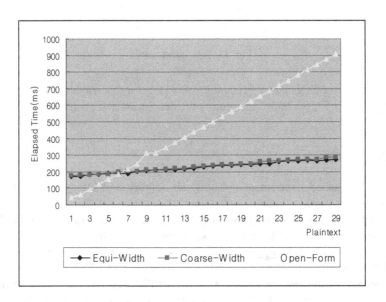

Fig. 15. Time per plaintext size (in milliseconds) required to decrypt plaintext.

5   Conclusions

It is necessary to consider the evident discrimination between the cryptograph for database security and the traditional cryptograph security. As various attack, such as inference attack, query execution attack, known-plaintext attack and so on, may possible in database, we have to design the cryptographic mechanism appropriated for the characteristic of database environment.

In this paper, we propose a bucket ID transformation scheme that is suitable for the range search without order-preserving for the encrypted data. We expect that our idea can make secure the data such as a personal information, a confidential document in database and provide the efficiency for the database query compared to the previous studies such as Sun[8], Agrawal[1], and Damiani[3]. We plan to verify the provable secure encryption mechanism.

Acknowledgment. This research was supported by Basic Science Research Program through the National Research Foundation of Korea(NRF) funded by the Ministry of Education, Science and Technology(No. 2010-0028122).

This work was supported by the Korea Science and Engineering Foundation(KOSEF) grant funded by the Korea government(MEST) (No. 2010-0027503).

References

1. Agrawal, R., Kiernan, J., Srikant, R., Xu, Y.: Order Preserving Encryption for Numeric Data. In: Proc. of the ACM SIGMOD Conf. on Management of Data, Paris, France, pp. 563–574 (2004)
2. Damiani, E., Vimercati, S.D.C., Jajodia, S., Paraboschi, S., Samarati, P.: Balancing Confidentiality and Efficiency in Untrusted Relational DBMSs. In: Proc. of the 10th ACM Conf. on Computer and Communications Security (CCS), pp. 93–102 (2003)
3. Damiani, E., Vimercati, S.D.C., Finetti, M., Paraboschi, S., Samarati, P., Jajodia, S.: Implementation of a Storage Mechanism for Untrusted DBMSs. In: Proc. of the International IEEE Security in Storage Workshop, p. 38 (2003)
4. Hacigümüs, H., Iyer, B., Mehrotra, S.: Providing database as a service. In: Proc. of the 18th International Conference on Data Engineering, p. 29 (2002)
5. Blum, L., Blum, M., Shub, M.: A Simple Unpredictable Pseudo Random Number Generator. SIAM Journal on Computing Archive 15(2), 364–383 (1986)
6. Hacigümüs, H., Iyer, B.R., Li, C., Mehrotra, S.: Executing SQL over Encrypted Data in the Database-Service-Provider Model. In: Proc. of the ACM SIGMOD Conf. on Management of Data, Madison,Wisconsin, pp. 216–227 (2002)
7. Iyer, B., Mehrotra, S., Mykletun, E., Tsudik, G., Wu, Y.: A Framework for Efficient Storage Security in RDBMS. In: Hwang, J., Christodoulakis, S., Plexousakis, D., Christophides, V., Koubarakis, M., Böhm, K. (eds.) EDBT 2004. LNCS, vol. 2992, pp. 147–164. Springer, Heidelberg (2004)
8. Chung, S.S., Ozsoyoglu, G.: Anti-Tamper Databases: Processing Aggregate Queries over Encrypted Databases. In: 22nd International Conference on Data Engineering Workshops (ICDEW 2006), p. 98 (2006)

Improvement of Message Processing Method for SOA Based Digital Set-Top Box System

Ji-Yeon Hwang, Seung-Jung Shin, and Dae-Hyun Ryu

Dept of IT, Hansei University,
604-5, Dangjung-Dong, Gunpo-Si,
Gyunggi-Do, Korea
dhryu@hansei.ac.kr

Abstract. In this paper, we reinterpreted the features of a set-top box system by applying a SOA (Service Oriented Architectures) like that used in the web-based Internet and improved the way messages are handled. Our set-top box system can respond to multiple requirements.

Keywords: Message Processing, Digital Set-top Box, Service Oriented Architectures.

1 Introduction

Digital television (DTV) is the transmission of audio and video by digital signals which is in contrast to using analog signals used as used by analog TV. Many countries are replacing over-the-air broadcast analog television with digital television to allow other uses of the radio spectrum formerly used for analog TV broadcast[1].

Leading digital broadcasting systems are DVB[3] in Europe, ATSC[2] in America, and ARIB[3] in Japan. Each country will broadcast services to meet these broadcast standards. The device which facilitates the reception of digital broadcasts via satellite or cable is called a digital set-top box. As the use of set-top boxes increase, a greater variety of content is being released. This new content is being driven by the demands of consumers, broadcasters, and operators Features such as web services, DLNA (Digital Living Network Alliance), FTP Server, Media, SI are being delivered via set-top box.

In this paper, we reinterpreted the features of a set-top box system by applying a SOA (Service Oriented Architectures) like that used on the web-based Internet and improved message handling. Our set-top box system can respond to multiple requirements.

2 Related Research

2.1 DVB(Digital Video Broadcasting)

The Digital Video Broadcasting Project (DVB) is an industry-led consortium of around 250 broadcasters, manufacturers, network operators, software developers,

T.-h. Kim et al. (Eds.): ISA 2011, CCIS 200, pp. 306–312, 2011.

regulatory bodies and others in over 35 countries committed to designing open technical standards for the global delivery of digital television and data services[4].

DVB have been adopted in most areas of the world except the United States. Canada, the Republic of Korea, Mexico, and others adopted ATSC and Japan has adopted their own standards. Satellite broadcasting player, Skylife TV in Korea, broadcasts using the DVB-S standard. Depending on the method of broadcasting, there are DVB-S (satellite), DVB-C (cable television), DVB-T (terrestrial), DVB-H (mobile only).

Table 1. Main Table Names of DVD

NIT	NETWORK NAME
BAT	BOUQUET
SDT	SERVICE NAME
EIT	Time, Program Information
TDT	Time Information
EMM	SMARTCARD Information (CAT)
ECM	SCRAMBLED (CAT)

2.2 MPEG-2(Moving Picture Expert Group)

MPEG-2 is a standard for "the generic coding of moving pictures and associated audio information". It describes a combination of lossy video compression and lossy audio data compression methods which permit storage and transmission of movies using currently available storage media and transmission bandwidth[5].

MPEG-2 refers to a series of standards on the audio and video encoding (coding) established by MPEG (Moving Picture Expert Group) and was announced as ISO Standard 13818 (13818-1 system, the video coding 13818-2, 13818-3 and audio). In general, MPEG-2 is being used for digital satellite broadcasting, digital cable TV and digital broadcasting of audio and video information transport. Also, a slightly modified encoding format of the MPEG-2 standard is being used with commercial DVD's standard Dolby Digital, DTS. MPEG-2 13818-2 video standard, which is similar to MPEG-1, supports interlaced video that is used in television broadcast. MPEG-2 video (part 2) is unsuitable in a low bit-rate (1 Mbit / s) environment, but is showing more advanced compression ratio requiring three megabits per second more than MPEG-1. One main feature of MPEG-2 which distinguishes it from MPEG-1 is that the transport stream is defined in a way which is suitable for an environment where data loss is common. It is currently being used for digital broadcasting. MPEG-2 is also included in the HDTV (high definition television) standard which was originally meant to be developed as MPEG-3. In addition, the MPEG-2 decoder that conforms to the standard can also play MPEG-1 streams because compatibility with MPEG-1 is guaranteed. This part of the standard was carried out in collaboration with ITU-T Video Coding Experts Group (Video Coding Experts Group, VCEG) and ISO / IEC of the Motion Picture Experts Group (Moving Picture Experts Group, MPEG). Therefore, the ITU-T's H.262 and MPEG 13818-2 is the same.

Table 2. Main Table names of MPEG-2

PAT	n- PROGRAM
CAT	SCRAMBLE
PMT	STREAM TYPE PID

2.3 SOA(Service Oriented Architectures)

The efforts to build a software system based on service-oriented concepts have resulted in the creation of the service-oriented architecture. Service-oriented architecture (SOA) is a flexible set of design principles used during the phases of systems development and integration in computing. A system based on SOA will package functionality as a suite of interoperable services that can be used within multiple, separate systems from several business domains[6].

The SOA implementations rely on a mesh of software services. Services comprise of unassociated, loosely coupled units of functionality that have no calls to each other embedded in them. Each service implements one action, such as filling out an online application for an account, or viewing an online bank statement, or placing an online booking or airline ticket order. Rather than services embedding calls to each other in their source code, they use defined protocols that describe how services pass and parse messages using description metadata. From the perspective of the architecture and implementation techniques, SOA is defined as a kind of architectural style including architectural principles and patterns which define how to design software systems for autonomous service to do message-based communication to another based on open standards as shown in Fig. 1.

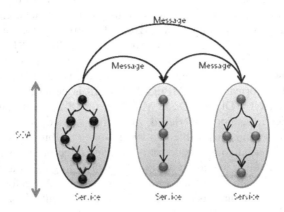

Fig. 1. SOA Architecture of Message Method

In SOA, a service is defined as action provided through an interface in contract between a component and other components. Requirements of SOA are defined as Layered, Rule, MVC, Service Hierarchy, Component, Class, Function, Data, Reuse [7].

3   Design and Implementation

3.1   System Architecture

In this study, we use a Linux-based UDS to provide independence between services to reinterpret the features of a set-top box system through the services provided by existing digital set-top boxes. We use shared memory to process large amounts of set-top box data. We use an embedded computer with a MPEG-2 Demux chip as the receiver and implemented a 4-layer set-top system.

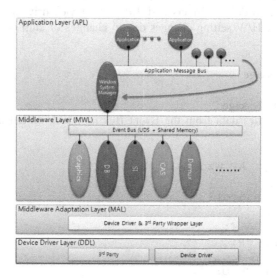

Fig. 2. SOA-based architecture of Set-top

3.1.1   APL(Application Layer)

APL is the part of the application shown on the screen. There are WSM (Window System Manager) and the many changes are available. Application can request an Event to the Event Bus from WSM and the data in shared memory ascends to the APL from the MWL to trigger the UDS event.

3.1.2   MWL(Middleware Layer)

MWL uses UDS for event communication and is implemented to use the shared memory to put data of each service to APL. It is possible for the set-top to play incoming video information via satellite or cable without having to draw the graphics on the screen because of the Demux chip. Also, we can see EIT information in real-time without a DB in which configuration information is stored, through DVB-SI or ARIB.

Using this feature, we constructed the basis of the SOA by re-interpreting DB, Graphics, and SI into independent unit from a service perspective. Using this method, it is possible to use the Europe set-top system in Japan, just by changing the SI

Service from the European DVB to the Japanese ARIB without changing other features. It is also possible to construct automatically operating system based on the information from satellite and cable by connecting DVB and ARIB together. We also implemented a method to use EEPROM or Flash module Instead of DB modules.

3.1.3 MAL(Middleware Adaptation Layer)

MAL is needed to ensure the independence of the MWL. We implemented MAL not to be affected by API changes or   3rd Party Device Driver versions.

3.1.4 DDL(Device Driver Layer)

DDL is divided into device drivers and 3rd party device drivers. We implemented DDL to guarantee H/W setting changes due to changes of chip or the Linux kernel version.

3.2 System Message

3.2.1 APL Bus Message

APL Message notifies data from the Event Bus in WSM. APL Bus Message is as follows.

```
APL_Result_t AP_Wzd_Main_Proc
{
switch (nMessage)
{
case WSM_CREATE:
case WSM_KEYUP:
case WSM_KEYDOWN:
case WSM_CLICKED:
....
```

3.2.2 Window Manager Loop of APL

The screen refreshes if the Window Message not come over 10 minutes of sleep time.. The window manager APL loop is as follows

```
ulMessage = MWL_EventBus_ReceiveTimeout

(&msg, sizeof(MSG), WAIT_10MS);

switch(ulMessage){

case MWL_EVENT_PAINT:

case MWL_EVENT_NO_EVENT:

/* Update Screen */

case MWL_EVENT_ALARM:

/* Alarm-MWL의 Timer */

....
```

3.3   System Message Manager

We improved the system message manager to enable asynchronous processing to solve problems where SI does not respond quickly or CAS event fires late due to delayed communication between CAS and SI using a UDS Event method.

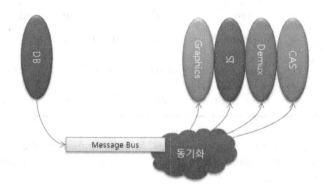

Fig. 3. Data processing procedure without Message Manager

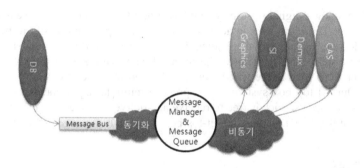

Fig. 4. Data processing procedure with Message Manager

Fig. 3 shows the data processing procedure before the implementation of the message manager and Fig. 4 shows the results after the message manager is implemented. In the existing system, when a message occurs, other services are not processed because of synchronous operation while checking all the services linked to Message Bus. Since the new message manager is asynchronously connected to a service during message distribution. The message manager uses a queue for asynchronous operation. For synchronous operation for real time messages, there should be synchronization between the message bus and message manager to avoid sending a message to multiple entities in the same service.

Table 3. Test Result of Message Manager Performance

Service		Message Count	Message Manager	
Send	Receive		o	X
DB	DB	10	about 1ms	about 1ms
DB	SI, CAS	10	about 1ms	about 1ms
DB	DB	1000	about 100ms	about 100ms
DB-CAS-SI Sequentially	SI, Graphics	1000	about 71ms	about 100ms
DB-CA-SI Randomly	SI, CAS	1000	about 73ms	about 100ms
DB-CA-SI Randomly	DB-CA-SI	1000	about 71ms	about 100ms

This test result is the average of 20 times. In order to measure the exact time, we made the function getting the message right at the point where it terminates except for message generation parts..

4   Results

By implementing a digital set-top system based on SOA, services can be easily added and removed. Therefore we can adapt our digital set-top system easily to be used in Europe, Korea, Japan, and the United States. In this paper, we reinterpreted the features of a set-top box system by the service by applying a SOA (Service Oriented Architectures) as used in the web-based Internet and improved the way messages are handled. Our set-top box system can respond to multiple requirements. Also, in our system, SOA-based service is free to receive and deliver messages by overcoming the problem that is inherent in existing set-top boxes which is message processing delay.

References

1. http://en.wikipedia.org/wiki/Digital_television
2. http://www.atsc.org/
3. http://www.arib.or.jp
4. http://www.dvb.org/
5. ISO/IEC 13818 MPEG-2 at the ISO Store
6. Bell, M.: Introduction to Service-Oriented Modeling. In: Service-Oriented Modeling: Service Analysis, Design, and Architecture, p. 3. Wiley & Sons, Chichester (2008) ISBN 978-0-470-14111-3
7. Bell, M.: SOA Modeling Patterns for Service-Oriented Discovery and Analysis, p. 390. Wiley & Sons, Chichester (2010) ISBN 978-0470481974

A Data Management Method to Secure Data in Cloud Computing Environment

You-Jin Song[1], Jae-Sang Cha[2], Jang-Mook Kang[3,*], and Wan-Sik Kim[4]

[1] Department of Information Management,
Dongguk University,
707 Seokjang-dong, Gyeongju, Gyeongsangbuk-do, 780-714, Korea
song@dongguk.ac.kr
[2] Department of Media Engineering,
Seoul National University of Science and Technology,
Seoul, Korea
chajs@seoultech.ac.kr
[3] Electronic Commerce Research Institute,
Dongguk University,
707 Seokjang-dong, Gyeongju, Gyeongsangbuk-do,
780-714, Korea
mooknc@gmail.com
[4] LIG Nex1 Co., Ltd. 148-1 Mabuk-dong, Giheung-gu,
Yongin-City, Gyeonggin-do, Korea
Wansik_kim@lignex1.com

Abstract. Rise in the use of mobile Internet is increasing the volume of data stored and managed on a daily basis beyond TB level. Google, Yahoo and Amazon, etc. are developing proprietary distributed computing platform technologies based on massive cluster to store and manage data in large quantity. One of the best-known applications of cloud computing is u-Healthcare service. u-Healthcare adopts cloud computing to enable consolidation and sharing of medical data. Notably, cloud computing may save system implementation costs in u-Healthcare service delivery process. Cloud computing may make sense for u-Healthcare service. However, since full trust in cloud computing service provider is a must, issues involving privacy violation or personal data disclosure may break out. Such issues occur as sensitive medical data relates to identifiable data of certain individual. To address such issues, this paper proposes AONT-based privacy protection method suited to support massive data processing in cloud environment. The method herein is suitable for processing large quantity of data, as AONT supports variation in size of fragment along with XOR operation. It can also minimize increase in DB size now appearing in relation to penetration of smartphone.

Keywords: Bucket ID Transformation, Encryption, Database, Inference Attack, AES, Range Query.

---

* Corresponding author.

T.-h. Kim et al. (Eds.): ISA 2011, CCIS 200, pp. 313–317, 2011.

1   Introduction

Smartphone is fast becoming a commodity. However, as conventional computing environment may not be suitable for processing massive load of data, it is necessary to develop methods to store and manage data in large quantity[1].Global Internet service providers such as Amazon, Google and Yahoo are developing distributed computing platform technologies based on massive cluster of affordable commercial nodes to address such issues and cloud computing is being noted as a distributed computing solution[2]. Cloud computing is defined as a computing method that uses Internet technology to offer highly extensible and flexible IT resources as services to a variety of 3rd party customers[3].

One of the major issues accompanying adoption of cloud computing is about security. Cloud Security Alliance (CSA)[4] and Gartner[2] announced 7 security threats to cloud computing and 7 security guidelines to assess such security risks, pointing out the abuse of cloud computing in relation to storage and management of distributed data, unethical use, data loss and disclosure and indicating needs for access right information and data separation.V. Ciriani et.al[7] ensures confidentiality by using fragmentation and encryption technologies to make it impossible to link and identify data. This paper proposes a distributed data storage and management method based on RSA-OAEP which is a variation of AONT method. In addition, outcomes of the method proposed herein are compared with those of AES-based preceding methods in RSA-OAEP-based test environment.

2   Main Body

2.1   AONT Method

AONT(All-or-Nothing Transform) methods[6] was proposed by Rivest who invented RSA encryption method. It was originally intended for OAEP[5] to strengthen RSA encryption.

When plain text is divided into fragments as shown in Fig. 1, the sum of such fragments and the plain text are the same in terms of size and, following conversion, AONT can be performed on the fragments to adjust the fragment count or size again.

2.2   AONT Method

Fragmentation and encryption method was proposed by V. Ciriani et.al[7] in 2008 to enhance data privacy. This method consists of confidentiality constraints relating to sensitivity and relationship of attributes, fragmentation of attributes in line with confidentiality constraints and physical fragments for encryption of fragmented attributes. CBC mode is used as encryption method used in physical fragmentation.

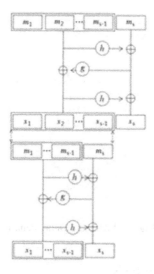

Fig. 1. AONT Method

3   Proposed Method

3.1   Overview of Proposed Method

This paper proposes a new method combining existing methods to address the following issues. First, conventional fragmentation and encryption method stores the same attributes in the relation schema of each fragment, which increases the size of fragmented data. Second, as massive quantity of data is stored or used in cloud computing environment, large volume of data used may compromise the efficiency by requiring more physical disc space. Therefore, when performing fragmentation and encryption method, AONT method was used to keep data size from increasing. First of all, healthcare flow scenario utilizing the proposed method is configured and described below.

3.2   Scenario Configuration

Fig. 2 describes a scenario of healthcare data flow adopting the proposed method in hospital information system in cloud environment. As an example of the scenario, patient attribute data including patient number, name, date of birth, address, name of disease and physician in charge generated when a patient receives medical treatment in hospital is stored in accordance with the following method.

As shown in Fig. 2, privacy can be safeguarded by separating relations between attributes with fragmentation and AONT method.

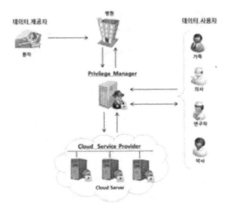

Fig. 2. Healthcare Data Scenario

4 Experiment and Analysis

The proposed method generates 3 Shares divided from each attribute by AONT and each Share is sized to be 2KB, 4KB, 4KB. Therefore, the 1st fragment requires 80KB, the 2nd fragment 112KB and the 3rd fragment 112KB and the remaining Share DB 96KB to store data. Ultimately, the aggregate size is 496KB, 224KB less than conventional method, indicating that the proposed method reduces the aggregate size of fragmented data, assuming that the number of fragments is identical.

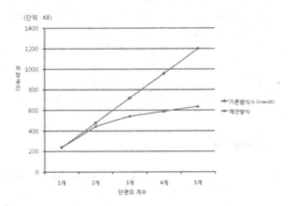

Fig. 3. As-is Method[7] vs. To-be Method Comparison

As Fig. 3 shows, physical fragmentation reduces the effective size of fragmented data, improving efficiency.

5   Conclusions

This paper has proposed an approach using AONT method to resolving the issue of increase in data storage requirement resulting from duplication of attribute data. The proposed data can protect privacy in the same manner as conventional fragmentation method and minimize data storage space requirement at the same time.

Acknowledgment. This research was supported by Basic Science Research Program through the National Research Foundation of Korea(NRF) funded by the Ministry of Education, Science and Technology(No. 2010-0028122)

This work was supported by the Korea Science and Engineering Foundation(KOSEF) grant funded by the Korea government(MEST) (No. 2010-0027503).

References

1. Shamir, A.: How to share secret. Comm. of the ACM 22, 612–613 (1979)
2. Gartner, http://www.gartner.com/DisplayDocument?id=685308
3. Chang, F., Dean, J., Ghemawat, S., Hsieh, W., Wallach, D., Burrows, M., Chandra, T., Fikes, A., Gruber, R.: Bigtable: A Distributed Storage System for Structured Data. In: Proc. of the 7th OSDI (2006)
4. CSA, Security Guidance for Critical Areas of Focus Cloud Computing V2.1 (2009)
5. Bellare, M., Rogaway, P.: Optimal asymmetric encryption. In: De Santis, A. (ed.) EUROCRYPT 1994. LNCS, vol. 950, pp. 92–111. Springer, Heidelberg (1995)
6. Rivest, R.L.: All-or-nothing encryption and the package transform. In: Biham, E. (ed.) FSE 1997. LNCS, vol. 1267, pp. 210–218. Springer, Heidelberg (1997)
7. Ciriani, V., Vimercati, S.D.C., Foresti, S., Jajodia, S., Paraboschi, S., Samarati, P.: Fragmentation and encryption to enforce privacy in data storage. In: Proc. of the 12th ESORICS, Dresden, Germany (2007)

VLSI Architecture of Adaptive Viterbi Decoder for Wireless Communication

Dongjae Song, Soongyu Kwon, Chun-Guan Kim, and Jong Tae Kim

School of Information and Communication Eng., Sungkyunkwan Univ., 300
Cheoncheon-dong Jangan-gu, Suwon, Gyeonggi-do 440-746, South Korea
jtkim@skku.ac.kr

Abstract. Wireless communication systems based on the Viterbi algorithm use various specifications which meets to error correction performance required by channel variations. Since decoder is designed with specification for the worst case channel state it wastes energy even in the good channel state. In this paper we present new Viterbi decoder architecture which can change its specification adaptively. It is simulated using WCDMA system model and results show that when it is adaptively controlled we can reduce the average energy consumption by 57%.

1 Introduction

Viterbi decoder is widely used in wireless digital communication system for FEC(forward error correction) since it has a simple architecture and fast decoding time. It is designed with different code parameter values for various error correction requirements. Decision on the required parameter values depends on the worst case channel state in order to ensure a stable BER(Bit Error Rate). However, it is not necessary to operate the Viterbi decoder in the worst case environment at all time since channel state varies. Viterbi decoder consumes much more power in the worst case channel state. If the channel is in good state we can lessen the required specification for the decoder that leads to saving power consumption for decoding. Therefore, it is necessary to design Viterbi decoder which can change its parameters dynamically according to the channel state variations. In this paper, we propose a Viterbi decoder architecture that can control decoding parameters (constraint length, number of soft decision bits, decoding depth). We verified the architecture by simulating the performance and energy consumption of the decoder. The proposed architecture is simulated with the WCDMA system model using Synopsys PrimePower.

2 Adaptive Viterbi Decoder Architecture

A simplified block diagram of the proposed adative Viterbi decoder architecture is shown in Fig. 1. It is mainly composed of four blocks, BMC(branch metric calculation) unit, ACS(add-compare-selection) unit, systolic array block, and controller. Operations are performed in a continuous manner. The reconfiguration of the soft decision bit and

T.-h. Kim et al. (Eds.): ISA 2011, CCIS 200, pp. 318–325, 2011.

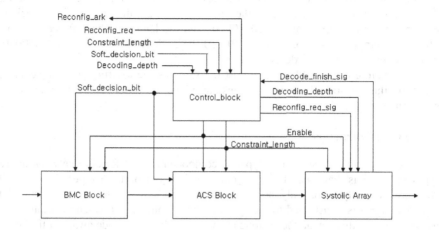

Fig. 1. Adaptive Viterbi Decoder Block Diagram

decoding depth is possible at any time. However, the reconfigure-request-signal must be used for the reconfiguration of the constraint length.

2.1 BMC and ACS Block

Figure 2 describes a block structure diagram for the BMC. The *codeword store* block is a memory that stores the codeword data for each constraint length. The *codeword converter* block is a codeword data extension block, which extends the codeword data from 2 bits to 8 bits according to the variation of soft_decision_bit signal. For example, when the codeword data is "01" and the length of the soft decision bit is 4bits, output data of the codeword converter is "00001111". As an another example, if the codeword data is "01" and the length of the soft decision bit is 2bits, then the output data is "00000011".

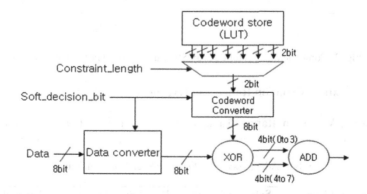

Fig. 2. BMC Block Structure Diagram

The *data converter* block is the input data converting block. It converts the data from 8 bits to 8 bits according to the variation in the soft_decision_bit signal. For example when the input data is "10110010" and the length of the soft decision bit is 4bits, the output of data converter is "10110010", whereas the output is "00100000" when the length of the soft decision bit is 2 bits.

The structure of ACS block is almost the same as the existing one. However, the input of the unused block has a constant value in order to avoid unnecessary switching.

2.2 Systolic Structure

The systolic array consists of two types of component. The difference between the two types in Fig. 3 is that type2 has load_out and final_out port but type1 does not. The structure of the type2 is only necessary at the end stage of the systolic array. The *load_out* signal is transmitted to the systolic array control block when the input data is assigned. Using this signal, the systolic array control block is made aware of the state of the data decoding operations. The *final_output* port is the data out port. In the systolic array, the total number of type2 components is sixteen. According to the constraint length and decoding depth, we should select one final_output data for the output of the Viterbi decoder among the sixteen possible values.

The reset signal for each component is controlled separately. Therefore, we can reduce the amount of unnecessary switching due to the existence of unused blocks.

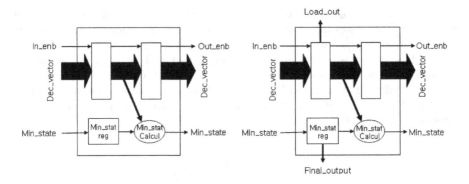

Fig. 3. Component of Systolic Array Structure (Left : type1, Right : type2)

2.3 Specification Variation Range and Overhead

Specification Variation Range. Table 1 shows the specification variation range of the Viterbi decoder.

Table 1. Adaptive Viterbi Decoder Spec Variation Range

Constraint length	Soft decision bit	Decoding depth (times of const)	Total available spec number
3 ~ 9	1 ~ 4	2 ~ 4	84

Overhead. The area overhead of the proposed adaptive Viterbi decoder is 19% of that of the fixed specification Viterbi decoder whose constraint length is 9, the number of soft decision bit are 4, and the decoding depth is 4 times. There is the time and energy overhead incurred by the refilling of the systolic array during the change in the constraint length. For example, if the current constraint length changes from 7 to 9 and the next decoding depth is 36, then the overhead incurred by the refilling of the systolic array is 72 clock cycles. Therefore, we should use an efficient changing policy which takes the overhead into account.

3   Viterbi Decoder Specification Decision

3.1   Viterbi Spec. Satisfying Target BER vs. Channel Eb/N0 Simulation

Because the Viterbi decoder specification changes to the dynamic mode depending on the channel state, we should determine the most suitable Viterbi parameters according to the current channel situation.

In this paper, we assume that the target BER is 1×10^{-5} and then simulate the value of the channel Eb/N0 in order to satisfy the target BER. We use the BPSK modulation method, the AWGN channel environment, and Matlab for the simulation.

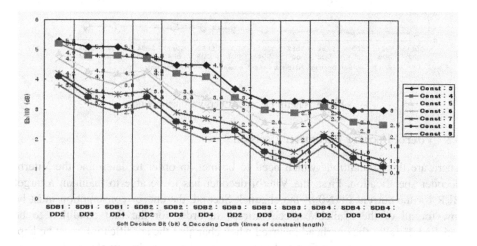

Fig. 4. Viterbi Specification Satisfying 1×10^{-5} BER VS Eb/N0

(SDB : soft decision bit, DD : decoding depth)

We can obtain the information about the minimum Viterbi specification required to satisfy the target BER and usable specifications in the same Eb/N0.

3.2 Energy Consumption Simulation

We measured the energy consumption of each Viterbi decoder and investigated the differences between them by simulation. We used a Synopsys PrimePower and performed the simulation at the gate level for the purpose of measuring the energy consumption. Fig. 5 shows the quantity of energy that is used to decode a data message consisting of 100 bits. According to fig. 5, the amount of energy consumed doubles as the constraint length is increased from 3 to 9.

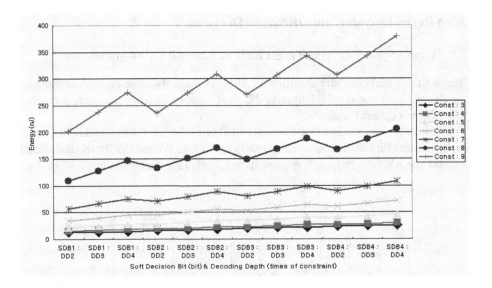

Fig. 5. Viterbi Decoder Energy Consumption

3.3 Viterbi Decoder Parameter Decision

There are three conditions which need to be met, in order to determine the Viterbi decoder specification. First, the Viterbi decoder has to be able to maintain a target BER for the current Eb/N0 of the channel. Second, the energy consumption must be low for all of the available specifications, in order for the first condition to be satisfied. Finally, the overhead incurred when changing the specification must be kept small. Data concerning the first and second conditions was already obtained from the simulation. (3.1 and 3.2) Therefore, we analyze about the overhead. As mentioned in section2, overhead is only generated by the change of the constraint length. If the constraint length changes, the pipeline of the systolic array is initialized and refilled. Therefore, the time required to fill the systolic array and the energy consumption can be considered as overhead. This overhead is able to be analyzed through the energy simulation.

For example, If we change the constraint length to 9 and the decoding depth to 4 times of the constraint length, the energy overhead is equal to the energy which the systolic array consumes for 72 clock cycles. In this way, we can calculate the energy consumption of the systolic array using the energy simulation result shown in Table2.

Table 2. Overhead Analysis

Constraint	3	4	5	6	7	8	9
Time(ns)	480	640	800	960	1120	1280	1440
Energy(nJ)	0.909	1.980	3.798	7.209	13.249	29.606	59.774

4   Adaptive Viterbi Decoder Energy Simulation

4.1   Simulation Method

Getting Eb/N0 Trace. Firstly, we trace the BER of the signal which is output by the rake receiver of the WCDMA system model. Secondly, we trace the BER of the signal using only BPSK modulation and AWGN channel environment. Third, we compare the result of the second operation with that of the first operation and, in this way, we generate the Eb/N0 variation profile of the channel. This profile represents the variation in the Eb/N0 of the channel during a period of 100ms. Figure6 shows 6 cases of Eb/N0 variation profile.

Adaptive Viterbi Decoder Parameter Decision. The specification decision of the Viterbi decoder involves the selection of the minimum specification in figure 4 according to the Eb/N0 of the channel. Figure 7 represents the Eb/N0 range of the minimum specification that is selected. The black bars of figure 7 are the minimum specifications.

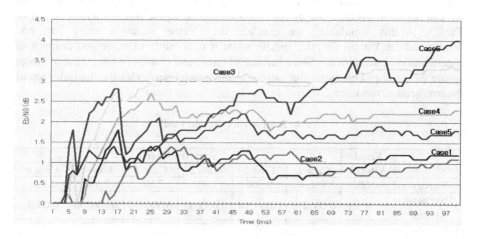

Fig. 6. Eb/N0 Variation Profile in WCDMA Model

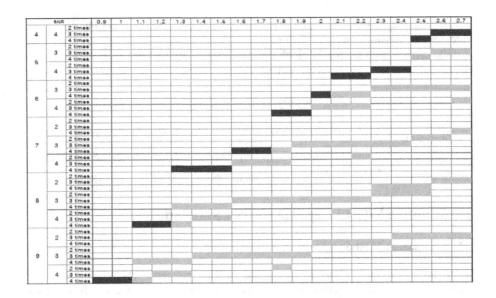

Fig. 7. Viterbi Decoder Minimum Spec VS Eb/N0 of the Channel

The simulation uses Synopsys PrimePower and executes for 100ms. During the simulation, the Eb/N0 varies as shown in figure6 and the Viterbi specification is decided according to the minimum specification priority policy.(black bars in figure7) The specification of the fixed Viterbi decoder is based on the worst case Eb/N0 in figure6. (constraint length : 9, soft decision bit : 4, decoding depth : 4times the constraint length)

4.2   Simulation Result

According to the channel variation, there is big difference at energy consumption. But we can see 57% average energy reduction compared to the fixed Viterbi decoder in Table3. In this simulation, we checked the channel situation every 1ms and determined the Viterbi decoder specification; it is possible to make 100 changes of specification at maximum.   Since the rate of parameter change is low, we can almost ignore the overhead energy.   But in the channel state varies rapidly, the influence of the overhead grows more.

Table 3. Simulation Results (mJ)

	Fixed Viterbi	Adaptive Viterbi					
		Case 1	Case 2	Case 3	Case 4	Case 5	Case 6
Energy	10.601	8.079	8.969	1.901	2.693	2.987	2.823
Overhead Energy	0	0.000479	0.000294	0.000033	0.000082	0.000293	0.0003
Total Energy	10.601	8.079	8.969	1.901	2.693	2.987	2.823

5   Conclusion

Viterbi decoder is widely used in wireless digital communication system for FEC(forward error correction) since it has a simple architecture and fast decoding time. In this paper, we propose a Viterbi decoder architecture that can control decoding parameters (constraint length, number of soft decision bits, decoding depth). We verified the architecture by simulating the performance and energy consumption of the decoder. The proposed architecture is simulated with the WCDMA system model using Synopsys PrimePower. Experimental results show that adaptive Viterbi architecture has an area overhead of 19%, but decrease the average energy consumption by about 57%.

References

1. Chan, F., Haccoun, D.: Adaptive Viterbi Decoding of Convolutional Codes over Memoryless Channels. IEEE Transactions on Communications 45(11), 1389–1400 (1997)
2. Glisic, S.: Advanced Wireless Communications. John Wiley & Sons, Ltd., Chichester (2004)
3. Truong, T.K., et al.: A VLSI Design for a Trace-Back Viterbi Decoder. IEEE Transactions on Communications 40(3), 616–624 (1992)
4. Shao, H.M., Reed, I.S.: On the VLSI Design of a Pipeline Reed-Solomon Decoder Using systolic array. IEEE Transactions on Computer 37(10), 1273–1280 (1988)
5. Hanzo, L., Liew, T.H.: Adaptive Coding and Transmission Paradigms for Wireless Channels. In: Proceedings of 2nd IMA International Conference on Mathematics in Communications, pp. 1–8 (December 2002)
6. Ikemoto, K., Kohno, R.: Adaptive Channel Coding Schemes using Finite State Machine for Software Defined Radio. In: The 5th International Symposium on Wireless Personal Multimedia Communications, vol. 3, pp. 1029–1033 (October 2002)
7. Lau, V.K.N.: Variable-Rate Adaptive Channel Coding for CDMA-Reverse Link. Bell-lab Technical Journal 5(4), 138–156 (2000)
8. Rahriema, M., Antia, Y.: Optimum Soft Decision Decoding with Channel State Information in the Presence of Fading. IEEE Communications Magazine 35(7), 110–111 (1997)

A Study for Security Scheme and the Right to Be Forgotten Based on Social Network Service for Smart-Phone Environment

Jang-Mook Kang[1], You-Jin Song[2], Jae-Sang Cha[3,*], and Seon-Hee Lee[3]

[1] Electronic Commerce Research Institute, Dongguk University,
707 Seokjang-dong, Gyeongju,
Gyeongsangbuk-do, 780-714, Korea
mooknc@gmail.com
[2] Department of Information Management, Dongguk University,
707 Seokjang-dong, Gyeongju,
Gyeongsangbuk-do, 780-714, Korea
song@dongguk.ac.kr
[3] Department of Media Engineering,
Seoul National University of Science and Technology,
Seoul, Korea
chajs@seoultech.ac.kr, seonhee@snut.ac.kr

Abstract. Republic of Korea became the norm in the smartphone. Especially social networking services have been spread with a smartphone. With the increasing use of social network service, privacy violations are increasing. A study deals with the privacy and the right of forgotten. Particularly the right to be forgotten has emerged recently. So the right to be forgotten is still under discussion. This article recently appeared in the right to be forgotten case revolves. According to the development of new and emerging security issues are also analyzed together. This article further expands the area of privacy and security policies and technologies are expected to be used.

Keywords: Smart-phone, SNS (social network service), the right to be forgotten, Privacy, Security, Information security.

1 Introduction

The European Union, apparently following former Google CEO Eric Schmidt's lead, is letting anyone and everyone know that it's ok to go wild, post embarrassing pictures of yourself on Facebook because they're going to see if you have the ability to remove it [1].

'The right to be forgotten' has been associated new to the concept 'The right to be left alone'. Therefore, 'The right to be forgotten' has as an extension of the right to privacy can be understood. 'name hits out personal information to Google, Facebook

---

* Corresponding author.

T.-h. Kim et al. (Eds.): ISA 2011, CCIS 200, pp. 326–332, 2011.

still on after the death of personal photos, reported more than 5 years before the newspaper turned out to be false information ....' they have in common is that you want to erase history [2]. But to get rid of those records must be authorized by an Internet company. The information rights of individuals, but the deletion of information in the enterprise is [2].

Republic of Korea to the last occurring in social network service are growing concerns about privacy. Republic of Korea, along with the emergence of the Internet, privacy is often the problem occurred. However, the advent of smart phones as mobile services, the concern about privacy is increasing rapidly. Therefore, this article is based on an understanding of privacy "the right to be forgotten" is analyzed. Research is processed discussion of privacy, understanding of the right to be forgotten, and how to resolve the problem.

2   Discussion on the Privacy

2.1   Concept of Privacy

Concern about privacy is concern about conditions of life, and it is so in the law as it is elsewhere [3]. That the concept of privacy figures prominently in recent philosophical and particularly legal scholarships is indisputable [4].

Fig. 1. Forgotten man [5]

Privacy (from Latin: privatus "separated from the rest, deprived of something, esp. office, participation in the government", from privo "to deprive") is the ability of an individual or group to seclude themselves or information about themselves and thereby reveal themselves selectively [6].

2.2   New Understanding Privacy under Mobile Environment

In our mobile life, we have concerned many privacy and personal information. So the Protected zone of privacy is changing. The below figure 1. illustrate the changing area of privacy protection.

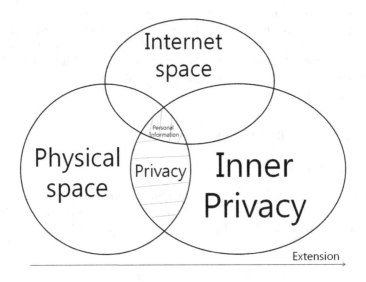

Fig. 2. New Concept for privacy

The concept of privacy is organized as follows. First, it is privacy in the physical realm. In the picture above is located to the left of the circle is a part. What is privacy in this area mainly in the real world experience is a privacy zone. For example, the right to be left alone in the room of the house would be like. Second, the Internet space is in privacy. The privacy in this area is closely related in information. In the picture above the top of the circle area is located. For example, Internet content, means wanderer. Third, human nature means the world (inner privacy). In the figure above on the right hand a large circle. For example, in the spirit world is peace.
Inner zone of privacy from the real world is expanding.

3   The Right to Be Forgotten

3.1   The Concept of "The Right to Be Forgotten"

Mounting concerns over privacy on the Internet have activists challenging their governments for the right to manage their personas online. The movement is particularly strong in Europe, where last year, privacy advocates proposed legislation to the European Union titled "The Right To Be Forgotten." [7].

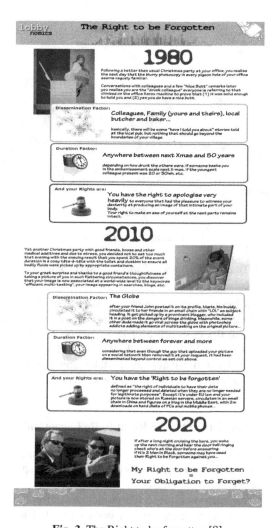

Fig. 3. The Right to be forgotten [8]

Upper fig. 3 shows that the balance between different rights (e.g. privacy Vs freedom of expression) is a well-known tension. But the creation of new rights that is so-called derivatives from privacy and seems to ignore both that tension and the fact that if you set up a right, it's always better if it's enforceable in practice, is a worrying trend [8].

So why do we need to assert our "right to be forgotten"? According to the article (A useful venn diagrm):

"Viviane Reding, Europe's rights commissioner, said the world of data protection had been transformed by popular new technologies in the 15 years since data protection legislation was last amended [9]. 'Internet users must have effective control of what they put online and be able to correct, withdraw or delete it at will,' she said."

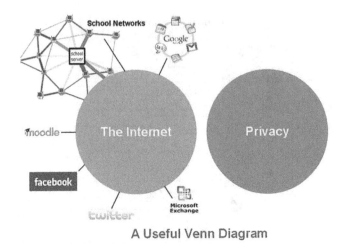

A Useful Venn Diagram

Fig. 4. Threats to privacy and social networking services [10]

'Internet users must have effective control of what they put online and be able to correct, withdraw or delete it at will,' she said." Privacy and social networking services is to fall in with the emergence of new threats. The figure 4. above shows social networking services as like Facebook, Twitter, Moodle, Google such as the advent of the Internet space and privacy are at stake, and that is showing. Therefore, when consumers want information about them and have the right to delete or erase personal information.

3.2 Social Network Service and "The Right to Be Forgotten"

The connection between social networks services have features that strong tie. Therefore, the content from one service to another service will spread. This is because the content can be moved between the free.

Content, including any personal information includes information about threats to privacy. Free movement of information has been expanded to a smart-phone. In addition to this, the software helps social networks service.

For example, data from a slide-sharing(www.slideshare.net) is linked automatically goes to the tweeter(www.twitter.com). In case of republic of Korea, location information from 'I'm in (www.im-in.com/) to 'me2days (www.me2day.net)' goes in automatically. Thus, consumers whether they go up to the writing just do not know where you can upload. In the past, these things have been delivered directly by the hand of man. However, in recent years through social networking services are handled automatically.

After all is getting harder to protect the privacy. A smart-phone is available in real time, frequent moves. The content of the spread of social network services increases. Thus, the proliferation of social networks and smartphones to privacy is a new set. The next chapter on this protection scheme is analyzed.

4   Security Scheme

So far only for the protection of 'the right to be forgotten' has not been introduced. Therefore, the existing privacy of policies and technologies can be applied to 'the right to be forgotten'. The figure 5. below is SSL(secure sockets layer)-based case.

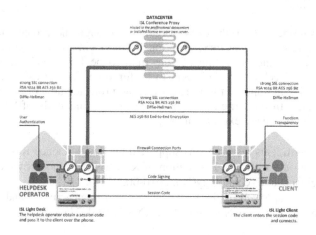

Fig. 5. Security Scheme by SSL [11]

As shown above encryption scheme is the primary means to protect privacy. This can be applied to the protection of 'the right to be forgotten'. In addition to this a number of privacy is the main tool has been developed. Than the ones based on technology, 'the right to be forgotten' can be protected.

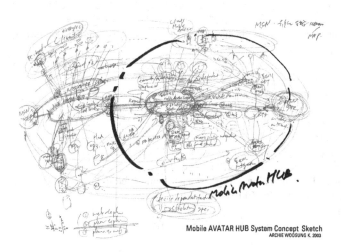

Fig. 6. Complex network and security for "the right to be forgotten" [12]

The figure 6. above shows the complexity of the network. Complex network is difficult as the protection of "the right to be forgotten". The prevalence of smartphones with the protection of "the right to be forgotten" is a factor more difficult. With the development of smart phones and social networking service, it is difficult getting the protection of privacy.

5   Conclusions

This study examines "the right to be forgotten" through the protection of privacy. While privacy has a long history, how much "the right to be forgotten" does not quicken. Therefore, the protection of "the right to be forgotten" was discussed in terms of privacy. Technically "the right to be forgotten" of the existing methods of encryption can be an important tool. However, the protected area of privacy, the need for change arises. In this article, the topics covered in the study of "the right to be forgotten" in the future are expected to help.

Acknowledgment. This research was supported by Basic Science Research Program through the National Research Foundation of Korea(NRF) funded by the Ministry of Education, Science and Technology(No. 2010-0028122).

This work was supported by the Korea Science and Engineering Foundation(KOSEF) grant funded by the Korea government(MEST) (No. 2010-0027503).

References

1. socialmediatoday,
   http://socialmediatoday.com/steve-olenski/280649/you-have- right-be-forgotten-online
2. dongA newspaper (2011), http://news.donga.com/3/all/20110208/34642846/1
3. Gross, H.:
   http://heinonline.org/HOL/LandingPage?collection=journals&
   handle=hein.journals/nylr42&div=16&id=&page=
4. Parent, W.A.: Rechnt work on the concept of privacy. American Philosophical Quarterly 20(4), 341 (2011)
5. beaglescout, http://www.news.unifiedpatriots.com/2011/03/18/eu-creates-a-bizarre-right-to-be-forgotten/
6. Wikipedia, http://en.wikipedia.org/wiki/Privacy
7. PSFK,   http://www.psfk.com/2011/05/the-right-to-be-forgotten-questioning-the-nature-of-online-privacy.html
8. lobby nomics,
   http://www.lobbynomics.com/2010/11/my-right-to-be-forgotten- your-obligation-to-forget/
9. Waterfield, B.: http://www.theage.com.au/digital-life/digital-life-news/eu-push-for-online-right-to-be-forgotten-20101105-17hht.html
10. utopianist,
    http://utopianist.com/wp-content/uploads/2011/03/privacy- chart.jpg
11. islonline, http://www.islonline.com/isl-light/security.htm
12. archiebrain, http://archiebrain.com/blog/attach/1/1135150647.jpg

Development of Integrated Adapter Based on Multi-sensor Networks for Tracking and Surveillance

Jun-Pil Boo[1] and Do-Hyeun Kim[2]

[1] ARA Communication Co., Ltd.,
801-7 Samdo-2Diong, Jeju-si, Jeju-do, 690-756, Korea
bip0389@nate.com
[2] Department of Computer Engineering, Jeju National University,
1 Ara 1Dong, Jeju-si, Jeju-do, 690-756, Korea
kimdh@jejunu.ac.kr

Abstract. Recently, two or three among them are being integrated and applying to many fields such as agriculture, livestock industry, construction, medical service and so on. Therefore, there is increasing research to make an interface to integrate them. Therefore, we present an integrated adaptor of video, sensor data, and location information collected in mobile sensing nodes for tracking and surveillance of mobile objects. This adaptor integrates and processes heterogeneous data from GPS devices, sensor networks, and video devices. We develop an integrated adaptor which receives from each of interfaces efficiently through filtering, distributing, queuing and etc. As a result, I'm considering it can supply good quality data to an application for various intelligence services.

Keywords: Integrated adapter, Multi-sensor, GPS, Location information.

1 Introduction

Recently, there is increasing the need of integrated interface for supporting various ubiquitous services in agriculture and livestock, construction, medical applications and, etc. Also, various intelligence applications are being developed based on GPS and sensor networks. GPS is mainly used for location-based applications, and sensor networks are deployed for collecting context information such as temperature, humidity, atmospheric pressure, and so on. Additionally, many researches on sensor web technology are carried out by OGC (Open Geospatial Consortium), Microsoft, etc. The sensor web or sensor map technology is for displaying and monitoring sensor data repositories connected to the Internet or World Wide Web. The current Sensor Web research focuses on providing real-time sensor data and video collected in sensor networks. Meanwhile, more studies are required on mobile sensor web technology dealing with data from mobile sensor networks composed of cars, ships, persons, and so on.

This paper proposes an integrated adaptor for video and sensor data in multi-sensor networks. This adaptor integrates and processes heterogeneous data from GPS, sensors, video devices to provide information of moving objects in mobile sensor networks. We develop an integrated adaptor which provides a common interface for the heterogeneous data and creates combined messages after parsing and queuing them.

T.-h. Kim et al. (Eds.): ISA 2011, CCIS 200, pp. 333–338, 2011.
© Springer-Verlag Berlin Heidelberg 2011

The rest of this paper is organized as follows: First, we review some of related work in Section 2, then Section 3 presents the integrated adaptor. Finally, the conclusion is given in Section 4.

2   Related Work

GPS is a constellation of satellites that broadcast signals to derive precise timing, location and velocity information. It can calculate position accurately to within meters or even centimeters, a most essential aspect for surveying work. This data, along with GIS software, has enabled surveyors to create more detailed maps for surveys. This information, when further combined with other systems such as communications devices, computers, and software can perform a wide range of tasks. GPS, along with GIS software, can provide a reliable and efficient system for navigation, vehicle tracking, and monitoring the routes of vehicles on land and ships on rivers and oceans LBS (Location-Based Service) using GPS as an information service, accessible with mobile devices have the ability to make use of the geographical position of the mobile devices. LBS include services to identify a person or object with location information. The location information can be provided to users with other context data like sensor data. LBS technologies include LDT (Location Determination Technology), mobile communication technology, LEP (Location Enabled Platform), and LAP (Location Application Program) [1-2].

A WSN (Wireless Sensor Network) is a wireless network composed of spatially distributed sensors, actuators, RFIDs, etc. to provide users with context information such as temperature, humidity, pollutants, or pressure [3, 4].

Sensor web is an environment in which users can discover and monitor various sensors, instruments, image devices, and sensor data repositories through the Internet Web. SWE standardization has been in progress by OGC to provide common bases for sharing and utilizing heterogeneous sensor data. SWE standards include SensorML, Observation & Measurement, sensor observation service, and web notification. Sensor web can be used for real-time detection and early warning system for forest fires, earthquakes, tidal waves, and so on [5-7].

Our previous research investigated a general architecture in vehicular sensor networks, and the problem of intermittently connecting from cars or other mobile devices to the Internet. This work did not address multimedia sensors issues, such as a camera, a microphone, multiple sensor, etc[8,9].

3   Development of Integrated Adaptor

This paper presents the integrated adapter architecture based on camera system, GPS system and sensor networks. This adapter can process an integrated data that received from each of interfaces efficiently through filtering, distributing, queuing and etc. Proposed adapter supports an open API of upper layer for transmitting the integrated frame to a middleware and application. Additionally, we present the integrated adapter architecture based on camera, GPS, and sensor networks. Integrated adaptor processes the data of a mobile node equipped with GPS, sensors, and camera, and then transmits the processed data to middleware or applications. Fig. 1 shows the implemented integrated adaptor structure composed of data processing module, data combining module, data transmission module, and interfaces with sensor networks and applications.

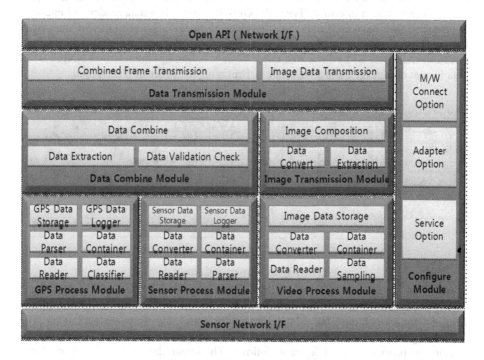

Fig. 1. Architecture of the integrated adaptor

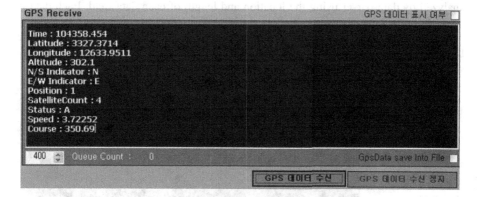

Fig. 2. Display of processed GPS data

For processing GPS data, we used Leadtek Wireless GPS Receiver made by Leadtek Research Inc. and Promi SD202 Bluetooth Serial Adaptor made by Promi, Inc. And Maxfor, Inc.'s TIP700 series and Logitech, Inc.'s QuickCam®E2500TM were used for sensor and video data processing, respectively.

The GPS we used provides NNEA-0183 data format. The operations of GPS data processing module are as follows: GPS receiver connected to a PC receives GPS data through the common interface. Then, the GPS data is read by data reader and encoded to primitive GPS data. GPS data classifier divides the GPGGA and GPRMC messages into each component such as latitude, longitude, altitude, velocity, GPS time, direction indicator, and others. We used '$' as a delimiter character, as NNEA-0183 data format does. Fig. 2 shows a window displaying the processed GPS data.

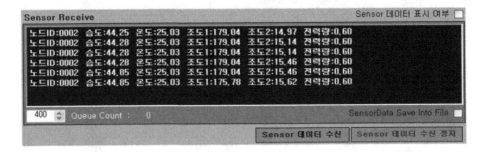

Fig. 3. Display of processed sensor data

We constructed a sensor network using Maxfor, Inc.'s TIP700 series. The sensed data include temperature, humidity, illumination, intensity of power, and so on. The node ID, group ID, and channel are used to identify sensor nodes. The operations of sensor data processing module are as follows: The sensor data receiver connected to a PC receives sensor data through the common interface. Then, the sensor data is read by data reader and encoded to primitive sensor data. The primitive sensor data is analyzed by data parser using the location and length of each data field. Each data is converted to a numerical value by data converter using a converting formula. Finally, we defined a data object as a temporary variable to store the sensor data such as node ID, channel, temperature, humidity, illumination, intensity of power, and so on. Fig. 3 shows a window displaying the processed sensor data.

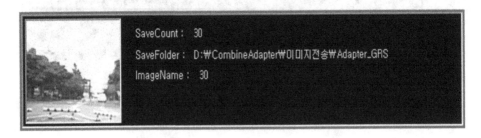

Fig. 4. Display of processed video data

Video data processing module receives video data from a camera, stores the data in a data object operating as a temporary variable, converts the data into image data files, and stores the files in image data storage. Fig. 4 shows a window displaying the processed video data.

Fig. 5. Combined frame creation and transmission

Combined frame creation module takes out GPS and sensor data objects from each data queue for data valid check, and creates a combined frame. Depending on the result of data valid check, a message mode is determined. As mentioned earlier, the message mode indicates which of GPS and sensor data is included in the combined frame. We defined three kinds of data objects for GPS data, sensor data, and video data. The data object has a few variables to store its data components. Every data object is made and inserted into a queue in sequence whenever the data is received. Fig. 5 shows a window for combined frame creation and transmission.

4   Conclusion

Recently, intelligent services is increasing among the aging population, many individuals are interested in ubiquitous environments. Therefore, this paper presents the integrated adaptor for multi-sensor networks. The proposed adaptor integrates heterogeneous data such as GPS, video, and sensor data. We develop the proposed adaptor which has functions of receiving GPS, video, and sensor data through a common interface, parsing and queuing them, and creating and transmitting a combined frame composed of GPS and sensor data.

Acknowledgments. This work was supported by the Industrial Strategic Technology Development Program funded by the Ministry of Knowledge Economy(MKE, Korea) [10033915, Adaptive fusion technology for large-scale sensor node based intelligent surveillance system]. "This work was supported by the National Research Foundation of Korea(NRF) grant funded by the Korea government(MEST) (No. 2011-0015009)."Corresponding author; DoHyeun Kim (e-mail: kimdh@jejunu.ac.kr).

References

1. Wang, S., Min, J., Yi, B.K.: Location Based Services for Mobiles: Technologies and Standards. In: IEEE International Conference on Communication (2008)
2. Küpper, A.: Location-Based Services: Fundamentals and Operation. Willey, West Sussex (2005)
3. Römer, K., Mattern, F.: The Design Space of Wireless Sensor Networks. IEEE Wireless Communications 11, 54–61 (2004)
4. Culler, D.: Overview of Sensor Network. IEEE Computer Society, Los Alamitos (2004)
5. Chu, X., Buyya, R.: Service Oriented Sensor Web. In: Mahalik, N.P. (ed.) Sensor Network and Configuration: Fundamentals, Standards, Platforms, and Applications. Springer, Germany (2007)
6. Bott, M.: OGC® Sensor Web Enablement: Overview and High Level Architecture. Open GIS Consortium (2006)
7. Open Geographic Information System, http://www.opengis.org/
8. Hull, B., Bychkovsky, V., Zhang, Y., Chen, K., Goraczko, M., Shih, E., Balakrishnan, H., Madden, S.: CarTel: A Distributed Mobile Sensor Computing System. In: Proceedings ACM SenSys (2006)
9. Eriksson, J., Balakrishnan, H., Madden, S.: Cabernet: Vehicular Content Delivery Using WiFi. In: Proceedings of the 14th ACM International Conference on Mobile Computing and Networking (2008)

High Speed and Low-Complexity Mode Decision for Advanced Video Coding

Byoungman An[1], Youngseop Kim[1], and Oh-Jin Kwon[2]

[1] Electronics & Electrical Engineering, Dankook University,
126 Jukjeon-dong, Suji-gu, Yongin-si, Gyeonggi-do, 448-701, Korea
{yesbman,wangcho}@dankook.ac.kr
[2] Electronics Engineering, Sejong University,
98 Kunja-Dong, Seoul 143-747, Korea
ojkwon@sejong.ac.kr

Abstract. This paper presents a low-complexity algorithm for an H.264/AVC encoder. The proposed motion estimation scheme determines the best coding mode for a given macroblock (MB) by finding motion-blurred MBs; identifying, before motion estimation, an early selection of MBs; and hence saving processing time for these MBs. It has been observed that human vision is more sensitive to the movement of well-structured objects than to the movement of randomly structured objects. This study analyzed permissible perceptual distortions and assigned a larger inter-mode value to the regions that are perceptually less sensitive to human vision. Simulation results illustrate that the algorithm can reduce the computational complexity of motion estimation by up to 47.16% while maintaining high compression efficiency.

Keywords: Advanced Video Coding (AVC), Motion Estimation, Video Coding, High-Efficiency Video Coding (HEVC).

1 Introduction

H.264/AVC is the newest international video coding standard [1]. It achieves higher compression efficiency than other standards [2] by using advanced coding techniques such as multiple-reference frame prediction and context-based adaptive binary arithmetic coding (CABAC) [3]. It enables the compression of video to 1.5–2 Mbps for standard-definition video and 6–8 Mbps for high-definition video by saving storage space, frequency spectrum, and channel bandwidth. Most of all, the variable block mode of H.264/AVC contributes to high compression efficiency; however, it also requires high computing power to determine the best compression mode. It is known that the motion-estimation process for determining the best mode occupies more than 60% of the computing time of the whole encoder [4]. Therefore, the development of fast and efficient motion estimation algorithms for H.264/AVC is a hot research topic [5–10].

Low-complexity motion-estimation algorithms for H.264/AVC were described in [5] and [6]. Fast inter-mode decision-making using the Lagrangian cost correlation proposed in [5] to determine the best coding mode for a given macroblock (MB) by

T.-h. Kim et al. (Eds.): ISA 2011, CCIS 200, pp. 339–348, 2011.

estimating the rate distortion (RD) cost from the neighboring MBs in the previous frame. In [6], an early prediction algorithm was used to reduce complexity by estimating the Lagrangian RD cost function using an adaptive model for the Lagrangian multiplier parameter based on local-sequence statistics. In [7], an RD performance-improved mode-decision method was proposed for H.264 intra-coding without changing the syntax and decoding process of H.264. This method uses inter-block mode-dependent decision criteria for the intra 4×4 mode of the original rate-distortion optimization (RDO) procedure. The authors of [8] proposed a system for managing the computational complexity of H.264/AVC video encoding in a real-time scenario. Their complexity management system controls the coding time of each frame of a video sequence with maintaining a high frame rate and avoiding significant frame quality loss.

On the other hand, taking human perception into consideration, the concept of perceptual image and video coding has been in existence for quite some time. The work reported in [9] used a rate control scheme at both the frame and MB levels. At the frame level, the algorithm estimated the target bits using a motion complexity measure which represented the amount of motion between two consecutive frames. In [10], a perceptual distortion masking measure was used for rate control, with the measure coupled into the RDO process. The success of this fast perceptual mode-decision algorithm depends heavily on accurate estimation of visual features, and therefore a more precise scheme needs to be developed. The contribution of this study is a method of managing complexity to reduce computational processing. The key concept of the proposed speed-dependent motion-estimation (SDME) algorithm is that, to save computation time, it assigns a larger intermode value to regions that are perceptually less sensitive to distortion than to more sensitive regions.

The remainder of this paper is organized as follows. Section 2 analyzes the problem of the H.264/AVC standard and describes the new low-complexity management approach in detail. Section 3 reports RD and execution-time results for the operation of the coding algorithm on both advanced video coding (AVC) test sequences and high-efficiency video coding (HEVC) test sequences [11]. The rate figures are calculated from actual compressed file sizes and on mean squared errors (MSE) or peak signal-to-noise ratios (PSNR) from the reconstructed videos as given by the algorithm. These results are put into perspective by comparison to JM 17.2, which is the original reference software version of MPEG and ITU-T. The conclusions of the paper are presented in Section 4.

2   Low-Complexity Motion Estimation

The proposed algorithm decreases computational processing by means of early identification of MBs. The proposed SDME model aims to reduce computation time by skipping certain MBs while maintaining RD performance. SDME is compared with a JM 17.2 encoder operating with the following parameters (hereafter called the "baseline encoder"):

1) baseline profile;
2) five reference frames, IPPP sequence type, CAVLC;

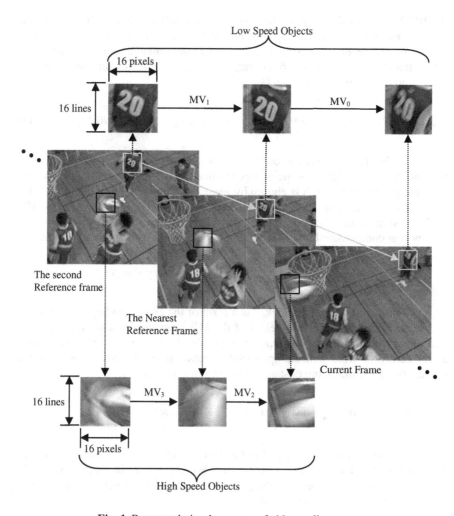

Fig. 1. Perceptual visual property of video coding sequences

3) asymmetrical multi-hexagon search (UMHexagonS);
4) RDO mode selection enabled.

First, the motion-estimation method used in the JM encoder will be presented, and then the low-complexity motion estimation model will be described.

2.1 Motion Estimation in the JM Encoder

In contrast to previous video coding standards, H.264/AVC considers the distortion and the occurrence rate for selecting the best mode within a number of possible modes. The RDO contributes to determining the motion vector and choosing the best mode. It consists of the Lagrangian coefficients with their weighted distortion values and occurrence rates.

The RDO method calculates the RD cost for each MB mode. For this reason, the motion-estimation process has high computational complexity. To determine the best motion-estimation mode, the inter-mode first has to determine a motion vector and a reference frame in terms of a current frame. The motion vector and the reference frame are determined using Equation (1):

$$J_{motion}(MV, REF \mid \lambda_{motion}) = SAD(s, r(MV, REF)) + \lambda_{motion} \cdot R(MV, REF). \tag{1}$$

where λ_{motion} is the Lagrangian coefficient which depends on the quantization coefficient, and $R(MV, REF)$ is the observed bitrate used to code the motion vector and the reference frame, which is chosen by means of a defined table. Equation (2) is used to calculate the sum of the absolute difference (SAD), where $SAD(s, r(MV, REF))$ is the sum of the absolute values of the differences between the original image and the motion-compensated image according to the motion-estimation algorithm:

$$SAD(s, r(MV, REF)) = \sum_{x \in H, y \in V}^{H,V} |s(x, y) - r(x - m_x, y - m_y)|. \tag{2}$$

where s is a pixel of an original block, r is a pixel of the corresponding reconstructed block, H and V are the width and height of the MB respectively, and (m_x, m_y) is the motion vector of the MB. In P8×8 mode, the encoder determines the optimized macro mode for each 8×8 block and the optimized direction in intra mode, along with the best mode, using the minimum cost as determined in Equation (3):

$$J_{mode}(s, r, M \mid \lambda_{mod\,e}) = SSD(s, r, M) + \lambda_{mode} \cdot R(s, r, M). \tag{3}$$

where λ_{mode} is the square of λ_{motion}. M is the MB mode; it is the predicted direction mode or sublevel of the MB. $R(s, r, M)$ is the observed bitrate in practice when the encoder codes the mode corresponding to M. Equation (4) describes the sum of squared differences (SSD), $SSD(s, r, M)$:

$$SSD(s, r, M) = \sum_{x \in H, y \in V}^{H,V} (s(x, y) - r(x - m_x, y - m_y))^2. \tag{4}$$

The H.264/AVC rate-distortion algorithm calculates and determines the best mode in such a way that it occupies more than 60% of the computation time for the whole encoder. Using Equation (3), the encoder decides on the best mode and computes the actual bitrate, which requires a DCT / Hadamard transform, quantization / dequantization, an inverse DCT / inverse Hadamard transform, and entropy coding. The entropy coding uses Exp-golomb code, context-adaptive variable-length coding (CAVLC), and the CABAC.

2.2 Human Visual System

The human visual system (HVS) plays a significant role in understanding perceptual video coding [12]. The eyes can track moving objects in a visual scene to keep the object of interest on the fovea and compensate for object motion to improve visual acuity, a phenomenon known as Smooth Pursuit Eye Movement (SPEM) [13]. Human beings cannot perceive fine-scale variations in visual signals because of the psychovisual properties of the HVS. Related psychophysical studies have demonstrated the level of contrast required to detect a flickering grating at different spatial and temporal frequencies [14]. The masking effect refers to the perceptibility of one signal in the presence of another signal in its spatial, temporal, or spectral vicinity [15]. Moreover, the sensitivity of the HVS relies on the background luminance and color of the stimuli. Visual sensitivity can be measured using a spatiotemporal contrast sensitivity function (CSF) [16].

2.3 ROI-Based Video Coding

Region of interest (ROI)-based perceptual video coding has been in existence for quite some time. Earlier ROI-based video coding methods included restrictions on how the ROI could be defined. The foreground/background video coding method uses this approach. Visual attention techniques have recently made it possible to identify multiple ROIs. Figure 1 shows the perceptual visual property of video coding sequences, in which the main observation to be made is that human vision is sensitive to movement of well-structured objects (MV_0 and MV_1) while tolerating large distortions in moving areas with random structures (MV_2 and MV_3). Note that the higher-speed objects have larger-magnitude motion vectors than the low-speed objects because the size of the motion vector is related to the distance between the current frame and the nearest reference frame.

The theoretical key to the SDME algorithm is that it considers the speed of an object between the current frame and reference frames and codes more distant MBs less accurately when an object moves fast. This coding makes an attempt to control block distortion so that the perceptual impression given by different blocks will be consistent, i.e., blocks which can tolerate higher distortion will be more coarsely coded. Nevertheless, perceptual redundancy cannot be completely determined without consideration of the foveal features of the HVS. In this way, both computational savings and low complexity of the H.264/AVC encoding can be achieved.

2.4 Speed-Dependent Motion Estimation

To reduce computation time, the capability of the HVS to detect distortions in video sequences must be taken into account. As described previously, the basic idea of the proposed low-complexity motion-estimation scheme is to allocate fewer bits to areas where coding distortions are less noticeable. The HVS is more sensitive to perceptual distortions of smoothly textured objects with regular motions that are recognizable by eye movements in the foreground. These objects are generally susceptible to encoding distortions because of the inefficiency of the block-based motion-prediction model.

The SDME was designed based on these properties. First, to determine whether an MB has large movements and causes motion blur, the movement of a motion vector can be estimated as:

$$\text{MVDistV} = | \overrightarrow{MV} | . \tag{5}$$

where MV is the motion vector used to code an MB between a current frame and a reference frame. It contains the direction of movement and the amount of motion. Next, let the distance value (DV) denote the maximum scale value as follows:

$$\text{DV} = \sqrt{(width)^2 + (height)^2} . \tag{6}$$

where width and height are the horizontal and vertical size of the input image respectively. To calculate MVDistV as a proportion of DV, these parameters are estimated using the offset value (OV), which can be obtained using Equation (7):

$$\text{OV} = \frac{MVDistV}{DV} = \begin{cases} 1, 0 \leq \text{OV} \leq 1 \\ 0, \text{otherwise} \end{cases} . \tag{7}$$

where OV is limited to the range $0 \leq \text{OV} \leq 1$.

Then, the lowest threshold (LT) and highest threshold (HT) were defined to judge whether or not the SDME is enabled. Equation (7) plays a significant role in implementing the SDME because the SDME algorithm is enabled only when OV is between LT and HT:

$$\text{Lowest Threshold (LT)} \leq \text{OV} \leq \text{Highest Threshold (HT)} . \tag{8}$$

To avoid reintroducing complexity into the coding process, the optimal choices for the LT and HT parameters are estimated before coding. To achieve computational savings, the LT and HT parameters are estimated using different LT and HT coefficients (Table 1). The appropriate values of LT and HT for the test sequence, BlowingBubble [QP (quantization parameter) = 28, frames = 30, search range = 64] were found to be LT ≈ 0.1 and HT ≈ 25. Through the experiments reported here, it was found that the threshold range between LT and HT is crucial because the SDME algorithm will not be beneficial and productive if the parameters are set too small or too large. In addition, fixed parameters LT = 1.5 and HT = 25 were found to provide an acceptable tradeoff between computational performance and rate distortion. Therefore, these fixed parameters were chosen to provide low complexity with minimal loss of rate-distortion performance (see Section 3).

Table 1. The Simulation results of proposed algorithm compared with that of reference software, QP=28

LT (%)	HT (%)	Original JM17.2				SDME				Original JM17.2 vs. SDME (%)			
		Total time (sec)	ME time (sec)	PSNR(dB)	Compression ratio (%)	Total time (sec)	ME time (sec)	PSNR (dB)	Compression ratio (%)	Total time	ME time	PSNR	Compression ratio
2	25	242.5	200.4	35.23	2.76	225.2	185.1	35.13	2.87	7.1	7.7	0.28	0.11
6	12	242.5	200.4	35.23	2.76	219.4	180.7	35.11	2.85	9.5	9.9	0.34	0.09
3	6	242.5	200.4	35.23	2.76	218.3	180	35.13	2.87	10	10.2	0.28	0.11
1.5	3	242.5	200.4	35.23	2.76	207.4	170.6	35.12	2.87	14.5	14.9	0.31	0.11
0.8	1.5	242.5	200.4	35.23	2.76	171.1	139.7	35.14	2.94	29.4	30.3	0.25	0.18
0.4	0.8	242.5	200.4	35.23	2.76	164	134	35.15	3.03	32.4	33.1	0.22	0.27
0.2	0.4	242.5	200.4	35.23	2.76	187.5	154	35.15	2.96	22.7	23.2	0.22	0.21
0.1	0.2	242.5	200.4	35.23	2.76	222	183.2	35.12	2.85	8.4	8.6	0.31	0.09
0.05	0.1	242.5	200.4	35.23	2.76	224	185	35.12	2.85	7.6	7.7	0.31	0.09
0.6	1.25	242.5	200.4	35.23	2.76	162.4	132.5	35.14	2.96	33	33.9	0.25	0.21
0.3	1.25	242.5	200.4	35.23	2.76	124.1	100.2	35.17	3.10	48.8	50	0.17	0.34
0.1	25	242.5	200.4	35.23	2.76	53.3	38.5	35.21	3.35	78	80.8	0.05	0.59

Table 2. Coding results for H.264/AVC sequences and high efficiency video coding (HEVC) sequences, QP=28

Input File		Search range	Frames	LT HT (%)(%)	Original JM17.2			SDME			Original JM17.2 vs. SDME (%)		
Resolution	Seq. Name				Total time (sec)	PSNR (dB)	Compression ratio (%)	Total time (sec)	PSNR (dB)	Compression ratio (%)	Total time	PSNR	Compression ratio
CIF (352*288)	Coastguard	64	30	1.5 25	3,393	35.43	3.40	1,792	35.22	3.62	47.16	0.59	0.22
	Foreman	64	30	1.5 25	2,507	36.83	1.35	1,356	36.72	1.64	45.91	0.29	0.29
	News	64	30	1.5 25	1,564	38.53	0.63	1,379	38.37	0.69	11.85	0.41	0.06
QCIF (176*144)	Coastguard	32	30	1.5 25	613	34.81	2.62	325	34.62	2.84	47.00	0.54	0.22
	Foreman	32	30	1.5 25	547	36.57	1.57	285	36.43	1.87	47.85	0.38	0.30
	News	32	30	1.5 25	371	37.12	0.89	327	37.01	0.93	11.64	0.29	0.04
	Partyscene	64	50	0.1 25	5,265	34.80	4.06	1,903	34.65	4.65	63.86	0.43	0.59
WVGA (832*480)	Partyscene	64	50	1.5 25	5,265	34.80	4.06	4,409	34.70	4.30	16.26	0.28	0.24
	Bqmall	64	60	1.5 25	4,334	36.70	1.81	2,531	36.63	2.16	41.58	0.19	0.35
	BasketballDrill	64	50	1.5 25	4,426	36.84	1.52	2,742	36.67	1.76	38.03	0.46	0.23
WQVGA (416*240)	BlowingBubble	64	50	1.5 25	1,212	34.97	2.31	1,072	34.87	2.46	11.52	0.28	0.15
	BQSquare	64	60	1.5 25	1,071	35.25	3.49	1,043	35.16	3.52	2.61	0.25	0.04

2.5   New Fast SDME Algorithm

One potential problem in performing mode prediction is error propagation due to a wrong prediction of the best mode and further prediction based on this nonoptimal mode. To avoid propagation of mode-prediction errors, a thorough mode-decision evaluation was carried out. In the proposed SDME algorithm, the motion vector and the reference frame are computed using Equations (1) and (2). MVDistV, DV, and OV are obtained when the proposed SDME algorithm is enabled, and then OV is compared with LT and HT. If OV is between LT and HT, the 16×16 mode is chosen as the best mode for calculating the MB without unnecessary computational processing, using Equations (3) and (4).

3   Experimental Results

All experiments were performed by encoding and reconstructing an actual bitstream to verify the correctness of the proposed algorithm. It is important to observe that the

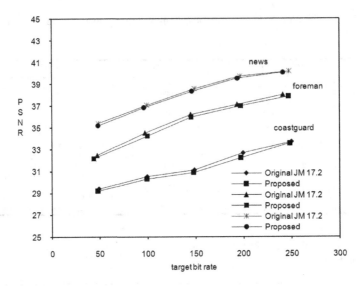

Fig. 2. Rate-distortion performance of QCIF sequences

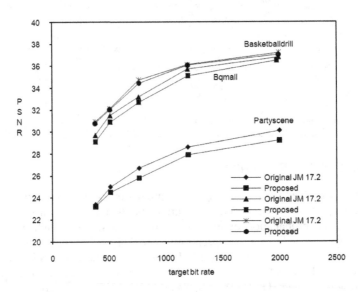

Fig. 3. Rate-distortion performance of WVGA sequences

bitrates are not entropy estimates; they were calculated from the actual size of the compressed files, and then the recovered image was compared with the original sequence. The distortion was measured using the PSNR.

Table 2 records the experimental results measured when the SDME algorithm is enabled, as well as the unmodified baseline profile encoder with respect to the total time, the Y-PSNR, and the compression ratio. The results shown in Table 2 indicate that the coding time has been reduced by 11.52% to 47.85% compared with the baseline encoder due to the algorithm's early selection of the best mode. The computational savings are greater for larger-movement sequences such as Coastguard, Foreman, and Bqmall and lower for smaller-movement sequences such as News, BlowingBubble, and Paryscene.

For the CIF and QCIF formats, Coastguard and Foreman show a time saving of approximately 45% with 0.4 dB PSNR degradation and 0.25% extra bits for Foreman, while News had the best RD efficiency and the worst time saving with 0.35 dB PNSR degradation, 0.04% additional bits, and a time saving of approximately 13%. For the HEVC test sequences such as WVGA and WQVGA format, Bqmall and BasketballDrill exhibited twice as much time saving as Partyscene and BlowingBubble, with percentage reductions of 41.58% and 38.03% respectively.

However, BQSquare, which was the smallest-movement sequence among the eight sample sequences, had the lowest time reduction, with 0.25 dB degradation, 0.04% extra bits, and a 2.61% time saving. Although the parameters for lower-speed sequences were set to provide an increased performance range (e.g., Partyscene with threshold values of LT = 0.1 and HT = 25), the computational time indeed decreased notably to half of its previous value, but the PSNR degradation and the number of additional bits dramatically increased to twice their previous values, with rates of 0.43 dB and 0.59% respectively. This is not desirable in applications with a constant-bitrate channel where perceptual quality should be maximized when processing power becomes limited as long as the bitrate limit is not exceeded.

However, it is worthwhile to evaluate the performance of the proposed SDME algorithm compared with that of the JM software with both bitrates and complexity set at comparable levels. This makes it possible to compare directly the original motion estimates and those from SDME for the perceptual qualities. The results for the Coastguard, Foreman, News, Partyscene, Bqmall, BasketballDrill, BlowingBubble, and BQSquare sequences with QP $\in$ {25•••33} are presented in Figures 2 and 3. In each case, the rate-distortion performance of the baseline profile and the low-complexity encoders is nearly identical across a range of test sequences and bitrates. Coding complexity and time are substantially reduced because RDO is selectively performed using the proposed algorithm. This reduction is particularly marked for high-activity sequences.

4   Conclusions

This paper has analyzed existing motion-estimation algorithms, as well as the HVS for perceptual video coding, and has presented the computation and performance tradeoffs involved in choosing appropriate values of LT and HT. This analysis directs the video coder to assign fewer bits to regions that can tolerate larger distortions, and accordingly computational savings are achieved. The proposed SDME algorithm is shown to be more effective than previous implementations of the JM17.2 reference software. The algorithm can reduce computational complexity by up to 47.16% with only about 0.25% extra bits and approximately 0.35 dB PSNR degradation. The authors believe that the results of this coding algorithm with HVS, along with its fast execution, are impressive.

References

1. Draft ITU-T recommendation and final draft international standard of joint video specification (ITU-T Rec. H.264/ISO/IEC 14496-10 AVC. In: Joint Video Team (JVT) of ISO/IEC MPEG and ITU-T VCEG, JVT-G050 (2003)
2. Chen, Z., Zhang, D., Ngan, K.N.: An efficient algorithm for H.264/AVC high definition video coding. IEEE Trans. Consumer Electronics 54(4), 1852–1857 (2008)
3. Wiegand, T., Sullivan, G.J., Bjontegaard, G., Luthra, A.: Overview of the H.264/AVC video coding standard. IEEE Trans. Circuits Syst. Video Technol. 13(7), 560–576 (2003)
4. Wang, Y.J., Cheng, C.C., Chang, T.S.: A fast fractional pel motion estimation algorithm for H.264/MPEG-4 AVC. In: Proc. ISCAS, pp. 3974–3977 (May 2006)
5. Ri, S.H., Vatis, Y., Ostermann, J.: Fast inter-mode decision in an H.264/AVC encoder using mode and Lagrangian cost correlation. IEEE Trans. Circuits Syst. Video Technol. 19(2), 302–306 (2009)
6. Kannangara, C.S., Richardson, I.E.G., Bystrom, M., Solera, J.R., Zhao, Y., Maclennan, A., Cooney, R.: Low-complexity skip prediction for H.264 through lagrangian cost estimation. IEEE Trans. Circuits Syst. Video Technol. 16(2), 202–208 (2006)
7. You, J., Choi, C., Jeong, J.: Modified rate distortion optimization using inter-block dependence for H.264/AVC intra coding. IEEE Trans. Consumer Electronics 54(3), 1383–1388 (2008)
8. Kannangara, C.S., Richardson, I.E., Miller, A.J.: Computational complexity management of a real-time H.264/AVC Encoder. IEEE Trans. Circuits Syst. Video Technol. 18(9), 1191–1200 (2008)
9. Yu, H., Pan, F., Lin, Z., Sun, Y.: A perceptual bit allocation scheme for H.264. In: 2005 IEEE International Conference on Multimedia and Expo (ICME), p. 4 (July 2005)
10. Tsai, C.J., Tang, C.W., Chen, C.H., Yu, Y.H.: Adaptive rate-distortion optimization using perceptual hints. In: IEEE International Conference on Multimedia and Expo, vol. 1, pp. 667–670 (2004)
11. Joint call for proposals on video compression technology. In: The Joint Collaborative Team on Video Coding (JCT-VC) of ISO/IEC MPEG and ITU-T VCEG, MPEG 91st Meeting, N11113, Kyoto, Japan (April 2010)
12. Wandell, B.: Foundations of Vision. Sinauer Associates, Inc., Sunderland (1995)
13. Girod, B.: Eye movements and coding of video sequences. In: SPIE Visual Communications and Image Processing (1988)
14. Robinson, D.A.: The mechanics of human smooth pursuit eye movement. J. Physiol. 180, 569–591 (1965)
15. Jayant, N., Johnston, J., Safranek, R.: Signal compression based on models of human perception. Proc. IEEE, 1385–1422 (October 1993)
16. Kelly, D.H.: Motion and vision II stabilized spatio-temporal surface. J. Opt. Soc. Amer., 1340–1349 (October 1979)

Robust Congestion Control Design for Input Time Delayed AQM System

Ji Hoon Yang[1], Seung Jung Shin[2,*], Dong Kyun Lim[3], and Jeong Jin Kang[4]

[1] Department of Electrical Engineering,
Hanyang University, Seoul, 133-791, Korea
[2] Department of Information & Technology,
Hansei University, Gunpo-City, 435-742, Korea
[3] Department of Computer Science,
Hanyang Cyber University, Seoul, 133-791, Korea
[4] Department of Information & Communication,
Dong Seoul University, Seongnam-City, 461-714, Korea
openyj@hanyang.ac.kr, expersin@hansei.ac.kr,
eiger07@hycu.ac.kr, iwit2000@gmail.com

Abstract. This paper proposes the LQ-Servo control for input-time-delayed AQM(Active Queue Management) using Loop-shaping method. The proposed controller structure is made by both taking a traditional servo mechanism based on Linear Quadratic approach and augmenting a new state variable. And, the new loop shaping method is developed by shifting all zeros to a larger pole of AQM model to determine the design parameters. And also, the proposed LQ-Servo controller is extended the control input with time-delay using Smith's principle.

Keywords: Congestion control, Flow-based traffic management, Loop-Shaping, LQ-Servo, Time-delay.

1 Introduction

During the past few years, computer networks have been explosively increased by their users, and have confronted severe congestion collapse problems according to growth of computer networks. In the last 80's, Jacobson and Karels[1] proposed the end-to-end congestion control algorithms which forms the basic for the TCP(Transmission Control Protocol) congestion control. It is content that a TCP sender keeps a sending window (packets) rate according to the rate of dropped packets when a buffer becomes full in the router queue. Floyd and Jacobson [2] presented the RED (Random Early Detection) In the last 90's. Its mechanism is that packets are randomly dropped before the buffer of queue overflows. And, Braden et al. [3] proposed the enhanced end-to-end congestion control for Active Queue Management.

In recent years, the more needs for the congestion controllers having enough ability which is more logically predictable and reliable are occurred. For this reason, the

---

* Corresponding author.

T.-h. Kim et al. (Eds.): ISA 2011, CCIS 200, pp. 349–358, 2011.
© Springer-Verlag Berlin Heidelberg 2011

traditional control algorithms which have been used only for mechanical or electrical systems are adopted to the area of congested network and their performances which are known as relatively good. Consequently, the more controllers which have various featured types have been adopted to the network congestion control area using control theories.

On the issue of applying control theories to the network, especially AQM Router, Misra *et al.*[4] developed a methodology to model and obtain expected transient behavior of networks with Active Queue Management Routers supporting TCP flows. And Hollot *et al.* approximated its linearized model[5] using small-signal linearization about an operating point to gain insight for the purpose of feedback control, and designed the PI controller[6] based on the linear control theory. Its main contribution is to convert the congestion control algorithm into the controller design problem within the framework of control theory in AQM system. And also, Aweya *et al.* [7] and Ren *et al.* [8] have used fundamental control theories to analyze and develop for AQM. More recently, Yang and Suh[9] have proposed the robust PID controller using LQ approach, and the robust AQM controllers have developed by the optimal control theory based on the Linear Matrix Inequalities (LMI) [10] and the robust μ-analysis technique [11] for the stability and performance issues in AQM. These controllers maintain the queue size which is given at the starting moment of the system without any fluctuation. In these types of system operation case, it is impossible to use all resources (memories) being occupied by another software application because all those resources were privately dominated by previous one. In order to deal with various unpredictable critical problems and share the memory resource peacefully, the LQ-Servo controller [12] for TCP/AQM system has proposed, and also the tuning method [13] of LQ-Servo has presented based on Loop-Shaping method [14] [15] in order to determine the weight factor of cost function of LQR. But, there have a problem that the time-delay of control input does not considered.

This paper proposed an improved version of previous work [12] and [13] in order to deal with time-delay of control input of TCP/AQM system. The proposed LQ-Servo controller is extended the control input with time-delay using Smith's principle [16], and also is formed by combining two features of LQ optimization and servo structure is proposed to select the suitable weighting factors Q using the loop shaping technique [15] by shifting all zeros closely to a larger pole of TCP/AQM model in order to meet the frequency domain specification as good disturbance rejection, command following and noise attenuation.

2   AQM System

This section describes a mathematical model of AQM based on a control theoretical approach.

2.1   Linear Model of AQM

A non-linear dynamic model for TCP flow control is developed using fluid-flow and stochastic differential equation in [4], which is as following:

$$\dot{W}(t) = \frac{1}{R(t)} - \frac{W(t)W(t-R(t))}{2R(t-R(t))}p(t-R(t)), \quad \dot{q}(t) = \frac{W(t)}{R(t)}N(t) - C \tag{1}$$

where $\dot{W}(t)$ denotes the time-derivative of $W(t)$, $\dot{q}(t)$ denotes the time-derivative of $q(t)$, $W \doteq$ Expected TCP window size (packets), $q \doteq$ Expected queue length (packets, $R_0 \doteq$ Round-trip time (seconds), $C \doteq$ Link capacity (packets/second), $N \doteq$ Load factor (number of TCP sessions), $p \doteq$ Probability of packet mark/drop, and $t =$ Time

For the control theoretical analysis, it was approximated as a linearized constant model by small-signal linearization about an operating point (W_0, q_0, p_0), see [5] for linearization details, which leads to the following (2):

$$\delta\dot{W}(t) = -\frac{2N}{R_0^2 C}\delta W(t) - \frac{R_0 C^2}{2N^2}\delta p(t-R_0), \quad \delta\dot{q}(t) = \frac{N}{R_0}\delta W(t) - \frac{1}{R_0}\delta q(t) \tag{2}$$

where $\delta W(t) \doteq W - W_0$, $\delta q(t) \doteq q - q_0$, $\delta p(t) \doteq p - p_0$.

The expected queue length q and the expected TCP window size W are positive value and bounded quantities. And also, the probability of packet mark (drop) p takes value only in $0 \le p \le 1$.

So, the plant transfer function which is denoted as $P(s) = P_{tcp}(s)P_{queue}(s)e^{-sR_0}$ can be expressed

$$P(s) = \frac{\dfrac{C^2}{2N}}{(s + \dfrac{2N}{R_0^2 C})(s + \dfrac{1}{R_0})}e^{-sR_0} \tag{3}$$

where $P_{tcp}(s)$ denotes the transfer function from loss probability $\delta p(t)$ to window size $\delta W(t)$, $P_{queue}(s)$ denotes the transfer function from $\delta W(t)$ to queue length $\delta q(t)$, and $C(s)$ denotes the transfer function of controller.

2.2 State-Space Model of AQM

Let the state variable $x(t)$ of (2) be defined as:

$$x(t) = [x_r(t) \quad y_p(t)]^T = [\delta W(t) \quad \delta q(t)]^T \tag{4}$$

and (2) can be represented with state-space model:

$$\dot{x}(t) = A_p x(t) + B_p u(t-R_0), \quad y(t) = C_p x(t) \tag{5}$$

where $y(t) = \delta q(t)$ is an output variable, $u(t-R_0) = \delta p(t-R_0)$ is a input-time-delayed control variable. And the system matrix, input matrix and output matrix of (5) can be expressed as following:

$$A_p = \begin{bmatrix} -\dfrac{2N}{R_0^2 C} & 0 \\ \dfrac{N}{R_0} & -\dfrac{1}{R_0} \end{bmatrix}, B_p = \begin{bmatrix} -\dfrac{R_0 C^2}{2N^2} \\ 0 \end{bmatrix}, C_p = [0 \quad 1] \tag{6}$$

3   Robust Control of AQM

This section presents the LQ-Servo control for AQM based on Linear Quadratic approach and augmenting a new state variable.

3.1   Augemented State-Space Model

In order to follow a reference input command trajectory which is continuously varying, our controller must have at least one integrator which is associated with proper state variables. For the AQM system model, the reference queue size is the reasonable state variable. In this paper, rectangular reference input commands are used for the test of continuous varying command. Thus just one integrator is adapted to AQM system.

Integrator adoption process which is finished to augmented system matrix A_p is formed via hiring new state variable $z_p(t)$. So, the augmented state-variable descriptions become

$$x(t) = \begin{bmatrix} x_r(t) & y_p(t) & z_p(t) \end{bmatrix}^T = \begin{bmatrix} \delta W(t) & \delta q(t) & \int_0^t q(\tau)\,d\tau \end{bmatrix}^T \tag{7}$$

Then, the state-space model of (5) becomes as following (8)

$$\dot{x}(t) = Ax(t) + Bu(t - R_0), \quad y(t) = Cx(t) \tag{8}$$

And also, the system matrix, input matrix and output matrix can be presented, respectively,

$$A = \begin{bmatrix} A_p & 0 \\ C_p & 0 \end{bmatrix}, \quad B = \begin{bmatrix} B_p \\ 0 \end{bmatrix}, C = \begin{bmatrix} C_p & 0 \end{bmatrix} \tag{9}$$

3.2   LQ-Servo Control

Without loss of generality, the optimal servo problem based on Linear Quadratic approach, that is called LQ-Servo, is to find the optimal control law $u(t)$ by minimizing the cost functions

$$J = \int_0^\infty \{x^T(t)\cdot Q\cdot x(t) + u(t)\cdot \rho\cdot u(t)\}dt \tag{10}$$

where a weighting matrix Q is symmetric and positive semi-definite, and a weighting factor ρ is positive value.

Then, we use the general control law for regulating

$$u(t) = -G\,x(t) \tag{11}$$

where $G = -\rho^{-1}B^T K$ and $K = K^T$ is a solution matrix of the algebraic Riccatti's equation:

$$KA + A^T K + Q - \frac{1}{\rho}KB\ B^T K = 0 \tag{12}$$

Suppose the gain matrix G is decomposed into $G = \lfloor g_r \quad g_y \quad g_z \rfloor$, the optimal control input of (11) can be expressed by the augmented state-variable $x(t)$ of 7) as following:

$$u(t) = -g_r x_r(t) - g_y y_p(t) - g_z z_p(t) \tag{13}$$

Therefore, the LQ-Servo structure of AQM is shown in Figure 1 to ensure that zero steady state error is robustly achieved in response to a constant reference commands

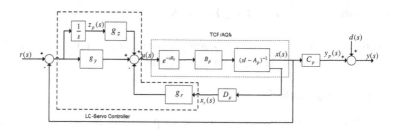

Fig. 1. LQ-Servo Control Structure for AQM

3.3 LQ-Servo Control with Input Time Delay

We extend the preceding design method to the time-delay system by Smith's principle [16]. It can decompose the state equation (8) into two stages:

(i)   when $0 \le t < R_0$, since there is no input signal to (8), that is $u(t - R_0) = 0$

$$\dot{x}(t) = A\,x(t), \qquad 0 \le t < R_0 \tag{14}$$

(ii)   when $t \ge R_0$, since the system has non-zero input signal,

$$\dot{x}(t) = Ax(t) + B\hat{u}(t), \qquad t \ge R_0, \tag{15}$$

where $\hat{u}(t) = u(t - R_0)$.

Through this decomposition, (14) and (15) are both delay free. So, the standard LQR results can be applied in the delay-free model. The LQR solution of Riccatti's equation (142) is

$$\hat{u}(t) = -G\,x(t), \qquad t \ge R_0 \tag{16}$$

where G is the control gain matrix, and K is determined by the (12). By converting $\hat{u}(t)$ into $u(t)$, the control input $u(t)$ is obtained as

$$u(t) = \hat{u}(t + R_0) = -Gx(t + R_0), \quad t \ge 0. \tag{17}$$

The control input $u(t)$ becomes a feedback of the future state at the time $(t + R_0)$. By combining (14) ~ (16), the following relationships can be obtained with $A_c = A - \rho^{-1} B B^T K$.

$$x(t + R_0) = e^{A_c t} x(R_0) = e^{A_c t} e^{A(R_0 - t)} x(t), \quad 0 \le t < R_0 \tag{18}$$

$$x(t + R_0) = e^{A_c t} x(R_0) = e^{A_c R_0} x(t) , \quad t > R_0 \tag{19}$$

Therefore, substituting (18) and (19) into (17), we have the control input as flowing:

$$u(t) = -G e^{A_c t} e^{A(R_0 - t)} x(t), \quad 0 \le t < R_0 \tag{20}$$

$$u(t) = -G e^{A_c R_0} x(t), \quad t \ge R_0 \tag{21}$$

4   Selection of the Weighting Factors

In this section, an optimal selection procedure of weighting factors Q and ρ by the limiting loop-shaping method based on Yang and Suh [15].

4.1   Loop-Shaping Method

To deal with the performance issues by the loop shaping method, a loop transfer function $h(s)$ obtained by braking at the AQM output point in Figure 1 must be considered as following:

$$h(s) = C_p (sI - A_p)^{-1} B_p \begin{bmatrix} s g_r & g_y & \dfrac{g_z}{s} \end{bmatrix} = \dfrac{-\dfrac{g_r R_0 C^2}{2N^2} s^2 - \left(\dfrac{g_r C^2}{R_0 N^2} + \dfrac{g_y C^2}{2N} \right) s - \dfrac{g_z C^2}{2N}}{s(s + \dfrac{2N}{R_0^2 C})(s + \dfrac{1}{R_0})} \tag{22}$$

And the loop transfer function $g_{LQ}(s)$ of LQR, is obtained as

$$g_{LQ}(s) = G(sI - A_{aug})^{-1} B_{aug} = \dfrac{-\dfrac{g_r R_0 C^2}{2N^2} s^2 - \left(\dfrac{g_r C^2}{R_0 N^2} + \dfrac{g_y C^2}{2N} \right) s - \dfrac{g_z C^2}{2N}}{s(s + \dfrac{2N}{R_0^2 C})(s + \dfrac{1}{R_0})} \tag{23}$$

Since (22) = (23), it can be obtained the equality as $h(s) = g_{LQ}(s)$.

Next, in order to associate the frequency loop shaping procedure with the weighting factors Q and ρ, we can use the frequency domain equality:

$$\rho \left(1 + g_{LQ}(-j\omega) \right) \left(1 + g_{LQ}(j\omega) \right) = \rho + g_{OL}(-j\omega) g_{OL}(j\omega) \tag{24}$$

where $g_{OL}(j\omega)$ is an open loop transfer function of LQR.

Since $g_{LQ}(j\omega) = h(j\omega)$ and $g_{OL}(j\omega) = N(j\omega I - A)^{-1} B$ where N_q is a partitioned matrix of the weighting matrix as $Q = N_q^T N_q$, (24) can be expressed as

$$\rho \left(1 + h(-j\omega) \right) \left(1 + h(j\omega) \right) = \rho + (N_q(-j\omega I - A)^{-1} B)(N_q(j\omega I - A)^{-1} B) \tag{25}$$

And, it can be described as

$$\left| I + h(j\omega) \right| = \sqrt{1 + \dfrac{1}{\rho} \left| N_q (j\omega I - A)^{-1} B \right|^2} \tag{26}$$

Also, (26) can be approximated as (27) since $|h(j\omega)| \gg 1$ in low frequencies and $|h(j\omega)| \ll 1$ in high frequencies. It is provided in [15] to be

$$|h(j\omega)| \approx \frac{1}{\sqrt{\rho}} \left| N_q (j\omega I - A)^{-1} B \right| \qquad (27)$$

To decompose $|h(j\omega)|$ into the low frequencies and high frequencies according to the matrix N_q, it can be partitioned as $N_q = \begin{bmatrix} n_0 & n_1 & n_2 \end{bmatrix}$, and then the loop transfer function can be developed into

$$|h(j\omega)| = \frac{1}{\sqrt{\rho}} \left| \frac{-\dfrac{n_0 R_0 C^2}{2N^2}(j\omega)^2 - \left(\dfrac{n_0 C^2}{R_0 N^2} + \dfrac{n_1 C^2}{2N}\right)(j\omega) - \dfrac{n_2 C^2}{2N}}{(j\omega)(j\omega + \dfrac{2N}{R_0^2 C})(j\omega + \dfrac{1}{R_0})} \right| \qquad (28)$$

4.2 Design Specifications

It is well known that the shape of $|h(j\omega)|$ should not be invade both the command following barrier or disturbance rejection barrier "$\alpha(\omega)$" with a boundary frequency Ω_r and the sensor noise barrier "$\beta(\omega)$" with a boundary frequency Ω_n in Figure 2. The LQ-Servo controller design taken satisfaction of the frequency domain design specifications is equivalent that the loop shaping of $|h(j\omega)|$ not be attacked by $\alpha(\omega)$ and $\beta(\omega)$. In other words, the shape of $|h(j\omega)|$ at the low frequencies should be located in the upper than the barrier $\alpha(\omega)$ and should be existed on the lower the barrier $\beta(\omega)$ at the high frequencies. So, there are establishing the design specifications in frequency domain.

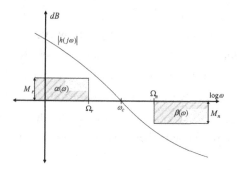

Fig. 2. Design specifications of a low frequency and a high frequency

Let M_r and M_n be a height of $\alpha(\omega)$ and $\beta(\omega)$, respectively. The barrier $\alpha(\omega)$ and $\beta(\omega)$ become:

$$\alpha(\omega) = \begin{cases} M_r &, \omega \le \Omega_r \\ 0 &, \omega > \Omega_r \end{cases} , \quad \beta(\omega) = \begin{cases} 0 &, \omega < \Omega_n \\ M_n &, \omega \ge \Omega_n . \end{cases} \qquad (29)$$

It is noted that the $\alpha(\omega)$ and $\beta(\omega)$ become the design specifications, and then the values of M_r, M_n, Ω_r, Ω_n are given by the design specifications. Therefore, we should consider that the values of n_0, n_1 and n_2 in (28) can be determined by satisfying (29).

4.3 Selection of Weighting Factor

The limiting behaviours of $h(j\omega)$ at low frequency and high frequency are approximated as

$$\lim_{\omega\to 0}|h(j\omega)| = -\frac{|n_2|}{\omega\sqrt{\rho}}\frac{C^2}{2N}, \quad \lim_{\omega\to\infty}|h(j\omega)| = -\frac{|n_0|}{\omega\sqrt{\rho}}\frac{R_0C^2}{2N^2} \tag{30}$$

In order to satisfy the frequency domain specifications, the ranges of the design parameters n_0 and n_2 are obtained from (30) as following:

$$|n_2| < -M_r\Omega_r\sqrt{\rho}\,\frac{2N}{C^2}, \quad |n_0| > -M_n\Omega_n\sqrt{\rho}\,\frac{2N^2}{R_0C^2} \tag{31}$$

However, these rages are too broad to choose the values of n_0 and n_2, and also the design parameter n_1 cannot obtained.

To solve these problems, a limiting loop shaping technique which made by shifting all two zeros formed by the LQ-Servo controller closely to a large pole of the AQM model is proposed. Denote poles and zeros of $|h(j\omega)|$ by p_1, p_2, z_1 and z_2. Let p_2 be larger than p_1. Then (28) can be expressed as

$$|h(j\omega)| = \frac{1}{\sqrt{\rho}}\left|\frac{-\dfrac{n_0R_0C^2}{2N^2}(j\omega+z_1)(j\omega+z_2)}{(j\omega)(j\omega+p_1)(j\omega+p_2)}\right| \tag{32}$$

Since poles of $|h(j\omega)|$, p_1 and p_2 are given by AQM model, the positions of poles on the Bode plot are fixed for a given AQM model. But two zeros of $|h(j\omega)|$ could be placed (or moved) to any position by selecting the design parameters n_0, n_1 and n_2. Also the suitable shape of $|h(j\omega)|$ could be obtained by controlling the two zeros of $|h(j\omega)|$. Suppose that z_1 and z_2 are moved closely to the larger pole p_2, the loop-shaping curve would be farther separated from the barrier $\beta(\omega)$.

5   Simulations

We can verify the tracking performance of some network congestion controller by simulation using the ns-2 simulator [17]. The parameters of AQM model are given as $R_0 = 0.246$ (second), $C = $ 15Mbps (3750 packets/sec) and $N = $ 60. Figure 3 shows the PI controller [6] performance for the continuous varying reference command. In this paper, the design specifications of frequencies domain are given as:

$$\alpha(\omega) = \begin{cases} 30 \ dB & ,\omega \le 10^1 \\ 0 & ,\omega > 10^1 \end{cases} \quad \text{and} \quad \beta(\omega) = \begin{cases} 0 & ,\omega < 10^5 \\ -40 \ dB & ,\omega \ge 10^5 \end{cases}.$$

The design parameters are computed to be $N_q = \begin{bmatrix} -0.6402 & 0.0654 & -0.0434 \end{bmatrix}$ by the proposed loop shaping method. So, the weighting factor matrix Q is obtained by $N_q^T N_q$. Finally, we can get the control gain as $G = \begin{bmatrix} -0.2595 & -0.0153 & -0.0155 \end{bmatrix}$.

The loop shaping of loop transfer function and tracking performance of LQ-Servo control for AQM is shown in Figure 4.

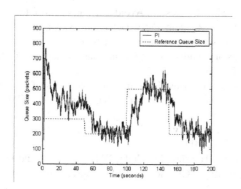

Fig. 3. Tracking performance of the PI controller

Figure 3 and Figure 4 indicate the simulation results of both the PI controller and the proposed LQ-Servo controller with respect to changed reference queue size. These results show that the proposed controller has the better performance in a trajectory tracking problem in AQM.

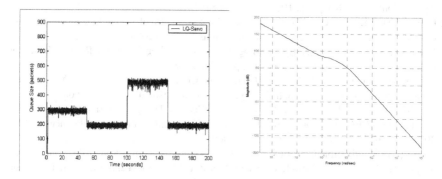

Fig. 4. Tracking performance and Loop-shaping of LQ-Servo controller

6   Conclusion

This paper proposed the LQ-Servo controller dealing with a control input with time-delay. This controller structure is made by taking a traditional servo mechanism based on Linear Quadratic approach and by augmenting a new state variable to the feed forward loop of LQ-Servo structure. In order to determine the frequency domain specifications, this paper proposes the limiting loop shaping method based on pushing all zeros closely to a larger pole of AQM model. The simulation results show that the proposed controller is more effective in getting the good tracking responses than PI controller for the varying reference queue size in AQM.

References

1. Jacobson, V., Karels, M.J.: Congestion Avoidance and Control. In: SIGCOMM'ss (1988)
2. Floyd, S., Jacobson, V.: Random Early Detection gateways for Congestion Avoidance. IEEE/ACM Transactions on Networking 1(4) (1997)
3. Braden, B., et al.: Recommendations on Queue Management and Congestion Avoidnace in the Internet, RFC2309 (1998)
4. Misra, V., Gong, W.-B., Towsley, D.: Fluid-based analysis of a nerwork of AQM routers supporting TCP flows with an application to RED. In: Proc. ACM SIGCOMM, pp. 151–160 (2000)
5. Hollot, C.V., Misra, V., Towsley, D., Gong, W.B.: A control theoritic analysis of RED. In: Proc. IEEE INFOCOM (2001)
6. Hollot, C.V., Misra, V., Towsley, D., Gong, W.B.: Analysis and Design of Controller for AQM Routers Supporting TCP Flows. IEEE Transcations on Automatic Control 47(6), 945–959 (2002)
7. Aweya, J., Ouellette, M., Monyuno, D.Y.: A control theoretic approach to active queue management. Computer Networks 36, 203–235 (2001)
8. Ren, F., Lin, C., Ying, X., Shan, X., Wang, F.: A robust active queue management algorithm based on sliding mode variable structure control. In: Proc. IEEE/INFOCOM (2002)
9. Yang, J.H., Suh, B.S.: Robust PID Controller for AQM based on Linear Quadratic Approach. In: IAENG International Conference on Communication Systems and Applications, Hong Kong, pp. 1083–1087 (2008)
10. Lima, M.M.A.E., Fonseca, N.L.S., Geromel, J.C.: An Optimal Active Queue Managemnet Controller, pp. 2261–2266. IEEE Communications Society (2005)
11. Chen, Q., Yang, O.W.W.: On Designing Traffic Controller for AQM Routers Based on Robust u-Analysis. In: IEEE Globecom, pp. 857–861 (2005)
12. Lee, K.M., Yang, J.H., Suh, B.S.: Congestion Control of Active Queue Management Routers Based on LQ-Servo Control. Engineering Letters 16(3), 332–338 (2008)
13. Lee, K.M., Yang, J.H., Suh, B.S.: LQ-Servo Control Design Based on Loop-Shaping Method for TCP/AQM Router. In: The 28th IASTED International Conference on MIC 2009, Innsbruck, Austria, February 16-18 (2009)
14. Athans, M.: Multivarible Control System. Athan's Control Lecture Note. MIT, Cambridge
15. Yang, J.H., Suh, B.S.: A New Loop-Shaping Procedure for the Tuning LQ-PID Regulator. Journal of Chemical Engineering of Japan 40(7), 575–589 (2007)
16. Marshall, J.E.: Control of Time-Delay Systems. Peter Peregrinus Ltd., Stevenage (1979)
17. NS-2 Network Simulator, Obtain from http://www.isi.edu/nsnam/ns

An Intelligent Clustering Method for Highly Similar Digital Photos Using Pyramid Matching with Human Perceptual 25 Color Histogram

Dong-Sung Ryu, Kwanghwi Kim, and Hwan-Gue Cho

Dept. of Computer Science,
Pusan National University, Busan, Korea
{dsryu99,kwanghwi,hgcho}@pusan.ac.kr

Abstract. Recently, as the number of photos to be managed grows, photo classification becomes one of the most burdensome tasks. Besides, these technical advances encourage people to take duplicate photos for the more clear and the more user-wanted photos. This paper presents an automated clustering method to classify hundreds of photos considering the people's recent photographing behavior. First, we partition the input photo sets into trivial event groups. Then, we employ an interval graph considering their color similarity from temporally consecutive photos to construct each similar photo group. For this clustering, we used 25 color block histogram based on pyramid matching. The user experiment shows that our algorithm is enough correct to classify hundreds of photos.

Keywords: photo clustering, pyramid matching, maximal clique finding.

1 Introduction

Widespread distribution of digital cameras and the low price of memory are acclimating people to taking many more photos than before. As the number of taken photos to be managed grows, the photo management tasks generally get more time-consuming and burdensome. Especially, photo grouping according to events is one of the most burdensome photo management tasks, since this task is usually performed manually by user. Therefore, it is a crucial work to group or cluster hundreds of photos [1]

Recently, photographers are interested in taking good quality photos, they do not take care of the number of taken photos. Therefore, it is not unusual to take more than 1,000 photos at once. They are also likely to take photos to memorize important and impressed scene comparing with film camera days. These practices make people to take many similar photos.

In this paper, we concerned on how to classify hundreds of photos automatically considering people's duplicate photographing behavior. Our approach consists of two: 1) In order to construct trivial temporal event photo groups, we employ a priority queue-based hierarchical photo clustering method. 2) For nearly similar photos group each other, we employ the interval graph method to construct similar photo

T.-h. Kim et al. (Eds.): ISA 2011, CCIS 200, pp. 359–366, 2011.

groups each other [2]. For this similar photo grouping, we coupled with 25 color histogram block and pyramid matching framework to measure these photos similarity.

2   Related Work

One of the most time-consuming tasks among photo management is the classification task of a huge number of photos. In order to improve this work, many studies have been carried out over the long term. Most photo clustering studies that used the photo taken time and content as a clustering criterion. GPS information is also a very useful clustering criterion because it includes the taken place information of each photo. However, current digital cameras with GPS receivers have not been widely distributed, since these cameras have a low capacity problem of battery.

Table 1. Related work about photo clustering

Study / Year	Clustering criteria	Description
AutoAlbum 2000 [3]	Time order and content based context	- Partitioning photos in the time order to make temporally contiguous groups - Best first probabilistic model merging algorithm
Graham 2002 [4]	Timing information	- Tree structured clustering by dynamic time gap - Calendar and hierarchical image browsers
PhotoTOC 2003 [5]	Temporal and content-based context	- Content based clustering - Table of Contents interface
Toyama 2003 [6]	Geographic location tag	- Query based interface for large number of photos
Cooper 2005 [1]	Temporal and content based context	- Temporal similarity using logistic function with taken time intervals - Visualization of clustering result using DCT
Boutell 2005 [7]	Temporal and content based context	- The first-order Markov property - Integration content-based and temporal context cues
Yang 2009 [8]	Vocabulary retrieved internet images	- Coarse grouping using bag-of visual-words model - Refining grouped results considering matched features such as visual words' position on the image
Jang 2009 [9]	Temporal and content based context	- A clustering algorithm for concurrent digital photos obtained from multiple cameras - Block matching similarity for content-based context

Most studies related to photo management cover how to deal with clustering many photos. We summarize photo clustering studies in Table 1. Toyama proposes an application built on top of the World Wide Media eXchange (WWMX) which is a light-weight travelogue-authoring tool providing auto clustering functions according to geographic location tags [6]

For grouping and summarizing scene images from the Internet, Yang employs the bag-of-visual-words model used in image retrieval applications. This model has the role to give similarity between images and divides the large image collections into separated coarse groups. AutoAlbum partitions photos in time and photo creation order to make a temporally contiguous photo group. Then, it uses the best-first probabilistic model merging algorithm to provide semantically meaningful photo groups with users [3].

As one of the most representative studies using temporal contexts, Cooper proposes an event clustering method by photo timestamp [1]. He also visualizes his clustering result using a DCT matrix. Graham proposes two photo browsers, Calendar and Hierarchical Browsers, to exploit the timing information [4]. He considers photo shoot times and semantically related photos tend to occur in bursts when he constructs a hierarchical photo structure. Boutell proposes a general probabilistic temporal context model in which the first-order Markov property is used to integrate content-based and temporal context cues [7]. He applies the context models to two problems, achieving significant gains in accuracy in both cases. Jang proposes a clustering algorithm for concurrent digital photos obtained from multiple cameras [9]. In order to consider the content-based context, he defines a new color-based similarity between two photos, a block matching similarity.

The studies using temporal and content context are Cooper [1], Boutell [7] and Jang [9]. They provide each clustering similarity and the method to couple with them. Especially, Jang proposed a clustering algorithm for concurrent digital photos obtained from multiple cameras.

3   Temporal and Color-Based Clustering

A photo timestamp is a powerful key to clustering photos because it is related to their events [1]. Most people tend to take many photographs, sometimes intensively, sometimes coarsely. Besides, general photographers implicitly take the next photo considering before taken photos for their event photographing. Therefore, it needs to apply the characteristic of sequential photo arrays to temporal photo clustering. For instance, lots of pictures may be taken at a good sightseeing area, but few if any pictures may be taken until going to another good sightseeing place. Figure 1 shows that the photo sequence reflects this situation. The four photos (a, b, c, d) may be taken at some sightseeing place. Then, five other photos (e, f, g, h, i) may be taken after going to another place. If we try to cluster these nine photos using a constant time gap, four photos (a, b, c, d) having a very small time gap were grouped into $C1$. However, the five other photos with a larger time gap between them were clustered into each cluster, $C2 \sim C6$, respectively. The goal of our clustering method is to group these clusters, $C2 \sim C6$, partitioned by the constant time gap into one cluster, $C2$, as shown in Figure 1 (b).

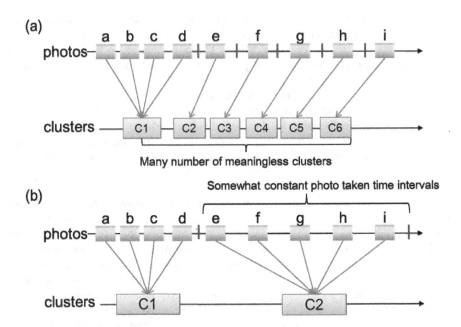

Fig. 1. Example of photo clustering using photo timestamp gap. (a) Partitioning result using constant time gap. Photos e, f, g, h and i are separated into other clusters, $C2, C3, C4, C5$, and $C6$, due to the large amount of time between them. (b) The goal of our proposed clustering in this paper. Photos e, f, g, h and i with larger intervals than photos a, b, c and d are clustered into one cluster, $C2$.

Figure 2 shows our proposed temporal clustering algorithm. For each photo timestamp, the Exif headers are processed to extract the timestamp. First, we sort the photos, $p = \{ p_0, p_1, ..., p_{n-1} \}$, in taken time order and extract the taken time gap from this sequence p. The ordered n-1 time gaps, $g = \{ g_0, g_1, ..., g_{n-2} \}$, in the user collection from n photos are ordered in time so the resulting timestamp gaps satisfy $g_0 \leq g_1, ..., \leq, g_{n-2} \}$, $g_0 \leq g_1 \leq ... \leq g_{n-2}$. Second, we conduct imputation for calculation of photo time gap variance in a window (its size is designated by user, w). By the time we reach the end of the time gap list, the photo list (p) is split into finer clusters based on the time gap variance.

We insert each split group into a priority queue. The priority is decided by the variance of the taken time difference. That is, the photo groups with wide-spread distribution have high priority. Then, these steps are recursively performed. As a result, our recursive clustering method based on the priority queue constructs hierarchical tree structure.

Now we can get temporally clustered photo sets. In this paper, we employ the interval graph to find similar photo sets each other using Ryu's method [2]. By construction interval graph and using maximal clique finding, he can find complete graphs whose photos consists of similar photos more than user designate similarity.

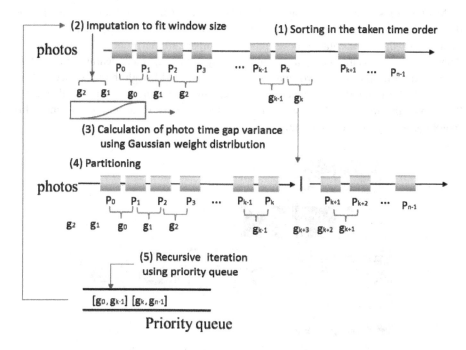

Fig. 2. Our temporal clustering method based on photo taken time. It consists of five steps.

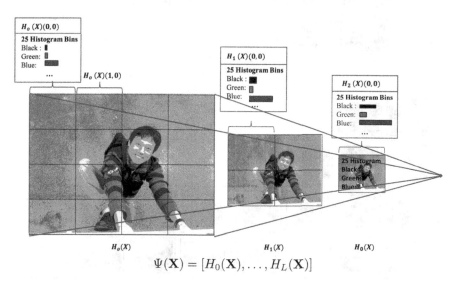

$$\Psi(\mathbf{X}) = [H_0(\mathbf{X}), \ldots, H_L(\mathbf{X})]$$

Fig. 3. 25 Color-based similarity using pyramid matching. The default block size is *64 px*.

Most studies relating to image similarity comparison used feature point as the descriptor. SIFT (Scale-Invariant Feature Transform) or Surf (Speeded-Up Robust Feature) are the representative descriptors to compare similarity between two images. They usually measure the image similarity by matching each feature point. This image similarity measured two images very correctly. Although they produce correct result its time complexity would be a problem in comparing many pairs of images. Therefore, the image similarity studies focused on how to accelerate it since this matching is very time-consuming.

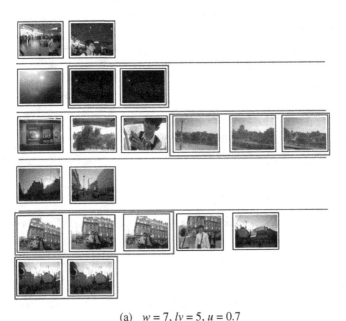

(a) $w = 7, lv = 5, u = 0.7$

(b) $w = 12, lv = 4, u = 0.7$

Fig. 4. Result of temporal and color clustering according to window size (w) and temporal clustering level (lv). The blue and red lines depict temporal and color clustering.

Pyramid matching is one of the most efficient frameworks to improve this time-complexity [10]. This matching function is a fast kernel function which maps unordered feature sets to multi-resolution histograms and computes a weighted histogram intersection in this space. This "pyramid match" computation is linear in the number of features, and it implicitly finds correspondences based on the finest resolution histogram cell where a matched pair first appears. We used 25 color histogram block based on pyramid matching instead of using feature point descriptor. This has the role to construct similar atmosphere of photos. If we want to construct same model and object, we also used feature point descriptors such as SIFT or Surf.

Figure 3 shows the pyramid matching structure to construct 25 color histogram bins. Each default block depicts the histogram distribution at the pyramid level zero. This is calculated by counting the number of 25 color quantized pixels. Equation 1 shows the 25 color histogram based similarity between two photos, p_k and p_j, using pyramid matching structure. In this equation, N means the common histogram according to each pyramid level [10].

$$S_C(p_k, p_j) = \frac{|N(p_k, p_j)|}{|N(p_k, p_k)||N(p_j, p_j)|} \tag{1}$$

The photo sequence clustered by temporal information generates intervals from consecutive photos with more color similarity to each other than the user-defined threshold u. The result of our clustering is shown in Figure 4. We set u is 0.7.

4   Experiment

In order to evaluate our clustering method, we asked photographers to make the true photo sets classified by manual operation for similar photo sets and temporally grouped photo sets. Then, we measured precision and recall between our clustering result and true photo sets classified by 6 participants. The input photo sets consists of three groups and 506 photos. The precision and recall of our temporal clustering are about 0.89 and 0.83. For a benchmark test, we implemented Cooper's similarity-based clustering algorithm. The precision and recall of the benchmarking method are also good result (0.87 and 0.82). For the similar photo group clustering, the precision and recall are 0.74 and 0.72 on average, respectively. We believe that our algorithm is enough superior to construct good quality photo sets, respectively.

5   Conclusion

In this paper, we present an automated clustering method to classify hundreds of photos considering the people's recent photographing behavior. Our approach consist of two steps: constructing temporal photo groups and more detailed clustering using interval graph with 25 color-based pyramid matching similarity. The user experiment shows that our algorithm is enough correct to classify hundreds of photos. For future work, we proposed the photo navigating interface to visualize similar photo groups. For example, these similar photo groups are very useful to provide users with a summarized view. Since this kind of interface keeps temporal context continuity, it is very helpful for users to manage their photos according to their travel itinerary.

References

1. Cooper, M., Foote, J., Girgensohn, A., Wilcox, L.: Temporal event clustering for digital photo collections. ACM Transactions on Multimedia Computing, Communications, and Applications (TOMCCAP), 269–288 (2005)
2. Dong-Sung, R., Kwang Hwi, K., Sun-Young, P., Hwan-Gue, C.: A web-based photo management system for large photo collections with user-customizable quality assessment. In: Proc. of the ACM Symposium on Applied Computing, pp. 1229–1236 (2011)
3. Platt, J.C.: AutoAlbum: clustering digital photographs using probabilistic model merging. In: Proc. of IEEE Workshop on Content-based Access of Image and Video Libraries, pp. 96–100 (2000)
4. Graham, A., Garcia-Molina, H., Paepcke, A., Winograd, T.: Time as essence for photo browsing through personal digital libraries. In: Proc. of the 2nd ACM/IEEE-CS Joint Conference on Digital Libraries, pp. 326–335 (2002)
5. Platt, J.C., Czerwinski, M., Field, B.A.: PhotoTOC: automatic clustering for browsing personal photographs. In: Proc. of the IEEE Joint Conference of the 4th Pacific Rim Conference on Multimedia, pp. 6–10 (2003)
6. Toyama, K., Logan, R., Roseway, A.: Geographic location tags on digital images. In: Proc. of the 11th ACM International Conference on Multimedia, pp. 156–166 (2003)
7. Boutell, M., Luo, J.: A generalized temporal context model for semantic scene classification. Multimedia Systems, 82–92 (2005)
8. Yang, H., Wang, Q.: Grouping and summarizing scene images from web collections. In: Proc. of the 5th International Symposium on Advances in Visual Computing, pp. 315–324 (2009)
9. Chuljin, J., TaeJin, Y., Hwan-Gue, C.: A smart clustering algorithm for photo set obtained from multiple digital cameras. In: Proc. of the ACM Symposium on Applied Computing, pp. 1784–1791 (2009)
10. Grauman, K., Trevor, D.: The Pyramid Match Kernel: Discriminative Classification with Sets of Image Features. In: Proc. of ICCV, pp. 1458–1465 (2005)

Requirements Analysis and Critical Requirement Derivation Method Using Macrostruktur

Yong-Kyun Cho and Young-Bum Park

Computer Science, University of Dankook
Anseo-dong, Dongnam-gu, Cheonan-si, Chungnam, 330-714, Korea
loveofworld@korea.com, ybpark@dankook.ac.kr

Abstract. As software is varied and grew in size, the importance of clear understanding and representing customer's need, has been emphasized. It is not easy to drive and define critical system needs, since requirements in early stage of the development, is abstract and conceptual. In this paper, to drive clear customer's requirements, Macrostruktur concept of textlinguistics is used. First, Macrostruktur of textlinguistics is used to analysis descriptive requirements. Second, Macrostruktur-rule is applied to analyzed Macrostruktur data in order to derive Macrostruktur-propositions. Finally, it is implemented to derived Macrostruktur-propositions.

Keywords: critical requrirement, requirement derication, requirements analysis, Macrostruktur, Macrostruktur-rule.

1   Introduction

As software industry got diversified and grew in size rapidly year after year due to development of IT technology, economic loss and risk from defect of software is increasing as well [1].

According to the U.S. Standish Group's report that analyzed cause of failure of software business, the cause are inaccurate definition of requirements and their frequent changes making the success rate of software business very low [2]. It was found that the problem is fault method of understanding and analyzing customers as well as fault managing and controlling all the changes not the lack of applied technology or methodology [3] [4].

The goals of customers are abstract and conceptual, it is not easy to express them, and fulfilling of those goals can be limited by various factors that cannot be controlled. Therefore, It is not easy to derive and define the critical system' needs clearly [5][6].

In this paper, requirements in early stages of development are analyzed using Macrostruktur of textlinguistics, and methods for driving the critical requirements are suggested. Various information that was derived by analyzing the requirements with Macrostruktur is used to clearly drive critical requirements. And analyzing tool are used to manage the critical requirements and various information.

T.-h. Kim et al. (Eds.): ISA 2011, CCIS 200, pp. 367–377, 2011.

2   Related Work

2.1   Macrostruktur of Van Dijk

Multiple propositions and sentences are combined to form a subtext, and multiple subtext are combined to form a text of high level. If linguistic factors and non-linguistic factors such as situation are added to this, it constructs a whole text. The overall structure focused on correlation based on large unit or whole text composed of propositions or sentences is called Macrostruktur [7][8][9].

The theme of a text with Macrostruktur is made by summarizing the whole text. This structure forms a single meaning unit at the level of the whole text composed of numerous propositions or at more comprehensive level. In addition, Macrostruktur can have multiple layers. Texts with Macrostruktur of high level can have summarized theme of subtext and consequently, the Macrostruktur can have hierarchial structure at various levels. One of features of Macrostruktur with hierarchial structure is its relativity. Top-level macro-proposition which represents the overall meaning can be understood by understanding macro-propositions in bottom-to-top order [10].

2.2   Characteristics and Principles of Macro-rules

Functions of macro-rules are reduction and organization of information, and formation of these macro-rules are essential for understanding. Fundamental objective of applying macro-rules in producing and interpreting texts is to clearly discern themes of texts. And since summarization is one of the important clues for confirming whether themes are clearly understood, it is a measure of verifying them. Propositions included in Macrostruktur through macro-rules are macro-propositions, and a text can be summarized or outlined with these macro-propositions [9].

Van Dijk said macro-propositions can be understood based on macro-rules of transcription type. Macro-rules applied in movement of information from text to proposition of higher level are important because they function as criteria for differentiation of important/not-important information, help smooth communication between text producer and consumer, and   construct unit propositions. Types of macro-rules are omission rules, selection rules, generalization rules, and construction rules [10][11].

3   Requirements Analysis Method Using Macrostrukur Concept

In this paper, critical requirements are derived by analyzing requirements using Macrostruktur of extlinguistics.

3.1   Requirement Analysis Using Macrostruktur

Semantic relations meanings connoted in requirements text are analyzed using Macrostruktur of textlinguistics to derive semantic propositions. Derived semantic propositions are essential information for deriving macro-propositions. The 3 steps of derivation process from requirements text to semantic propositions can be organized like Table 1.

Table 1. Steps of derivation process of requirements semantic propositions

step 1) Semantic relations among each sentence in requirement text R are analyzed to form a group of sentences representing the same meaning. The sentence group becomes requirements sentence S which is divided by (n), and it is completely included in the text R semantically.

step 2) In the requirements sentence S, each function and behavior that represent or indicate something are divided into discrete meanings. Those discrete meanings are organized by objects, behaviors or functions of objects, and features of the behaviors and functions.

step 3) Semantic relations among the discrete meanings are analyzed to derive semantic proposition P, and they are organized by objects, behaviors or functions of objects, and features of the behaviors and functions. The semantic proposition P derived are completely included as components of the requirements sentence S semantically.

To clearly analyze meanings connoted in requirements text, the requirements text should be divided into each proposition unit, and its semantic relations should be analyzed. To analyze semantic relation of each step in the 3 steps of requirements semantic-propositions derivation process represented in Table 1, a series of conditions are needed. The continuity condition [10] suggested in textlinguistics of Van Dijk can be used for finding and analyzing semantic relation to delete repeated conditions or those that includes higher concepts. And the conditions can be reorganized as conditions for clearly analyzing proposition's precedent meaning and subsequent meaning like the 4 conditions suggested in the Table 2.

Table 2. 4 conditions for semantic relations analysis of propositions [10]

1) A causes B, or A is reason of B.
2) A is result of B. A is a kind of behavior, or result of it.
3) A and B take place in the same situation.
  A and B belong to the same scope of concept and the followings are allowed.
  - A and B take place simultaneously.
  - A takes place in part of period of B, or vice versa.
  - A and B overlap each other
4) A is necessarily a part of B, or vice versa. A necessarily result in B, or vice versa.

The derivation process of requirements semantic propositions will be explained in detail in 3 steps.

In step 1, semantic relations among each sentence constructing requirements text R are analyzed to form the requirement sentence S through grouping of sentences representing the same meaning. Requirements text R is composed of general sentences.

$$t \quad : \text{sentence constructing R}$$
$$n \quad : \text{the number of sentences constructing R} \qquad (1)$$
$$R = \{ t_0, t_1, \ldots\ldots, t_n \}$$

Requirements text R is complex sentence composed of 1 or more sentences (t). To form independent requirement sentence S composed of the same meaning from each sentence (t) of requirements text R, semantic relations should be analyzed with the conditions for semantic relation analysis and the sentence representing the same meaning among sentences (t) should be selected. If t_i analysis (where $0 \leq i \leq n$) is precedent sentence selected among those composing requirements text R for analysis, the selected sentence t_i and subsequent sentence t_j analysis (where $0 \leq j \leq n$, $i \neq j$) for are analyzed with the conditions for semantic relation analysis.

Sentence t_i, selected for analyzing semantic relations, is included as an initial component of requirements sentence S_k.   And if semantic relation between t_i and t_j is analyzed with the 4 conditions for semantic relation analysis, the meanings connoted in sentence t_i and t_j are the same. So, t_j is grouped by components of requirements sentence S_k.   Sentence t_i and t_j, which are grouped by components of requirements sentence S_k, become components of requirements sentence.

If semantic relation between sentence t_i and t_j is analyzed without 4 conditions for semantic relations analysis, meanings connoted in t_i and t_j are different. So, whether t_i has semantic relation with t_{j+1} is analyzed which is the next sentence for semantic relation analysis.

In this way, all the sentences are selected the sentence t_i which is precedent sentence chosen for semantic relations analysis, and they construct requirements sentence S_k through semantic relations with other sentences. If sentence t_i is included in requirement sentence S, sentence t_j whose semantic relation with t_i is analyzed is grouped as component of requirements sentence S.

$$S_k = \{ t_0, t_1, \ldots\ldots, t_i, (\text{where } 0 \leq i \leq n) \}$$
$$R = \{ S_0, S_1, \ldots\ldots, S_k, (\text{where } 0 \leq k \leq n) \} \qquad (2)$$

Requirement sentence S_k can be organized into one sentence or a group of sentences according to semantic relations analysis. And since S_k organized through semantic relations analysis is organized into a group of sentences (t),   all the derived S_k are included in requirements text R.

In step 2, all the discrete meanings in requirements sentence S composed of sentences (t) are derived.

Like requirements text R, requirements sentence S is complex sentence composed of 1 or more discrete meanings. Sentences (t) organized from requirements text R are organized by 1 or more discrete meanings (m). Since requirements sentence S composed of multiple sentences (t) is composed of multiple sentences with the same meaning, requirements   can be divided by the discrete sentences (m).

$$S = \{ t_0, t_1, \neq \neq, t_k, (\text{where } 0 \leq k \leq n) \}$$
$$t_k = \{ m_0, m_1, \neq \neq, m_i, (\text{where } 0 \leq i \leq p) \} \qquad (3)$$
$$S = \{ m_0, m_1, \neq \neq, m_j, (\text{where } 0 \leq j \leq q, q \leq p \neq n) \}$$

Discrete meanings (m) derived from requirements sentence S are organized by objects, behaviors or functions, features of behaviors or functions.

Objects have interaction with system to achieve their goals through behaviors or functions provided by the system. Behaviors or functions are provided by the system for the objects to achieve their goals. Features of behaviors or functions are additional information necessary for implementing system's functions that cannot be expressed with objects, behaviors, or functions.

The reason of expressing discrete meanings using the 3 components is that it is the form of sentence representing propositions which can express meanings using minimum information. If Objects are expressed as subjects and behaviors and functions are expressed as verbs, objects, or complements, they form a sentence of third form. Since it organize discrete meanings using minimum information, meanings are expressed clearly with ambiguous expressions reduced.

Objects in discrete meanings are expressed as subjects in form of nouns in requirement sentence. Behaviors or functions in discrete meanings are expressed in forms of verbs, objects, and complements that modify subjects. However, not all forms of verbs, objects, and complements that modify subjects and nouns expressed as subjects become objects, behaviors, and functions. If a noun that represents too broad meaning is selected as object, nouns that represents narrow meanings belong to the noun of broad meaning abstractly. So, the system is for correcting the nous with too broad meaning. If selected system is for development, it can include every behavior or function. So, the system for development is excluded from objects. Like objects, abstract behaviors or functions are excluded from behaviors or functions.

The way to derive conceptual meanings from requirements sentence that has been explained so far is like the following.

Object which is noun representing subject that can be object in sentences constructing requirement sentence is derived. And function which is information composed of verbs, objects, and complements representing behaviors or functions in sentences constructing requirement sentence is derived. If selected object among derived objects for writing proposition is $object_i$, whether $fuction_j$ representing behaviors or functions for $object_i$ exists is investigated. If $fuction_j$ for $object_i$ is found, $object_i$ and $fuction_j$ are generated as proposition. If it is not found, the next $fuction_{j+1}$ is investigated. In this way, whether behaviors or functions for derived object exist is investigated all and proposition is generated. Discrete meaning can be derived by writing features of behavior or function in generated proposition.

In step 3, semantic relations among discrete meanings derived from requirement sentence are analyzed to derive semantic propositions. The reason of deriving semantic propositions by analyzing semantic relations among discrete meanings derived is that not all the discrete meanings derived represent requirement sentence S. Certain discrete meaning of requirement sentence S can construct a requirement sentence through semantic relations with other discrete meanings, but it can be inessential for composition. Therefore, to derive semantic propositions from requirements sentence, semantic relations among all the discrete meanings that can be derived from requirements should be analyzed.

The way to derive semantic propositions from conceptual meanings that has been explained so far is like the followings.

If relation between discrete meanings m_i and m_j is analyzed with the 4 conditions for semantic relation analysis, the sentence m_i and m_j form semantic relations in constructing requirements sentence S. So, m_i is derived as P_k.

If relation between discrete meanings m_i and m_j is analyzed without the 4 conditions for semantic relation analysis, m_i and m_j do not form semantic relations in constructing requirements sentence S. So, relation of mi with the next discrete meaning m_{j+1} is analyzed. The analysis is repeated until relations among every discrete proposition (m) is analyzed semantically. And by adding information on discrete meaning m_i selected as P_k and information on semantic relation analysis of discrete meaning m_{ij} that has semantic relation, semantic proposition P_k, can be formed. The discrete meaning mij is written as semantic proposition P_k.

When relations of all the discrete meanings are analyzed, discrete meanings that have no semantic relation with one of the others are omitted.

$$S = \{\ t_0, t_1, \ldots\ldots, t_i\,, \text{(where } 0 \leq i \leq n) \ \}$$
$$t_i\ = \{\ P_0, P_1, \ \neq \neq\ , P_j\,, \text{(where } 0 \leq j \leq q) \ \} \tag{4}$$
$$S = \{\ P_0, P_1, \ \neq \neq\ , P_k\,, \text{(where } 0 \leq k \leq q) \ \}$$

Because semantic propositions P are derived based on sentences (t) constructing requirements sentence S, all the derived P are included in requirements sentence S.

3.2 Definition of Critical Requirements Using Macrostruktur

Requirements text are analyzed by Macrostruktur to derive semantic propositions. Semantic propositions are components of requirements text. If macro-rules are applied in semantic propositions of requirements text, the overall meaning of the semantic propositions which is the macro-proposition can be derived.

Because macro-rules are measure of clear understanding of theme of requirements text, derived macro-proposition can be used to define critical requirements. Macro-rule [10] in textlinguistics of Van Dijk, can be applied in this paper like the followings. First, in omission rules, additional semantic propositions which are not critical can be omitted because not all the semantic propositions of each requirement sentence is critical. Second, in selection rules, only representative semantic propositions should be selected among all of them derived by semantic relations. Third, in generalization rules, semantic propositions are expressed after generalized to semantic propositions of higher concept. Fourth, in construction rules, various semantic propositions can be replaced with integrated and comprehensive expressions such as certain state, event, process, general condition, situation, facto, and result.

Macro-rules have correlation one another and be influenced by the semantic relations. Semantic proposition of the overall theme can be selected   among many semantic propositions and the rest of them can be omitted applying the mission rules above. Selections rules are applied when selecting the semantic proposition of them overall theme, and the rest of them can be omitted applying the omission rules. Construction rules are replaced with propositions by conditions such as selection rules. The difference is that construction rules represent macro-propositions by integrating multiple semantic propositions. Generalization rules are applied in all the semantic propositions that derive macro-propositions using selection rules and construction rules. Macro-rules that have been explained so far can be applied in semantic propositions to derive macro-propositions, and the derive macro-propositions are defined as critical requirements representing the overall theme of requirements text.

Macro-propositions are expressed as M, they are essential summaries of requirements sentence S. Macro-rules are applied in P with semantic relation among multiple P in requirements sentence S to derive macro-propositions. Among macro-rules, selection rules and construction rules can be applied to derive macro-proposition.

If analyzed semantic relations of P in requirements sentence S are found to have one of the 4 conditions listed in the Table 2, P_i which represents every semantic proposition P can be selected to derive macro-proposition M. semantic propositions P which were not selected are not omitted and become components of P_i, which is selected macro-proposition by omission rules.

If analyzed semantic relations of P in requirements sentence S are found to have condition 3) among the 4 conditions listed in the Table 2, construction rules can be used to write new proposition of higher concept which represents every semantic propositions P, for deriving macro-propositions M. Derived macro-proposition M   is written in forms of discrete meanings, or objects, behaviors, or functions like semantic propositions. Every semantic propositions P is not omitted and becomes components of macro-proposition M which was written as new proposition of higher concept.

Because macro-propositions and semantic propositions which derived by applying macro-rules represent customers' critical needs, they can be used as tools for accurate and smooth communication between analyzers and customers.

4   Case Study

In this paper, macro-propositions are derived by applying suggested method and critical requirements are defined.

4.1   Application of Semantic Propositions Using Macrostruktur

In step 1 of requirements semantic propositions derivation, semantic relations between each sentence constructing requirements text R are analyzed to construct requirements sentence S.

Table 3. Requirements text R for semantic propositions derivation

requirements text R :
A student registers for courses. After registration, he uses system to check his registration information. Administrator registers the new student, and modifies or deletes student information.

To analyzed semantic relations among multiple sentence, requirements text R can be divided by the sentences (t) and organized like the Table 4.

Table 4. Divided sentence from requirements text R

t_0 : A student registers for courses. t_1 : After applications, he uses system to check his registration information. t_2 : Administrator registers the new student, and modifies or deletes student information.

To derive requirements sentence S from all the sentences constructing requirements text R, semantic relations among t_0, t_1, t_2 should be analyzed.

Precedent sentence t_0 which was selected for semantic relation analysis is included as component of requirements sentence S_0 And semantic relation of t_0 with other sentences are analyzed.

t_0 and t_1 can be analyzed by semantic relation of "t_0 is cause of t_1" or "t_0 is reason of t_1". Because t_0 and t_1 have semantic relation of cause, they construct requirements sentence S_0.

Because t_0 and t_2 are not analyzed by semantic relation, they are not grouped as components of requirements sentence S_0, It can be organized like Table 5.

Table 5. Derived requirements sentence S

requirements sentence S_0 : t_0 : A student registers for courses. t_1 : After applications, he uses system to check his   registration information. requirements sentence S_1 : t_2 : Administrator registers the new student, and modifies and deletes student information.

In the step 2, all discrete meanings are derived from requirements sentence S composed of sentences (t). Table 6. shows an example of applying the step 2.

Table 6. Requirements sentence S for deriving discrete meanings

requirements sentence S_0 : t_0 : A Student registers for courses. t_1 : After applications, he uses system to check his registration information.

Discrete meanings necessary are derived to derive semantic propositions from requirements sentence S.

In requirements sentence S_0, host of the whole meanings is "student" and behaviors or functions   that can be derived are discrete meanings such as   "registers for courses", "checks registration information.", "registration is completed", "uses system". The derived information can be organized as discrete meanings   like the Table 7 and Table 8.

Table 7. Discrete meanings about course registration

m_0	object : student behavior or function of object : Registers for courses feature of behavior or function : None

Table 8. Discrete meanings about checking course registration information

m_1	object : student behavior or function of object : checks course registration information. feature of behavior or function : after course registration

There ware 3 behaviors or functions of objects derived from requirements sentence S_0. However, because "uses system" represents behaviors or functions of system for development, it is not derived as discrete meaning. And because "course registration is completed" is feature of "checks course registration information", it is written as features of behaviors or functions of m_1.

In step 3, semantic relations of discrete meanings derived from requirements sentence S are analyzed to derive semantic proposition P. Semantic relation between discrete meaning m_0 of the Table 7 derived from requirements sentence S_0 and discrete meaning m_1 of the Table 8 are analyzed to derive semantic proposition.

m_0 and m_1 satisfy the condition of "m_0 is the cause of m_1." among the 4 conditions for semantic relation analysis of the Table 2. As discrete meaning, "a student registers for courses" can be expressed as the cause of "a student confirms course registration information". They also satisfy the condition of "m_1 is the result of m_0." As discrete meaning, "a student confirms course registration information" can be expressed as the result of "a student registers for courses".

Table 9. Portfolio made by analyzing requirements text

requirements sentence S_0 : t_0 : A student registers for courses. t_1 : After registration, He uses system to check his registration information.	
P_0	object : student behavior or function of object : registers for courses feature of behavior or function : None semantic relation analysis : 1) cause condition of P_1
P_1	object : student behavior or function of object : checks course registration information. feature of behavior or function : after course registration semantic relation analysis : 2) result condition of P_0

Since discrete meanings m_0 and m_1 have semantic relation, they can be derived as semantic propositions P_1 and P_2. The method to derive semantic proposition P and requirements sentence S from requirements text which has been derived so far can be applied in requirements text of the Table 3 like the Table 9.

4.2 Derivation of Macro-Proposition Using Macro-Rules

In paragraph 4.1, macro-proposition is derived by applying macro-rules in the **Table 9** which represents information of semantic proposition derived from requirements text, and the derived macro-proposition becomes critical requirement representing critical meaning in the requirements.

Because semantic propositions P_0 and P_1 of requirements sentence S_0 has conditions of 1) and 2) from the **Table 2**, P_0 which represents cause is selected as macro-proposition according to selection rule.

Since semantic propositions P_0, P_1, P_2 of requirements sentence S_1 have semantic relation for the same situation of managing student information, they can be replaced with comprehensive and integrated expression according to the construction rule. The comprehensive and integrated macro-proposition is "administrator manages student information".

Table 10. Semantic proposition about confirming course registration information

S	semantic proposition	Macro-rule	macro-proposition
S_0	P_0 : A student registers for courses. P_1 : A student checks his registration information.	selection	M_0 : A student registers for courses.
S_2	P_0 :Administrator registers student information. P_1 :Administrator modifies changed student information. P_2 : Administrator deletes changed student information.	construction	M_1 : Administrator manages student information.

5   Conclusion

In this paper, critical requirements are derined using Macrostruktur of textlinguistics to clearly define critical requiremetns that customers want.

To understand, analyze, and document requirements and control changes, various technologies and methods are being used. However, clearly defining and manaing requirements are very difficult and need much flexibility.

Requirements analysis method suggested in this paper tries to improve these problems and derives critical requirements through derivation of critical meanings by analyzing meaning of pure languages (oral/spoken) based on spoken words from a person. Rather understanding and analyzing requirements after deriving needed information from simple form of writings or texts, clearly analyzing customers' needs after deriving meaning connoted in the writings or texts is better way to understand, analyze, and document requirements. Since information is analyzed and expressed in minimum unit hierarchically, the method can be applied in every form of proposition constructing writings or texts. Therefore, through various analysis that is used much theoretically in technological aspect as well as verification method, comparison, and complementary researches, not only derivation method of requirements but also application method for software design will be implemented.

References

1. Soonll cha, The Present and Prospect of Software Testing Industry, Korea Information Science Society, Communications Of The Korea Information Science Society, 28(11), 79–85 (2010); The Standish Group, Standish Group Report (2005)
2. The Standish Group, Standish Group Report (2005)
3. Lee, B.G., Hwang, M.S., Lee, Y., Lee, H.J., Baik, J., Lee., C.-k.: Design and Development of a Standard Guidance for Software Requirement Specification, Korea Information Science Society. Journal of KISS: Software and Applications 36(7), 531–538 (2009)
4. Choi, J.-E., Choi, S.-K., Lee, S.-A.: The Case Study of Software Requirement Management. Korea Information Science Society 291(B), 445–447 (2002)
5. Easterbrook, B.N.S.: Requirements Engineering: A Roadmap. In: ICSE 2000 Proceedings of the Conference on The Future of Software Engineering (2000)
6. Kung, S.H., Lee, J.-K., Namgoong, H.: Analysis and Verification of Functional Requirements for GLORY using UML. The Korea Contents Society, Journal Of The Korea Contents Association 8(5), 61–71 (2008)
7. Kang Changu, Understanding Textlinuistics (2004)
8. 김재봉, 텍스트 연구회 편 : 문 주제 중심의 텍스트 요약과 거시규칙, 한국텍스트언어학회 텍스트언어학 (1995)
9. 서혁, 요약 능력과 요약 규칙, 국어교육학회 국어교육학연구 (1994년)
10. van Dijk, Textlinguistics (1995)
11. 텍스트 요약 전략에 대한 국어교육학적 연구, 김재봉 (1999)
12. Einführung in die Textlinguistik. Tübingen: Niemeyer. , de Beaugrande, Robert-Alain/Dressler, Wolfgang Ulrich (1981)
13. Eine Einführung in Grundbegriffe und Methoden., Brinker, Klaus, Linguistische Textanalyse. 3., durchges. und erweit. Aufl. Berlin: Schmidt (1992)
14. Textlinguistik., Coseriu, Eugenio, Eine Einführung. Tübingen: Narr (1980)
15. Textlinguistik. Eine Einführung., Heinemann, Wolfgang/Viehweger, Dieter, Tübingen: Niemeyer (1991)
16. van Dijk, T.A.: The Study of Discourse. In: van Dijk, T.A. (ed.) Discourse Studies: A Multidisciplinary Introduction. Bd. I: Discourse as Structure and Process, pp. 1–34. Sage, London (1997)

A Scheme for Role-Based 3D CCTV Using CS-RBAC (Context-Sensitivity Role-Based Access Control)

Jang-Mook Kang[1], Jae-Sang Cha[2,*], You-Jin Song[3], Goo-Man Park[2],
Eun-Young Ko[4], Myong-chul Shin[4], Jeong-Jin Kang[5], and You-Sik Hong[6]

[1] Electronic Commerce Research Institute, Dongguk University,
707 Seokjang-dong, Gyeongju, Gyeongsangbuk-do, 780-714, Korea
mooknc@gmail.com
[2] Department of Media Engineering,
Seoul National University of Science and Technology, Seoul, Korea
chajs@seoultech.ac.kr, gmpark@seoultech.ac.kr
[3] Department of Information Management, Dongguk University,
707 Seokjang-dong, Gyeongju, Gyeongsangbuk-do, 780-714, Korea
song@dongguk.ac.kr
[4] Department of Information & Communication Engineering,
Sungkyunkwan University, 300 Cheoncheon-dong, Jangan-gu,
Suwon, 440-746, Korea
key@keit.re.kr, mcshin@skku.edu
[5] Department of Information & Communication,
Dong Seoul University, 423, Bokjeong-Dong, Sujeong-Gu,
Seongnam, Gyunggi, 461-714, Korea
iwit2000@gmail.com
[6] School of Information and Communication Engineering,
Sang JI University, Wonju, Kangwon, 220-702, Korea
yshong@sangji.ac.kr

Abstract. A CCTV to ensure the safety of the routine has been used as a tool. Especially in recent years, CCTV has improved the performance of the hardware. As an example, CCTV were realized connection to a smart phone and supporting high-definition CCTV with the advent of CCTV images. This paper is part of the study for an effective monitoring of the object to define the role of private CCTV Multiple CCTV at the same time. Multiple CCTV and dynamic roles are needed to define to separate between the algorithms and policies. To this end, this article was fused of CS-RBAC concept with 3D CCTV. In this article, the proposed scheme for effective use of CCTV is expected to be available in various environments.

Keywords: 3D CCTV; CCTV; CS-RBAC; context awareness.

1 Introduction

A closed circuit television (CCTV) is being installed and been used in a long time. In recent years, CCTV has been linked to the internet. Recent evidence indicates that

---

* Corresponding author.

T.-h. Kim et al. (Eds.): ISA 2011, CCIS 200, pp. 378–383, 2011.
© Springer-Verlag Berlin Heidelberg 2011

nearly half of all metropolitan and non-metropolitan councils already have installed CCTV within their town centres, However, very few of these systems have been systematically evaluated. There is growing concern at this lack of evaluation, particularly amongst retailers who contribute significantly to the financing of many of these systems [1].

In addition, the presence of CCTV cameras has increased enormously in the past few years all over the world. Therefore, enough to increase the CCTV is growing concern about privacy. Anyway, few, if any, clear patterns of opinions emerged. Instead, what was more remarkable was the broad diversity of positive and negative opinions regarding CCTV and their responses to it. This diversity served to defy any obvious or common sense categorization of offender reaction to CCTV surveillance [2]. A CCTV used for this study is growing into the center on the effectiveness of the use and the privacy concerns.

In this article, ways to improve the efficiency of CCTV technology and policy are analyzed. Today, in addition hand carry portable CCTV is growing. Of course, fixed type and high resolution of the CCTV was generalized. Thus, out of hardware performance issue has been emphasized collaboration between networks CCTV.

This article in the fundament analysis of role based CCTV as aspect to communication and service for collaboration.

In this article the notion of CS-RBAC (Context-Sensitivity Role-Based Access Control) is applied to CCTV. The concept of control CCTV is an effective idea within a distributed network environment. In this article, the proposed dynamics-based CCTV scheme is expected to be utilized in various fields in the future.

2   3D CCTV

2.1   Computer-Enhanced CCTV

The adoption of computer-enhanced CCTV surveillance systems should not be an automatic response to a public space security problem and their deployment should not be decided simply on the technology's availability or cost [3]. Even with the help of computers, software need to maximize effectiveness are raised CCTV for enhanced precision.

Therefore, S. Akhtar Ali Shah etc. focuses on the system architecture of the model and tests its performance by comparing its predicted values with a real incident data. As per present practice in Korea, the traffic managers use a heuristic approach for incident analysis based on their experience of similar scenarios. However, this approach induces uncertainty thereby reducing the overall effectiveness of the subsequent incident management and rescue operations [4].

This article is proposed a CCTV image and network that enables collaboration scheme.

2.2   3D CCTV Based on Web and Smart-Phone

3D CCTV is the trend of connection between smartphone and web. Therefore, based on the recorded video in various aspects of reality can be reproduced. This trend in the convergence of broadcasting and telecommunications has accelerated. Figure 1 is based on the same 3D CCTV is fuse the analysis of a schematic diagram.

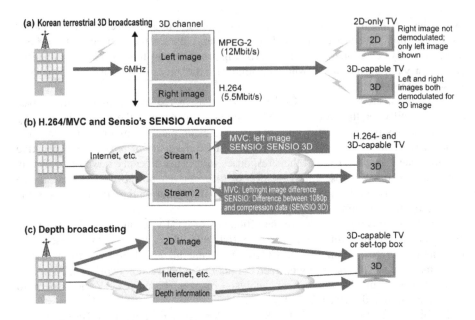

Fig. 1. Higher-Definition 3D Broadcasting [5]

3 Role-Based 3D CCTV

3.1 CS-RBAC

Role-based Access Control (RBAC) based on the user's role is to control access. In this article we based the user's role is to transition into the role of CCTV-based. Since Ravi S. Sandhu have been proposed the basic model proposed by various models. Since It has been incorporated into the standard reference model [6][7][8][9].

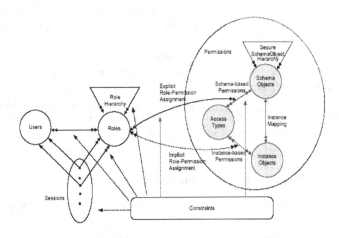

Fig. 2. The System architecture of CS-RBAC [8]

The above Figure 2 shows a CS-RBAC system for role based policies and technologies to provide role-permission and role-assignment. The above figure 2 is a configuration as 'session', 'roles', 'users', 'role hierachy', and so on.

3.2   Role-Based 3D CCTV Using CS-RBAC

Role-based CCTV to be implemented as in Figure 2 and the right to access CCTV should be sensitive. In a number of networked CCTV environments, the CS-RBAC can be offered to the principle for the algorithm and the right to access in particular CCTV based in policy. The following figures 3 are for this analysis.

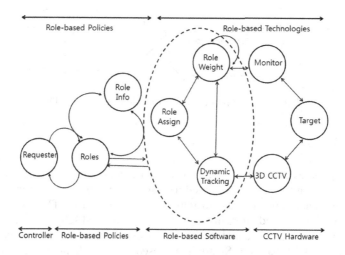

Fig. 3. Role-based 3D CCTV using CS-RBAC

4   Scheme for 3D CCTV Using CS-RBAC

Based on the above discussion, this article may suggest the scheme for 3D CCTV based on CS-RBAC. This scheme has module for precise detection using 3D CCTV supporting CS-REAC.

The proposed scheme for role-based 3D CCTV using CS-RBAC is organized as "install 3C CCTV as hardware", "Role-based access control as software", "context sensitivity role-based access control", "mash-up 3D image and map" and so on. Future, features for each module and function describe the details.

The proposed scheme was composed to easy control the hardware to be useful to process role-based 3D CCTV. In particular, the role of CCTV-based, which helps formulate policy.

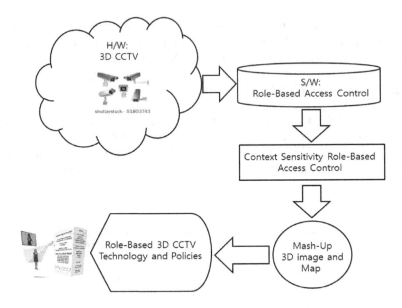

Fig. 4. The proposed scheme for role-based 3D CCTV

5   Conclusions

Role-based policies and technologies introduced earlier studies is considered to be a user object. But, in this article we based the user's role is to transition into the role of CCTV-based. Therefore, in order to implement role-based CCTV detailed modules and algorithms are needed later. In this article, the proposed scheme based on the role of CCTV in policy and technology can be applied widely. For example, that the schema applies "LBS-based or Smartphone-based CCTV role model" etc. This article can be applied to various fields such as the main feature is role-based CCTV.

Acknowledgment. This research was supported by Basic Science Research Program through the National Research Foundation of Korea(NRF) funded by the Ministry of Education, Science and Technology(No. 2010-0028122).

This work was supported by the Korea Science and EngineeringFoundation(KOSEF) grant funded by the Korea government(MEST) (No. 2010-0027503).

References

1. Webb, B.: CCTV in Town Centres: Three Case Studies, p. 6. Police Research Group (1995)
2. Short, E., Ditton, J.: Seen and Now Heard: Talking to the Targets of Open Street CCTV. British Journal of Criminology 38(3), 404 (1998)
3. Surette, R.: os and cons of second generation CCTV surveillance systems. Policing: An International Journal of Police Strategies & Management 28(1), 152

4. Shaha, S.A.A., Kim, H.J., Baek, S.K., Chang, H.H., Ahn, B.H.: System architecture of a decision support system for freeway incident management in Republic. Transportation Research Part A: Policy and Practice 42(5), 799 (2008)
5. BroadcastEngeering,
   http://broadcastengineering.com/production/looking-past-side-by-side-3-d-broadcasting-20100622/
6. Zhang, L., Ahn, G., Chu, B.: Rule-Based Framework for Role-Based Delegation. In: Proceedings of ACM Symposium on Access Control Models and Technologies, Chantilly, VA (2001)
7. Barkley, J.F., Cincotta, A.V., Ferraiolo, D.F., Gavrilla, S., Kuhn, D.R.: Role Based Access Control for the World Wide Web. In: 20th NISSC National Information Systems Security Conference, pp. 331–340 (1997)
8. Ferraiolo, D.F., Barkley, J.F., Kuhn, D.R.: A Role Based Access Control Model and Reference Implementation within a Corporate Intranet. ACM Transaction on Information System Security, 34–64 (1999)

Vessel Tracking Using Adaboost Algorithm and AIS Information

Jangsik Park[1], Hyuntae Kim[2], Gyuyeong Kim[3], and Yunsik Yu[3]

[1] Department of Electronics Engineering, Kyungsung University,
Daeyeon3-dong, 110-1, Nam-gu, Busan, 608-736, Korea
jsipark@ks.ac.kr
[2] Department of Multimedia Engineering, Dongeui University,
Gaya-dong, San 24, Busanjin-ku, Busan, 614-714, Korea
htaekim@deu.ac.kr
[3] Convergence of IT Devices Institute Busan,
Gaya-dong, San 24, Busanjin-ku, Busan, 614-714, Korea
{nz90nz,ysyu}@deu.ac.kr

Abstract. A vessel tracking method is proposed to support port monitoring. The proposed method is co-operated with Automatic Identification System including various data of vessels. To reduce computation of searching, Cartesian coordinates of images are mapped into latitude and longitude based on landmarks. Vessels are searched near received position data of AIS information and detected by Adaboost algorithm. By computer simulations and experiments, it is shown that the proposed method can be applied to port monitoring system.

Keywords: Adaboost Algorithm, AIS, Vessel Tracking.

1   Introduction

Various researches and standardizations are performed to support safe and efficient maritime transportation. The Automatic Identification System(AIS) is a short range costal tracking system using on vessels and by Vessel Traffic Services(VTS) for identifying and locating vessels by electronically exchanging data with other nearby vessels and VTS stations. Information such as unique identification, position, course and speed can be displayed on a monitor.

Video surveillance systems have been widely deployed in harbors or along coastlines. These systems provide a continuous surveillance of the transportation in a certain area, however, it is difficult to position a specific vessel and keep tracking it on these systems in an automatic way[1].

To overcome difficulties of vessel tracking, this paper put forward a method of tracking a vessel by combining video and AIS information, which can provide continual positions of the vessel. First, Cartesian coordinates of images are mapped into latitude and longitude based on major landmarks. And moving vessels are detected by searching around received AIS positioning information. Adaboost algorithm is used to detect vessels in the images.

T.-h. Kim et al. (Eds.): ISA 2011, CCIS 200, pp. 384–388, 2011.
© Springer-Verlag Berlin Heidelberg 2011

Simulation results show the proposed method has a high tracking precision and a user-friendly characteristic. This research shall be helpful for tracking specific vessels with video surveillance.

2   Vessel Detection and Tracking

The proposed video based vessel detection and tracking consists of two stages: (i) vessel detected by Adaboost algorithm, (ii) matching with AIS information. Flow chart of tracking vessels and displaying their information is illustrated in Fig. 1. Cartesian coordinates of the image converted into AIS position(latitude and longitude) in the process of initializing. Server generates files including AIS information transmitted from vessels near port. AIS information is displayed on a moving vessel detected by video processing.

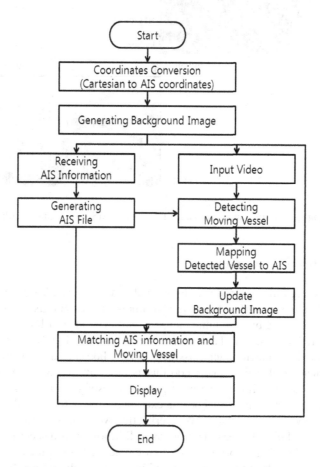

Fig. 1. Flow chart of detecting and displaying moving vessel and its information

2.1 Matching with AIS Information

Image coordinates of camera are mapped into latitude and longitude based on major landmarks. Mapping example is depicted in Fig. 2. The latitude and longitude of a moving vessel can be obtained by mapping. To reduce computations, latitude and longitude in the images are processed with integer operations. Moving vessels are detected by searching around received AIS positioning information.

Fig. 2. Mapping from Cartesian coordinates of images to AIS positioning coordinates(latitude, longitude)

2.2 Vessel Detection Algorithm

The Adaboost algorithm, introduced by Freund and Schapire[2], solved many of the practical difficulties of earlier boosting algorithms[3]. Boosting is a general strategy for learning classifiers by combining simpler ones. The idea of boosting is to take a "weak classifier" that is, any classifier that will do at least slightly better than chance and use it to build a much better classifier, thereby boosting the performance of the weak classification algorithm. This boosting is done by averaging the outputs of a collection of weak classifiers. The most popular boosting algorithm is Adaboost, so called because it is adaptive. Adaboost is extremely simply to use and implement(far simpler than SVMs), and often gives very effective results. There is tremendous flexibility in the choice of weak classifier as well. Boosting is a specific example of a general class of learning algorithms called ensemble methods, which attempt to build better learning algorithms by combining multiple simpler algorithms. It is adaptive in the sense that subsequent classifiers built are tweaked in favor of those instances misclassified by previous classifiers.

Haar-like features are used to detect vessels from video in harbor. The purpose of Haar-like features is to meet the real-time requirement. Each Haar-like features consists of two or three jointed black and white rectangles illustrated in Fig. 3.

Vessel images are taken from the MPEG4 harbor video. Images contain vessels of variable quality, different expressions and taken under a wide range of lighting conditions, with sea background shown in Fig. 4. The data set of vessel images are contains 100 images and non-vessel images were collected from web.

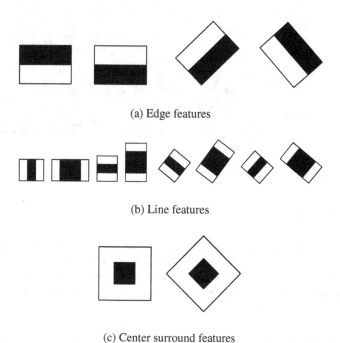

(a) Edge features

(b) Line features

(c) Center surround features

Fig. 3. A set of extended Haar-like features

Fig. 4. Vessel images for Adaboost training

3   Experimental Results

Simulations are performed to evaluate the performance of the proposed vessel detection and tracking. The tracking results are shown in Fig 5. Each of AIS information is displayed on the detected vessels. Simulation results show that moving vessels are well detected by the proposed method.

Fig. 5. Tracking vessels with AIS information

4   Conclusions

In this paper, a method has been developed using Adaboost algorithm from CCTV camera images and AIS information to track vessels automatically in harbor. Simulation results show that the proposed method performs well. Further works will evaluate the performance of this approach monitoring system in field and improve the performance of vessel tracking.

Acknowledgement. This work was supported in part by MKE(NIPA), Busan Metropolitan City and Dong-Eui University.(08-GIBAN-13, Convergence of IT Devices Institute Busan).

References

1. Chen, J., Hu, Q., Zhao, R., Guojun, P., Yang, C.: Tracking a Vessel by Combing Video and AIS Reports. In: Proceedings 2nd International Conf. on Future Generation Communication and Networking, FGCN 2008, pp. 374–378 (December 2008)
2. Viola, P., Jones, M.: Rapid object detection using a boosted cascade of simple features. In: Proceedings IEEE Conf. on Computer Vision and Pattern Recognition (2001)
3. Freund, Y., Schapire, R.E.: A Short Introduction to Boosting. Journal of Japanese Society for Artificial Intelligence 14(5), 771–780 (1999)

Relative Self-Localization Base on Fish-Eye Lenses and SIFT Algorithm for Indoor Mobile Robot

Xing Xiong and Byung-Jae Choi

School of Electronic Engineering, Daegu University
Jillyang, Gyeongsan, Gyeongbuk
712-714, Korea
GaleWing@gmail.com,
bjchoi@daegu.ac.kr

Abstract. In this paper, we consider the problem of mobile robot indoor position estimation using only visual information from a single camera. A camera which has a fish-eye lens is mounted on the top of the mobile robot and pointed to the ceiling. At the beginning of the visual positioning, we assume that we know the initial orientation and position of the mobile robot. Through the key point extraction, non-ceiling key point removal, key point calibration, ellipsoid construction and so on; the robot position and orientation can be determined after a short time moving.

Keywords: Ceiling Key Point Extraction, Scale Invariant Feature Transform (SIFT), Radial Distortion Calibration.

1 Introduction

Mobile robot self-localization is a mandatory task in accomplishing full autonomy during navigation. Various solutions in the robotics community have been developed in order to solve the self-localization problem. The solutions can be categorized into two groups: relative localization (dead-reckoning) and absolute localization. Although very simple and fast, dead reckoning algorithms tend to accumulate errors in the system since they utilize only information from proprioceptive sensors, such as odometer readings (e.g. incremental encoders on the robot wheels). Absolute localization methods are based on exteroceptive sensor information. This method yields a stable locating error but is more complex and costly in terms of computation time. Relative localization requires a high sampling rate in order to maintain an up-to-date pose, whereas absolute localization is applied periodically with a lower sampling rate in order to correct relative positioning misalignments [3].

Visual positioning method plays an important role in the self-localization of autonomous service mobile robots working in indoor environments [5]. Generally, the knowledge existing in indoor environments can be used to determine the position and orientation of a mobile robot via visual positioning approaches. The features used by different approaches for mobile robot's localization range from artificial markers such

T.-h. Kim et al. (Eds.): ISA 2011, CCIS 200, pp. 389–394, 2011.

as barcodes and more natural objects such as ceiling lights and doors to geometric features such as straight wall segments and corners. Indeed, the selected visual features have apparent influence on the performance of the positioning approach.

In an indoor environment, the floor is assumed to be planar. The ceiling consists of a series of blocks, which form a chessboard pattern parallel to the floor. A camera is mounted on the top of a mobile robot working on the floor. Its orientation is upright, directs to the block ceiling, as shown in Fig. 1.

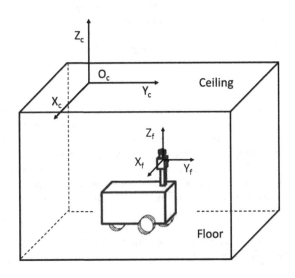

Fig. 1. Model of ceiling based visual positioning

In the remainder of this paper, extraction of feature points is introduced using SIFT algorithm in Section 2. The detail of the image calibration method is described in Section 3. The detail of the non-ceiling key point removal and construction of elliptic are described in Section4. Some experimental results are described in Section 5, followed by conclusions in Section 6.

2   Feature Point Extraction and Matching

In the past, SIFT has been proven to be one of the robust image –matching techniques that use local invariant feature descriptors with respect to different geometrical changes. To allow efficient matching between images, each image is processed to extract feature point, each of which is then represented as a SIFT feature vector, as mentioned previously.

The following figure shows two image's feature extraction and matching.

Fig. 2. Feature point extraction and matching (in short time interval, the camera rotated 45°)

3   Radial Lens Distortions and Its Correction

Radial lens distortion causes points on the image plane in the wide-angle/fish-eye camera to be displaced in a nonlinear fashion from their ideal position in the rectilinear pin-hole camera model, along a radial axis from the center of distortion in the image plane (Fig. 3). The visual effect of this displacement in fish-eye optics is that the image wills a higher resolution in the fovea areas, with the resolution decreasing nonlinearly towards the peripheral areas of the image.

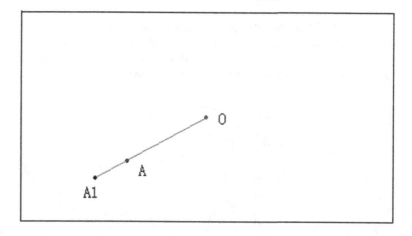

Fig. 3. Displacement of points in radial distortion, where A is the distorted and A1 is the undistorted radius

$$\begin{cases} x1 = x + \cos a * (k * OA^3) \\ y1 = y + \sin a * (k * OA^3) \end{cases}$$

where (x,y) represent the coordinate of A, $(x1,y1)$ represent the coordinate of A1, OA is the length, a is angle between OA and X-axis positive direction, k is the coefficient.

The distortion removal result as following:

Fig. 4. This is a corrected version of Fig.2 left

4   Removal of Non-ceiling Key Point

After using the SIFT algorithm, the image contain a large number of points which not in ceiling. The distance between these points and the camera are different. Before determining the relative position, the non-ceiling key point must be removal. The following show the change of the feature point in two images.

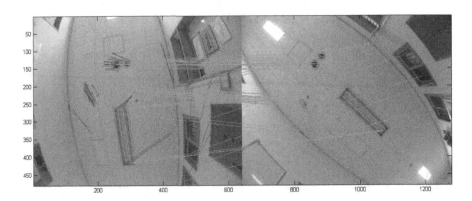

Fig. 5. Change of the feature points

From the above image, we know that, when robot move or rotate, the feature points are the changes according to certain rule. So the histogram as following:

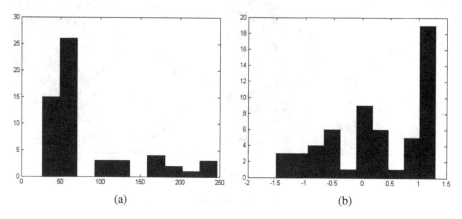

(a)   (b)

Fig. 6. The histogram of the feature point's angles and distance change (a) is the distance change (b) is angel change

From the above Fig 6, the key points in ceiling have high degree of polymerization. Their change angle or distance is within a certain range. So the non-ceiling key point can be removal according to the histogram.

5   Simulation Result

The experiment system consisted of a mobile robot and a camera. The camera was mounted on the top of a mobile robot, whose orientation was upright, pointed to the block ceiling, as shown in Fig. 1. The following image produced that robot, movement in short time, change in the position and orientation. The left images are the previous shooting image. The right images are the current shooting images, and show the previous location and current location.

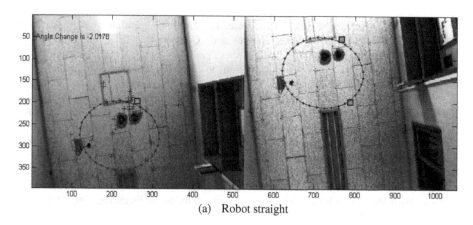

(a)   Robot straight

Fig. 7. Experimental result of the position and orientation

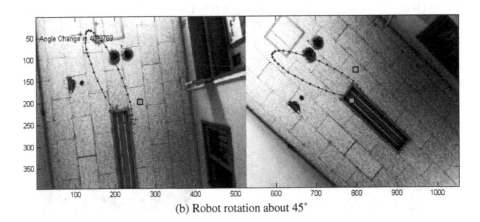

(b) Robot rotation about 45°

Fig. 7. (*Continued*)

6   Conclusions

Our main contribution is that a new visual positioning method based on the features on ceiling is presented for an indoor mobile robot. The method is based on the use of a SIFT-based key point image-matching process. The positioning procedure consists of three main parts: feature point extraction and matching, radial lens distortions and removal of non-ceiling key point. The experimental results verify the effectiveness of the proposed method.

Acknowledgments. This work was supported in part by the Basic Science Research Program through the National Research Foundation of Korea (NRF) funded by the Ministry of Education, Science and Technology under Grant 2010-0006588.

References

1. Yuen, D.C.K., MacDonald, B.A.: Vision-Based Localization Algorithm Based on Landmark Matching, Triangulation, Reconstruction, and Comparison. IEEE Transactions on Robotics 21(2), 217–226 (2005)
2. Kitanov, A.: Mobile robot self-localization in complex indoor environments using monocular vision and 3D model
3. Koenig, A., Kessler, J., Gross, H.-M.: A Graph Matching Technique for an Appearance-based, visual SLAM-Approach using Rao-Blackwellized Particle Filters. In: IEEE/RSJ International Conference on Intelligent Robots and Systems, pp. 1576–1581 (2008)
4. Chen, K.-C., Tsai, W.-H.: Vision-Based Autonomous Vehicle Guidance for Indoor Security Patrolling by a SIFT-Based Vehicle-Localization Technique. IEEE Transactions on Vehicular Technology 59(7) (2010)
5. Xu, D., Han, L., Tan, M., Li, Y.F.: Ceiling-Based Visual Positioning for an Indoor Mobile Robot With Monocular Vision. IEEE Transactions on Industrial Electronics 56(5) (2009)

User-Oriented Pseudo Biometric Image Based One-Time Password Mechanism on Smart Phone[*]

Wonjun Jang, Sikwan Cho, and Hyung-Woo Lee

School of Computer Engineering, Hanshin University, Korea
{jangwjfly,whtlrdhks3355,hyungwoo8299}@hanmail.net

Abstract. User authentication procedures should be enhanced its security on Smart phone. And more secure system should be implemented to minimize the user's privacy disclosure. Although image-based authentication mechanism was introduced recently, replay attack is also possible on existing one-time password based authentication system. In this paper, we implemented pseudo biometric image based OTP generation mechanism, which uses transformation function on captured biometric image from each user for providing enhanced secure authentication service on smart phone.

Keywords: Pseudo Biometric Image, Authentication, One-time password, Smart phone.

1 Introduction

With a recent rapid increase in smart phone users, various applications are being used. It is possible to use an e-financial service or an Internet banking service by use of a smart phone so a correct authentication process for smart phone users should be set up, together with a solution for security. In case an Internet banking service is used through a smart phone, a more reinforced user authentication process should be made than the existing environment. Otherwise, it can create a serious problem. Therefore, it is necessary to use other approach which has more improved security than one-time password (OTP) approach applied to the existing financial services, and it is also necessary to associate user-related information with an OTP-generating process and offer a multi-factor authentication feature.

The existing OTP approach [1,2,3] can't offer an identification process for the real owner of OTP token so it can't offer identification/verification features for users when it is lost. In addition, in the process of issuing OTP token, it creates a one-time password, using a previously-set identification number, but it doesn't include the information on a real user so there is no way to identify or detect the use by a third party. That's because man-in-the middle (MITM) attack can be given to OTP information. Therefore, a method of offering it more safely should be suggested [4,5].

[*] This research was supported by Basic Science Research Program though the NRF of Korea funded by the MEST (No.2010-0016882) and also partially supported by MKE (Ministry of Knowledge Economy), Korea, under the ITRC (Information Technology Research Center) support program supervised by NIPA (National IT Industry Promotion Agency)" (NIPA-2011-(C1090-1031-0005)).

T.-h. Kim et al. (Eds.): ISA 2011, CCIS 200, pp. 395–404, 2011.
© Springer-Verlag Berlin Heidelberg 2011

As a solution, this study intends to offer an authentication feature for a real owner or user of OTP token. For this, it has implemented a system that OTP value is created from pseudo biometric information owned by an individual and used for authentication. Pseudo biometric information (PBI) suggested in this study means quasi-biometric information that a smart phone user himself/herself captures. For example, it means an image including a part of a user's identity, like an image of the back of his/her hand. This system can solve a matter of privacy that can be raised in the process of using a smart phone. Besides, it can offer OTP-based multi-factor authentication feature using an information instrument, like a smart phone. It also has an advantage of coping with replay attacks in case conversion function is applied to pseudo biometric information to generate OTP.

This study has analyzed vulnerabilities of the existing smart phone authentication technology and OTP technology, and suggested results of system design and implementation for B-OTP approach with pseudo biometric information and OTP technology applied. And it has implemented the system in smart phone applications and then, analyzed its stability

2   One-Time Password on Smart Phone

2.1   Existing One-Time Password Mechanisms

OTP-generating method is this. Once a user enters his/her personal identification number (PIN) or password (PW) by use of OTP-generating media, the server transmits a challenge value. And then, hash function, like MD5 or SHA-1, is applied to the challenge value to get a one-way digest value. This one-way digest value is encoded and then, by use of it, OTP value is generated [1,2]. By adding time-based, event-based, and challenge-response mechanisms to this algorithm, different OTP is generated. The server and the OTP-generating media should use the same algorithm all the time to generate OTP, which can prevent any authentication failure resulting from inconsistent OTPs. OTP-generating method uses hash function, which is one-way function, so it is difficult to find out the original value (PIN + time, event, question-answer) of the encoded OTP so user information can't be easily decoded when it is exposed to a hacker, which is strength of OTP-generating method [2].

OTP authentication process is this. Once a user makes the initial registration in order to use OTP, OTP server delivers PIN value (a random 4-digit value) to the user. After delivering, the server generates OTP value, using the PIN value, the time value when the user registered OTP, and the current time value, and OTP–generating media generates OTP value in the same way. And then, the user requests authentication to the server, using the OTP value coming out of the OPT-generating media. The server makes authentication if its OTP value and the OTP value entered by the user are same [4].

Currently in Korea, in order to reinforce financial safety, customers of Internet banking and telebanking are classified into three security grades as shown on the below table, and a different money transfer limit is set for each security grade. Of the three security graders, the first security grader is obliged to use OTP for a financial transaction. The method of using an OTP generator and an authentication certificate at the same time is for a high security grade. Two-channel authentication method, which is based on a security card and an authentication certificate, is available too, but recently, the method of using an OTP generator is being extensively used.

An OTP-based operation scenario is as follows: OTP user generates OTP value and enters it into his/her PC, and the authentication server verifies it. The user generates OTP, using his/her own PIN and synchronization information, and then, enters it into his/her PC. The entered information is delivered to OTP authentication server of a financial institution and goes through comparison/verification against the OTP value generated in the server.

2.2 Image Based User Authentication

Recently ConfidentTech suggests an image-based authentication approach, which is this: a user sets up an image title in advance to use and enters ID; and in response to the challenge value composed of various combinations of image values, he/she transmits a title value of the image title chosen by him/her. For example, if a user chooses three categories of dog, car, and ship, 3-digit access codes, which are combinations of 5, X, and V, are transmitted in response to the challenge images in the below figure. In the next step, the images and their arrangements are changed so one of the combinations of F, z, and N is input as a new access code [6,7,8].

This method is similar with OTP method. The image title set by a user can be a secret of each user and different images are differently arranged and different access codes are assigned each time so it can be said that it is a kind of OTP method. However, if a user chooses 3 different image titles and 9 image samples are offered, only 6 out of 504 combination codes (9*8*7) can be suitable access codes, which means 1.19% probability. This method has a problem that three image categories can be easily found out through the analysis of similarities and commonness of 9 images that are given when an attacker tries to have access several times. However, in that a one-time access code is generated by use of image information, this method shows that it is possible to connect the existing general OTP method with images or other multimedia information. Therefore, this study intends to suggest a user authentication process that each user generates a one-time password from a random image captured by the user through his/her smart phone, and performs user authentication.

Fig. 1. Image-Based User Authentication

3   Pseudo Biometric One-Time Password Mechanism

3.1   Proposed Pseudo Biometric Image Based OTP Mechanism

In order to acquire safety in a financial transaction, like Internet banking, a safer, more efficient approach should be used. And a security feature for privacy should be offered too. Therefore, in case the existing facial recognition system is used for Internet banking, there can be some problems like an error in facial recognition and abuse of the obtained bio information. Therefore, a new approach, which can solve those problems, needs to be offered. In order to overcome technical limits of the recognition system which is based on biometric information (fingerprints or face) and to solve an error in recognition, the following new approach is proposed.

This study intends to use pseudo biometric data, image information that a user provides by use of the camera of his/her smart phone. That is, a user is asked to perform a real-time capture feature for his/her face or other information by use of his/her own instrument. The obtained information includes pseudo biometric information of each individual. For example, let's assume that LENA image is transmitted through a smart phone. A user can obtain an image that he/she wants as shown on the below, and he/she can give several effects to it. A blurring effect can be given too. However, in case that biometric information of an individual's face is transmitted as it is, a matter of privacy can be raised and overall security can't help going down. Therefore, a more effective way is that an individual transmits an image including his/her own biometric information as per the below image.

Pseudo Biometric Information: It means the information related with a user's body. It is quasi-biometric information that is used for solving a matter of privacy. For example, it is the image information including a part of a user's body.

In the case of using partial biometric image information as per the above, a matter of privacy happens less than the case that the whole image of a face is transmitted. It is true that in this case, the identification feature for biometric information in the image can have a problem, but it uses partial biometric information, that is, pseudo biometric information, so any problems resulting from privacy can be solved. And a matter of a real owner can be raised too even though the image of a face is used.

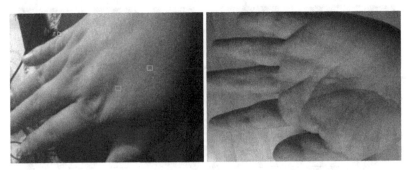

Fig. 2. OTP Application Based on User Images (or pseudo biometric information)

Therefore, this study proposes an approach of generating B-OTP by use of pseudo biometric information that a user captures through the camera in his/her smart phone. It abstracts pixel information in a specific random position of an image and generates B-OTP information by use of it.

3.2 Using Pseudo Biometric Image on OTP Generation

Currently security-related technology, like biometric information-used user authentication, is getting attraction and researches of it are being actively conducted, but the technology is not used a lot because of its high cost. However, dissemination and use of smart phones have been rapidly increased and activated after 2009 so through this environment, one of the problems with using biometric information, which is high cost, can be solved.

By use of a camera, a microphone, and a sensor of a smart phone, it is possible to receive such information as a user's voice, image, and actions, and through a mobile communication network and Wi-Fi network, it is possible to smoothly receive and transmit information so the use of biometric information through a smart phone can be done very efficiently in terms of cost and convenience.

The existing OTP-generating method through a terminal device has many restrictions and inconvenience so if a software-like OTP-generating approach is implemented through a mobile phone, the use of OTP will be very efficient and activated in terms of convenience. However, this approach has a problem of security so if biometric information is used in the process of generating OTP, high-security OTP can be used more efficiently and conveniently.

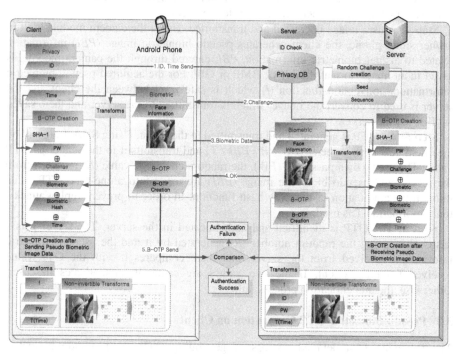

Fig. 3. A User-Image-Based OTP System Architecture on Smartphone

The process of performing B-OTP by use of a smart phone can be designed like this. First, a user transmits his/her identity (*ID*) value only, except for password (*PW*), to the server and the server checks if the *ID* has been registered. If it has not been registered, no further progress will be made. Now the server creates a random challenge value and transmits it to the client. At this time, the client generates OTP, using PW created by him/her, and transmits it to the server. Likewise, the server compares the OTP value generated by it with the OTP value received from the client and if they are same, it works on authentication.

OTP authentication architecture, which this study has developed with a smart phone, is as per the below. An Android phone, which is a recent issue, has been used for designing. As shown on the below figure, the client generates OTP, using the random challenge value received from the server after transmitting his/her *ID* to the server.

The way of enhancing safety of the above architecture is using biometric information. Its detailed process is as follows:

Step 1: An *ID* is transmitted to the server. A smart phone user transmits his/her *ID* to the server and makes a request for OTP generation. At this time, he/she transmits the request time T too.

Step 2: The *ID* is confirmed in the client. The server searches the received *ID* in database and confirms it.

Step 3: A random challenge value is generated and transmitted. The server applies conversion function to the *ID* and time information *T* received from the client, generates a random number (*R*), using seed and sequence values and hash algorithm like SHA-1 or MD5, and then, transmits it to the client.

Step 4: A user image is created and transmitted. Using the camera module built in his/her smart phone, the client generates pseudo biometric image (*PBI*) information related to his/her biometric information. *PBI*, entered through the camera module, is saved in an image format, like JPG, BMP or GIF. For the acquired pseudo biometric information, conversion function (*f*) which is safely set between the client and the server is used to convert the image, which is transmitted to the server and then, saved as 'PBI' by the server.

Step 5: An OTP is generated and transmitted in the client. Using SHA-1 algorithm, the client gets hash value $H (PW \mid R \mid PBI \mid T)$ and transmits it to the sender as OTP value. The user's own password (*PW*), the random challenge value (*R*) received from the server, and pseudo biometric image (*PBI*) are made into a one-time OTP value through the application of one-way hash function. In order to prevent replay attacks, time information T is used.

Step 6: The OTP is identified and authenticated in the server. The server gets a hash value, using the random number (*R*) generated by it and the pseudo biometric information received from the server, and then, compares it with the OTP value received from the client. If the two values are same, it authenticates the user. Otherwise, the authentication process fails.

3.3 Pseudo Biometric OTP Generation on Client

The following is a detailed process of generating OTP using pseudo biometric information in the client:

Step 1: Enter *ID/PW*-based privacy information into the *ID/PW* field and press the Login button.

Step 2: Focus the camera on your face or other part and press the shutter to abstract biometric privacy information.

Step 3: Apply conversion function (*f*) to the PW entered in step 1, the challenge value received from the server, and the pseudo biometric information abstracted from step 2, and then, calculate biometric hash value. Generate B-OTP value by use of time information.

The conversion or transformation function (*f*) can be re-defined as follows: Referring to the existing researches of biometric salting or non-invertible transformation methods [11,12,13], conversion is performed to the biometric information that a user entered from a smart phone. That is, cancelable biometric technique [11, 12, 15] is applied to pseudo biometric information to divide PBI data captured by the user into x × y blocks, and then, conversion function (*f*) is applied. Conversion function $f = H(ID | PW | T)$ can be created and defined by use of user *ID/PW* and time information. Therefore, using this defined conversion function, conversion is performed to the pseudo biometric information (*PBI*) obtained by the user.

3.4 Pseudo Biometric OTP Verification on Server

The biometric OTP generation architecture in the server is as follows:

Step 1: Make a judgment if the ID received from the client is in the ID list in the privacy database of the server.

Step 2: If the ID is not valid, the server invalidates the ID received from the client. If it is valid, the server generates a 5-byte random seed value and a 10-byte random challenge value as a sequence value.

Step 3: In the same way as the client, the server generates B-OTP. In case the ID in step 1 is valid, conversion function is applied to the PW of the relevant ID in privacy database, to the 10-byte challenge value generated in step 2, and the PBI value received from the client, through which B-OTP value is generated.

Conversion function f that was generated in the client can generate its identical function f' in the server too. Using user PW/ID/time information T that are saved already, the server can calculate conversion function $f' = H(ID | PW | T)$. Therefore, using conversion function f', the server can work on the conversion process for PBI' received from the user, and using it, it can generate and verify OTP value.

4 Implementation and Security Analysis

4.1 Implementation Results

This study has used Android OS as a client system and SQL server as a server system. Android-based development environment is composed of JAVA JDK 1.6.x version, Android software development kit (SDK), and eclipse galileo-SR2. The SQL server is MySQL-based. In Android environment, a user performs a process of receiving an account from the server in advance. This study has implemented biometric OTP login in Android environment.

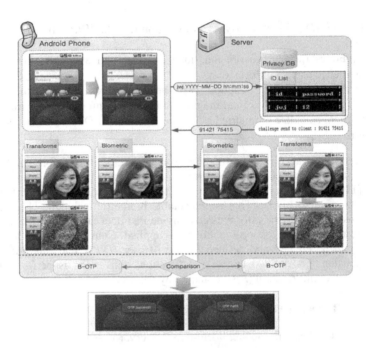

Fig. 4. A Biometric OTP Implementation

4.2 Security Analysis

This study has analyzed safety of OTP system which uses implemented pseudo biometric information (PBI). OTP token used for Internet banking can be faced with MITM attacks, but in the case of the technique used by this study, the client transmits different pseudo biometric image information to the server each time. And the transmitted biometric information can be used for personal authentication because it is not a fingerprint or a whole face which can cause a privacy problem. Therefore, more reinforced security can be given.

Multi-factor authentication feature: The technique suggested by this study is combined with OTP method through the use of PBI so it can enhance safety more than the existing method. The existing OTP method doesn't offer an authentication process for the real owner of OTP token. When issuing OTP, PIN is used to generate PW, but it doesn't include the information on a real user so in case it is used by a third party, there is no way to verify it. However, PBI is used so an identification feature can be improved.

Smartphone-based owner authentication/identification feature: In case OTP token is lost or stolen, both synchronous and asynchronous methods don't present a countermeasure. When OTP token is lost, an identification process for its original owner is not offered at all. That is, the existing OTP method just purports to create a one-time password and it doesn't offer owner authentication/identification processes for OTP instrument and modules. Therefore, this study has applied conversion function to a pseudo biometric information image in order to authenticate the real owner of OTP token, changed the image, and applied it to the process of generating OTP. This method can solve the privacy matter happening when biometric information is used, and it can be also used for OTP information-based multi-factor authentication.

Replay-attack prevention feature: This study has applied conversion function f to PBI in the process of generating OTP so it provides the feature of privacy protection for the biometric information obtained by a user, and it can also perform an authentication process on the basis of a one-time password so finally, it can prevent replay attacks. In the process of applying conversion function (f), time information (T) value is used so even though a replay attack is done by an attacker, it can be detected. If an attacker generates OTP by use of ID, PW and time information included in conversion function (f), it will be different from the information generated by the server so it is possible to detect one-time password transformation made by replay attacks.

The proposed mechanism has been found to have similar computation complexity to existing mechanisms. In the mechanism, human voice information is used for user authentication and OTP generation on a smartphone. For biometric information available in the authentication process, the existing mechanisms [14,15,16] use face or fingerprint information, while the proposed mechanism allows a user's face information to be used for authentication. Actually, the new mechanism has been designed with considerations for the convenience of OTP users and the environment where smartphones are used. It is also applicable to fingerprint information like the existing ones.

5   Conclusions

This study has designed and implemented a pseudo biometric information-used OTP system in order to strengthen the authentication feature for users in the process of using smart phone applications and to offer a safe user authentication feature in an e-financial system like Internet banking.

Unlike the existing general OTP method, the system implemented in this study uses the method that a user obtains biometric information (a part of his/her body) from the camera module of a smart phone, converts it by use of conversion function that offers the feature of "inverse conversion not allowed", and then, applies it to the process of generating OTP.

References

1. Lamport, L.: Password authentication with insecure communication. Communications of the ACM 24, 770–772 (1981)
2. Haller, N.M.: A one-time password system. Tech. Rep. RFC 1938 (May 1996)
3. Haller, N.M., Metz, C., Nesser II, P.J., Straw, M.: A one-time password system. RFC 2289 (February 1998), http://www.ietf.org/rfc/rfc2289.txt
4. Jang, W.J., Lee, H.W.: Biometric one-time password generation mechanism and its application on SIP authentication. Journal of the Korea Convergence Society 1(1), 93–100 (2010)

5. Lin, M.H., Chang, C.C.: A secure one-time password authentication scheme with low-computation for mobile communications. ACM SIGOPS Operating Systems Review 38(2), 76–84 (2004)

6. http://confidenttechnologies.com/products/confident-imageshield

7. http://www.darkreading.com/authentication/security/client/showArticle.jhtml?articleID=228200140

8. http://www.marketwire.com/press-release/Confident-Technologies-Delivers-Image-Based-Multifactor-Authentication-Strengthen-Passwords-1342854.htm

9. Ang, R., Rei, S.N., McAven, L.: Cancelable Key-Based Fingerprint Templates. In: Boyd, C., González Nieto, J.M. (eds.) ACISP 2005. LNCS, vol. 3574, pp. 242–252. Springer, Heidelberg (2005)

10. Hirata, S., Takahashi, K.: Cancelable Biometrics with Perfect Secrecy for Correlation-Based Matching. In: Tistarelli, M., Nixon, M.S. (eds.) ICB 2009. LNCS, vol. 5558, pp. 868–878. Springer, Heidelberg (2007)

11. Kong, B., et al.: An analysis of Biohashing and its variants. Elsevier - Pattern Recognition 39(7), 1359–1368 (2006)

12. Lee, Y.J., et al.: One-Time Templates for Face Authentication. In: International Conference on Convergence Information Technology (ICCIT 2007), pp. 1818–1823 (2007)

13. Savvides, M., Vijaya Kumar, B.V.K., Khosla, P.K.: Cancelable Biometrics Filters for Face Recognition. In: Int. Conf. of Pattern Recognition, vol. 3, pp. 922–925 (2004)

14. Wang, D.-S., Li, J.-P.: A new fingerprint-based remote user authentication scheme using mobile devices. In: International Conference on Apperceiving Computing and Intelligence Analysis, ICACIA 2009, pp. 65–68 (2009)

15. Yoon, E.J., Yoo, K.Y.: A secure chaotic hash-based biometric remote user authentication scheme using mobile devices. In: Chang, K.C.-C., Wang, W., Chen, L., Ellis, C.A., Hsu, C.-H., Tsoi, A.C., Wang, H. (eds.) APWeb/WAIM 2007. LNCS, vol. 4537, pp. 612–623. Springer, Heidelberg (2007)

16. Khan, M.K., Zhang, J.S., Wang, X.M.: Chaotic hash-based fingerprint biometric remote user authentication scheme on mobile devices. Chaos, Solutions & Fractals 35, 519–524 (2008)

Author Index